Behind the Screen

Behind the Screen

Tap Dance, Race, and Invisibility During Hollywood's Golden Age

BRYNN W. SHIOVITZ

Oxford University Press is a department of the University of Oxford. It furthers
the University's objective of excellence in research, scholarship, and education
by publishing worldwide. Oxford is a registered trade mark of Oxford University
Press in the UK and certain other countries.

Published in the United States of America by Oxford University Press
198 Madison Avenue, New York, NY 10016, United States of America.

© Oxford University Press 2023

All rights reserved. No part of this publication may be reproduced, stored in
a retrieval system, or transmitted, in any form or by any means, without the
prior permission in writing of Oxford University Press, or as expressly permitted
by law, by license, or under terms agreed with the appropriate reproduction
rights organization. Inquiries concerning reproduction outside the scope of the
above should be sent to the Rights Department, Oxford University Press, at the
address above.

You must not circulate this work in any other form
and you must impose this same condition on any acquirer.

CIP data is on file at the Library of Congress

ISBN 978–0–19–755310–7 (pbk.)
ISBN 978–0–19–755309–1 (hbk.)

DOI: 10.1093/oso/9780197553091.001.0001

*In celebration of Sophia,
my first labor of love*

and

*In loving memory of my aunt Toni,
who first inspired me to write*

Contents

Acknowledgments		ix
Note on Language		xiii
Preface		xv
	Introduction: Masks in Disguise	1
1.	Integrating the Screen: Sound Synchronization, Sonic Guises, and Pre-Code Blackface, 1927–1930	31
sing-along	"Dinah," a Fleischer Screen Song	73
2.	Optical Illusion and Design: Exposure Values, Protean Guises, and Eddie Cantor's Blackface, 1930–1933	75
cartoon short	The Three Little Pigs, an excerpted Walt Disney Silly Symphony	121
3.	Public Works and Accolades: Race Film, Southern Repossession, and the Rise of Bill Robinson, 1929–1935	123
dance break	"Have You Got Any Castles," Featuring Buck and Bubbles	171
4.	Bon Homage: Female Figures, the Tribute Guise, and Pre-War Departures, 1934–1939	173
travel ad	Skirting Censorship: Brownface and Technology in Transit	219
5.	With a Glory Be: The Gabriel Variation, Jazz, and Everything In-Between, 1934–1942	227
war bond ad	"Any Bonds Today?" Produced in Cooperation with Warner Bros. and U.S. Treasury Dept. Defense Savings Staff	280

viii CONTENTS

6. Hays Is for Horses: Cartoons' Crossover Appeal, Dis-figuration, and the Animated Bestiary, 1934–1942   281

Coda Enlisting the Tropes: Covert Minstrelsy in Action, 1942–1954   331

Appendix: Excerpts from the Production Code (1934–1954)   353
Index   359

Acknowledgments

Remember your teachers; dance for your ancestors; challenge; share your craft; be challenged; learn from your students. Tap dance honors its legacy while continuing to build up its community. In keeping with such a tradition there are many members of my community to whom I would like to extend my gratitude.

To my very first teachers—my parents—Esther and Tom, whose love from day one has been unwavering and given me the very best model to love and adore my youngest teacher, Sophia. To Sophia for keeping me company "inside" while I wrote—you shimmied to every swingin' piece of archival footage I watched—and for continuing to be my dynamic dinosaur—RAWR—and biggest motivation every day. To Josh for being such a great dad to our little mover and shaker, giving me the time to write, acting as my eternal sounding board, and being the one who challenges me most to see things from new angles. To Becca, who made it easy to trust someone other than my immediate family to care for our little one while I write. To my sister Zoe whose love and generosity know no bounds. And to my aunt Toni who first inspired me to perform, to write, and to teach.

Susan Leigh Foster has championed my scholarly endeavors from the moment we first connected and has had such a profound impact on my writing that a phantom Susan forever sits on my left shoulder as I type. My heartfelt thanks to Anthea Kraut who has been such a generous mentor in all things professional and personal. I admire her deeply and hope to approach my scholarship and motherhood with as much grace and integrity as she has. To the Department of World Arts and Cultures/Dance (otherwise known as WAC/D) at the University of California, Los Angeles, for taking me in, challenging me, and supporting me. A very special thank you to my dissertation committee, Susan, Anthea, Jay O'Shea, Yogita Goyal, and David Rousseve, who helped me think through the earliest stages of this project. To Lynn Dally for her committed mentorship and friendship. Her honesty, excitement, and wisdom mean so much. To Margaret Morrison who always offers great enthusiasm and support for my work. To Constance Valis Hill for carving out a space for tap dance within dance studies and to Thomas

X ACKNOWLEDGMENTS

DeFrantz for being such a staunch supporter of percussive dance practices and consistently saying things in a way that resonates.

To my friends and colleagues who have offered their support in numerous forms: to my village, who lifts me up, challenges me, and lets me share not only my craft, but my soul self. I do not know where I would be without those frequent phone dates, Facetimes, and fireside chats. To Melissa for helping strip the layers that no longer serve me, discover a better version of self, and sit with those big feelings in the process. To Beth for your honesty, patience, and intentions. Gwyneth Shanks, Elyan Hill, Kelly Midori McCormick, AB Brown, and Aileen Kaye Robinson have all offered incredible feedback and accountability at varying stages of this manuscript. Gwynn and Elyan deserve special recognition for reading more than they bargained for. I am so appreciative of Rebecca Rossen, Rosemary Candelario, Melissa Blanco Borelli, and Emily Wilcox who let me join their second book club and offered invaluable insight into the book's second and fifth chapters. Rebecca's reading recommendations and insights into the Jewish studies components were so helpful. To Elizabeth Leone and my dad who read the very roughest of drafts. To Archer Porter, Mika Lior, and Ryan Rockmore who read versions of the complete manuscript and offered excellent points of view in the final stages. And to everyone I consulted at various points during the writing process— Nic Gareiss, Michael Love, Steve Zee, Reggio McLaughlin, and Marv Goldberg, to name a small number.

I am so fortunate to have made a habitat for myself at Chapman University. The dance department has become a second home. I am especially grateful for my chair, Julianne O'Brien, who runs a tight ship and also always has time for a heart-to-heart and tuna. To Clara Harnett who keeps everything running smoothly and whose warmth makes work homey. To Robin Kish for making space for me (in the department and in your office). And to Liz Maxwell, Wilson Mendieta, Jenny Backhaus, Alicia Guy, and Brandee Lara for including me in all sorts of ways. Over the years, my students have taught me so much and it is only fitting that a few of these Chapman alums have left their artistic mark on this book. Aaron Woo helped me navigate the graphic design of my opening diagram and Kira Bartoli turned my cover design ideas into a reality, skillfully drawing the shadows and gloves adorning *Behind the Screen*'s first impression.

Support for this book was provided by the Office of Research and the College of Performing Arts at Chapman University. Joann King deserves a round of applause for her help ironing out the details associated with this grant as does my Dean, Giulio Ongaro, who always has my back. Special thanks to Michael Spinella and the Textbook and Author's Association (TAA) who also offered support with some of the book's image acquisition and copyright.

Were it not for the help of Genevieve Maxwell and the Margaret Herrick Library, I would have had no access to the PCA's censorship files. The New York Public Library for the Performing Arts and Derek Davidson at Photofest were also instrumental in helping me track down some rare photographs.

Last, but certainly not least, Norman Hirschy at Oxford University Press has been a godsend. He expressed great enthusiasm for this project and offered such valuable insight from the get-go. I am grateful for the chance he took on this book. The insightful feedback I received from him and from my anonymous reviewers at various stages has been vital to both the content and construction of this book. Thank you, everyone.

Note on Language

Language carries a history, and its usage reflects a particular historical moment with specific geographic boundaries. The discursive context laid out here reflects what I believe makes the most sense in the United States in 2022 and may be less suitable in a different time and/or place. While not wanting to preserve the use of certain words in everyday speech, I wish to communicate certain ideas with historical accuracy. Some song lyrics and titles in *Behind the Screen* contain offensive language. In those instances, I have either placed said words in quotations to emphasize their *historical* circulation or will use the Latin [*sic*] next to the first letter, denoting that the word originally used was erroneous.

For decades, scholars have been distinguishing between "Black-on-White" minstrelsy, or the act of a White person donning black makeup, and "Black-on-Black" minstrelsy, which requires that the person under the mask identify as Black. While motivations behind the blackface performances of Black and White performers may differ, bolstering arbitrary race-based distinctions risks further alienating Black performance from history; I refer to all iterations of visible blackface minstrelsy simply and inclusively as "blackface," specifying the individual when necessary.

While I understand and respect the AP standard of capitalizing the *b* in "Black" and leaving the *w* of "white" lowercase, I have chosen to capitalize "Black" *and* "White" in keeping with two lines of inquiry that resonate for me at this particular moment: the first comes from the Center for the Study of Social Policy, which made a collective decision to capitalize "White" in addition to "Black" in spring of 2020 because it calls attention to how "Whiteness functions in our social and political institutions and our communities. Moreover, the detachment of 'White' as a proper noun allows White people to sit out of conversations about race and removes accountability from White people's and White institutions' involvement in racism."[1] One might be quick to point out that White Supremacist organizations have capitalized "White" and that by capitalizing the *w*, I may be lending those organizations support. Kwame Anthony Appiah has insightfully suggested that one might instead choose to see the flip side: if anti-racists begin capitalizing the *w*, then "the supremacists' gesture would no longer be a provocative defiance of the norm and would lose all force. Supremacists would have to find another way to ennoble themselves."[2]

I do not wish to recognize "brown" as I do "Black" and "White"; instead I offer the qualifier as a way of highlighting Hollywood's indistinctive use of the term during the Golden Age, which really was more as a color than as representative of any kind of lived experience. Accordingly, my use of "brown" in this book will remain lowercase (with a few exceptions of self-identification) because of the way I use it to describe Hollywood's historic flattening of Native Hawaiian, Spanish, Mexican, Latin, Indigenous, and Middle Eastern people. That is, when discussing the stereotype, I will refer to "brown" people, but when I'm talking about who or what is the basis for the caricature, I will be as specific as possible, naming people with real lived experiences. Additionally, in keeping with the National Congress of American Indians' (NCAI) current practice, I use "Native Hawaiians" to refer to *Kanaka Maoli*, the Indigenous people of the Hawaiian archipelago and "American Indians" to refer to the Indigenous people of the mainland. Since "red" is generally not a way that Indigenous people across the United States self-identify and is often just a color used in drawn caricatures, this term will also remain lowercase.

Finally, performances such as blackface, brownface, yellowface, redface, and jewface will remain lowercase since they, by definition, imply a caricature rather than a lived experience. That is, in general, use of the uppercase here denotes a lived experience whereas the lowercase first letter draws attention to the performance, masquerade, or literal color of something.

Notes

1. Ann Thúy Nguyễn and Maya Pendleton, "Recognizing Race in Language: Why We Capitalize 'Black' and 'White,'" Study for the Center of Social Policy, March 23, 2020, https://cssp.org/2020/03/recognizing-race-in-language-why-we-capitalize-black-and-white/.
2. Kwame Anthony Appiah, "The Case for Capitalizing the *B* in Black," *The Atlantic*, June 18, 2020.

Preface

The movies make everything seem effortless—the makeup, the coloring, the dancing—it all looks so natural to young, unassuming eyes. Growing up I idolized Shirley Temple. Not until I was much older, did I question her use of blackface in *The Littlest Rebel* or her relationship with Bill Robinson. Nor did I problematize how easy it was for me to identify with other White girls I saw on the screen, girls who, like me, loved tap dancing. What I recognize now is that many of the things I took for granted as a young aspiring tap dancer boil down to privilege: that not everybody can utilize blackface as a disguise; that having the greatest living tap dancer simplify his own dancing in order to make a White child shine brighter so that White audience members can identify with her is a form of entitlement; having someone onscreen who shares my skin color as an inspiration is a freedom. This is a book about the various strata of White privilege that have and continue to exist in Hollywood as much as it is a book about the donning and doffing of burnt cork.

Burnt cork has long been used as a facial additive. The Ancient Romans used its ash for an effect comparable to modern-day mascara. French makeup artist Stéphane Marais used burnt champagne cork to create a smokey eye shadow for Jean Paul Gaultier's models at a 2018 couture show. He claimed it created a "strange beauty but very captivating."[1] But in the United States, paste derived from burnt cork has long been associated with the minstrel stage, where the substance's deeply colored and toxic features have been used to exaggerate not just the eyes, but the sight and sound of Blackness, all-encompassing. This applied mask produces an unstable dialectical relationship between self and Other. This dialectic is, in the well-articulated words of Ryan Friedman, "reflexively determined but demands no reciprocity in recognition."[2] The history of burnt cork application is thus one of specular mimesis, the performance of trying on the Other in one's mirror image.

The makeup itself is dense with imagery—auditory and visual—put on as a temporary solution to alleviate power struggles and identity crises. The mask it creates is temporary for the wearer but comes with lasting consequences for the one(s) it seeks to emulate. This covering is also ambivalent both in its presentation and in its reception: burnt cork often presents itself as something that is not quite; the disguise tends to hide something deeper. Michael Rogin has argued that one way Jewish immigrants were able to take the focus away from their ethnic differences was to highlight their Whiteness through the donning of burnt cork. Meanwhile, Louis Chude-Sokei has discussed the potentially liberating powers and racial progress insinuated by burnt cork worn by Black performers like Bert Williams. Many scholars have discussed the blackface mask's inherent ambivalence, how it has the power to simultaneously fascinate and repulse those whom it intends to entertain—a *strange* but *captivating* attraction that has kept this racial masquerade tied to the American narrative for centuries. Its sublime embodiment of fear and horror sanction it to the realm of the almost-but-not-quite, the ambivalent, and the unstable. Thus, the act of "blacking up" always tells at least two stories: at the same time burnt cork provides amusement for one, its performativity effects violence for another. *Behind the Screen* addresses this violence through a deconstruction of the many masks involved in a deceptively simple process of makeup application.

Similarly, holding on to some of the reasons a performer might don a mask in the first place could help to provide some empathy for those performers I identify as engaging in minstrel practices; it is easy to point fingers retrospectively, so it is important to keep in mind our common human desire for belonging. Finally, recognizing the inherent ambivalence in all types of minstrelsy will support a deeper understanding of the *many* factors and thus complications involved in disassembling a practice that has existed for centuries.

To fully understand the thrust of covert minstrelsy, the mask should be deconstructed from the interior. The structure of *Behind the Screen* performs the act of layering while taking a performative approach to masking. At the same time, this book takes a performative approach to writing, seeking to undo its act of masking through its utterance. As such, *Behind the Screen* is best read from start to finish because each chapter builds on the last, adding new levels of complexity to the issues at hand as the chapters progress. Reading this book as presented will engage you in the *process* of layering, allowing you to reflect on all iterations of covert minstrelsy in each of its guises and variations. The makeup must first be removed in order to understand its application, and my hope is that this performative approach will better outfit readers to strip away the individual masks on their own, preventing the passive consumption of films, their imagery, and their soundtracks.

PREFACE xvii

Much of the text situates readers in the position of an American, White moviegoing public, Hollywood's target audience during its Golden Age. Short interludes exist between the chapters: a sing-along, a seven-minute cartoon, a Vitaphone short (here categorized as a dance break), a travel advertisement (here labeled a transit narrative), and various pitches to buy war bonds would have been common additions to any feature film seen by this audience; their presentation unfolds in a time-specific manner within a book that is organized chronologically with some temporal overlap between chapters. Descriptions of what you might have seen along with what more attuned ears might have heard appear in italics. The chapters' analyses are meant to fill in some of the sonic, technological, historical, and social gaps that exist in these performance descriptions while also building a framework of covert minstrelsy. For those looking for a methodological quick reference to covert minstrelsy, I have created a descriptive diagram.

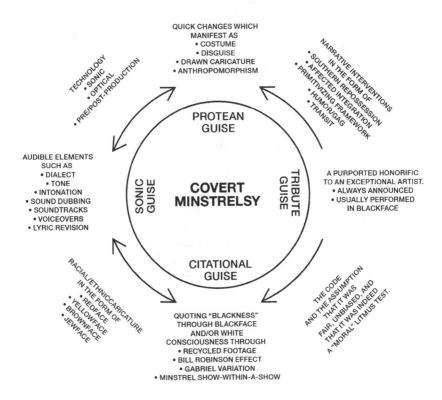

Covert minstrelsy is not linear, and its four guises often bleed together. The sonic, protean, tribute, and citational guises comprise covert minstrelsy; each guise is influenced by a set of attributes and variations designated by the map's short descriptors and bullet points. Arrows on the diagram denote which ways the guises are capable of flowing. The outermost orbit represents the major distractions involved in the process: technology, narrative interventions, the Production Code, and racial/ethnic caricature. All of this will be explained in the introduction and subsequent chapters. Additionally, an excerpted version of the Production Code (1930–1954) can be consulted as a resource in the Appendix at the back of the book.

Blackface minstrelsy, no matter what its intent, effects racial violence. Several visual references to the specific performances about which I am writing appear throughout *Behind the Screen*. The reproduction of black-face imagery in this book is not meant to further mark or mythify Blackness but instead to confront readers with the historical reality of American performance. In including such visuals, I am entrusting the reader to both see and share such imagery only in context. Furthermore, some cited language in *Behind the Screen* is offensive. Naming such language is meant to contextualize the ways that racial caricature manifests in more ways than through darkening the skin. In printing original text, I do not wish to reify the fiction that blackface has sought to emulate, but instead to highlight the realness of its existence in history.

Notes

1. Delphine Achard, "Haute Couture Fall 2018: Beauty Looks from Fashion Week: Jean Paul Gaultier," *Women's Wear Daily*, July 6, 2018,, https://wwd.com/beauty-industry-news/beauty-features/gallery/haute-couture-fall-2018-beauty-looks-from-fashion-week-1202742377/jean-paul-gaultier-show-backstage-fall-winter-2018-haute-cout ure-fashion-week-paris-france-04-jul-2018/, accessed May 30, 2021.
2. Ryan Jay Friedman, *Hollywood's African American Films: The Transition to Sound* (New Brunswick, NJ: Rutgers University Press, 2011), 161.

Introduction

Masks in Disguise

Astaire in his tap solo in blackface equals his best work as a dancer who uses imagination as well as his feet. This striking production . . . hits high with a silhouette background on which Astaire seems to be casting three gigantic shadows of himself in action.[1]

This review of Fred Astaire's "Bojangles of Harlem" number from *Swing Time*, which appeared in the *Hollywood Reporter* in August of 1936, is one of several from this era that captures the appeal that blackface still held in the 1930s for the majority of White journalists and White spectators. What most people do not understand is that *blackface was never banned* from the American stage or screen, and it persists in the twenty-first century. The screen itself was born from a fractured lens; the perception of racial difference lives in its optics. This book traces a history of blackface onscreen and the covert means by which it entered Hollywood cinema, despite the Motion Picture Producers and Distributors of America's (MPPDA) decades-long efforts to censor such racial caricature, and specifically visible blackface like Astaire's, from appearing.

The Hays Code (also known as the Production Code, or just Code, all used interchangeably throughout this book) professed to regulate the "purity" of motion pictures. However, contrary to what the MPPDA conditioned the general US public to believe was the purpose of this Code, Will H. Hays (first chairman of the MPPDA) put the Code in place to deter public backlash at Hollywood's provocative imagery and to offend the smallest percentage of members comprising the country's cultural and legislative leadership. This leadership included nationally federated civic and religious organizations (e.g., the PTA, YMCA, and various women's clubs).

Behind the Screen. Brynn W. Shiovitz, Oxford University Press. © Oxford University Press 2023.
DOI: 10.1093/oso/9780197553091.003.0001

2 INTRODUCTION

In the eyes of Hays, public relations were key to the moviemaking industry's success, and thus the board could not "ignore the classes that write, talk, and legislate"; these were those classes.[2] But it was no secret to the nation's Black journalists that "negroes can expect little from this crusade because the moralists themselves define 'cleanliness' in traditional terms." *The Crisis*, the official voice of the National Association for the Advancement of Colored People (NAACP), knew that purity for those on the MPPDA's board was not opposed to "Jim Crow and all that it mean[t]."[3] Thus, inasmuch as the leadership behind the Hays Code claimed to regulate Hollywood's imagery from an impartial moral standpoint, its definition of decency was highly subjective.

Behind the Screen considers the Code to be one of many ruses used during Hollywood's Golden Age (here defined as 1927 to 1963) to distract the White moviegoing public from *seeing* the ways Hollywood projected nineteenth-century minstrel logic through a modern lens. While the NAACP and other Black-run organizations were free to comment on the integrity of the motion picture industry and the films it produced, the Black voice had little sway in Hollywood's visual spectacle. The Production Code exemplifies what Slavoj Žižek might refer to as a constitutive ideology, an ideological form that "provides the coordinates of the very space within which the content is located."[4] Understanding such structural racism helps not to justify the cracks in the system but rather to explain how certain representational politics have persisted over time. Biased apparatuses of power, like the Code, are central to *covert minstrelsy*, the term I offer—and this book's focus—to refer to theatrical practices that assist in creating national unity through the exclusion of an Other by way of masking.

Anti-Black sentiments were not the only logics operating behind the screen. The various iterations of the Code directly reflect the makeup of their contemporaneous review boards as well as certain external factors; this was certainly the case with anti-Jewish sentiments before US involvement in World War II. Shortly after Hitler consolidated power in Europe, the Reichsfilmkammer (RFK)—the corporation that regulated the film industry in Nazi Germany—began censoring imported American films and proceeded to eliminate Jewish and part-Jewish artists from stage and screen. This included removing "every [European] Jewish film man employed in all of the American film offices and branches."[5] Because American offices "could not afford" to lose the European market, they complied; this attitude bled over into film censorship so that "Jewishness

INTRODUCTION 3

in content or in person qualified as prima facie justification for condemnation."[6] Joseph I. Breen, an "influential layperson" in the Catholic community and the man Hays appointed to spearhead the Production Code Administration (PCA) in 1934 was a staunch anti-Semite who did not do much to censor anti-Semitic material until pressure from the Catholic Church motivated him to issue a statement in 1938.[7] Thus purity in motion pictures has always been more related to the economics of representation and the more global political stakes than about virtue. The Production Code tracks a history of what White Catholic men determined was in the best interest of the country over a span of three decades. This book asserts that the Code has worked to reinforce and perpetuate racial, ethnic, and sexual inequity by allowing the privileges associated with a very particular type of Whiteness to endure.

Blackface Minstrelsy as Performance

The notion of blackface minstrelsy may be understood through a consideration of its constituent parts: minstrelsy and blackface. The term "minstrel," on its own, means a singer, or more broadly a musician, who would recite poetry for the noble class during medieval times.[8] Generally speaking, the word "blackface" denotes the use of any prosthetic applied to the skin to imitate an imagined version of Blackness. Both minstrelsy and the darkening of one's skin date back to the Middle Ages. Some of the earliest uses of blackface occurred in medieval miracle plays where "the souls of the damned were represented by actors painted black or in black costumes."[9] During the Elizabethan Era, actors commonly used makeup to darken their skin when depicting Moors, Africans, and Turks. Shakespeare's *Othello* notoriously features a role written for a White actor to perform in blackface, whether it was called "blackface" in 1604 or not. But "blackface minstrelsy" specifically references a practice that began in the early nineteenth century.

Rather than dwell on who was the originator of blackface minstrelsy— there were conceivably many—I want to trace a few patterns that seem to be consistent throughout all these so-called origin stories. Blackface minstrelsy is the imitation of a "*Negro type*." I italicize and set this phrase off in quotations to show that these words were both ascribed and prescribed to any visibly Black American during the antebellum period. The Negro type

4 INTRODUCTION

included a look, a way of speaking, and a specific ontology. Early examples of this "type" can be seen in Charles Mathews's *A Trip to America* (1824) where he imitated Black Americans' way of speaking and darkened his skin. Thomas "Daddy" Rice began *Jumping Jim Crow* around 1830, a performance in which he "blacked-up" and adopted a similar "Black dialect." Both Mathews and Rice claimed that their impressions were based on empirical data: Mathews professed to have "studied [Black peoples'] broken English carefully," and specifically that of a real life "specimen" in the form of a Black Methodist.[10] T. D. Rice asserted that his Jim Crow character was based on a "deformed" enslaved person with a "laughable limp."[11] But no evidence outside of Mathews's or Rice's travelogues exists for either of these.

Rice and his contemporaries quickly began building on these so-called Negro types, developing a set of Negro archetypes that would become as tied to the nineteenth-century minstrel stage as Pantalone, Pulcinella, and il Capitano were linked to *Commedia dell'arte*. Of the many stock characters that found their way onto the minstrel stage, the Jim Crow, Zip Coon, and Long Tail Blue characters were the three most popular: Jim Crow was the simpleton or dumb fool, a figure whose iconography Barbara Lewis has described as confirming the "chattelization or demotion of the black body, an attitude that would find legal sanction in the 1857 Dred Scot decision that decreed that black bodies were only fractionally human."[12] As almost an opposite, Long Tail Blue represented the Black Dandy who dressed decorously and spoke eloquently. Zip Coon offered the stage a more ambivalent identity, straddling these extremes, with ostentatious dress, and undignified speech. But the value of each of these archetypes increased when juxtaposed, each extreme enhancing the comic effect of the other. Lewis perfectly captures the nature of this dynamic when she writes, "The correct and necessary equilibrium between the races was re-established as Crow symbolically ripped Blue Dandy's coat, leaving it so full of holes, no tailor could ever fix it again."[13] What each of these three archetypes—and all those that would follow— shared were their ascribed and prescribed ways of looking, speaking, and being in the world. Those who performed these types took on authoritative roles. They sold these fictitious representations as exact replicas of real "specimens" while also assuring audiences that the attributes they assigned to these Negro types were natural.

The blackface minstrelsy I discuss in *Behind the Screen* stems from this specific nineteenth-century history: archetypes created by White men in the image of Black American subjects (the "Negro") who claimed to imitate the real qualities of objectified Black bodies, speech patterns, and ontologies. Although White men created these archetypes, Black performers have participated in this practice since 1822.[14] In some instances Black engagement with Black stereotypes is not a choice; in others—to borrow a phrase from Greg Tate—"Black irony and contrariness are never far away."[15] I explore the many reasons that both Black and White performers *may* have participated in this practice recognizing that we can never fully *know* one's intentions or limitations. I can only offer speculations based on my observations and interviews, and what I have encountered in the archive.

The book also attends to other forms of racial and ethnic caricature—brownface, redface, jewface—but each of these has a unique history separate from the nineteenth-century practice of blacking-up on the minstrel stage and will be singled out as a form of racial or ethnic caricature accordingly. When I write about brownface I am talking about the act of using brown makeup or full-body bronzer as Juliet McMains discusses in relation to competitive Latin ballroom dance. I also include the use of props, clothing, and hairpieces that signify a range of people assumed to be of Latin, Mexican, Spanish, Polynesian, Middle Eastern, and Southeast Asian descent. However, brownface generally fails to be specific in its representation, and the flattening of these disparate locales that occurs onscreen tends to be part of the caricature itself. Similarly, my use of redface refers to both an actor's or animator's application of red or brown paint as well as costumes, props, and/or vocal transmogrification that is meant to indicate someone of American Indian or "Native" origin. The lines between these racial caricatures become less clear when animation is discussed because of the variety of paint shades available to artists. The term "jewface" refers to a popular vaudeville act from the late nineteenth century that featured Yiddish-speaking, large-nosed, bearded caricatures played by both Jewish and non-Jewish performers.[16] I deploy the term "jewface" when discussing audible and visible references to the caricatured Jewish body in live action film and animation. I do not use the term to describe the performances of Al Jolson and Eddie Cantor; I argue that they double coded their Jewishness by utilizing a variety of masks, resulting in a perpetual and imperfect assimilation. Finally, I distinguish between caricature, racial/ethnic caricature, and blackface minstrelsy. Understanding how we use these different labels makes the nuances of each clearer and thus leaves open the possibility for an artistic medium like

6   INTRODUCTION

animation, based entirely on the principles of exaggeration and imitation, to be funny without also causing harm.

Blackface Minstrelsy as Theory

Minstrelsy as a scholarly subject began with Ralph Ellison's fêted essay, "Change the Joke and Slip the Yoke" (1958),[17] wherein the author claims that the minstrel mask inverts shame into laughter through a process of identification with the audience. While provocative, it took a few decades for academics to catch on to the idea that blackface minstrelsy was a worthwhile topic, and only now, two decades into the twenty-first century, are mainstream media outlets discussing its prevalence. *Behind the Screen* builds on minstrel scholarship of the last thirty years and hopes to reroute the path along which current conversations around blackface are headed.

Although there are many theories on blackface performance, the ideas in this book stem from a few essential concepts: Eric Lott has famously argued—albeit almost exclusively from a White, working-class perspective—that blackface stages a racial counterfeit, one that develops from a desire to "try on" Black culture and use it for one's purposes; a "white ventriloquism through black forms."[18] This book tracks how blackface in Hollywood enabled White social mobility at the expense of real Black artistry performed by Black artists. That is, for performers like Al Jolson and Eddie Cantor who continuously "tried on" Blackness as a costume onscreen, their success was indelibly tied to their masquerade *and* supported the ongoing fetishization of Black culture. Central to this idea is that when non-Black performers utilize the blackface mask, their association with Blackness is only temporary and can be abandoned at any time. The impermanence of this mask is also what has allowed various ethnic groups to assimilate into the American mainstream. Which is to say, Al Jolson and Eddie Cantor reinforce their Whiteness through their temporary identification with Blackness, which seemingly downplays their Jewishness in the process. Such "racial cross-dressing," as Michael Rogin describes it, helped White immigrants (e.g., Irish, Jewish, German) look Whiter. Put differently, the very act of "blacking up"—a phrase historically used to describe the process of applying burnt cork or other black substance—in fact washed away one's distinguishing ethnic features. Moreover, because so much emphasis is placed on the *act* of "becoming" Black, in the films I discuss audiences will almost always see White performers donning—and often doffing—their blackface masks. "Primal scenes" such as these "expose the illusion that the individual was in charge of his or her voice, that it issued from an authentic interior."[19] Such scenes also seem to justify the inclusion of such racial masquerade in films that were otherwise meant to uphold certain moral standards.

We cannot apply the same intents to Black performers who performed in blackface: there are many reasons non-White individuals may have used burnt cork, not least of which is the reality that many Black performers in the nineteenth and early twentieth centuries had few employment options. This book mainly discusses White artists who chose to wear blackface and Black artists who had little choice but to engage in the act, visible and not. Bill Robinson and the Three Eddies are exceptions. Because I discuss their performances at length, I must offer another theory for why Black artists might have performed in blackface. Scholars like Louis Chude-Sokei have explored how the blackface mask worn by Black performers may have been an act of empowerment: for example, a performer like Bert Williams could erase his Caribbean identity as a means of gaining exposure in America by indulging audiences in African American stereotypes. He was in on a joke that his White audiences were not, and, at the same time he carved out a space for Black artistry on an otherwise White stage. Relatedly, Daphne Brooks views Williams's performance as "walking a fine line between disrupting the master narratives of theatrical 'race' performance and simultaneously capitulating to familiar and debilitating caricature."[20] In Brooks's view, Williams's career in blackface may have ruptured dominant narratives of race performance but simultaneously reinforced damaging stereotypes. Brooks's and Chude-Sokei's readings offer helpful insight for understanding Black artists who performed in blackface—overtly and covertly—and support a principal argument in this book: all masks perform from multiple vantage points depending on who is the masker and who is witness to such masking.

Blackface performance is fundamentally ambivalent because it operates on multiple registers simultaneously. It stabilizes and destabilizes racial/ethnic categories; it is lack but also desire; it is Lott's "love and theft" and Stéphane Marais's "strange but captivating beauty."[21] The mask is both social fetish and a Hegelian "self-consciousness." It is master and slave; self and Other. Blackface is the simultaneous attraction to and repulsion from

8 INTRODUCTION

the Other—what Julia Kristeva would consider a primary site for the "I's" becoming.[22] Blackface can, at least superficially, mediate between opposing forces. Recognizing that most race performance exists in this liminal space leads us to one of *Behind the Screen*'s essential concepts: the underlying ambivalence of blackface (and other ethnic/racial caricature) implicates the relationship between abjection and appropriation; one can both fear the Other and revere its artistry and aesthetic contributions.

On the one hand, minstrelsy is built on a series of contradictions. W. T. Lhamon has made a compelling argument for Jim Crow's doubleness. Long before blackface minstrels sold Jim Crow as a token of segregation through fantastical depictions of Blackness filtered through the lens of White desire, Jim Crow in fact "figured freedom, integration, and unity," evidenced by the original lyrics to "Jump Jim Crow." But this Jim Crow became too popular, "exceed[ing] the categories, spilling dangerously over into the consciousness of disaffected whites."[23] Those threatened by Crow tried to eradicate his image, but he forever lived on in the shadows. Over time, Jim Crow's totem accrued a wealth of meaning "across gulfs of difference." These interpretations "came to undergird both the politics of segregation and the politics of inclusion."[24] This Jim Crow anecdote provides a metaphor for blackface minstrelsy's larger stakes for the United States: no matter how hard one tries to wipe out the practice of "blacking up," blackface minstrelsy and all of its more covert iterations forever live behind the screen because the screen itself was built on the tokens (and totems) of racial difference.

On the other hand, blackface minstrelsy necessitates ambivalence through its competing narratives of power and subjection, an intricate cycle of intention and reception determined subjectively by time, place, and subject. Stephen Johnson captures this interplay when he describes the complexity of blackface performance as building up "in layers over time, adding radical meaning to the accepted imagery without entirely erasing the old, haphazardly accumulating ways of reading blackface that reshape, refocus, and redirect its intentions."[25] Because blackface minstrelsy depends so much on context and because it is impossible to ever know a masker's intent or how the mask will land on the object of its gaze, accepting the profusion of meaning that each and every performance contains is the only way to understand the practice.

FIGURE I.1 (*Top*) Al Jolson in *The Singing Fool*, 1928; (*Bottom*) Bing Crosby "blacks up" Marjorie Reynolds for "Abraham," in *Holiday Inn*, 1942. (Private collection)

10   INTRODUCTION

Interjecting in the Literature

Up until now minstrel scholarship has assumed a certain visibility when speculating on the psychological, political, or economic intents and ramifications of blackface performance. The theories that tend to hold the most weight all take sight for granted. Except for Susan Manning's breakthrough that minstrelsy could be metaphorical—that White dancers' bodies could become "vehicles for the tenors of nonwhite subjects"—and that minstrelsy could reference Otherness rather than overtly engaging in impersonation, most writing on the subject understands minstrelsy to be both literal and visible.[26]

On the contrary, music and sound studies have addressed aural perception for quite some time. In the last two decades, several scholars have invited Blackness into this conversation in exciting ways: Matthew Morrison's notion of "blacksound," Nina Eidsheim's "sonic blackness," Daphne A. Brooks's "sonic blue(s)face," and Barbara Savage's "aural blackface" have all had profound impacts on this book.[27] *Behind the Screen* imagines a sonic intervention at the crossroads of minstrel studies and dance scholarship, attending specifically to the ways that technology and systemic racism choreograph our senses, arranging the steps and patterns of *how* and *what* we perceive on the screen's surface. Even if blackface is first and foremost a visual phenomenon, its imbrication in aural practices such as dialect, music, and tap dance cannot be ignored. Sound becomes even more crucial in discussions of film because of the ways in which optical and sonic technology extend the types of possible projections. Everything from sound synchronization to dubbing affects our ability to hear, while camera angles and colorization alter how we see.

This book sets out to explore what it would mean to define blackface minstrelsy as simultaneously visible and invisible, audible and inaudible, overt and covert. Unlike conventional forms of minstrelsy, *covert minstrelsy* relies on several layers of disguise working together simultaneously to create a spectacle whose process remains hidden by the layers' very synchronicity. That is, covert minstrelsy is a specific type of minstrel performance wherein simultaneous sense perception, narrative, technology, and biased apparatuses of power (e.g., the Production Code) work together to reinforce pre-existing notions of race as well as to create new stereotypes through distraction.

Using covert minstrelsy as its primary lens, *Behind the Screen* makes three central arguments: first, race performance, and specifically blackface minstrelsy, need not be visible to be effective. This does not mean that such racial masquerades are metaphorical or even imperceptible, but it proposes that our vision may not always be reliable. Second, blackface performance has been a part of the American narrative since the 1820s, and accordingly, the imagery, music, and dance linked to the minstrel stage might carry an element of nostalgia for Americans who were never directly hurt by its portrayals; sometimes this nostalgia is confused with patriotism. Third, Africanist aesthetics have pollinated American entertainment in such a way as to mistake blackface performance for lived experience and furthermore to write Black artists out of the equation in favor of White bodies who utilize Black sensibilities. This book looks specifically at how less visible forms of blackface minstrelsy transitioned White audiences away from associating an Africanist aesthetic with visible Blackness while at the same time removing Black visibility from the screen.

Covert Minstrelsy

Covert minstrelsy sits at the center of a complex system of deception. It is itself a series of forces that exert themselves on and through individuals' sense perception. When covert minstrelsy is at play, several factors engage. Four primary guises comprise this orbit: the sonic guise, the protean guise, the tribute guise, and the citational guise. Sometimes covert minstrelsy manifests sonically, through audible elements such as dialect, tone, intonation, sound dubbing, soundtracks, voiceovers, or lyric revision; at times it surfaces through quick changes—costumes, disguises, drawn caricature, or anthropomorphism; on occasion covert minstrelsy appears as a purported honorific to an exceptional artist and is called a "tribute"; other times covert minstrelsy appears citationally: it quotes a fabricated concept of "Blackness" through blackface and/or the filter of White consciousness and can present as the Bill Robinson effect, the minstrel show-within-a-show, or the Gabriel variation. These four guises often bleed together. The protean can take on aural qualities, as with vocal transmogrification and voice throwing; the protean, at least in animated iterations, always accompanies the citational; and tributes are usually also exemplary of the citational guise, but not the other way around. These four guises work together to obscure the inner workings of an entertainment industry that thrives on racial caricature and masks an even more concealed infiltration of an Africanist aesthetic into the White mainstream.

12 INTRODUCTION

Tracking how an Africanist aesthetic not only entered the American vernacular but came to be associated with White bodies remains an integral part of this book. By Africanist aesthetic, I am referring to a range of recognizable *Black sensibilities*, or "the enlivened, vibrating components of a palpable black familiar [that] demonstrate[s] the microeconomics of gesture that cohere in black performance," as described by Thomas DeFrantz and Anita Gonzales in their introduction to *Black Performance Theory*.[28] Drawing heavily on the work of Robert Farris Thompson, who conceived of a terminology for these aesthetic commonalities, and Brenda Dixon Gottschild, who fine-tuned these aesthetic principles and applied them to dance specifically, this book *excavates* the "presences, trends, and phenomena" the African diaspora has generated.[29]

When referring to an Africanist aesthetic or Black sensibility in this book, I am specifically looking at ten traits: from Gottschild (and Thompson), *contrariety, polyrhythm, polycentrism, high-affect juxtaposition, ephebism*, and the *aesthetic of the cool*; from Thompson and Jacqui Malone the patterns of practice recognized as *improvisation* and *call-and-response*; and from Lindsay Guarino in *Rooted Jazz Dance*, the concept of *groove*.[30] Finally, *flexibility*; like Thompson's "*les tresors de souplesse*," flexibility—much like the aesthetic of the cool—is its own quality but is also inherent in the other nine.[31] These ten traits are interrelated and apply to a range of Africanist forms, but they are especially salient in discussing the rhythmic sensibilities of tap dance and jazz music. Being "in the groove" requires dancers and musicians to be rhythmically flexible, "in the pocket," neither here nor there, but "in it." Improvising requires a certain alacrity and elasticity; call-and-response demands that the participants listen, watch, be in the moment, be adaptable. Whether we are discussing the vitality of ephebism or the supple spine necessary for polycentric movement, flexibility sits at the base of these ten traits and at the heart of tap dance and jazz music.

The focus this book gives to tap dance is especially notable, considering the subject's lack of scholarly attention. Indeed, tap dance is often overlooked within dance studies despite its racially complicated history and rich aural offerings. Tap dance is deeply rooted in the nineteenth-century minstrel show and, like the figure of Jim Crow, has accrued a wealth of meaning over time, becoming a token of segregation as well as a prime space for the continuation and fertilization of racist ideologies, old and new. As demonstrated through my analyses of performances by famed tap dancers such as Fred Astaire, Bill Robinson, Eleanor Powell, and the Nicholas Brothers, tap's sonic component offers minstrel scholarship a different vantage point, one steeped in rhythm, sound, and corporeality. Studying the dance as itself an act of masking offers covert minstrelsy an exemplary model of all that is overlooked in more occularcentric studies.

Behind the Screen commences with the introduction of synchronized sound film and therefore establishes its theory of covert minstrelsy through the sonic guise. The sonic guise is the most versatile of the four and will appear in some version in each of the book's six chapters and a coda. Some foundation for this *first layer* is in order: by sonic I mean the sound one hears when Bill Robinson tap dances; by sonic I mean the notes one identifies when Cab Calloway scats *Hi-Di-Ho*; by sonic I mean the tone and intonation of Stepin Fetchit's voice; by sonic I mean the dialect Hollywood gives southern Black characters versus that assigned to African "Natives"; by sonic I mean the Stephen Foster songs played in the background of minstrel shows; by sonic I mean the audible lyrics of a song; by sonic I mean "a theory of historical embodiment to trace the ephemerality and materiality of the sounds produced by Black bodies within the history of popular music in the United States," or "blacksound" as Matthew Morrison defines it.[32] The sonic guise manipulates sound in order to alter one's perception of its remnant audibility.

The sonic guise stems from an interaction between sound and technology and how the novelty of new sound technologies radically transformed both the practice of listening as well as the sound itself and, in the process, taught the audience what to hear consciously and what to hear on a subceptional level.[33] The sonic guise involves sound dubbing and voiceovers, confusing the real with the imagined or post-produced. The sonic guise also deals with what Mendi Obadike refers to as acousmatic Blackness, or the idea that sound may summon the presence of Blackness even without the attendance of Black bodies;[34] the sonic guise refers to a film's soundtrack and how that soundtrack signifies according to certain musical, cinematic, and cultural codes. These codes help shape what an audience hears, which, as Kathryn Kalinak asserts, forces audiences to engage in a "quasi-magical" process of transference and slippage between sound and image. And finally, the sonic guise refers to lyric substitution, or exchanging a new word for N[*sic*] but keeping a song's melody intact; the specters of minstrelsy remain present even in certain words' absences.

To sketch the remaining three guises, it will be helpful to define them in context. *Mickey's Mellerdrammer* provides a good introduction to many of

FIGURE I.2 (*Top*) Mickey Mouse lights a stick of dynamite backstage as part of "the gag" in Disney's *Mickey's Mellerdrammer* (1933); (*Bottom*) Mickey completes the gag and cites Al Jolson's "Mammy" in blackface. (Private collection)

the concepts this book will explore in more depth. *Mellerdrammer* is a minstrel show-within-a show, one of many variations of the citational guise that offers directors and animators an opportunity to *cite* the minstrel show vis-à-vis its replica, while at the same time reproducing an original minstrel show. The citational guise, generally speaking, is any mention of a person, performer, or practice who/that has a well-known connection to blackface expressed physically, aurally, or both. When in *Mellerdrammer* Mickey appears in blackface and then sits on one knee, arms outstretched reciting "Mammy," he both physically and aurally *cites* Al Jolson's *Jazz Singer* performance. This same citation appears in live and animated films for decades to come, justifying the reproduction of Jolson's minstrel performance as "just in quotations" and therefore not the real deal.

Mellerdrammer's narrative not only helps to explain Mickey's blackface and provides an excuse to *cite* Jolson's famous "Mammy" moment [FIG. I.2], but it also introduces a cast of minstrel archetypes (Topsy, Uncle Tom, Little Eva), rehashes Dan Emmett's famous song "Dixie," and reinforces a connection between tap dance, the minstrel stage, and a kind of White privilege that allows White characters to temporarily become "Black" as a form of entertainment. While there is nothing covert about Mickey's blackface, the fact that it is part of the gag within a grander homage to the early roots of American entertainment, speaks to how embedded these tropes are in the White American psyche. That is, even if the point of *Mellerdrammer* was not to directly offend or put down Black individuals, it makes clear that a large percentage of Americans have long viewed race performance as a form of entertainment.

Nicholas Sammond offers a helpful lens through which to view cartoons like Mickey Mouse and Clarabelle, suggesting that by the 1930s, cartoons had become *vestigial minstrels*, "carrying the tokens of blackface minstrelsy in their bodies and behaviors yet no longer immediately signifying as such."[35] In Sammond's view, neither Mickey nor Clarabelle is *like* a minstrel; they *are* minstrels. If we view blackface minstrelsy as constantly adapting to the "social and material relations of its day," then animation *is* minstrelsy in the 1930s.[36] *Behind the Screen* views many of America's most popular cartoons as vestigial and posits that because the attributes that define these cartoons as minstrel are so covert and embedded in the cartoons themselves—Mickey's famous gloves, for example—cartoons were an ideal vessel for presenting minstrel material that also passed the censors. Cartoons were and are also perfect vehicles for performing the protean guise, which requires quick transformations.

16 INTRODUCTION

Blatant forms of blackface necessitate that the masker undergo some kind of physical transformation. Recall Charles Mathews, one of the earliest blackface minstrels on record. He was known both for the verisimilitude of his transformations and also the alacrity with which he underwent them: "Mathews, the mimic, could effect [an] extraordinary . . . change in the appearance and expression of his face, by simply [t]ying up the tip of his nose with a piece of catgut."[37] I refer to these transformations as exemplary of the protean guise. In animation, the protean guise accompanies all illustrations of the citational guise. In live action film this is usually the case but is not definitive. The protagonist offers a series of quick changes through wardrobe (costume, makeup, props), dialect, and embodied caricature, which all help to converge and collapse notions of Otherness. Eddie Cantor's frequent engagement with the protean is part of what both obscures and permits his use of blatant blackface. Whether the protean manifests aurally through a skill such as voice throwing, or visually by means of expedient costume changes—within a few minutes of screen time, Cantor morphs from White middle-class hypochondriac to Greek chef and then again from American Indian to Jewish salesman—these processes occur so quickly that the audience has no time to process the individual stereotypes. This looks similar in animation, but because of the ease with which a cartoon can transform, and special effects in cartoons such as clouds of dust or invincibility, animated versions of the protean guise occur even faster and more seamlessly than is possible with real actors. Furthermore, because of animation technology, artists can easily detach one element of a cartoon's body or voice, make it disappear, reattach it to another part of the body, or even create a completely new form. Such protean transformations allow the racial imaginary to run wild thus creating new stereotypes and upholding old.

Often overlapping with the protean and related to the citational guise, but heavily influenced by a film's narrative, is the tribute guise, or the act of one using the "tribute" label in conjunction with burnt cork and various stereotypes to convince the audience that their makeup merely acknowledges a historical moment or honors an individual. Not only did tributes provide an exemption from the Code in matters of blatant blackface, but they also gave directors and animators carte blanche to display themes that threatened to "lower moral standards." Crimes against the law, illegal drug trafficking, the use of liquor, and gambling were strictly prohibited by censors when executed by a film's White characters. These themes more easily snuck by the censors when implemented by Black characters or White characters performing in blackface. Fred Astaire's tribute "Bojangles of Harlem" exemplifies this: Lucky's (Astaire) gambling addiction is highlighted most prominently in his swingin' tribute to Bill Robinson performed in blackface. A correspondence letter between the film's producer B. B. Kahane and head of the PCA Joseph Breen explicitly advises the creative team to remove any references to gambling. In the final version of the script, Astaire's rendezvous with Blackness vis-à-vis blackface, swing music, and tap dance pardons his lower moral standards as a race problem.[38] The double standard to which Black performers were held in Hollywood applied both to the Code and more generally to moral guidelines.

The Modes of Distraction

One mechanism through which Africanist aesthetics subtly and pervasively infiltrate American culture is through the technique of distraction. Several modes of distraction operate within this landscape of covert minstrelsy. Sonic technology has the ability to modify how we hear as well as what we see. Some examples include early sound synchronization, which forced audiences to reconcile sound and image in a way silent film had not required. It brought "increasingly subtle means of punctuating scenes without putting a strain on the acting or the editing . . . unobtrusive ways to emphasize a word, scan a dialogue, close a scene."[39] It opened up a world of sound dubbing and voiceovers, where taps could be pre-recorded and reassigned to a new body, and a single person could be the voice behind a whole cartoon menagerie. As Michel Chion notes, "Sound superimposed on an image is capable of directing our attention to a particular visual trajectory."[40] Sonic technology thus augments the sonic guise and helps obfuscate certain visuals.

Optical technology also has profound effects on how we perceive. This book examines everything from Busby Berkeley's distinctive eye for the camera to later developments in camera technology including Technicolor's introduction of a three-color camera in 1932, which captured separate color records onto three strips of film, as well as Paramount Pictures' high-resolution, wide-screen variant known as VistaVision.[41] Like sound synchronization, which ostensibly allowed people to hear more transparently but in fact removed a level of audience autonomy by influencing a certain visual trajectory, optical technology like Technicolor and VistaVision made things appear more clearly on the surface but in fact offered audiences more densely saturated content than was available in black and white. As these examples

18 INTRODUCTION

demonstrate, technology operates in several directions, manipulated by and manipulating our senses: technology utilizes physics, which in turn influences our senses; our senses and internal biases then determine our perceptions.

Persistence of vision, for example, is a perceptual/physiological phenomenon wherein "our eyes hold on to images for a split second longer than they are actually projected, so that a series of quick flashes is perceived as one continuous picture."[42] This illusion forms the basis of film and television and is responsible for viewers' experience of movement on the screen; the images themselves do not move, but one's persistence of vision (when viewing still images in quick succession) allows one to experience motion. Persistence of vision occurs unconsciously with the blink of an eye at the same time numerous other slippages and displacements fail to register on the conscious level. Such physiological phenomena are further impacted by racial/ethnic biases, privilege at the structural level, and narrative framings.

Behind the Screen suggests that sometimes subtle forms of racial and ethnic caricature were used to distract film censors from flagging more blatant racial distortions. In *Honolulu*, Eleanor Powell's masquerade as a Native Hawaiian helps divert one's attention away from her unconcealed use of blackface. Powell's body produces a "multiplicity of discourses and acquired a range of meanings for different people at different times," engaging in several conversations simultaneously throughout the film.[43] In *Whoopee!* Eddie Cantor's obvious references to Jewish culture redirect an audience's attention away from his unconcealed redface, and that same redface guides censors away from his flagrant blackface in the previous scene. Multimodal racial and ethnic caricature were also used to avert White audiences and censors from acknowledging the presence of a swing aesthetic, since swing was classified as "hot" and dangerous due its ties to sexuality and Blackness. In *Ali Baba Goes to Town*, the film's location in fictional Baghdad helps deflect censors away from Cantor's unabashed swing number in blackface. In *Three Little Pigs*, the Wolf's jewface intercepts his engagement with Africanist body percussion. In *The Kid from Spain*, the Goldwyn Girls' brownface forfends from the conspicuousness of their polyrhythmic Charleston-infused tap dance while at the same time thwarting the visibility of Cantor's blackface. At the heart of all these examples is the ability for racial and ethnic caricature to mediate between extremes—Black and White, here and there, us and them—allowing exceptional non-White performers finite opportunities for imperfect assimilation.

INTRODUCTION   19

The process of redirection made possible through the simultaneous use of racial and ethnic caricature—among other things—creates a masking effect, making invisible and silencing what would seem blatantly minstrel in a performance that was singularly visual or sonic. Unlike other forms of minstrelsy, the simultaneous modes, or processes of masking, at play in covert minstrelsy work together to obscure underlying aesthetic and racial ideologies. Thus, covert minstrelsy refers not only to a particular type of masking, but also requires that the masking itself mask the mask(s) at play.

Narrative intervention exhibits the final mode of distraction that interacts with the four guises to produce this systemic blurring and fading of covert minstrelsy's various strata and coatings. This can take many forms including southern repossession, transit narratives, affected integration, a primitivizing framework, and the "gag," five patterns I track as being the most common during the Golden Age. Simply put, southern repossession locates a film or a segment of a film in a Civil War or glorified old South context and through such narrative framing justifies the use of blackface (e.g., Shirley Temple in *The Littlest Rebel*) or songs tied to the minstrel stage such as "Dixie Land," "Turkey in the Straw," or "Old Black Joe."

Several of the dances occur in transit: Eddie Cantor performs in blackface alongside the Nicholas Brothers en route to Egypt in *Kid Millions*, Eleanor Powell performs a tribute in blackface en route to Hawaii in *Honolulu*, a caricatured Uncle Tom performs Bill Robinson's stair dance on a showboat in *Mississippi Swing*. Transit narratives are neither here nor there; they mediate between the exotic island and the American mainland, the self and Other, the local and the foreign. Transit narratives mirror minstrelsy's ambivalence and offer an excuse to skirt Production Code guidelines in virtue of their constant state of becoming.

Affected integration encompasses film plots that either advertise their progressive racial politics or sell themselves as "integrated" when in fact such integration is only a ruse for more covert forms of racism. The animated *Boogie Woogie Bugle Boy of Company 'B'* marks a perfect example: Hot Breath Harry (a jazz musician) who is drafted into the army swing dances with one of the Andrews Sisters. While such depictions of race-mixing were extremely progressive—and went against the Code—for a 1941 cartoon, the animators' use of a Negro dialect, giant minstrel-like lips, and a shuffle walk often used to caricature the Black enslaved completely undermine the final dance scene.

Primitivizing frameworks often create scenarios wherein someone White visits lower-class Black neighborhoods, shantytowns, or Africa and appears

20 INTRODUCTION

to introduce or be the expert on Black vernacular forms that are normally assumed to originate in these locations. Sometimes the Black artists in these scenes wear some combination of animal skin, chains, shells, and/or feathers implying a loose association to the jungle or a "primitive" lifestyle. Primitivizing frameworks assist in the transfer of audibly Black forms to visibly White bodies while providing a way to sidestep a Code that advised against the use of such "dangerous," "hot" rhythms.

The "gag" was the most common of these narrative interventions during this period. In live action film, gags naturalize blackface through cause and effect. In both live action and animated film this generally takes the form of either a disguise or an explosion. Eddie Cantor hiding in a stove that spontaneously combusts epitomizes the faulty household appliance approach while Mickey's reckless use of a firecracker in *Mickey's Mellerdrammer* exemplifies a typical cartoon gag. [Figure I.2] In this same cartoon, Clarabelle cow "blacks up" with chimney soot. What these gags share along with almost all other blackface gags is their superfluousness to the plot. While narratively justified, the stove "joke" does not drive the plot forward but instead accentuates Cantor's reputation as *the* blackface comedian. The use of an explosive and soot in *Mellerdrammer* make no sense outside of being the supposed cause of Mickey's and Clarabelle's blackface, which is further justified because of the cartoon's overarching plot as a recreated minstrel show.

Finally, it would be irresponsible of me to discuss the Hollywood musical *without* mentioning aesthetic camp; the Golden Age is teeming with excess, impersonation, and quotation marks. But camp plays a very specific role for covert minstrelsy. The function of aesthetic camp I explore in *Behind the Screen* is not the kind that is tied to queer agency as scholars like Moe Meyers have explored in depth; the "queer aura" will be found throughout this book.[44] Instead, I am specifically interested in the way that camp *sensibilities* (*a la* Susan Sontag) became a primary mode of distraction during World War II, an adornment that was "consciously stagey" in a continued effort to shift audiences away from "what a thing *is* to how it looks," all while upholding two of film's primary functions during the war, namely, to galvanize and to entertain.[45]

As the stories in this book unfold, the nuances of each of the four guises along with the four main modes of distraction will continue to surface at the same time they will become more concentrated. All the examples I discuss are representative rather than exceptional to the ethos of the period. What I hope to expose by the end is, first, the way that the Code operated as a "White [male, Catholic] given" which, to use the important words of

Michael Eric Dyson "boast[ed] an *a priori* manner of evaluating white ideas and actions," and second, the way that Hollywood has used multiple—often invisible—means of disguise to silence real lived experience by continuously inscribing, and re-ascribing blackface ("the Negro type") as a stand-in for real Black artistry.[46]

Chapter Preview

Chapter 1, "Integrating the Screen: Sound Synchronization, Sonic Guises, and Pre-Code Blackface, 1927–1930," situates Al Jolson's blackface within a technological revolution. Understanding the impact that the "coming of sound" had on the visual image and its role in offsetting racial caricature from 1927 to 1930—the "pre-Code" era—lays the framework and foundation for future, more discreet iterations of covert minstrelsy that develop in the years following 1930. Jolson's iconic sound/lip-synchronous performance of "Mammy" in *The Jazz Singer* (1927) not only transitions the nineteenth-century practice of "blacking up" into the sound era, but it offers blackface, and specifically blackface tied to sound, as the key to national integration. Establishing the *sonic guise* as both motivated by these early sound-synch experiments and Hollywood's strong desire to avoid censorship in a rapidly changing industry, I analyze Irving Berlin's song "Puttin' on the Ritz" in the 1930 film by the same name as exemplary of the kind of micro-manipulations that would become so popular in future years. This includes the film's sound-track as well as small changes Berlin made to the musical compositions and their lyrics. Furthermore, "Puttin' on the Ritz" has been inaccurately labeled the first "interracial" song and dance to be performed on the silver screen. This chapter examines this misleading label—a kind of affected integration—in combination with Berlin's unique use of syncopation and lyricism, to show how even in the absence of visible blackface, Hollywood directors engaged in more covert forms of masking, teaching viewers how to *see* Blackness in a modern, urbanized context.

Adding a level of optical technology to the novelty of sound in the wake of the Great Depression, chapter 2, "Optical Illusion and Design: Exposure Values, Protean Guises, and Eddie Cantor's Blackface, 1930–1933," investigates Busby Berkeley's unique use of the camera as a means of choreographing female sexuality and Eddie Cantor's blatant gender-bending and use of blackface during the Great Depression. These two performances,

FIGURE I.3 (*Top*) Eddie Cantor poses in front of Follies/War Bonds advertisement, 1917 (Bains News Service/Library of Congress); (*Bottom*) Busby Berkeley inspects Goldwyn Girls, 1935 publicity portrait. (Private collection)

in tandem, allowed such "perversions" to slide by the newly established Hays Code that forbade "undue exposure" and "pansy gags" of any kind. Cantor's extremely quick, almost imperceptible character changes—here introduced as the protean guise—allow Cantor to edge past the censors almost as seamlessly as he transforms himself. I also introduce the citational guise, a form of embodied caricature usually evoked through physical gestures and/or the voice. These two guises (i.e., the protean and the citational) along with redface and brownface, help to illustrate the ways in which the very simultaneity of layers further obscures the conscious image, making it easier for taboo body parts and racial caricature to "slip in." In *The Kid from Spain*, the Goldwyn Girls' brownface justifies their exposed cleavage; their breasts distract from Cantor's blackface; Cantor's mask validates his Whiteness. Cantor's redface in *Whoopee!* similarly disguises his aural blackface, both of which de-emphasize his Jewishness, while his Jewishness and blackface are what allow him to act "effeminately" to destabilize new forms of working-class consciousness and organization by flipping perceived gender paradigms on their head during the country's worst economic crisis to date.

Chapter 3, "Public Works and Accolades: Race Film, Southern Repossession, and the Rise of Bill Robinson, 1929–1935," looks beyond Hollywood's high-budget films intended for White spectatorship by reading independently produced race films alongside the racial caricature produced in mainstream Hollywood. Beginning with an analysis of race film, this chapter demonstrates four directions that depictions of Blackness took on the screen between the years 1929 and 1934: blackface performed by Black artists who capitalize on a successful White performer's use of the blackface mask; all-Black films made by all-White creative teams that utilize a range of overt and covert disguises to uphold a set of imaginary beliefs about Black life and the Black body; the minstrel show-within-a-show and southern repossession formulas that allowed for flagrant uses of burnt cork; and finally the material realized through Oscar Micheaux and other Black filmmakers who linked themselves to White consciousness only insofar as it impacted the funding of their films. The remainder of this chapter recounts the concealed ways White audiences utilized covert masks through a handful of exceptional Black artists, the most popular of which was Bill Robinson. Robinson pioneered an era onscreen, often making sacrifices through casting, song choice, choreography, and even his own relationship to the NAACP. This chapter introduces the Bill Robinson effect through which romanticized

24 INTRODUCTION

portrayals of an individual allow audiences access to a nostalgic and unquestioned slave-owning past while shielding them from the shameful parts of this narrative.

Covert minstrelsy becomes more pervasive in Hollywood when Will Hays appoints Joseph Breen to lead the censorship review board. Chapter 4, "Bon Homage: Female Figures, the Tribute Guise, and Pre-War Departures, 1934–1939," begins during this shift in the Production Code Administration (PCA). The minstrel show-within-a-show continues to justify blatant blackface, minstrel music, and the tried-and-true formula of popular song, *olio* (variety), and *afterpiece* (which usually included slapstick and tap dancing). But more covert than the minstrel show-within-a-show is the use of the tribute guise. This chapter focuses on the benefit of labeling a performance a "tribute," analyzed through two representative examples: Fred Astaire's performance of "Bojangles of Harlem" in *Swing Time* and Eleanor Powell's tribute to Bill Robinson in *Honolulu* three years later. Beyond its more visible use of excusing blackface during a time when the Code clearly stated that "entertainment which tends to degrade human beings" should be avoided, the "tribute" label allows White performers to re-introduce an Africanist rhythmic sensibility through their "blacked-up" White bodies.[47] In this way, Hollywood "authenticates" the tap dancing of Astaire and Powell at a time when the industry was employing fewer Black artists, thus creating a distance between a polyrhythmic aesthetic and Black corporeality. Simultaneously, by *masquerading* as Robinson, Astaire and Powell could present gambling and "sex perversion," themes that the PCA viewed as moral offenses when delivered by White actors, but acceptable material when performed through a Black filter.

Storylines that relied on overblown racial caricature mostly disappear by the end of 1934. What remains, however, is a strong use of the citational guise in the form of "Black heaven," a subset of covert minstrelsy I refer to as the Gabriel variation. Chapter 5, "With a Glory Be: The Gabriel Variation, Jazz, and Everything in Between 1934–1942," returns to both the sonic and citational guises, examining both a general shift in attitude toward syncopated rhythms and the significance of blacksound when offered in a "holy" context. Beginning in 1934, Hollywood's White stars flirted with an increasingly popular swing aesthetic, one that had hitherto been tied to the devil and subject to unforgiving censorship laws. To circumvent the Code, directors utilized two primary strategies: the first was to cast Black actors and White actors in blackface within a White conception of Black heaven—caricatured to the point of Black dystopia—which housed not only dozens of minstrel caricatures but also foregrounded these fictions in a swing aesthetic. The Gabriel variation allowed Hollywood to sidestep many of the rules surrounding racial representation while simultaneously pulling "hot" rhythms out of the depths of hell. Alternatively, a swing-inspired scene or film would encode a classic primitivist framework—often signaled through a generalized brownface—into its overarching narrative. Concurrently this chapter tracks how, during the Code's most unforgiving period, the transit narrative functioned in the background to help establish a racial in-between-ness or "safe" exoticism, and to assist in the passage of swing from the audibly Black to the visibly White.

As the penultimate chapter, "Hays Is for Horses: Cartoons' Crossover Appeal, Dis-figuration, and the Animated Bestiary 1934–1942," examines the radical aesthetic shift that animation technology made possible. It documents how this transition not only aided in what was imaginable artistically, technically, visually, and sonically, but also how it naturalized laws of the appropriate and ethical as governed by Breen's iteration of the Production Code. Much of what the Code deemed unacceptable in live action film for the censors was excused when the representation was not "real." Focusing on those qualities that give animation a "moral" advantage, I assess how anthropomorphism, technology, and dis-figuration contributed to the censors' "blindness." The art of animation lends itself more freely to concepts such as imitation, exaggeration, and buffoonery; the protean takes on the ability to transform humans into animals and vice versa, animation technology's capacity to sever voice from visible image further nuances covert minstrelsy's sonic component, altering the citational soundscape at the most minute levels; the protean guise, along with the sonic, allows a single body part to either perform on its own, disappear, or re-assemble itself to another part of the body to create a new form; technology allows this transformation to appear seamless. In a world where humans can become animals, animals can become racialized, and body parts can detach from one object and re-attach to another almost instantaneously, "Hays Is for Horses," stands as a testament to the innumerable coatings that have been applied to our screen.

For a brief moment in the 1940s, the United States was forced to reconsider Black representation in cinema as part of supporting Black involvement in World War II. Activated by the Double V campaign, people of color and liberal Whites worked together to instigate change, both onscreen and

26 INTRODUCTION

out in the world. However, many of Hollywood's efforts were thwarted by a stronger economic desire to satisfy the industry's biggest markets, often polarized in their social and moral viewpoints. In the book's coda, "Enlisting the Tropes: Covert Minstrelsy in Action, 1942–1954," I argue that patriotism was something both markets could agree on and that appealing to a camp aesthetic was the most effective way of reaching these divided values. The willfully hackneyed nature of some of the musicals made during the War are what allowed them to be both adored by both sides *and* overlooked by the censors.

Read separately, each chapter offers the basic obstacles Hollywood directors faced and the various means by and through which White privilege enabled them to circumvent such hurdles. Each chapter also sheds light on the individual masks involved within a much more complex operation of covering up structural racism while seeking to recuperate the stories of some of Hollywood's most talented Black artists who were written out of the credits. When considered together, the chapters highlight these disparities and discrepancies on a much grander scale, exposing not just the charades that occurred behind the scenes but also the mere spectacle these synchronous façades produced for Hollywood's target audience in the 1930s and 1940s. This process has perfected itself over the years at the same time our senses have been manipulated.

Visible blackface began fading from the screen shortly after World War II, and by the time Breen's tenure was up in October 1954, its blatant manifestations were a rare occurrence. But the belief that someone can temporarily try on race has in no way disappeared. Racial masquerades continue to haunt mainstream media, and only a small percentage of these are brought to our attention. Training ourselves not just to see, but to listen for even the most covert manifestations, breaks this silence and teaches us the value in delving *behind* the screen.

Notes

1. "Astaire-Rogers 'Swing Time' Triumph of Comedy, Music Equals Their Best on Every Count," *Hollywood Reporter* (Los Angeles, CA), August 24, 1936.
2. "Will Hays and the MPPDA in the 1920s," MPPDA Digital Archive, Flinders University Library Special Collections, https://mppda.flinders.edu.au/history/mppda-history/will-hays-and-the-1920s/, accessed June 1, 2021.

INTRODUCTION 27

3. Quoted in Thomas Doherty, *Pre-Code Hollywood: Sex, Immorality, and Insurrection in American Cinema, 1930–1934*, Film and Culture (New York: Columbia University Press, 1999), 340.

4. Slavoj Žižek, *Living in the End Times* (New York: Verso, 2011), 55.

5. Ibid., 94.

6. Ibid.

7. Thomas Doherty, "Was Hollywood's Famed Censor an Antisemite?," *Jewish Daily Forward* (New York), December 11, 2007, https://forward.com/culture/12234/was-hollywood-s-famed-censor-an-antisemite-00948/, accessed February 27, 2021.

8. From the French *menestral*, meaning "entertainer, servant," via the Latin *ministerialis*, meaning "servant." See Merriam Webster and Oxford English Dictionaries.

9. Anthony Gerard Barthelemy, *Black Face, Maligned Race: The Representation of Blacks in English Drama from Shakespeare to Southerne* (Baton Rouge: Louisiana State University Press, 1987), 3–4.

10. Quoted in *Mrs. Mathews, The Life and Correspondence of Charles Mathews, the Elder, Comedian* (London: Routledge, Warne, and Routledge, 1860), 284.

11. Quoted in Tracy C. Davis, "Acting Black, 1824: Charles Mathews's Trip to America," *Theatre Journal* 63, no. 2 (2011):177–78.

12. Barbara Lewis, "Daddy Blue: The Evolution of the Dark Dandy," in *Inside the Minstrel Mask*, ed. Annemarie Bean (Middletown, CT: Wesleyan University Press, 1996), 267.

13. For an analysis of how the juxtaposition of these three archetypes on the minstrel stage simultaneously created and threatened racial and class binaries, see Lewis's "Daddy Blue," 265–66.

14. For evidence of the first Black blackface performer, Billy Waters, see Ayanna Thompson, *Blackface* (New York: Bloomsbury, 2021), 28–30.

15. Greg Tate, *Everything but the Burden: What White People Are Taking from Black Culture* (New York: Broadway Books, 2003).

16. Talya Zax, "Remembering the Days of Vaudeville and Jewface," *Forward*, December 8, 2015.

17. Ralph Ellison, "Change the Joke and Slip the Yoke," in *Shadow and Act* (New York: Random House), 1964.

18. Eric Lott, *Love and Theft: Blackface Minstrelsy and the American Working Class* (New York: Oxford University Press, 1993).

19. Michael Rogin, *Blackface, White Noise: Jewish Immigrants in the Hollywood Melting Pot* (Berkeley: University of California Press, 1996), 119–20.

20. Daphne Brooks, *Bodies in Dissent: Spectacular Performances of Race and Freedom, 1850–1910* (Durham, NC: Duke University Press, 2006), 213.

21. Eric Lott, *Love and Theft*; as mentioned in my preface, French makeup artist Stéphane Marais used burnt champagne cork to create a smokey eye shadow for Jean Paul Gaultier's models at a 2018 couture show. He claimed it created a "strange beauty but very captivating." Delphine Achard, "Haute Couture Fall 2018: Beauty Looks from Fashion Week: Jean Paul Gaultier," *Women's Wear Daily*, July 6, 2018.

28 INTRODUCTION

22. Julia Kristeva and Leon S. Roudiez, *Powers of Horror: An Essay on Abjection* (New York: Columbia University Press, 1982).

23. W. T. Lhamon, "Turning Around Jim Crow," in *Burnt Cork: Traditions and Legacies of Blackface Minstrelsy*, ed. Stephen Johnson (Amherst: University of Massachusetts Press, 2012), 26–27.

24. Ibid., 24.

25. Stephen Johnson, *Burnt Cork: Traditions and Legacies of Blackface Minstrelsy* (Amherst: University of Massachusetts Press, 2012), 3.

26. Susan Manning, *Modern Dance, Negro Dance: Race in Motion* (Minneapolis: University of Minnesota Press, 2004).

27. Matthew Morrison, "Race, Blacksound, and the (Re)Making of Musicological Discourse," *Journal of the American Musicological Society* 72, no. 3 (2019): 790–91; Nina Sun Eidsheim, *The Race of Sound: Listening, Timbre, and Vocality in African American Music* (Durham, NC: Duke University Press, 2019); Daphne A. Brooks, " 'This Voice Which Is Not One': Amy Winehouse Sings the Ballad of Sonic Blue(S) Face Culture," *Women & Performance: A Journal of Feminist Theory* 20, no. 1 (2010): 37–60; Barbara Dianne Savage, *Broadcasting Freedom: Radio, War, and the Politics of Race 1938-1948* (Chapel Hill: University of North Carolina Press, 1999).

28. Thomas DeFrantz and Anita Gonzales, *Black Performance Theory* (Durham, NC: Duke University Press, 2014), 8.

29. Brenda Dixon Gottschild, *Digging the Africanist Presence in American Performance: Dance and Other Contexts* (Westport, CT: Praeger, 1998), xiv.

30. I am intentionally using "excavates" as it relates to "digging up" for Gottschild. See Gottschild, *Digging*, 12–16. See also Lindsay Guarino, "Where's the Jazz? A Multilayered Approach for Viewing and Discussing Jazz Dance," in *Rooted Jazz Dance: Africanist Aesthetics and Equity in the Twenty-First Century*, ed. Lindsay Guarino, Carlos R. Jones, and Wendy Oliver (Gainesville: University of Florida Press, 2022), 107.

31. Robert Farris Thompson, *African Art in Motion: Icon and Act in the Collection of Katerine Coryton White* (Berkeley: University of California Press, 1979), 10.

32. Matthew Morrison, "The Sound(s) of Subjection: Constructing American Popular Music and Racial Identity through Blacksound," *Women & Performance: A Journal of Feminist Theory* 27, no. 1 (2017): 13–24.

33. Subception, or subliminal auditive perception, refers to the effect that visual simulations of sound can have on their viewer. See Mervyn Cooke, *A History of Film Music* (New York: Cambridge University Press, 2008).

34. Mendi Lewis Obadike, "Low Fidelity: Stereotyped Blackness in the Field of Sound" (PhD diss., Duke University, 2005).

35. Nicholas Sammond, *Birth of an Industry: Blackface Minstrelsy and the Rise of American Animation* (Durham, NC: Duke University Press, 2015), 3.

36. Ibid., 5–6.

37. Quoted in Tracy C. Davis, "Acting Black, 1824: Charles Mathews's Trip to America," *Theatre Journal* 63, no. 2 (2011): 177–78.

38. George Stevens, *Swing Time* (RKO Radio Pictures, 1936), April 11–September 18, 1936, MS Hollywood, Censorship, and the Motion Picture Production Code,

1927–1968: History of Cinema, Series 1, Hollywood and Production Code Administration, Margaret Herrick Library, Archives Unbound, accessed April 27, 2021.

39. Michel Chion, *Audio-Vision: Sound on Screen* (New York: Columbia University Press, 1994), 49.

40. Ibid., 11.

41. According to the George Eastman Museum, the three-strip process worked as follows: "Light entered the camera through the lens and was divided by the beam-splitting prism into two paths. One strip of film recorded the green record onto black-and-white film, while the other two records were exposed onto two black-and-white film strips in 'bipack' (sandwiched together); the front film was blue-sensitive only, while the back film was sensitive to red." See "Technicolor 100," George Eastman Museum, https://www.eastman.org/technicolor/technology/three-strip-camera, accessed June 12, 2021; "Widescreen Museum—The VistaVision Wing—2," *www.widescreenmuseum.com*, accessed April 3, 2021.

42. Kit Laybourne, *The Animation Book: A Complete Guide to Animated Filmmaking—from Flip-Books to Sound Cartoons to 3-D Animation* (New York: Three Rivers Press, 1998), 19.

43. Anthea Kraut, "Between Primitivism and Diaspora: The Dance Performances of Josephine Baker, Zora Neale Hurston, and Katherine Dunham," *Theatre Journal* 55, no. 3 (October 2003): 438.

44. Moe Meyer, ed. *The Politics and Poetics of Camp* (London: Routledge, 1994), 5.

45. Esther Newton, *Mother Camp: Female Impersonators in America* (Chicago: University of Chicago Press, 1979), 107.

46. Michael Eric Dyson, *Entertaining Race: Performing Blackness in America* (New York: St. Martin's Press 2021), 6.

47. Quoted in Doherty, *Pre-Code Hollywood*, 348.

FIGURE 1.1 (*Top*) "God appears" and (*Bottom*) "POOF, God is now a satanic alien." (Private collection)

1

Integrating the Screen

Sound Synchronization, Sonic Guises, and Pre-Code Blackface, 1927–1930

A flurry of angels in striped leotards and whimsical tulle capes flutters across the foreground of an enchanted forest of cardboard geodes and stalactites. The glissando of a turn-of-the-century piano comically accents their frantic flying. POOF. A puff of smoke tries to conceal the shaky set change as the paper rock/ crystal formations vanish into "thick" air and two masked tumblers jump out of the two-dimensional set. Somersault. Handstand. Backflip. Roll. CUT. Four masked men with flambeaus leap out of nowhere. They conduct the space with their flaming torches providing the accompanist several opportunities to synch his sound with their movement while also presenting what appears to be an extreme fire hazard for the spectator aware of early film's flammability and the extremely low-budget nature of this predominantly wood-furnished set. It's beginning to look a bit like a Hieronymus Bosch hellscape. JUMP CUT. God (who bears a great resemblance to the Jesus found in nineteenth century Danish paintings) appears.[1] He makes big prophetic gestures, but his exact message is lost in translation. Without audible dialogue, God's memorandum is difficult to decipher. CUT. God, played by the film's director Georges Méliès, is now a Baphomet (also played by Méliès) clothed in an outfit resembling that of a court jester. POOF. More smoke and mirrors. A flambeau appears in the Baphomet's hand, and he performs a solo fencing match. He drops the torch, and a small piece of the stage goes up in flames. CUT. The Baphomet vanishes and fireballs float through the air so seamlessly that the men guiding their suspension are almost invisible. POOF. Two White dancers in blackface, dressed like the American stars Aida Overton Walker and George Walker, strut onstage and proceed to perform their rendition of the cakewalk, the most popular dance of 1903. It almost looks like the dance the Black enslaved were performing half a century earlier. Little do these French performers know they are impersonating White plantation owners, or more accurately, these White performers in blackface are copying the performance of two Black stars who are imitating the

Behind the Screen. Brynn W. Shiovitz, Oxford University Press. © Oxford University Press 2023.
DOI: 10.1093/oso/9780197553091.003.0002

32 BEHIND THE SCREEN

performance of the Black enslaved mimicking their "masters." CUE PASTRY. Two White performers in blackface dressed like Dahomean warriors transport a giant cake to center stage. Is Méliès further alluding to Aida Overton and George Walker in their successful run of In Dahomey, *which is currently on tour in England and France?[2] Is he commenting on the French takeover and colonization of the kingdom of Dahomey, which would very soon be absorbed into French West Africa?[3] Winner takes the cake. POOF. A man (Méliès) dressed as a Sabbatic goat/circus strong-man emerges from the cake's center with calf muscles as round as the softballs with which he has stuffed his tights and horns as big and narrow as those of an Ibex. Prance. Hop. Leap. Kick, kick. The live accompanist is really having fun keeping up with this one. Only one minute left. Let's go out with a bang and show the audience just how far stagecraft has come since Loïe Fuller.[4] Amputated legs appear in the background. SPLICE. Now amputated arms. CUT. The live ragtime music escalates with the excitement of all these optical and technical illusions on the screen. POOF. Grand finale. CUE ENSEMBLE. CUE CAKEWALK. CUE PYROTECHNICS. CUE TRAPDOORS. CUE BLACKFACE DANCERS. Sensory overload.*

The earliest film technology may have lacked an ability to "move" sound, but it did not lack the capacity to broadcast deeply entrenched Euro-American attitudes of "Blackness." In fact, silent film had mastered the art of presenting Black artistry as something dangerous and all dances tied to Blackness as satanic. *Le Cake-Walk Infernal* (1903) effectively communicates this pairing through its use of narrative—the title alone says so much—and easily interpreted visible markers like blackface, Baphomets, and the dark underworld.[5] This film, like so many others of the silent era, relied on images, visible fragments, and loaded signifiers to deliver a complex, yet accessible vision of the various stratum of White privilege: depicting God as White and presenting Black dance as "of the underworld" offers one layer; showing White dancers in blackface who can seemingly "try on" race highlights another; the film's allusions to American slavery and French colonization are just icing on the cake for an audience intent on preserving such dispensation.

While cutting edge for their time, the stagecraft and filming techniques used in *Infernal* make the film's process highly transparent to modern eyes; yet to someone watching in 1903, their novelty likely obscured some of these secrets. Turn-of-the-century cinema was primarily concerned with visual effects, manipulating what could be seen rather than heard. That is, technologically speaking, the various "scopes" and "oramas" invented over the nineteenth century were methods for looking and modes of being seen. The smoke and mirrors implemented during cinema's early years helped to conceal rudimentary camera technology while at the same time advertising modern science.

In a sense, the "special effects" employed in films like *Infernal* helped audiences to see and not to see. Everything from stage science (e.g., pyrotechnics and trapdoors) to camera science (e.g., substitution splices or stop tricks) helped to cover up some aspects while flaunting others.[6] The live (often improvised) music that accompanied these films in the theater allowed fugitive sounds, or sounds displaced from their inscribing object, the ability to run free without any accountability. The inability to record sound meant that neither music nor dialogue left any trace on the film itself. Which is also to say that the general lack of sound technology—and upsurge in highly visible science—leading up to the mid-1920s helped produce a certain ocularcentrism. And, because movies were mostly for *watching*, the medium itself included *no expectation* for listening. This lack of expectation, combined with the novelty of sound that arose in 1926, forms the nucleus of the *sonic guise* and is foundational for understanding covert minstrelsy between 1927 and 1930.

The pairing of sound with film was not an instantaneous shift that began clearly in 1927 as many have theorized; instead, it was an ongoing technological and commercial pursuit. This "coming of sound" in fact took the better part of a decade to materialize.[7] Long before movie palaces had sound, audiences could hear live music at vaudeville houses and nickelodeons. Pianists, like the one referenced in *Infernal*, had creative freedom. They held a certain autonomy and were often free to improvise with the action observed on the screen. Because of this, each screening was slightly different, and the accompanist in many ways determined audience pathos.

Around 1906, these screening houses began experimenting with new modes of communication, which included everything from canned sound to live actors standing behind the screen and narrating the visual. Nickel theaters became synch-sound experiments and politicians some of the first test subjects.[8] Inventors and experimenters were constantly tweaking technology: the first sound-synch system used in theaters was the Chronophone (1907), but E. E. Norton's Cameraphone (1908) quickly superseded its predecessor, finding its niche market in synching image with the "inexpensive reproduction of high-priced vaudeville stars."[9] That same year, Jules

34 BEHIND THE SCREEN

Greenbaum's Synchroscope, which synchronized image with phonograph records; L. P. Valiquet's Photophone (which combined a Mutoscope and a Phonograph);[10] and the German Biographon competed for theaters' business as well. While the Cameraphone had a longer shelf-life than some of these other synch-sound systems, it too did not last.[11] Thus, in the decade preceding the first universally recognized talkies, competing technologies drove the industry. Rick Altman posits that it was a lack of standardization that "condemned each synch-system to a tiny market"[12] and ultimately led to their decline. These early "novelties" stand in contrast to the industry's conversion to sound in the late 1920s when "modern" *electronic* technologies were driving such transfiguration.

This chapter examines these electronic technologies and the effect such science has had on sound itself—something Mark Katz refers to as the "phonograph effect"—and the impact such modern sound has had on the visual image. Understanding the process by and through which American audiences learned *how* to listen as mediated by technology and a certain sensory overload lays a framework for future iterations of covert minstrelsy. This emerges both in response to an invisibilizing process spawned by the phenomenon of sound and as a byproduct of distraction.

Thus, we might understand the function of sound technology in this first chapter as characterizing both the dominant means of disguise in pre-Code Hollywood (i.e., sound technology on its own, its impact on recorded music and film, and the science behind aural processing) and as scaffolding an understanding of a primary premise of covert minstrelsy writ large. While sound technology acts as the primary pretense for offsetting racial caricature from 1927 to 1930, this technological layer will continue to play a central role in covert minstrelsy for the next two decades. Because it continues to haunt the dances of Code-informed Hollywood musicals, it is important to recognize its success as motivated by the rapid changes that occurred during this so-called paradigm shift. Furthermore, understanding the way in which technology and sound interact lays the groundwork for understanding how covert minstrelsy depends on *multi*-masking. The success of minstrel performances that are covert in nature depends on the use of multiple signs that work together, in synch, to convey both a superficial and a veiled meaning.

The earliest examples of covert minstrelsy in Hollywood surface around 1930, the same year that the Production Code goes from an insouciant list of "Don'ts and Be Carefuls" to a more official set of regulations.[13] This parallel is no coincidence: as external surveillance became more robust, certain messages (especially ones related to race, sex, politics, and religion) had to find ways to "slip in" to the narrative. New sound technology meant more modes of expression which, naturally, meant Hollywood and its supporting organizations had to put more rules in place to "protect" American viewers from *seeing* anything deemed "dangerous."

While true covert minstrelsy begins in 1930, *The Jazz Singer* (1927), starring Al Jolson, represents an important in-between moment in Hollywood. The most successful films during these early years of sound synchronization boasted new science and recognizable vaudeville performers.[14] *Le Cakewalk Infernal* and *Jazz Singer* share the same polarizing idea that one kind of music/dance is religious or "good," and another is full of sin. The silent *Infernal* effectively communicated this through its *mise-en-scène*, use of blackface, and multiple suggestions of "cakewalking." *The Jazz Singer* successfully transmitted this not only through its *mise-en-scène*, use of blackface, and multiple suggestions of "jazz," but also through its new sound technology that allowed for a more nuanced narrative. For the first time on film, *The Jazz Singer* presented blackface with a tune other than improvised ragtime, and it paired (Black) jazz music with the performance of blackface, including Jolson's visible burnt cork and his audible "Mammy."

As the first feature-length motion picture to include synchronized dialogue, *The Jazz Singer*'s target (White) audience was less concerned with what its *images* were doing and more taken by its innovative use of sound. It is precisely Jolson's pairing of *aural* blackface with the visible act of "blacking up" that sets the stage for the sonic guise to flourish in films like *Puttin' on the Ritz* (1930). Beginning with an analysis of Jolson's pivotal performance in *The Jazz Singer*, this chapter establishes the sonic guise as both an effect of early sound technology and as affecting how audiences "viewed" these early films in light of the newly established Production Code. Through a close analysis of the title song and dance "Puttin' on the Ritz" from the film by the same name, I explore how covert minstrelsy can manifest sonically through a film's soundtrack, including micro-manipulations within the musical compositions themselves as well as through lyric revisions. Locating these "edits" not only complicates Irving Berlin's music in *Ritz* but will become the foundation on which later sonic guising builds, becoming increasingly more layered over time. But before I embark on an explication of the sonic guise, a history of how early sound technology developed through film is in order.

The Sound Behind the Screen

The Jazz Singer was not the first film to synch sound. Animators began experimenting with new sound technology much earlier. Max and Dave Fleischer were the first to attempt animated sound shorts with the experimental *Come Take a Trip in My Airship* (1924) and then the more successful (and well-known) *My Old Kentucky Home* (1926).[15] A major moment in sound experimentation occurred when composer/director Hugo Riesenfeld introduced Max Fleischer to Dr. Lee DeForest who had created a synchronization process under the *Phonofilms* label.[16] Major movie houses rejected DeForest's technology, but Fleischer's recent success with sing-alongs and his desire to advance the technological development of animation made him a prime collaborator for this new science.[17] While the dialogue in *Come Take a Trip in My Airship* is fairly rudimentary, this cartoon successfully synched sound, allowing music to emanate from the animated piano in perfect time with the lady mouse's fingers on the keys. By 1926, DeForest and the Fleischer brothers had a fully synched seven-minute cartoon with dialogue that moved beyond grunting. *My Old Kentucky Home* also succeeded in "moving" sound from something static and meant for the ears to a complementary mode of storytelling that the eyes could partake in as well.

That same year, Warner Bros. released *Don Juan*, the first full-length feature to use Vitaphone's sound-on-disc system. It was likely the company's strong financing along with the Vitaphone partnership and an industry-wide standardization that made the Vitaphone technology more effective than all of its predecessors.[18] However, even with a fully synchronized score, *Don Juan* lacked any sort of synchronized dialogue. Moreover, the score was constantly in flux: musical directors re-commissioned new musical settings for *Don Juan* even eight months after the film premiered.[19] Thus, the coming of sound was not clear-cut nor was it purely a matter of technological pursuit. Internal debates about the utility of sound, pre-existing theaters' architectural restrictions, and the sheer expense of new science were also complicating factors. It took a while before everyone in the industry saw the "cost benefit" of these new specifications. I am interested in this particular moment in Hollywood's history: the point in this process of moviemaking when Hollywood accepted an industry-wide standard in sound and when *listening* superseded hearing due to the aesthetic reprioritization that took place with Vitaphone's new sound technology.[20]

One year after Warner Bros. released *Don Juan*, the company made history with *The Jazz Singer*, a film that marked the "official" beginning of a new era in Hollywood as it became the first feature-length motion picture to include synchronized dialogue. It was about eighty minutes longer than the animated shorts the Fleischer brothers were producing with sound, included real humans rather than a combination of mice and men, and had a narratively contingent score that could not be changed.[21] Despite the massive growth that occurred between 1926 and 1927 for sound and the noticeable differences between cartoons and live action films, *My Old Kentucky Home* and *The Jazz Singer* shared quite a bit: they both marked the end of the silent film era and the beginning of the age of Hollywood musicals. More specifically, they shared many visible traits typical of pre-Code Hollywood as well as invisible attributes that would come to covertly define cinema of the 1930s.

Shifts to the cinema's soundscape directly impacted audiences' sensory experience. Just as sound technology took time to mature, so too did people's ability to listen. Prior to 1910, movie houses were social spaces where customers came to converse. As sound entered the picture, audience members were asked to talk less.[22] One way that movie houses accomplished this was to try to draw audience attention toward the sound source. This meant putting a musician in plain sight or placing the new technology in the orchestra pit, front and center. Sing-alongs asked audiences to participate in the sound image, and new seating patterns made it easier to hear but more difficult for audience members to engage with each other.[23] Therefore the very process of bringing sound into the theater was also a matter of re-training the audience to participate in the visual image differently. Rick Altman explains that spectators were muted in this process, and what they "gained in visual access, they lost in opportunities for speech." This silencing—and circumscription—democratized the visual landscape of the theater while simultaneously "de-democratizing the theater soundscape."[24] As the industry silenced audiences, so too did they instruct them on how to listen, not just hear.

The need to draw audience attention toward the sound source was mitigated as audiences became more equipped to listen. In fact, new technologies assisted in a necessary redirection away from the sound source: loudspeakers, for example, were placed behind the screen "offering an invisible and, as it were, unauthored sound source." Disguising the logic and source of film music allowed for more covert means of sonic transmission. Over time, audiences developed new listening standards that in turn allowed for more passive consumption. Altman has distilled the accomplishments of these new listening standards, points that are crucial to understanding a process of mystifying the visual that occurred alongside the development of Hollywood's early soundscape. First, such changes replaced spectator individuality with a temporary homogeneity, contingent on an audience's immersion in the film. Hence the communally experienced soundscape helped to streamline spectator experience through the film's pathos. Second, Altman argues, these new specifications "transformed each spectator from recognized (audible) interlocuter in an overtly discursive situation to (invisible) voyeur and (silent) *écouteur* of a distanced history."[25] The coming of sound included a loss of audience autonomy—a silence and a complacence—a disappearance of sound sources, and a willingness to be lost in the Hollywood sound/imagescape. That is, the new sonic layer—made possible by new sound technology—which entered Hollywood in the 1920s removed a degree of audience visibility. Audiences were now shown how to think and taught what to feel, collectively. This homogenizing process not only silenced spectators but also integrated them into an industry built on assumed White spectatorship and disguise. Such a "screening process" was tied to modernity and laid the groundwork for the use of more complex sonic veneers with future consumers. Technology thus manufactured a new kind of sensory processing, one that conveniently (even if not intentionally) would aid in sidestepping censorship laws of this new era. But technology also changed the sound itself, not just the source or the way we process such sound.

Sound technology influences the music itself as well as the way we listen. The ability to pre-record sound sanctions sound's reification, allowing it to be transportable, manipulable, and commodifiable as never before. Mark Katz identifies this phenomenon as a "phonograph effect," or "any change in musical behavior—whether listening, performing, or composing—that has arisen in response to sound-recording technology."[26] Understanding this occurrence is an important facet of covert minstrelsy because the phonograph effect defined as such determines the technological limits of the sonic guise, even if only accounting for a fraction of its expressions. Even more than the phonograph effect's impact on the sonic guise, Katz's theory facilitates my understanding of the significance of Jolson's performance in *The Jazz Singer*—and specifically the pairing of "blacksound" with blackface and "Mammy," a topic to which I will soon return.

Sensory Processing

While a soundtrack inevitably contributes to a film's overall effect,[27] films need not have sound to convey a series of sentiments and/or to elicit meaning. Subception, or subliminal auditive perception, refers to the effect that visual simulations of sound can have on their viewer.[28] Everything from the image of a crying baby to the action of a knock at the door can simulate a sound effect for its viewers. As Deborah Kapchan notes, "listening acts" are performative in complex ways: they "do not simply represent sound, as waves reach the ears and are relayed to the brain, but they transduce these sound waves, changing them in the process."[29] Similar to the impact that sound effects have on viewers, music also shapes how audiences perceive a particular interaction, scene, or plot line. Hence, whether absent or present, sound and music can have profound effects on what is being viewed, either because it agrees with the images projected on the screen, because it disturbs one's sonic expectations, or even because the sound waves themselves are transformed in transit. We can understand this process of pairing sound (or silence) and image by looking at some of the ways animated films of the era used visual signifiers to effectively communicate sound. For example, pictures of musical notes and/or sheet music might convey the presence of a composition as they do in Disney's animated short *The Four Musicians of Bremen* (1922), where floating bar lines with notes indicate the presence of a song.[30] Lines or puffs of smoke shown to emanate from objects that make noise in real life also suggest the presence of sound, such as those connected to a car horn or a tea kettle. Often dancing animations were enough to intimate a particular kind of music. For instance, the black bears who accompany the combination buck dance/jig with saxophones and fiddles in Disney's *Cinderella* (1922) ask the audience to conjure up a specific rhythmic feeling.[31] This is different from the sound expected of an audience watching the haloed white mice dressed in tutus doing slow *grand jetés* across the screen as they do in the Fleischers'

Ko-Ko's Paradise (1926).[32] But if the dancing itself could not convey a particular sound or rhythmic feel, words could be used to better define the type of music an audience was supposed to imagine, such as the opening frame in Disney's *Oswald the Lucky Rabbit in Bright Lights* (1928) where a marquee reads: "VODVIL MLLE ZULU, Shimmy Queen."[33] This text presupposes the rhythm that might be associated with a hula skirt and coconut bra–wearing black cat that appears a few frames later. As confusing as this mélange might be to modern viewers, theatergoers of the late 1920s were familiar with the likely signified "siren of the tropics" Josephine Baker, and likely not confused by this strange apposition of wished-for sounds and visual signifiers.[34] In this example, each sound one hears "loses its autonomy, surrendering the power and meaning of its own structure to the various contexts in which it might be heard, to the varying narratives it might construct."[35] The visual images in this cartoon dictate what the audience hears and the sounds produced reinforce this story in light of historic sound/signified relationships. We see this relationship most recognizably when animators use onomatopoeic language to guarantee that an audience hears exactly what is intended: "boom," "pow," "ding" all tell an audience exactly what to hear and when.

Visual sound worked similarly in live action films. Even though *The Jazz Singer* was the first full-length talkie, it still relied heavily on these old techniques. The sound synchronization was reserved for only a handful of isolated scenes. Most of the story was told through intertitles, or "full-screen image[s] of text inserted into the body of a film or television programme."[36] Thus, even at the dawn of the sound era, written language was still of primary importance to audiences' narrative understanding.

Historically, filmmakers have used music as a means of conditioning their viewers' responses to visual stimuli on the screen. Kathryn Kalinak has theorized that music allowed the silent image of early films a three-dimensionality that was otherwise impossible. This process of projecting an image from front (the screen) to back and sound from back (the invisible sound source) to front created "a kind of transference or slippage between sound and image, the depth created by the sound is transferred to the flat surface of the image."[37] Whether or not the sound and image were in synch, the audience was forced to reconcile this "quasi-magical" process.[38] Others have argued that music, especially that played in the background, appeals to our subconscious and allows us to forget.[39] What one hears largely affects what one sees as well as one's interpretation of the image, action, and film as a whole, a process Michel Chion identifies as "audio-vision," the undeniable reality that the audio influences and transforms vision and vice versa.[40]

Prior to the age of talking pictures, audiences were not accustomed to listening (consciously) while watching. Sonic pairings in these early years depended on paired associations that live theater had helped to construct over time. But sonic engineers also had a unique opportunity to explore sound and knowledge production from a *tabula rasa*. That is, not only could the directors of these films choose to pair the songs of Stephen Foster with blackface masks or certain types of movement associated with the minstrel stage, but they could also choose to couple the act of donning blackface with klezmer or classical music, just because it was easy. Many cartoon composers began as film accompanists, which accounts for the frequent use of generic melodies used to establish musical identities.[41] The short piece of ragtime piano that we hear during a chase scene or a similar scene accompanied by a familiar classical overture might have had little to do with the creative team wanting to pair the act of running with Scott Joplin or Wagner and instead been a carryover from the silent film era. Likewise, using a traditional Jewish wedding song "Mazel Tov" in the background of a scene where the "unnamed dog" in *My Old Kentucky Home* washes its face in a bowler hat could have had no visible meaning. Many people in the industry were Jewish, and naturally they would gravitate toward familiar tunes they would have known how to play. We see an alarming number of soundtracks utilize this yoking of pseudo-Negro spirituals, cultural leitmotifs (one of which is the Jewish *nigun*),[42] and blackface rituals (legible and covert) throughout the Golden Age. The ramifications of this practice will continue to unfold, but we begin with one of the best-known and identifiable pairings of this nature in *The Jazz Singer*, where the blackface mask acts as the redeeming element in Al Jolson's American assimilation story.

Assimilating to Sound

The purpose of the blackface mask in *The Jazz Singer* was not to caricature Black people in the same manner as did nineteenth-century minstrel shows;[43] Jolson's performance represented the blackface mask as the key to "national integration" and is a common thread in films of this era. This cinematic trend

42 BEHIND THE SCREEN

of White actors donning blackface in pursuit of cultural assimilation was one mode of accomplishing this visibly; pairing cultural "*niguns*" with the act of donning blackface was one method of attaining this narrative aurally. *The Jazz Singer* achieves both and helps to broaden the spectrum of aural signifiers American audiences come to recognize as palpable ties to the minstrel stage.

While the blackface mask served many different functions for performers in the nineteenth century, its use was particularly prevalent among White immigrants and ethnic groups. White immigrants often used the mask to distinguish themselves from Black people so they might move up the social ladder. One's ability to don a black mask and become something one was not in reality, as well as one's power to remove that mask at will, were ways of visibly marking one's position as someone White enough to temporarily "become" Black.[44] Michael Rogin speculates that Jewish immigrants might have used the blackface mask to take the focus away from their ethnic differences and instead shine a light on their perceptible Whiteness. Rogin's theory of "racial cross-dressing" is directly applicable to Jolson's performance in *The Jazz Singer*, which substantiates this theory through its assimilation narrative and also through its lead actor. Both Jakie Rabinowitz (the film's protagonist) and Jolson (in his life story and also more specifically in his performance as Rabinowitz) support how the blackface mask transitions various White ethnic groups into the American mainstream "melting pot" while defining a larger concept of (White) national identity and outlining the parameters of citizenship.[45] Thus the mask that serves to protect one person, or group of people, may at the same time work to undermine another or destabilize the identity of a group.

The function of blackface in early Hollywood cinema not only "rooted the present in the past; it also made the entertainment business the vehicle for national integration."[46] During the 1910s and 1920s, it is likely that many White Americans were drawn to the image of the blackface mask on screen as it conjured up a certain nineteenth-century nostalgia, recalling a time when a good laugh trumped a guilty conscience, and putting down the Other shaped collective identity without fear of consequence. Many films with Civil War plots gave production houses an excuse to project the clear racial divide they believed existed between Black and White people while also hinting at the "source of division in American life."[47] The blackface mask in this context represented enslaved life rather than the lives of archetypal figures such as Zip Coon or Jim Crow. Subject matter unrelated to southern plantation life also permeated celluloid expression. Shows that were about theater, like *The Jazz Singer*, often used the blackface mask to signify the passing down of a tradition. When Jolson performs jazz music for his mother, he upholds the family tradition of song, while simultaneously assimilating into the American mainstream through his choice of "popular" music over religious.

Kneeling down, Rabinowitz in blackface links eyes with his mother sitting in the front row of a full house. Seeing tears in her eyes, Rabinowitz comforts her with song: "I know where the sun shines best! My little Mammy. My heart strings are tangled around . . . Al—a-baaamy. Mammy, I'm comin'—I hope I didn't make you wait!" Slowly rising, Jolson opens his arms embracing his White audience, his painted-on black skin offers a deep contrast to his exaggerated white lips, and the sincere gaze of his eye whites. He accents the mood with sound, cupping his large white gloves together to produce a faint but audible pah pah pah—"Mammy, I'm comin, oh, God, I hope I'm not late—MAMMY! Don't you know me? It's your little baby! I'd walk a mil-lion miles, for one of your smiles, my MAAA—MAAAAAM—MYYY."

Jolson's use of the blackface mask in this film signals the beginning of a new era for blackface in sound film. While Jolson's blackface mask might on the surface resemble the mask used in silent films like *Infernal*, sound technology grants Jolson's iconic "Mammy" performance a whole new level of meaning. Jolson's hyper-visible blackface mask functions as both protection and as a marker of identity similar to that of the cakewalkers' masks in *Infernal*, by "safely" offering Rabinowitz and Jolson (superficial) access to national integration. However, Jolson's use of the mask also normalizes "blacking up" in a way that future Hollywood performances would come to use as a way around the Production Code—an "excuse" well into the 1950s.

While Hollywood could not have predicted the future ramifications of Jolson's blackface performance, *The Jazz Singer*'s souvenir program demonstrates a conscious decision on the part of Warner Bros. to simultaneously promote Jolson and his range of talents while naturalizing his blackface and its "sincere" relationship to Blackness. Arthur Knight aptly notes how the positioning of the "displaced ur-text" as well as an omitted scene connects Jolson's real life with that of Rabinowitz and conjoins blackface and Black performance.[48] Warner Bros. juxtaposes the program's centerpiece "Al Jolson's Own Story: the Jazz Singer in Real Life," with "The Making of the

Jazz Singer," asking audiences to conflate Jolson's own upbringing as an immigrant with that of the film's protagonist, the son of a cantor who dreams of nothing more than becoming a singer of jazz music. This so-called biography motivates Jolson's blackface and writes it off as a constituent part of the modern assimilationist story, not something tied to nineteenth-century racism. The omitted scene involves Jolson's interaction with his Black dresser who ultimately gives the actor the idea—essentially "permission"—to perform in blackface: "Boss if yo' skin am black they always laugh."[49] The "relationship" between Jolson and his servant hopes to offer *The Jazz Singer*'s White audience a more sympathetic narrative of blackface while also promoting the *idea* of equality. This kind of covert justification would become a hallmark in Hollywood films featuring visible blackface at the height of Code enforcement. But in the meantime, Jolson's synchronous sound film debut (including this souvenir program's ur-text) helped paint a new picture for American entertainment.

While not policed, Hollywood had some rules in place at the time of *The Jazz Singer*'s blackface. A 1915 Supreme Court ruling propagated film censorship by excluding movies from First Amendment protections,[50] but this only applied to state and city censors, rules that were external to Hollywood. The real changes took place in the mid to late 1920s when Hollywood's trade organization, the Motion Picture Producers, and Distributors of America Inc. (henceforth MPPDA) began "self-regulating" script content to protect the industry from public criticism.[51] *The Jazz Singer* managed to bypass this self-regulating iteration of the Code. Jolson's blackface performance in "Mammy" went completely unquestioned and would be celebrated for decades to come.

By March 31, 1930, this cautionary set of rules congealed into the Motion Picture Production Code (Production Code). Matthew Bernstein writes of the Code:

> Drafted by Catholics and revised by Hollywood executives. . . . Under this latter system individuals at the MPPDA's Studio Relations Committee (SRC) and Production Code Administration (PCA) intervened in the writing of script drafts and the shooting and editing of finished films from the major Hollywood studios, indicating what might and what would not provoke local censorship against a particular movie and trying to shape films to avoid such consequences.[52]

A growing concern that any disruption to the existing state of affairs in America—social, political, and otherwise—could stymie economic growth for the industry, was enough to codify a set of rules that would keep the public "comfortable."

Jolson's "Mammy" is Hollywood's first use of a blackface mask tied to song. Stage iterations of blackface assumed a certain coupling of the mask with sound (e.g., a Negro dialect, popular songs classified as "coon" songs by White salesmen, and tap dancing), but the sonic component of blackface faded with the advent of silent films. Unlike uses of the blackface mask on the nineteenth-century stage, camera technology allowed for a repetition of Jolson's performance that permitted it to be widely disseminated, well known by the American public, and therefore referenced as a loaded "signifier" for decades to come. I offer Jolson's performance as a new kind of minstrel act, one that points to a fresh beginning in American entertainment while also summonsing a mask of the past. This one performance— and specifically the moment when Jolson shouts "Mammy" while on one knee—becomes a point of reference for countless dance routines over the next three decades. Not only does Jolson's "Mammy" help to define blackface of the twentieth century, but its particular aesthetic (visual, aural, and corporeal) will become even "more important if [and when] it is repeated."[53]

Until the spring of 1930, Hollywood paid little attention to the Code's rules and recommendations, and not until July 2, 1934, did anyone start enforcing this set of guidelines. This four-year span became an essential time for the development of covert minstrelsy, as it mediated between old ways of presenting caricatures of Blackness and new. Like the gradual transition from hearing sound to active listening that audiences made toward the end of the 1920s, the first few years of the 1930s allowed for a visual evolution as it concerned racial representation. Knowing that it would only be a matter of time before blatant blackface would be censored, Hollywood directors might have used this period to find ways to circumvent obvious ties to the nineteenth-century minstrel stage. The first step would be to "integrate" the Black performer without blackface into the silver screen while still maintaining widely established (and old) assumptions about Blackness. *Puttin' on the Ritz* builds on *Infernal* and *The Jazz Singer*'s presumption that Black music is tied to sin, but it situates this narrative in a modern Harlem context, devoid of blackface but still loaded with allusions to the nineteenth-century minstrel stage,

FIGURE 1.2 A scene from the title number in *Puttin' on the Ritz* featuring lead Harry Richman *front and center*. (Private collection)

INTEGRATING THE SCREEN 47

Puttin' on the Ritz

The well-recognized opening notes of "Puttin' on the Ritz" fill the onscreen theater. The curtains part, exposing two Black chauffeurs who jump off the back of a 1920s-style Rolls Royce to wait on the car's White owner who steps out of the assumed-to-be leather interior wearing a top hat and tails. Following an 8-bar instrumental intro, Harry begins to sing, "Have you seen the well to do, up on Lenox Avenue . . ." and it becomes unclear as to whether he is boasting of the Black servants who taxied him onstage in their pristine uniforms or whether he is remarking on others of his own racial and social status who have the money and leisure to gallivant uptown to Harlem to witness the wealthy Black class. His black shadow is prominent on the upstage cyclorama as are the silhouettes of teetering black buildings hedging out from either side of the backdrop. He moves very little and awkwardly at that—some box steps, hand sways, and small pivots— making the lyrics the focus of this opening. After completing the second chorus, an all-female, all White ensemble enters from both sides filling the stage with bodies. The cyc lifts and reveals a cityscape of rectangularly- shaped black apartment buildings with ghoulish facial features positioned as windows. The eyes and mouths shine prominently through the black boxes as candle-lit jack-o-lanterns. The architecture dominates the majority of the stage, but in fact accentuates the eyes and smile of the adjacent chewing gum advertisement occupying stage left. In this ad for "Chewy Gooey Gum" a woman wearing some cross between a medieval knight's helmet and a nun's habit stares down the audience with her shifty eyes and painted smile. And despite the energetic dance number taking place on the main stage, the backdrop itself requires audience attention.[54]

Around the time that Al Jolson was crooning "Mammy" to American audiences, Irving Berlin was hard at work on what would become an international hit and the title song for a musical by the same name just three years later. "Puttin' on the Ritz," which Berlin wrote in 1927 and published in 1929, was exactly the kind of upbeat carryover from the roaring twenties that the country needed as it headed into the Great Depression. Perhaps a less common use of the popular slang for dressing fashionably, Berlin's original lyrics spoke of the flashy Harlemites who would parade up and down Lenox Avenue: *Have you seen the well-to-do; Up on Lenox Avenue.*[55] Harry Richman and Fred Astaire helped to popularize the instant hit on phonograph records during 1929. Because of the portable and repeatable nature of such recording

48 BEHIND THE SCREEN

technology, film audiences were already familiar with the tune by the time United Artists released its film by the same name. This song's filmic realization is significant because its production qualities allowed it to accomplish something much more than the song could as a sonic standalone.

"Puttin' on the Ritz" has been inaccurately labeled the first "interracial" song and dance to be performed on the silver screen. The first talkie to utilize Black and White dancers on the same stage was *On with the Show*, which Warner Bros. released a little less than a year prior to United Artists' *Puttin' on the Ritz*.[56] While the big song and dance "Welcome Home" in *On with the Show* includes a mix of White and Black dancers, the featured tap dance performed by the Four Covans is isolated from the rest of the ensemble's performance. That is, the onstage White ensemble pauses its routine to watch the Covans perform; White dancers wait for the Black dancers to exit before resuming their choreography. Similarly, the "interracial" label given to the number "Ritz" is misleading in that it neither implied that Black and White dancers would share the same stage, nor did it attempt to separate Black artists from age-old minstrel stereotypes. Even in a pre-Code Hollywood, strategic and unconscious attempts were made to reinforce a long-standing association between minstrel archetypes and real Black people. Despite the lack of blackface, this musical's title number projects on the screen "with blunt force and unmistakable meaning," a set of unspoken racial stigmas that thickened amid the Harlem Renaissance.

Neither the title dance nor the film *Puttin' on the Ritz* contain blackface makeup, but covert expressions of the minstrel stage are plentiful. The four-minute integrated performance is a critique of race, class, and gender as it exists at the tail end of the Harlem Renaissance and at the dawn of the Great Depression. It also heralds an era of duplicitous methods for skirting Code guidelines and regulations. Our understanding of covert minstrelsy's elusiveness begins here, within this film, hidden between the lines and masked by the multisensory revelry of its title number.

The film itself offers a complicated critique of class as it exists interracially but also within entertainment strata. Perhaps the fulcrum of the narrative is the transition that Harry Raymond (Harry Richman) and Dolores Fenton (Joan Bennett) make from vaudeville to Broadway. This shift carries with it huge monetary gain as well as a complete transformation of status. In fact, this transition is responsible for the decline of their friendship with James Tierney (James Gleason) and Goldie Devere (Lilyan Tashman)—their original vaudeville partners—because in addition to the geographic move that

INTEGRATING THE SCREEN   49

Harry and Dolores must make to achieve their goals of Broadway fame, they shift into an entirely unrecognizable social class, one that alienates them from their former associations with the vaudeville working class. Yet despite the high-rollers Harry and Dolores begin associating with after their rise to fame on Broadway, the true White aristocracy—and in particular Mrs. Teddy Van Rennsler (Aileen Pringle)—refuses to see the performers as equals, clearly marking the divide between the *nouveau riche* and the *vieux riche*. But the class divide that develops throughout the film becomes much more complex during the title song and dance.

Mrs. Teddy Van Rennsler and her date scoff when they read the title of the upcoming number aloud as if the mere idea that one could "put on" ritz as if class were an article of clothing is sickening. This jab combined with Van Rennsler's extravagant fur coat, diamond jewelry, and way of speaking establishes a clear divide between the White people who perform on Broadway and the White people who attend, a distinction we see mirrored across racial lines in real life between wealthy White Park Avenue dwellers and the talented 10 percent of Black Harlemites who were enriching a corpus of Black literature during the 1920s and early 1930s.[57] But Van Rennsler and her date seem to forgive such divides in favor of the routine's entertainment quotient and the Mrs.' "boy-crush" on Harry.

The White ensemble dancers cover the stage with a geometrically complex yet unpolished routine of grapevines, chorus-line kicks, and chassés while singing the song's chorus. After a short refrain of the bridge, half of the large ensemble escorts Harry off stage right. The chorus dancers who exited stage left re-enter along with some White chorus men. The upbeat instrumental dance break accompanies what appears to be a variation on the Varsity Drag en masse with remnants of the Charleston.[58] This clump choreography features vertical highlights from the popular drag along with popular tap steps of the day, including a reworking of the recently introduced half break (final section) from the shim sham which was likely "borrowed" from the nearby Apollo theater or Cotton Club.[59] The White ensemble exits stage right after completing an 8-bar chorus, 4-bar bridge, and 4-bar chorus of instrumental accompaniment. What follows initially feels like a drastic tempo shift but in fact is a complex series of layered syncopations.

Berlin, likely influenced by a polyrhythmic aesthetic for a more Harlem feel, used a "four-pitch arpeggiated figure four times" tweaking it rhythmically each time. The sonic effect of having a pattern of seven eighth-notes within 4/4 time and a series of syncopated upbeats make it so that over time, certain notes end up falling a half beat behind where one might expect them to fall. Berlin highlights this sonic peculiarity by timing the cadence of certain lyrics—that is, his percussive accenting allows listeners to hear the words "blue/know/to/go" as syncopated rhymes.[60] In other words, the rhythm of the melody shifts in relation to the beat. Understanding Berlin's unique use of syncopation and lyricism in this song and how these fit into his popular "American" aesthetic will allow us to parse out what distinguishes the sonic guise from a more generalized musical pastiche.

Irving Berlin (b. Israel Beilin) emigrated from Russia in 1893 after his family's house was burned down in a pogrom. His family settled in New York City's immigrant community of the Lower East Side and changed the family's last name to Baline. When Israel's father died in 1901, "Izzy" (only thirteen) dropped out of school to work as a singing waiter. He became known as the "sly, bawdy parodist of popular songs issuing from Tin Pan Alley."[61] Although Izzy could neither read nor write music, he composed on the side and had published his first song "Marie from Sunny Italy" (1907) by the time he was nineteen.[62] With the publication of "Alexander's Ragtime Band" (1911), which sold 2 million copies in the first year, Berlin became known as the "Ragtime King" and one of the country's most popular composers. While the ragtime style is certainly present in Berlin's extensive musical corpus, his success might be better attributed to a musical *macédoine* of forms considered both high and low.

We might attribute Berlin's penchant for eclectic taste to his identity as a Jewish outsider. Ronald Sanders has argued that such pastiche is the "gift of people who live in culturally ambivalent situations."[63] Irving Howe has observed this trend in a generation of artists who were likely influenced by American Yiddish theater's yoking of "*shund* (trash) and *literatur* (literature)."[64] For Berlin, this can be seen in his merging of musical forms deemed high and those deemed low, such as the blending of minstrelsy and opera. But more important for my argument is Berlin's use of an Africanist aesthetic in conjunction with this cross-bred style of high and low, and particularly that of the low.

Berlin's use of an Africanist aesthetic appears on many levels. One sonic overlap surfaces in the way he flirts with ragtime syncopation. Ragtime as a musical genre exhibits Africanist qualities in both its rhythmic complexity and the organic spontaneity of its improvised structure. In the years following the Civil War, ragtime became the most popular musical form in America. While Berlin tends not to rely on traditional ragtime rhythms, he does "rag" other styles, meaning he plays with "syncopated melody against a regular, *oom-pah* or march-style, bass."[65] Many of Berlin's compositions make up "a big part of his rhythmic vocabulary." Most famously is his "repetition of the opening lyric and musical phrase; short, punchy phrases that push off from a strong bass-defined downbeat; and the restatement of a principal melodic phrase up (sometimes down) the interval of a perfect fourth."[66] Berlin's distinct approach to syncopation avoided the cliché cakewalk figure that marked other Tin Pan Alley ragtime songs. Rather than follow the cakewalk figure, Berlin used what Jeffrey Magee has pinpointed as augmentations (rhythmic expansions), diminutions (rhythmic contractions), tied variants, and the "reverse cakewalk." He combines these rhythmic tools with elements of the blues and jazz (specifically swing) of the period, commonly utilizing "riff-based construction with instrumental fills; swing-like eighth notes; across-the-bar syncopation and chains of syncopation; and even call-and-response patterns." Berlin also went on to incorporate quarter-note triplets and the "resulting three-against-two pattern."[67] Berlin never denied his use of Africanist syncopation nor his regular inclusion of a call-and-response format.[68] The sonic guise requires us to look beneath Berlin's sophisticated syncopations and monosyllabic language.

Despite the complexity of Berlin's syncopation, the composer strove for simplicity. Musically he relied on diatonic scales and triads, short rhythmic patterns, and the conventional 32-bar AABA or ABAC pattern. When it came to lyrics, he preferred single-syllable words and conversational English. That is, he coupled "textual repetition and musical syncopation."[69] Overlaying musical syncopations with monosyllabic language gives listeners the sense that the words too are syncopated. The sonic guise necessitates such an act of substitution, where one element of a song (rhythmic, tonal, musical, or lyric-related) conceals another. Generally, this happens on several levels instantaneously such that the very simultaneity of masks distracts the audience from hearing the song's (or performance's) subtext. It is important to note that the sonic guise—or any other form of masking I outline in this book—is not necessarily produced consciously.[70] While Berlin *was* intentional in his coupling of language and rhythm, his goal was not necessarily to deceive the audience. Rather, these small audible gestures add up and help to distract the audience from seeing all the layers at play in "Ritz." Thus, covert minstrelsy

52 BEHIND THE SCREEN

here surfaces not in Berlin's use of an Africanist aesthetic but instead in his juxtaposition of Africanisms alongside more blatant references to minstrelsy.

Due to the synchroneity of senses required to view this number as a whole, it would be very difficult for viewers to immediately identify all of the number's Africanisms and inherent messages when situated within the larger *mise-en-scène*. Recall that even by 1930, synchronized sound was still a recent addition to movies, and audiences were still processing what it meant to see and listen simultaneously.[71] These small manipulations or coatings function in a manner similar to the invisible eighth notes against Berlin's seemingly transparent 4/4—or common—backdrop. It is Berlin's precise musical structure and use of rhythm that results in certain notes falling a half beat behind. When this scenario plays out on the grander scale, the audience can easily forget (or truly not understand) how complex Berlin's rhythm is and what lay at the core of his syncopations. When all the parts work in synch, covert minstrelsy succeeds in transmitting a variety of sociopolitical messages while making the audience think they witnessed something as simple as a slight change in tempo. This will become more evident as I begin to break down the individual components of the production number.

The syncopation lasts for the duration of the dance number but the energy shifts when the Black ensemble enters the stage. Immediately following the White ensemble's exit, the Black ensemble enters with cakewalk prancing in droves of male/female pairings. While there is some crossover with Donald Tomkins's coined Varsity Drag as it appears in the 1930 film Good News, *this chorus makes use of the elements that require the lower body, a clear distinction from the very upright hand tosses and synchronized hops executed by the White ensemble. The lines are less vertical—more polycentric—and physical contact between the sexes determines much of the vocabulary. As such, we see less of the Varsity Drag lexicon and more of the types of movements that might have been familiar in jook joints and other dance clubs of the time such as elements of the turkey trot, the grizzly bear, Black Bottom, and a more generalized "jookin' style."[72] The crossover step known in both tap dance and future lindy hop circles also makes an appearance.*

While the movement and rhythmic qualities of the Black ensemble are suggestive in and of themselves, their dancing studied in comparison to that of the White dancers is even more revealing. Furthermore, the fact that White and Black dancers never appear on the same stage is worthy of attention. It is in these discreet attempts to segregate Blackness from White that we begin to see the corporeal elements of covert minstrelsy rise to the surface. In high contrast to the White ensemble, the Black performers add a percussive element of clapping, slapping, and vocals. Call-and-response helps to distinguish the social nature of the Black ensemble's performance from the solitary executions of the White performers who dance solo, but in synch. The Black performance is louder, perceptibly joyful, and certainly more raucous, perfectly exemplifying Brenda Dixon Gottschild's understanding of an Africanist aesthetic in dance.[73] Thus, despite the reputation that "Ritz" has acquired as being Hollywood's first interracial song and dance, the segregated ensembles make it clear that a lot still stands between the two racial groups. When juxtaposed, these two ways of dancing speak to larger social codes, especially as they relate to 1930s values surrounding public display of sexual conduct, no matter how innocuous.

A crucial component of the MPPDA's agenda during the early years of self-regulation was to advise filmmakers on issues concerning race and ethnicity. Staging scenes wherein Black people and White people were viewed as social equals was not appropriate, as many people in the industry feared that this would offend their southern market.[74] This is a plausible cause for clearly delineating "Black movement" from "White" during the "Puttin' on the Ritz" routine. In a pre-Code era, films relied heavily on the blackface mask to do this work for them. In *Infernal*, the blackface mask helps to qualify the cakewalk as morally hazardous and to distinguish it from the kind of dancing that God condones. Here, in the absence of blackface and satanic costuming, unmasked Black dancers must perform a dance that is perceptibly immodest in comparison to the way that the White dancers perform. This not only helps to define Whiteness as moral and chaste, but it also allows sexual conduct to be present at a time when the Catholic Church had considerable influence on the MPPDA. "Suggestive movement" was unlawful when performed by White people, and yet presenting Black people as overtly sexualized— as this dance number does—was a way of delivering sexual content in an agreeable manner. That is to say, fewer people took issue with distributing "forbidden" material via the Black performer. In fact, presenting the Black body as a vessel of demoralizing movement reinforced stereotypes that had long been in place; popular dances that stemmed from Black culture (e.g., the Black Bottom and slow drag) were still perceived to be as dangerous as the cakewalk was in 1903. Integration in this context thus strategically defined Black and White in a manner that appealed to northern and southern

54 BEHIND THE SCREEN

film audiences alike and satisfied Hollywood's influential organizations; the Catholics, YMCA, PTA, and Boy Scouts of America could condone sexuality in this highly specific racial context.

> *The grand finale of this title number brings all the elements together. Harry Richman hums while the White ensemble struts on stage from both sides singing the chorus. But this time a second stage is revealed so that while the White cast struts on the bottom (mainstage), the all-Black ensemble floods the lofted stage and breaks into a tap dance chorus. Simultaneously the backdrop breaks into a dance as well. The once-static apartment buildings begin swaying from side to side, moving their arms up and down, and horizontally, in a slow robotic fashion. The most prominent building raises and lowers what appears to be a top hat. The woman in the Chewy Gooey Gum ad also comes to life as her eyes begin shifting from side to side, exposing the whites; her mouth starts opening and closing. It becomes hard to ignore the set and the prominent features of both the woman and the monstrous buildings; both seem to overpower the dancing of the White and Black ensembles. The dance and song become secondary and tertiary to the production's powerful visual markers of past, present, and future. The buildings speak to grotesque imagery that has long been tied to Blackness while simultaneously gesturing at an age of architectural feats and scientific discovery. With the very recent detection of Pluto[75] and the near completion of the Chrysler Building, American science was in a propulsive state.[76] Yet the backdrop foregrounds a fundamental ambivalence, stabilizing and destabilizing racial categories through a modern façade.*

The woman in the gum ad, on the other hand, makes blatant reference to the minstrel stage with her prominent red lips and white eyes. The motion of her pupils, rolling in on themselves, along with the timed opening and closing of her mouth resembles the facial repertoire of the Jolly N[sic]Bank which for so many years would "chew" your money up and give you the same sort of show.[77] And while the spokeswoman for this pseudo chewing gum company recalls a whole minstrel enterprise, she also gestures at a present steeped in the increasing presence and prominence of advertising culture. This phony ad was likely a take on the ads for Wrigley's pepsin gum. The "Spearmint Girl with the Wrigley Eyes" had been a familiar mascot for the popular chewing gum company since 1911.[78] Thus the backdrop alone critiques America's past—entertainment steeped in blackface and a clear divide between the races—as well as its future—skyscrapers, machines, scientific discovery, and capitalist desire. Taken together, the set invites a modernist gaze of racial Othering.[79]

While United Artists did not use literal blackface in *Ritz*, the title number uses a backdrop of nineteenth-century minstrel allusions while also hinting at female sexuality and modern capitalism. The scenery used in "Puttin' on the Ritz" is a strange mix of grotesque imagery dating back to nineteenth-century print culture that used Black caricatures to sell food as well as contemporary pin-up material used to sell consumer products (like chewing gum) in the twentieth century. Such imagery accentuates an ambivalence akin to what Ann Anlin Cheng has described in terms of reading the Black body as a site of modernist desire and racial Othering.[80] For Cheng, viewers project an unconscious ambivalence onto the Black body such that "modernism and primitivism are intertwined, at times even identical phenomena."[81] The black buildings in this production number represent machine and animality while the chewing gum ad stands in as both female ornament and capitalist desire. The backdrop that directly alludes to modernism is complemented by the sexualized Black dancers who seem to exemplify a material sculpturalness. Positioned alongside the specters of capitalism, these Black dancers are reduced to flesh. These bodies are, to take a phrase from Eva Cherniavsky, "fully opened to and penetrated by the abstracting force of capital."[82] Thus the collocation of the two—that is, a theatrical set signifying capital and the remnant flesh of Black people—becomes a site of what Hortense Spillers has aptly identified as "pornotroping," or the "signifying property plus" historically embedded and overdetermined in the signifying chain of this ambivalent landscape.[83] These bodies are subjected to the "commodification of 'life and personhood'" in the wake of slavery, which includes traces of nineteenth-century minstrelsy re-apposed within a capitalist landscape of the twentieth century.[84] The stage itself becomes a site of transfiguration "where human skin morphs into modern surface" and the modern surfaces cite the same tropes of Black representation as did the minstrel stage.[85]

Consequently, in the absence of blackface, "the captive body is all surfaces; it is the scene of the evacuation of the captive person rendered wholly soluble in capital."[86] Covert minstrelsy—and specifically the set design in "Ritz"—provides a new, modern structure for looking at Blackness. The exposed surface—a new skin—covers up old ways of seeing while defining a new way of looking. What have been "integrated" are not Black artists, but instead their bodies, with the interior removed. Hollywood's first interracial musical number incorporates a modernist way of looking at Blackness within a colonial context rather than a new way of seeing Blackness as on par with Whiteness. This production perfectly exemplifies the ways in which the *juxtaposing* of Black and White—rather than the *integration* of these dancers—teaches viewers how to *see* in a modern, urbanized context. As Cheng proposes, visual technologies [such as these ways of seeing] affect our perception of racial difference and "racial difference itself influences how these technologies are conceived, practiced, and perceived."[87] Thus, just as sound recording technology shapes music production—the phonograph effect—these visual technologies (in *Ritz*, *mise-en-scène* specifically) shape how the dancers themselves are perceived. At a time when visual and audio technologies were rapidly changing, the modern eye was as vulnerable as the modern ear. Gone were the pyrotechnics and observable elementary camera techniques of the silent era. Smoke and mirrors in the age of talkies became a figurative phenomenon, one not so easily discernible by movie-theatergoers. While being taught how to listen, American audiences were simultaneously learning how to look and how *not* to see.

Rhythm in Vogue

Come with me and we'll attend their jubilee
And see them spend their last two bits; Puttin' on the Ritz.

The set in "Ritz" communicates (somewhat overtly) a racial distribution that will continue to surface in *mise-en-scènes* throughout the Golden Age. The apportioned stage speaks to this divide most literally, but the lyrics of this song also do their part to sequester Black dancers and to distinguish Black wealth from White. At the time Irving Berlin wrote this iteration of the lyrics, the Harlem Renaissance was reaching its peak. Recognizing the economic and social context out of which Berlin's lyrics evolve is crucial to understanding the many levels at which the sonic guise operates.

Two Berlin signatures assist in the lyric component of this production's sonic guise: repetition and antithesis, or "opposite language." Berlin relied on dynamic repetition for a continuous attack. This is often the title phrase (e.g., "Ritz") and repeatedly lands on the downbeat in order to create a feeling of suspense. He combines this with antithesis, which, according to Jeffrey Magee, helps give a song affect: antithesis serves to "highlight the contrast" between two conflicting sets of ideas or behavior.[88] The combination of repetition and antithesis sets up another way in which Berlin relies on an Africanist aesthetic—the first a form of "ephebism" (the attack or surprise) and the second a form of "contrariety" to use Robert Farris Thompson and Gottschild's vocabulary. But these two in combination also accentuate the narrative contrast Berlin sets up between Black people and White.

Narrative—often masked by lyric and lyric substitution—is another key component of covert minstrelsy. On the surface an audience might hear the punch and the dynamic contrast. Underneath the surface lay a much more complex story. As such, the significance of Berlin's lyrics as they pertain to class and race can only be understood in context. There was much more going on behind the scenes (i.e., socially, economically, and geographically) during the Harlem Renaissance than can possibly be gleaned from the story this spectacle tells.

Historian David Levering Lewis understands the Harlem Renaissance to have evolved out of a "rigidly segregated United States."[89] He and others identify Charles Johnson as being a central figure in the development and endurance of the Harlem Renaissance. Johnson believed that the arts were the one place where there was a "small crack in the wall of racism." No one had laid down exclusionary rules prohibiting Black Americans from making art. According to Johnson, art was to be the "sole battle plan affording both high visibility and low vulnerability." Each work of art, he urged would become a "weapon against the old racial stereotypes."[90] Many talented Black artists found this to be reasonable and so, together with Johnson, helped to inaugurate the movement. Alain Locke's widely read essay, "Enter the New Negro" (1925), for example, expressed with the most hopeful of intentions that Harlem was the race capital of the world. Harlem was, as Locke saw it, "rehabilitating the race in world esteem from that loss of prestige for which the fate and conditions of slavery have so largely been responsible."[91]

It became clear to many, however, that no amount of artistic output would equate to political shifts or long-lasting economic gain.[92] Levering Lewis writes of the period that Black Americans deceived themselves into "thinking that race relations in the United States were amenable" to a certain type of assimilation, when in fact the social uplift translated to only a small percentage of the Black population.[93] While there are many conversations to be had here, I am particularly interested in reading Berlin's account of Harlem as representative of White spectatorship at this time. This song is but

58 BEHIND THE SCREEN

one of many examples of White America feeding a logic of assimilation and production, a musical theater steeped in racial capitalism.[94]

Why don't you go where Harlem sits; Puttin' on the Ritz
Spangled gowns upon the bevy of high browns
From down the levy, all misfits; Puttin' on the Ritz

On the surface the lyrics set up a series of high contrast relationships. They make a pointed reference to Black migration from the rural South ("from down the levy") to the urban North and juxtapose "high browns" with "misfits." Underneath this lyric façade sits a critique of Harlem's provisional success.

In *Big Sea* (1940), Langston Hughes writes of the renaissance as "mere 'vogue' set in motion and largely financed by White downtowners while Negroes played minstrel and trickster roles in it all."[95] Hughes recalls White people taking an interest in not just Black music and dance but in Harlem itself with the premiere of the all-Black cast Broadway musical *Shuffle Along* (1921).[96] His vivid description of this mass migration uptown shares one side of minstrelsy's Janus-faced coin; the exotic pull of the visibly Black human was often enough to counteract an implicit fear of Black corporeality that so many White Americans outwardly expressed (and repressed) during the 1920s and 1930s. Hughes writes:

> White people began to come to Harlem in droves. For several years they packed the expensive Cotton Club on Lenox Avenue. But I was never there, because the Cotton Club was a Jim Crow club for gangsters and monied Whites. They were not cordial to Negro patronage, unless you were a celebrity like Bojangles. So Harlem Negroes did not like the Cotton Club and never appreciated its Jim Crow policy in the very heart of their dark community.[97]

The all-Black Broadway musical with a stellar cast intrigued White people so much that they began traveling uptown to see Black artists in their element. Harlem thus became the new center of entertainment.[98] The irony was that as White people took an interest, Black performers and establishments began catering to their White audiences as they had been for quite some time, again replicating this pattern of the "machine" altering production itself, where capitalism in the 1930s functions like sound technology in the aughts. Unlike a half century prior, however, Harlemites were gratifying White consumers in the one area that had previously been deemed their space, an isolated plot of land where they could be and do for themselves instead of for the enjoyment of others. A small percentage of Harlem residents sacrificed their space in order to meet the desires of the wealthy White class. Consequently, many of the neighborhood's *en vogue* nightclubs began banning Black patrons thinking this would raise the value of the entertainment. This policy often backfired, as these owners failed to recognize that Black patronage was part of the spectacle for these wealthy White customers. Hughes writes, "A large part of the Harlem attraction for downtown New Yorkers lay in simply watching the colored customers amuse themselves." Moreover, White visitors to Harlem assumed that what they experienced on their visits was the "authentic" Harlem. They neglected to see that unfeigned Harlem included rent parties,[99] not fancy night clubs with first-class entertainment and White spectatorship.[100] As Black authors and artists gave into this construct, White authors and artists did what they could to keep the fiction in motion.[101]

"That's where each and every lulu-belle goes." Berlin's lyrics speak directly to these racialized logics of American (White) assimilation. This song, viewed within the broader narrative of the film and the predominantly White institution known as Hollywood, unveils the social and economic value the industry (and White society in general) derived from associating with individuals with non-White racial identities.[102]

The song itself, which relies heavily on an Africanist aesthetic, has nothing to do with White people visiting Harlem to partake in Black art. Instead, it speaks to a modernist gaze and critiques racial difference. Berlin's choice of words speaks to White voyeurism and the tacit joy of watching Harlemites in their assumed environment. Three words stand out as carrying particular weight: *"high browns,"*[103] *"Lulu-Belles,"*[104] and *"misfits"* imply a type of racial Othering unique to working-class Black people.

Broadway increased the visibility of Harlem for White New Yorkers.[105] In particular the show *Lulu Belle* (1926), which portrayed Harlem street life, brought White New Yorkers up to Harlem in droves to see the "real thing."[106] That a show like *Lulu Belle* written by two White men and performed in blackface could have such an effect on theatergoers should say something both about the crowd who went in search of "authentic" Black life and something about Berlin's choice of words in this song.

Besides the racially charged designations, the original lyrics make blatant moral judgments about the way Harlemites live; they imply a certain

60 BEHIND THE SCREEN

excess: *High hats and arrow collars; White spats and fifteen dollars; Spending ev'ry dime; For a wonderful time.* Rather than discussing the huge economic inequalities between the two races, Berlin's lyrics speak to a certain enjoyment gleaned from watching Black profligate consumers run themselves into the ground: *". . . we'll attend their jubilee and see them spend their last two bits."*[107] The song examines Blackness as spectacle and provides a narrative within a narrative for the film: the song's lyrics mirror the relationship that Mrs. Van Rennsler has to the Broadway performers.

While not racial, the class dynamic between the character Harry Raymond and the wealthy aristocrat who is temporarily enamored of him offers a parallel critique of class to the dynamic between Black artists living in Harlem and their White supporters. Van Rennsler is not so much interested in Harry's talent as a singer or dancer as she is in the performer as spectacle; she uses the word "clown" to describe him to others of her social status. She knows very well that no matter how much fame Broadway brings him and no matter how she supports him financially, his social status will never actually change. He is temporarily "en vogue" and her fellow wealthy White class can decide when he and his art must fall out of fashion. As was made clear in this scene's opening when Van Rennsler and her date scoff at the concept of temporarily "putting on the ritz," those White dancers who performed on Broadway were merely *dressing up.* Those who perform are a small percentage—perhaps the most talented 10 percent—of the larger class, but however talented and temporarily flush with cash, their status is temporary. Whether racially motivated and the result of the wealthy White class funding the talented tenth of all Black people living in Harlem, or the non-racially motivated funding of Broadway performers by White, fur-coat wearing *vieux riche,* their class status is always in flux. Working class is still working class no matter how White; no amount of assimilation nor even cultural production would have lasting economic benefits nor positive social impacts on Black Renaissance artists. Such "ritz" was, to use Hughes's words, "not so gay and sparkling beneath the surface as it looked."[108]

If not demonstrated through the song's lyrics and surrounding *mise-en-scène* in *Ritz* (1930), then the lyric revision made in 1946 for Fred Astaire's reprising in the film *Blue Skies* should confirm that Harlem's role—and by extension its inhabitants—within the grander American caste system was only temporary.[109] The song's changing lyrics further support Langston Hughes's theory that Harlem was "merely in vogue" and demonstrate the impermanence of Harlem's fashionable nature in the eyes of Hollywood. The lyrics as

Berlin originally wrote them only appeared in one other film. Clark Gable sang a very condensed version of the song in 1939 within the context of a nostalgic musical revue in the film *Idiot's Delight*.[110] The director Stuart Heisler brought Berlin's hit number back seven years later in *Blue Skies*. Though in Fred Astaire's version—known to many as his "last dance"[111]—Berlin completely revamped the lyrics.[112] In an interview with Carol Saltus, Astaire claimed that one reason the lyrics might have been changed was because the old lyrics might have required the use of blackface: "In the only blackface number he ever did, 'Bojangles' in *Swing Time* . . . he danced with shadows of himself; since he intended to dance with images of himself in 'Puttin' on the Ritz,' that parallel would be close and might violate his almost obsessive rule about not repeating himself."[113]

> *Have you seen the well-to-do; Up and down* Park *Avenue?*
> *On that famous thoroughfare; With their noses in the air . . .*

The first major change was geographical in nature. While it is just a one-word substitution, the replacement of "Lenox" with "Park" carries both racial and monetary significance. This shift one mile downtown implies that Astaire is referring to wealthy White people rather than Black and therefore, a different kind of money altogether. This is further accented in the following stanza where Berlin replaced the line *White spats and fifteen dollars* with the line *White spats and lots of dollars*, implying a ceiling for Black wealth where there is not one for White. Not to mention the name dropping—*Come let's mix where Rockefellers walk with sticks . . .*—that insinuates not just any kind of wealth but the wealthiest.

Lyrics aside, the Black dancers who were present—albeit segregated—in the original number have been replaced by two nods at blackface in Astaire's rendition of this routine. The first appears right before Fred Astaire begins singing: backstage a man in blackface is very intentionally framed behind him. The second is less obvious as it is merely a reference to the dance Astaire performed in 1936 in blackface referred to earlier. The body replication in this routine's dance break mirrors (literally and figuratively) the "Bojangles of Harlem" routine in the film *Swing Time*.[114]

While I cannot use this retrospective knowledge of a 1946 version of the song to bolster my argument surrounding the version filmed in 1930, the shifting lyrics speak to a larger trend in Hollywood to re-use modified versions of songs and dances. As I will continue to argue throughout this book, such manipulations are a product of more rigid censorship laws: covert minstrelsy often relies on audiences' paired associations to old versions of a song or dance to fill in the gaps for elements that went missing as censorship became more tightly enforced. *Tributes* and *citations* constitute a large number of such performances and changing lyrics are just one of the many elements at play. As censorship laws became more strictly enforced, more and more minute manipulations occurred.

The sonic guise rears its head most glaringly in Hollywood's 1946 version, as the restaging serves to mask not only the intent of Berlin's original composition but also its underlying Africanist sensibility. The new lyrics sever Berlin's sophisticated syncopations—which were, I argue, initially intended to bring to mind the "hot" Harlem feel—from Black dancers. Whether this was an intended consequence is less important than the ramifications of re-assigning what were once dangerous rhythms to Park Avenue residents. Furthermore, Astaire becomes the new (visible) vestibule of such rhythmic impulses. This new arrangement—that is, the 1946 manipulation of the original—records a process of "creation, interpretation, and performance." Ryan Bañagale has argued that arrangements (as opposed to originals) serve as "musical vehicles for the delivery and maintenance of individual and communal narratives.[115] The re-debut of "Ritz" in *Blue Skies* marks the end of a particular racial transaction between Black corporeality, Black flesh, and finally, Astaire's White body. The sonic guise's "success" can thus be viewed when Berlin (behind the scenes) and Astaire (onstage) espouse an Africanist tradition without leaving any *visible* trace of Blackness.

***

"Ritz" slips in just on the cusp of Hollywood's first big censorship transition. Had the film been released even thirty days later, its portrayal of sex, use of an integrated stage, and references to Wrigley's Gum would have probably looked quite different. But even with little pressure from the Catholic Church and other influential organizations, this film makes clear that changes were being made in anticipation of the future. Unlike the blatant kind of blackface that we see in *The Jazz Singer*, it is the simultaneous modes, or processes of masking, at play in *Ritz* that work together to obscure underlying aesthetic and racial ideologies.

The power of this show is its ability to prime culture at the same time that it exposes racial fictions. The transition away from explicit burnt cork combined with new sound technology, and this show's specific narrative context lay the groundwork for future camouflage. The soundscape, which is elementary in its sophistication, but also novel, denotes one layer of distraction. Audiences could hear a catchy tune without immediately labeling it "Africanist" or identifying its syncopated-ness because this was just one of many senses being aroused during this production. Furthermore, audiences' ability to listen while watching was still embryonic. At the same time, audiences were expected to re-schematize racial caricature: the creative team extracted the eyes and lips of a familiar nineteenth-century blackface mask and placed these facial features in a modern context. Audiences were unlikely aware of such racial transference in the moment from using blackface makeup to signify racial inferiority to using just elements of the blackface mask to similar effect. The resultant mask reads more as a second skin, one that pendulates between the modern and the primitive and helps to set a precedent for future pairings. Thus, even in the absence of a recognizable blackface mask, audiences likely experienced parts standing in for the whole. These parts will become the new foundation for more invisible means of masking during a period of strict censorship around racial caricature.

The simultaneous presentation of all of these "technologies" distracts the audience from seeing what exactly the spectacle masks. Covert minstrelsy in this early context conceals this routine's heavy use of an Africanist sensibility—seen most clearly in Berlin's use of complex syncopations but also ever-present in the dancing itself—and masks economic inequality by offering a narrative of Black wealth. It further covers up the pleasure White people glean from spectating ersatz Black life. Placing this narrative alongside an analogous narrative between the White working class and old White money further disguises the racial implications. Thus, with or without the aid of burnt cork, the minstrel stage—or in this case the ghosts of the minstrel stage—establishes American identity through racial subordination. "Ritz" mislabeled itself as America's first interracial song and dance. This routine, along with countless others, in fact facilitated a false sense of national unification by making Blackness something "visible" yet voiceless on Hollywood's White stage. While more narratively disguised than Civil War films of the era, musicals like *Ritz* conjured up a certain nineteenth-century nostalgia while at the same time projecting a clear racial divide.

Puttin' on the Ritz, unlike the blatant blackface performances in *Le Cake-Walk Infernal* and *The Jazz Singer* masterfully circumvented a Code—albeit unenforced—that banned miscegenation and suggestive dances while at the same time drawing on Africanist music and dance traditions. It also managed to "integrate" the screen without the use of blackface while still masking a sociopolitical subtext surrounding Black artistry and corporeality. Over the

64 BEHIND THE SCREEN

next four years the Code would tighten around matters of sexual conduct, "profane and vulgar expression," and miscegenation, making the techniques implemented in *Ritz* more difficult to execute. The idea of integrating the dance stage would remain but the blackface mask would reappear as a form of integration and now also as a ritual of disguise and citation.

Notes

1. See, for example, Carl Heinrich Bloch's *The Resurrection*.
2. *In Dahomey* opened on Broadway on February 18, 1903, and ran for fifty-three performances. Not only was it Broadway's first full-length musical written and performed by Black men, but it exemplified the concept of the New Negro. After its successful run on Broadway, it toured London for six weeks, and then toured the rest of England and France for two months after that. See Camille F. Forbes, *Introducing Bert Williams: Burnt Cork, Broadway, and the Story of America's First Black Star* (New York: Basic Civitas, 2008), and Sean Mayes and Sarah K. Whitfield, *An Inconvenient Black History of British Musical Theatre: 1900–1950* (New York: Bloomsbury, 2021).
3. The French takeover of Dahomey (present-day Benin) began in 1872, resulting in the *Colonie du Dahomey et dépendances* in the 1890s and then finally Dahomey's incorporation into French West Africa in 1904. For a much more nuanced history of this period, see A. I. Asiwaju, "Anti-French Resistance Movement in Ohori-Ije (Dahomey) 1895–1960," *Journal of the Historical Society of Nigeria* 7, no. 2 (June 1974): 255–69, and Robin Law, "Dahomey and the Slave Trade: Reflections on the Historiography of the Rise of Dahomey," *Journal of African History* 27, no. 2, Special Issue in Honour of J. D. Fage (1986): 237–67.
4. The American modern dance pioneer Loïe Fuller was best known for her contributions to stagecraft and specifically stage lighting for which she held several patents including the chemical compounds for creating color gels and chemical salts used in treating her fabrics for a luminescent effect.
5. Georges Méliès, *Le Cake-Walk Infernal* (June 13, 1903; France/USA: Star-Film), Film.
6. A substitution splice (sometimes called a "stop trick") is most likely how Georges Méliès achieved some of *Infernal's* magic. This involves the appearance, disappearance, or transformation of something (e.g., the goat's legs and arms) by altering one aspect of the film's set between two shots but maintaining the same framing in both shots and then splicing the two shots together. See Alan Larson Williams, *Republic of Images: A History of French Filmmaking* (Cambridge, MA: Harvard University Press), 36.
7. Rick Altman, *Silent Film Sound* (New York: Columbia University Press, 2004), 391.
8. Politicians were also some of the first to use this technology, so filmed campaign speeches were synched to dialogue during this "trial" phase.

INTEGRATING THE SCREEN   65

9. Altman, *Silent Film Sound*, 163. *Moving Picture World* described the Cameraphone: "A combination of the moving picture and the graphophone. The two are operated by one man who controls them by electricity. The moving picture machine is operated by a spring motor, as is the graphophone, which is concealed behind the screen on which the pictures appear. The gestures, steps, or sounds, indicated in the pictures are heard, if there is any sound connected with them, from the graphophone behind the screen, thus giving the effect of speaking, as well as moving pictures. They are perfectly synchronized; that is, the movement of the lips in the pictures coincides with the words from the graphophone." See *Moving Picture World*, April 25, 1908, 369–70.

10. *Scientific American*, April 25, 1908, 292.

11. For a full list and history of silent film sound technology, see Altman's *Silent Film Sound*.

12. Ibid., 163.

13. The "Don'ts and Be Carefuls" were soft guidelines created for motion picture censorship in 1927.

14. Alan Crosland, *The Jazz Singer* (October 6, 1927; USA; Warner Bros.), Film.

15. Dave Fleischer, *Come Take a Trip in My Airship* (March 9, 1924; USA: Out of the Inkwell Films), Animation.

   Max and Dave Fleischer, *My Old Kentucky Home* (June 1926; USA: Out of the Inkwell Films), Animation.

16. Lee de Forest invented the Phonofilm system in 1923. This system allowed sound to be recorded on film. In 1925, Fox bought the patent for this system, followed by the patent for the German system Tri-Ergon, and finally merged the two systems into Movietone in 1927. See Pauline Reay, *Music in Film: Soundtracks and Synergy* (London: Wallflower, 2004), 7–8. Meanwhile Vitaphone, Warner Bros. and Western Electric developed their own sound-on-disc system in 1925, creating steep competition for Fox and the rest of the moviemaking industry. See Leonard Maltin, *Of Mice and Magic: A History of American Animated Cartoons* (New York: Penguin, 1987).

17. While sing-alongs were nothing new to the entertainment industry, Max Fleischer was the first to invent the concept of the bouncing ball in 1924. Contrary to popular belief, these bouncing balls were not animated but were instead the effect of a Fleischer employee holding a luminescent white ball on the tip of a long stick. The employee would, Leonard Maltin explains, bounce the ball "by hand in time to music while another man turned a large drum-like cylinder on which the lyrics were printed. One line at a time was exposed to the camera, which filmed this action with high contrast film; the pointer itself was never visible." Maltin, *Of Mice and Magic*, 91–92.

18. Altman, *Silent Film Sound*, 165.

19. Ibid., 391.

20. I return to this distinction in the coming pages.

21. Many of these early cartoons included a mix of live action and animated sequences. In Max and Dave Fleischer's *Out of the Inkwell* series (1918–1929), for example, audiences are privy to the pen-and-ink process and quite literally watch the animations come to life. See, for example, "Out of the Inkwell: The Cartoon Factory," YouTube video, March 20, 2014, https://youtu.be/B4bYfiQ0_pQ, accessed October 27, 2022.

66 BEHIND THE SCREEN

22. Altman explains that "early sound strategies drew constant attention to the sound apparatus while leaving room for audience chatter. . . . In a sense it was the campaign to standardize sound in the early 1910s that first turned cinema into an audiovisual medium, long before Hollywood's conversion to synchronized recorded sound. . . . Moving from intermittent silence to continuous music and from verbal popular song accompaniment to dependence on light classical 'songs without words,' film music henceforth concentrated audience attention on identification with the image." Altman, *Silent Film Sound*, 283.

23. There might be an interesting parallel to explore here between the birth of the museum and sound theaters. See Tony Bennett's *The Birth of the Museum: History, Theory, Politics* (London: Routledge, 1995).

24. Altman, *Silent Film Sound*, 283–84.

25. Ibid., 283–84 and 285.

26. Mark Katz, *Capturing Sound: How Technology Has Changed Music*, rev. ed. (Berkeley: University of California Press, 2010), 2.

27. Pauline Reay defines this soundtrack as having three basic components: dialogue, sound effects, and music. See Reay, *Music in Film: Soundtracks and Synergy* (London: Wallflower, 2004).

28. Mervyn Cooke, *A History of Film Music* (New York: Cambridge University Press, 2008).

    Annabel Cohen demonstrates that the part of the brain that responds to music and rhythm is associated with the cerebellum which is a more primitive part of the brain that is also involved in dance and motor responses to music. See Reay's *Music in Film*, 2.

29. Deborah Kapchan, *Theorizing Sound Writing* (Middletown, CT: Wesleyan University Press, 2017), 6.

30. Walt Disney, *The Four Musicians of Bremen* (August 1, 1922; USA: Laugh-O-Gram Films), Animation.

31. Walt Disney, *Cinderella* (December 6, 1922; USA: Laugh-O-Gram Films), Animation.

32. Dave Fleischer, *Ko-Ko's Paradise* (February 27, 1926; USA: Out of the Inkwell Films), Animation.

33. Walt Disney, *Oswald the Lucky Rabbit in Bright Lights* (March 19, 1928; USA: Robert Winkler Productions and Walt Disney Productions), Animation.

34. Perhaps one of Josephine Baker's best-known films released just one year prior (1927) to this *Oswald* short.

35. Altman, *Silent Film Sound*, 19.

36. These images were usually used to "express dialogue or to explain the plot, especially in silent films." See definition of "intertitle" in the *Oxford English Dictionary*.

37. Kathryn Kalinak, *Settling the Score: Music and the Classical Hollywood Film* (Madison: University of Wisconsin Press, 1992), 44.

38. See Cooke's understanding of Adorno and Eisler's writing on the subject in Cooke, *A History of Film Music*, 6.

39. Ibid.

40. Michel Chion, *Audio-Vision: Sound on Screen* (New York: Columbia University Press, 1994).

INTEGRATING THE SCREEN   67

41. Daniel Goldmark, *Tunes for 'Toons: Music and the Hollywood Cartoon* (Berkeley: University of California Press, 2005), 31.
42. From the Hebrew word "נִיגּוּן" (nigun) meaning "tune" or "melody."
43. Eric Lott has attributed much of the success of nineteenth-century blackface minstrelsy to its ability to bring people from disparate classes together; the blackface mask on the screen did not differ much in function. Blackface played a big part in shaping American entertainment, specifically musical theater; reenacting this mask was an opportunity for spectators to reminisce together, as a (visibly White) nation, on the basis of a history deeply rooted in strict subjugation of Black people. Eric Lott, *Love and Theft: Blackface Minstrelsy and the American Working Class* (New York: Oxford University Press, 1993).
44. Lott has discussed this in terms of Irish immigrants, suggesting that the blackface mask was one way that Irish immigrants could identify as White. Lott, *Love and Theft*.
45. For an understanding of how, in promoting "identity exchange," Jewish immigrants' blackface performances transitioned various ethnic groups into the American mainstream "melting pot" at the expense of other racial groups, see Michael Rogin, *Blackface, White Noise: Jewish Immigrants in the Hollywood Melting Pot* (Berkeley: University of California Press, 1996).
46. Michael Rogin, "New Deal Blackface," in *Hollywood Musicals, the Film Reader*, ed. Steven Cohan, 176 (London: Routledge, 2002)..
47. Ibid., 175.
48. For a superb analysis of this ur-text, see Arthur Knight, *Disintegrating the Musical: Black Performance and American Musical Film* (Durham, NC: Duke University Press, 2002), 54–57.
49. *The Jazz Singer* [1927], in *Souvenir Programs of Twelve Classic Movies 1927–1941*, ed. Miles Kreuger (New York: Dover 1977), 8.
50. Matthew Bernstein, *Controlling Hollywood: Censorship and Regulation in the Studio Era* (New Brunswick, NJ: Rutgers University Press, 1999), 2.
51. Ibid., 1–2.
52. Ibid., 2. Also, I believe that this quote misidentifies the Producers Appeal Board (PAB) as the Production Code Administration (PCA) which was not created until 1934.
53. Jakob Lothe, *Narrative in Fiction and Film: An Introduction* (Oxford: Oxford University Press, 2000), 71.
54. Edward Sloman, *Puttin' on the Ritz* (March 1, 1930; USA: Joseph M. Schenck Production Co.), Film.
55. I intersperse Berlin's lyrics throughout the remainder of this chapter. For full original lyrics, see *The Complete Lyrics of Irving Berlin*, ed. Robert Kimball and Linda Emmet, 262–63 (New York: A. A. Knopf, 2001).
56. Alan Crosland, *On with the Show* (July 13, 1929; USA: Warner Bros.), Film.
57. I am thinking specifically here of relationships between White patrons and Black artists such as Charlotte Osgood Mason or "Godmother" who sponsored many of the Harlem Renaissance geniuses including Langston Hughes, Alain Locke, and Zora Neale Hurston. David Levering Lewis writes of these patrons, the "aged, well-preserved White dowager of enormous wealth and influence" had always taken an interest in "Primitives" and "paid well when . . . pleased" (151). See David Levering

Lewis, *When Harlem Was in Vogue* (New York: A. A. Knopf, 1981), and Arnold Rampersad, *The Life of Langston Hughes*, vol. 1, *1902–1941, I Too, Sing America* (New York: Oxford University Press, 2002).

58. The Varsity Drag, introduced by Donald Tomkins and commercialized by Zelma O'Neal, became extremely popular in 1927 when it debuted in the Broadway show *Good News*. It continued to gain popularity with the release of MGM's film of the same name in 1930.

59. While several theories exist around the origins of the Shim Sham, I subscribe to the theory that places its origins in the hands of the chorus line dancers of the mid-1920s. See Brynn Shiovitz, "The Shim Sham: A Tap Tradition," *Dance Spirit* 14, no. 12 (December 2010).

60. For more on the theoretical breakdown of this song, see the Music Theory ProfBlog's article, "Take a Few Pitches; Shake; Strain." January 24, 2014. http://musictheoryprof. com/2014/01/take-a-few-pitches-shake-strain/, accessed August 23, 2019.

61. Jeffrey Magee, *Irving Berlin's American Musical Theater Broadway Legacies* (Oxford: Oxford University Press, 2012), 3.

62. A simple typo on the printed version of this song is responsible for his more assimilated name "I. Berlin."

63. Ronald Sanders, "The American Popular Song," in *Next Year in Jerusalem: Portraits of the Jew in the Twentieth Century*, ed. Douglas Villiers (New York: Viking, 1976), 202.

64. Irving Howe, *World of Our Fathers: The Journey of the East European Jews to America and the Life They Found and Made* (New York: Galahad Books, 1976), 483–92.

65. John Hasse, *Ragtime: Its History, Composers, and Music* (New York: Schirmer Books, 1985), 2.

66. Magee, *Irving Berlin's American Musical* Theater, 16–17.

67. Ibid., 17–18.

68. In an interview published in late 1913/early 1914, Berlin denied originating modern ragtime as many claimed. Instead, he felt his contribution was introducing the syncopated ballad. See Frederick James Smith, "Irving Berlin and Modern Ragtime," *Dramatic Mirror*. Unidentified clipping in IB scrapbook #1 on LC-IBC microfilm, New York Public Library for the Performing Arts.

69. Magee, *Irving Berlin's American Musical Theater*, 19.

70. When analyzing these covert practices, I maintain that my critique is merely one of observation rather than one of assigning blame to particular choreographers, directors, and composers.

71. We might also attribute this perceptible shift in tempo to the recording process itself, which was still in its infancy at the time this film was produced. As Rick Altman reminds us, "Recorded sound thus always carries some record of the recording process, superimposed on the sound event itself," acknowledging that audiences are always exposed to a trace of the process. Rick Altman in Kathryn Kalinak, *Settling the Score: Music and the Classical Hollywood Film* (Madison: University of Wisconsin Press, 1992), 26.

72. Katrina Hazzard-Gordon, *Jookin': The Rise of Social Dance Formations in African-American Culture* (Philadelphia: Temple University Press, 1990), 76–84.

73. Brenda Dixon Gottschild, *Digging the Africanist Presence in American Performance: Dance and Other Contexts* (Westport, CT: Praeger, 1998).

74. Bernstein, *Controlling Hollywood*, 8.

75. Clyde W. Tombaugh discovered the ninth planet on February 18, 1930, using a brand-new astronomic technique of a blink microscope and photographic plates to detect subtle changes and movements.

76. Architect William Van Alen completed the Art-Deco inspired skyscraper in May 1930. It would stand as the world's tallest building (1,046 feet) until the following year when the Empire State Building surpassed it. "Chrysler Building." The Skyscraper Center. http://www.skyscrapercenter.com/building/chrysler-building/422, accessed November 1, 2019.

77. A cast iron object that would devour money and roll its eyes back on being fed, popular from the late nineteenth up through the mid-twentieth centuries.

78. Matt Haig, *Brand Royalty: How the World's Top 100 Brands Thrive and Survive* (Philadelphia: Kogan Page, 2006), 50–52. Also worth noting is that Jerome Remick & Co. published a song one year prior, "Oh You Spearmint Kiddo with the Wrigley Eyes," depicting a woman dressed almost identically to the onstage Chewy Gooey poster woman with her pupils shifted all the way to the right.

79. Had this film come out just thirty days later, this direct reference to Wrigley's gum would likely not have been allowed, as product placement was one of the most tightly policed sectors of the Code during these early years. Ruth Vasey discusses this in her chapter "Beyond Sex and Violence: 'Industry Policy' and the Regulation of Hollywood Movies, 1922–1939" wherein she discusses how the advertising power of Hollywood was so influential that "their ability to stimulate consumer demand gave them a privileged standing within the institutions of capitalist enterprise. . . . Consequently companies tended to be very touchy about the ways in which their products were deployed on the screen." Bernstein, *Controlling Hollywood*, 104.

80. According to Cheng, Baker's Black body—whether clothed or naked—represents both "creativity" and "acute allergy" for Modernist architects like Adolf Loos (31), "machine" and "animality" for Le Corbusier (87), human flesh and material "sculpturalness" (102) in art, "ornament" and "essence" (110) in photography, "irresistible" and "destructive" (119) in sexuality, and "cipher" and "citation" in film (153). Thus, her Black dancing body constitutes ambivalence between the old and new; the familiar and strange. Anne A. Cheng, *Second Skin: Josephine Baker and the Modern Surface* (New York: Oxford University Press, 2011).

81. Ibid., 4.

82. Ibid., 84.

83. Hortense Spillers, "Mama's Baby, Papa's Maybe: An American Grammar Book," in *Diacritics* 17, no. 2, Culture and Countermemory: The "American" Connection (Summer, 1987), 64–81.

84. Eva Cherniavsky, *Incorporations: Race, Nation, and the Body Politics of Capital* (Minneapolis: University of Minnesota Press, 2006), 85.

85. Cheng, *Second Skin*, 12.

86. Cherniavsky, *Incorporations*, xvii.

87. Cheng, *Second Skin*, 6.

88. Magee, *Irving Berlin's American Musical Theater*, 21.

89. Houston Baker sums up Lewis's theory nicely when she writes: "Afro-Americans turned to art during the twenties precisely because there was no conceivable chance of their assuming *patria*—or anything else in White America. Art seemed to offer the *only* means of advancement because it was the only area in America—from an

70 BEHIND THE SCREEN

Afro-American perspective—where the color line had not been drawn . . . Afro-Americans adopted the arts as a domain of hope and an arena of possible progress." Houston Baker, *Modernism and the Harlem Renaissance* (Chicago: University of Chicago Press, 1987), 11.

90. Levering Lewis, *When Harlem Was in Vogue*, 48.

91. Alain Locke, "Enter the New Negro," *Survey Graphic*, Harlem: Mecca of the New Negro, March 1925.

92. Du Bois had a growing concern that " 'the criteria of Negro arts' were ruled by Whites." Du Bois writes: "I will say that there are today a surprising number of White people who are getting great satisfaction out of these younger Negro writers because they think it is going to stop agitation of the Negro Question." See citation in Levering Lewis, *When Harlem Was in* Vogue, 178.

93. Ibid., 304–5.

94. I am using the term as defined by Nancy Leong where "racial capital" is the "process of deriving social and economic value from the racial identity of another person." See Nancy Leong, "Racial Capitalism," *Harvard Law Review* 126, no. 8 (June 2013).

95. Baker, *Modernism and the Harlem Renaissance*, 110, note 17.

96. Hughes, in *Big Sea*, recalls seeing *Shuffle Along* numerous times because of its infectious "pre-Charleston kick" that then spread to the other arts. He writes that it gave a "scintillating send-off to that Negro vogue in Manhattan, which reached its peak just before the crash of 1929." See Langston Hughes, *The Big Sea: An Autobiography* (New York: A. A. Knopf, 1940), 223–24.

97. Ibid., 224–25.

98. In 1929, *Variety* wrote of Harlem: "Harlem's 'night life now surpasses that of Broadway itself. From midnight until after dawn it is a seething cauldron of Nubian mirth and hilarity.' 'You go sort of primitive up there,' Jimmy Durante—certainly an expert—warned, 'with the bands moaning blues like nobody's business, slim, bare-thighed brown-skin gals tossing their torsos, and the Negro melody artists bearing down something terrible on the minor notes' " (quoted in Levering Lewis, *When Harlem Was in Vogue* 208).

99. Rent parties originated in Harlem as a means of escape and often as a way to raise money. Musicians would play at these informal gatherings and a hat would be passed around to collect money to help defray the cost of rent. Cutting contests, jazz music, and swing dance are said to have evolved at these types of social gatherings. Ted Gioia, *The History of Jazz*, 2nd ed. (New York: Oxford University Press, 2011).

100. Hughes, *Big Sea*, 225 and 107–8. It is this mindset to which Hughes refers in his famous essay, "The Negro Artist and the Racial Mountain" (1926) where he writes paragraph one of the essay: "This urge within the race toward Whiteness, the desire to pour racial individuality into the mold of American standardization, and to be as little Negro and as much American as possible." The essay was originally published in *The Nation* on June 23, 1926.

101. For example, Carl Van Vechten has been criticized by many of his contemporaries as well as modern scholarship for reinforcing certain stereotypes of Blackness. Lewis writes of the ally, "Van Vechten's motives for writing what amounted to two books in one were a mixture of commercialism and patronizing sympathy. For the sake

INTEGRATING THE SCREEN 71

of sales, he intended *N[sic] Heaven* to create a sensation, while not disturbing his White readers' most basic perceptions of the Negro." See Levering Lewis, *When Harlem Was in Vogue*, 208.

102. See Leong, "Racial Capitalism," 2154.

103. Also known as "high yellow," this term was slang for a fair-skinned person of color who might have been able to pass for White or at least tried to emulate certain "high White" ways of life. Edward Ball, *The Sweet Hell Inside: The Rise of an Elite Black Family in the Segregated South* (New York: Harper Collins, 2002).
At the time this song was written, certain Harlem clubs like the Cotton Club had a strict policy around only hiring chorus dancers who were of this lighter complexion. Thomas J. Hennessey, *From Jazz to Swing: African-American Jazz Musicians and Their Music, 1890–1935* (Detroit, MI: Wayne State University Press,1994), 100.

104. A generic name often given to Black maids and also the title of a play in four acts that ran at the Belasco Theater from February 9, 1926, through March 19, 1927. See original Playbill, http://www.playbill.com/production/lulu-belle-belasco-theater-vault-0000010908, accessed September 10, 2019.

105. Note that Hughes cites *Shuffle Along* (1921) as the show that piqued White interest, while scholars like David Levering Lewis credit shows like *Lulu Belle* (1926) with having this impact. Regardless of the particular show, Broadway clearly influenced the flow of White traffic uptown. Levering Lewis writes of the exposure *Lulu Belle* caused: "Overnight, there was a real danger that in the stampede to the exotic and forbidden, Harlem's intellectual and artistic elite would be crushed by frantically stimulated whites." Lewis, *When Harlem Was in Vogue*, 165.

106. The popular show was written by Charles MacArthur and Edward Sheldon. Lenore Ulric played the lead role in blackface thereby complicating the "reproduction" of Black life.

107. In 1927 the Urban League concluded that 48 percent of Harlemites spent more than twice as much on rent as White New Yorkers. And yet "Harlem ballyhoo" distorted these findings in leading Black papers and obscured many of the truths behind "real" Harlem. Levering Lewis, *When Harlem Was in Vogue*, 109.

108. Hughes, *Big Sea*, 227.

109. Stuart Heisler and Mark Sandrich, *Blue Skies* (October 16, 1946; USA: Paramount Pictures), Film.

110. Clarence Brown, *Idiot's Delight* (January 27, 1939; USA: Metro-Goldwyn-Mayer), Film.

111. According to John Mueller, Fred Astaire wanted to "retire with a dance that was a knockout." See Mueller, *Astaire Dancing: The Musical Films* (New York: A. A. Knopf, 1985), 267.

112. For full original and updated lyrics, see Robert Kimball and Linda Emmet, eds., *The Complete Lyrics of Irving Berlin* (New York: A. A. Knopf, 2001), 262–263.

113. Carol Saltus, "The Modest Mr. Astaire Talks with Carol Saltus," *Inter/View*, June 1973, 9–16, and Mueller's *Astaire Dancing*, 426, note 20.

114. My critique of this appears in Chapter 4.

115. Ryan Raul Bañagale, *Arranging Gershwin: Rhapsody in Blue and the Creation of an American Icon* (Oxford: Oxford University Press, 2014), 3.

FIGURE 1.3 The Mills Brothers—Donald, Harry, Herbert, and John—sing the title song "Dinah" in Max Fleischer's Bouncing Ball Cartoon, 1933. (Private collection)

SCREEN SONGS
WITH THE FAMOUS BOUNCING BALL

MAX FLEISCHER
PRESENTS
DINAH

Copyright MCMIII

♪♪

PRESENTING RADIO'S GREATEST SENSATION

THE MILLS BROTHERS

Note: The music throughout this cartoon is furnished
by the Mills Brothers Quartette.
They employ no musical instruments of any kind—except the guitar.
There is no tuba, no trumpet, and no saxophone.

The Mills Brothers, who began as a barbershop quartet under the name of the Four Kings of Harmony, were the first African American singers to have their own national radio show (1930). Billed as "Four Boys and a Guitar" and known for their amazing ability to each sound like a different instrument, they imitated two trumpets, a trombone, and a tuba, and could trick listeners into thinking that they were a full jazz band. They appeared in several big films including The Big Broadcast of 1932 *and an uncredited performance in* Broadway Gondolier *(1935) as well as several shorts like* I Ain't Got Nobody *(1932) and* When Yuba Plays the Rumba on the Tuba *(1933). This short,* Dinah, *was the second of three bouncing ball shorts they made with the Fleischer Brothers. These cartoon/live-action shorts would appear in movie houses prior to the main attraction. Due to the Brothers' popularity on mainstream radio, such bouncing ball animation combined with these hit songs would guarantee a true sing-along.*

FIGURE 2.1 (*Top and Bottom*) The Goldwyn Girls (including starlets Paulette Goddard, Betty Grable, Mary Stewart, and Jane Wyman) perform "What a Perfect Combination," in *The Kid from Spain*, 1932. (Private collection)

2

Optical Illusion and Design

Exposure Values, Protean Guises, and Eddie Cantor's Blackface, 1930–1933

An ensemble of Goldwyn Girls dressed in giant hats and matching white lace bras and leggings rises from the Café Sevilla's cocktail tables. Beginning first with simple double basic time steps and slowly transitioning into sexualized shimmies and hip bumps, the dancers then make their way to an interior and exterior circular formation in the center. After a few bars of Charleston-infused tap dancing, the women in white lace are joined by the rest of the film's Goldwyn Girls dressed in identical costumes made of black lace. The patterns become increasingly more intricate now with twice the number of dancers and the two-toned color scheme. The classic passing parade of Goldwyn faces is made more interesting as women's hands frame each passer-by with the opening and closing of their rotations, framing each new face like the opening and closing of a camera's iris. Their bodies then chug toward center becoming more and more tightly interwoven until Berkeley's view from fifteen feet above captures nothing but a sea of white lace hats, out of which emerges Eddie Cantor in blackface.[1] This will become a typical choreographic move in the Berkeley/Cantor/Goldwyn trifecta films: The Goldwyn Girls never don burnt cork themselves but instead mask and unmask Cantor amid his big blackface routine. The camera captures a perfect top shot of the Girls in their low-cut lace, a frame that initially reads as capturing pure cleavage. However, their overexposed chests are soon overlaid by the slight tilt of their heads on which have been painted the faces of animated minstrel men. Their jet-black scalps support Cantor's more blatant burnt cork and offer their own "safe" nod at blackface. While it consumes only five seconds of screen time, the visual impact of Cantor's blackface surrounded by a sea of cartoon-like minstrels is striking. A protean patchwork of minstrels engulfed by a pageant of titillating body parts. The camera zooms in for a closeup of Cantor's mask while the surrounding Goldwyn Girls evacuate the stage. A new crop of women enters the theatrical space from all angles, surrounding Cantor's body with large sheets

Behind the Screen. Brynn W. Shiovitz, Oxford University Press. © Oxford University Press 2023.
DOI: 10.1093/oso/9780197553091.003.0003

76 BEHIND THE SCREEN

of metal that fit together as pieces of a puzzle. Code prohibits that the final image in this scene be one of blackface masks. The metal structure that these women construct brings viewers back to the Café Sevilla and the film's loose references to Spain. The final image of a bull's head reminds the audience that these dancers are neither White nor Black and layers their perception in such a way as to make them forget.

Busby Berkeley's use of a single camera eye to capture the synchronized movement of America's beauty ideal in the early 1930s was technologically simple yet sociologically complex. In fact, this iconic—albeit forgotten—calisthenic dreamscape, which was only Berkeley's fourth attempt at dance for camera, speaks to the intricacies of America's social values during the early years of the Great Depression. This dance scene from *The Kid from Spain* (1932) exposes the nation's insecurities surrounding the economic trauma brought about by the Depression while disclosing many of the ways it coped with a national shift in American employment: Busby Berkeley's organizing and display of beautiful White women into kaleidoscopic patterns provided a new type of optical distraction. Berkeley's choreography took the focus off a film's caricatured presentation of Indigenous, "Brown," and Black bodies—the identities of whom were seen as threats to the American workforce—in favor of close-ups and top shots of the White female body. That is, Berkeley's making of "animated poster art out of shapely showgirls" offered its own form of escapism and was one way that Hollywood kept weary viewers from acknowledging some of the major shifts occurring across racial, gender, and ethnic lines, onscreen and off.[2]

Just as the Wrigley's-inspired Chewy Gooey Gum ad of chapter 1 stands in as female ornament and capitalist desire at the same time the Black bodies onstage become "remnant flesh" when juxtaposed to the specters of the minstrel stage, so too do Berkeley's Goldwyn Girls mediate between the human body—sex—and modernity when placed in the imaginative worlds of Eddie Cantor. While the objectification of these women's bodies mirrors some of the acts of objectification that occur on the pseudo-integrated stages of this era, one key choreographed feature separates Goldwyn's girls from Black dancers during these early years of the Code: unlike the wild and "hot" presentations of Black dancers on the 1930s screen, the camera's duty was to organize these White bodies into patterns and formations that gave off a sense of order and productivity. Not only was it important for Hollywood to offer stability during this era, but it was also tactical to place the tight geometry of these

White bodies alongside the more unruly actions of these films' differently raced performers and Cantor's black face.

Berkeley's highly sexualized camera angles and Cantor's overt references to the minstrel stage in this climactic number from *The Kid from Spain* are questionable even within the Code's relaxed guidelines, but the film's narrative, combined with strategic representation, allowed Goldwyn a lot of leverage in moviemaking. In theory, the Production Code helped the industry "persuade its domestic audiences that its products were neither morally nor economically damaging."[3] The obvious way around a lot of the Code's restrictions was to either avoid politics altogether or to place the plot of the movie off American soil. Through this combination of Berkeley's optical effects and bracketing these early Cantor films in mythical settings, this film, along with *Whoopee!* (1930) and *Roman Scandals* (1933), sidesteps many of the Code's considerations.[4] Humoring these two seemingly inconsequential façades, the Cantor/Goldwyn/Berkeley team freed up the latitude with which they could explore sexuality and race.

This chapter examines the role Berkeley's Goldwyn Girls played in enacting the protean and citational guises, two common covert minstrel tropes of the early 1930s, specifically as they surface in the films of Eddie Cantor. Films of this era collectively represented prevalent anxieties that were spawned by the Great Depression.[5] But the four films Cantor made between 1930 and 1933 address more than the nation's fears of economic failure and the downfall of normative gender roles. Cantor's films get at the heart of changing class, racial, and ethnic formations through conventional comic narratives that address the socially constructed nature of gender and ethnicity while highlighting race as fixed through blackface and other covert means of masking.[6]

With the newly introduced Production Code in 1930, film studios trod lightly with regard to issues of race and sexuality; the majority of blackface performances between 1930 and 1933 manifest through false integration and rapidly changing technology, specifically of the sonic type. Yet Cantor seems to mark an exception, especially when coupled with the Goldwyn Girls. Though not the mask of the nineteenth-century stage, nor even that of early talkies, Cantor continues a tradition of citing past references to blackface of a previous era and also finds utility in the blackface mask as a means of disguise. The masks that surface between 1930 and 1933 on Cantor's screen combine the optical distractions of Busby Berkley with a simultaneous use of *protean* and *citational* guises. The protagonist offers a series of quick changes

78 BEHIND THE SCREEN

through wardrobe (costume, makeup, props), dialect, and embodied caricature which all help to converge and collapse notions of Otherness. Cantor's use of the protean is generally accompanied by the citational guise, or references to simulated impressions of "Blackness" through blackface and/or through a White filter. Looking at three of Cantor's films from this era, this chapter locates the protean guise as the predominant mask used during the brief period between Hollywood's adoption of the Code (1930) and its enforcement of it (1934).

Eddie Cantor was not only proficient in playing multiple kinds of roles but also displayed a certain alacrity for switching between them. Unlike other words that denote change like "morphic" or "mutable," "protean" captures an aspect of being able to take on or play *multiple* kinds of roles. "Protean" also implies an ease with which a man or object can change. "Blacking up" usually comprised one of Cantor's personas, and it is within this framework of the protean and his seamless ability to play to multiple races and ethnicities that such racial masquerade was normalized.

While the protean guise is the focus of this chapter, the protean generally accompanies some version of the citational guise. The citational—any mention of a person, performer, or practice who/that has a well-known connection to blackface expressed physically, aurally, or both—surfaces in the majority of Cantor's transformations. During this transitional moment, when Hollywood was not strongly enforcing the Code, the coupling of the protean and citational guises helped to divert attention away from more overt performances of blackface.

Finally, covert minstrelsy operates most successfully when multiple forms of racial/ethnic caricature operate alongside one another. Cantor frequently double-coded his performances as a means of de-emphasizing his Otherness. While Jewishness was always a part of his schtick, his use of blackface often helped to underplay his ethnic differences. However, the films explored in this chapter offer prime examples of the ways in which Hollywood utilized redface and brownface—forms of racial and ethnic caricature that would never be censored—to minimize vis-à-vis distraction Cantor's overt references to nineteenth-century minstrelsy. Situating Cantor's characters in ambiguous (non-American) locations, Hollywood could both appeal to international markets and avoid offending them. It could also write off questionable behavior as belonging to the Other while also blurring the line of who that Other was beyond the color of their skin. This muddling of specificity both allowed provocative material to slip past the censors and

OPTICAL ILLUSION AND DESIGN   79

reinforced an "us (the West) versus them (non-West)" mentality while simultaneously creating a "safe exotic," one capable of giving Americans the opportunity to "sightsee and tune in without ever leaving their theater seats."[7]

> "Well, what are my bids for this sturdy little [chap] here." The auctioneer slaps Eddie-pus on the back. "Isn't anybody gonna bid? What nobody?!" Yells the auctioneer. "Well, if nobody wants me I might as well go home," Eddie-pus says. He starts walking off the auction block. A man with a Spartan costume stops Eddie-pus in his tracks: "Slaves who are not sold are thrown to the lions." Eddie-pus looking petrified, backs up: "Well, well what are we waiting for—let's have a bid." The auctioneer starts in again: "Will somebody say five dinars (pronounced diners)? Do I hear five dinars?" Eddie-pus becomes anxious and starts to beg: "I don't even hear four dinars. What's the matter with you people? Don't you know a bargain when you see one? Look at me. I can cook a little. I can take care of the children. If there are no children, I can take care of that. . . . By being a son to you. Doesn't anybody want me?" "It looks like you're going to the lions," the auctioneer announces as he grabs Eddie-pus by the wrist. Now desperate Eddie wails, "Oh come people. You may never get a chance like this again. I can sing—'all of me, why not take all of me.'[8] Look, I can dance—'ya-da da da,(2-beat pause) ya-da da da—humming the oft-cited "Buck Dance" tune while performing a short soft- shoe.[9] He finishes his dance with a Bill Robinson citation: "hah, hah, hah," he says as he rolls his eyes back and forth with his mouth open wide. "TAKE HIM TO THE LIONS!" Someone in the stands shouts "100 pipiks!" Eddie-pus, relieved, places his hands on his heart: "Oh mister, you'll never be sorry for this." But when he finds out that 100 pipiks (yiddush for bellybuttons) is only equivalent to 1/10 of one gold dollar he exclaims that this isn't Woolworths, and he needs another bid. Josephus (David Manners) bids one gold dinar. Eddie-pus likes the sound of one gold dinar but when he finds out who has placed the bid, he opts for the man with the pipiks (bellybuttons). "One dinar is bid. One dinar is bid. . . . Do I hear two?" Eddie-pus shuffles to the foot of the stage: "Look people, look what you can get for two dinars. Look at these skins." He grabs his arms. "Imported." He grabs his thighs. "All the way from Russia." The bids keep escalating. Partially because Eddie-pus contorts his voice and shouts out random dinar bids. "Now let me hear another dinar," the auctioneer hollers. Eddie-pus breaks into song: "Dinah, is there anyone finer," reciting lyrics to the popular 1925 song.[10] The bids keep going up. Finally, Josephus places the winning bid for ten diners. Going, going, gone.

The slave auction in *Scandals* elucidates the covert nature of Cantor's citations and marks one example of how the protean guise often camouflages the heft of particular racial encounters when they emerge in rapid physical and aural succession. The scene is full of cultural references, all of which happen faster than one can digest on a conscious level. The comedic work that Cantor does to undermine the institution of slavery is quickly overwritten when he advertises his value as a commodity who can sing and dance. As an open referent, this carries little weight—anyone can sing and dance—but his sonic declaration that follows attaches specific meaning to this performance: the tune he sings—a famous "buck dance" rhythm famous on the vaudeville circuit and stemming from an Africanist tradition—infers a certain racial designation that is further confirmed in Cantor's physical citation of Bill Robinson's famous time step. The subsequent "ha ha" vocal combined with his wide mouth and rotating eyeballs not only quotes a Bill Robinson trademark but also alludes to Robinson's complicated suggestions of minstrelsy, even where no blackface makeup was present.

Yoo-Hoo! and Whoopee! for Eddie Cantor

Eddie Cantor is funny—to some. He can be really funny if you appreciate fast quips, word play, cultural references, and a comedian who can use his physical size (or lack thereof) to invert normative gender paradigms. In fact, a lot of Cantor's schtick involves challenging history, inviting levity to exaggerate and highlight the absurdity of certain social dynamics. In this scene from *Roman Scandals*, Eddie Cantor as Oedipus (pronounced *Eddie-pus*), finds himself on the auction block in ancient Rome for reasons beyond his own comprehension. While buried in all kinds of humor, Cantor, in due course, draws attention to the ways in which trying to place a dollar amount on the human body is ludicrous. So preposterous that we may as well be talking about belly buttons. Moreover, he underlines the intrigue sparked by the "exotic" body—he only starts receiving bids when he emphasizes how his "skins" have been imported all the way from Russia. On the outside, Cantor appears to destabilize everything from the institution of slavery to roles that have historically been assigned to women. His comic material, which is less overt, complicates Cantor's humor and perhaps undermines what he sought to expose.

Cantor's performance is also double coded, a term Henry Bial uses to describe performances that can "communicate one message to Jewish audiences while simultaneously communicating another, often contradictory message to gentile audiences."[11] Just as Cantor might read funny to some and not to others, he will likely read Jewish to some and not Jewish to others. This is because Cantor worked hard to de-emphasize his Jewishness, even if at times he said things that an audience equipped to see and hear as Jewish will read as so. Cantor offers a series of "visual and aural signs which are open to double meaning" depending on the audience. During the slave auction, some viewers will understand its allusion to a tension between the Jews and the Romans that spanned two thousand years. Others not schooled in Jewish history might instead pick up on Cantor's mention of Woolworth's, a famous five-and-dime store that scholars like Bial and comedians like Lenny Bruce would surely label "goyish."[12] As Cantor's performance demonstrates, being Jewish on the screen is "not about being so much as it is about performing," and the actor frequently double-coded his performances as a means of fitting in as White rather than standing out as Jewish.[13]

Born Isador Iskowitz on January 31, 1892, on the Lower East Side, Eddie Cantor was raised by his maternal grandmother Esther from age two, after both of his parents (both Russian Jewish immigrants) died. His poor upbringing would continue to surface in his comedic persona—always aware of class and "framed from the perspective of the hardworking immigrant Little Guy aspiring to the American dream."[14] He dropped out of school early to take on a bunch of odd jobs, one of which was in a vaudeville show at the Old Clinton Theater. He was quickly picked up by Gus Edwards and played in his *Kid Kabaret*. From then on, he would make a living in the performing arts. His big break came in 1917 when Florenz Ziegfeld hired Cantor for his midnight revue, *The Frolics*. Despite some turbulence between Ziegfeld and Cantor in the early 1920s, the two reconciled and Cantor returned to Ziegfeld's stage to do a series of successful shows, including Cantor's first full-length part on Broadway in *Kid Boots* (1923). He remained a headliner for the remainder of the decade, becoming one of the highest paid theater performers of the time. His success in *Ziegfeld's Follies* in 1927 and then in *Whoopee!* the following year led to his success in Hollywood.[15]

In addition to his triumph on stage and screen, Cantor had a successful career in radio and publishing.[16] A few things were consistent across these four mediums. When the stock market crashed in 1929, much of Cantor's comedy revolved around satirizing the economic and political crises of the

82   BEHIND THE SCREEN

early Depression, including but not limited to, a prevalent anxiety among White males. The film medium, however, allowed him to address this anxiety in ways that the other outlets did not: Cantor combined what many would perceive as an effeminate, sexually liminal persona along with burnt cork in foreign (yet fantastical) settings to construct a new form of Whiteness while establishing a clear divide between White Americans and non-White Others. [FIG. 2.3] Margaret McFadden captures Cantor's approach nicely when she sums it up in the following way: "Cantor's film characters condense the intersecting crises of the economy, of gender roles and relations, and of ethnic and racial identity into whimsical plots, but then invariably resolve all the narrative conflicts in ways that reestablish economic fairness, restore normative gender roles and relations, and construct a more inclusive version of White ethnicity, one with clear boundaries between White and non-White Americans."[17] We see this formula play out in the screen adaptation of *Whoopee!*, *The Kid from Spain*, and *Roman Scandals*.[18]

For Americans living through the Great Depression, the economic crisis and the gender crisis were related. Men were laid off and women were thrust into the workforce. As a result, women's social and economic power swelled but they were still expected to fulfill the same sexual and marital expectations they had shouldered at home before the Depression. According to McFadden, films made during this era relied on female characters to "raise and symbolically elide the threat of women's growing social and economic power" by defusing "male fears of female sexual and economic independence."[19] Cantor plays off this reality in all of the films he made between 1930 and 1933. Through a series of disguises, Cantor reinvents the heterosexual, White working-class male as fluid in his relationships with women, yet still economically competent and successful romantically.

But Cantor's humor also serves another function: Cantor's accentuation of his own Jewish identity—performed through a "repertory of tropes and framing mechanisms"—represents the comedian's ambivalent ties to ethnicity specifically as it relates to masculinity and Whiteness.[20] We see an overt display of this layering in the afore-described auction block scene in *Scandals*. As a whole, this film insinuates a history of Jewish enslavement by the Romans, which is accentuated in moments where Cantor plays up his Eastern European roots. His Russian "skins," the *pipiks*, and even his name Eddie-pus—likely a play on and Eddie-"*putz*," Yiddish for "fool" or

OPTICAL ILLUSION AND DESIGN 83

"penis"—showcase his ethnic roots to culturally informed audiences.[21] At the same time, he plays up his more effeminate side, which, on the surface, speaks to the nationwide gender crisis. However, this gender fluidity, read as a mechanism for defusing White male fears of women's sexual and economic independence amid the Great Depression, serves to mask Cantor's own ambivalence around ethnic difference. That is, Cantor uses what Sander Gilman has asserted as the most pervasive symbol of Jewish difference, the "feminized male Jew," to in fact alleviate the fears of a more widespread economic crisis.[22] The coding that Cantor performs in this scene, especially his references to African American culture—for example, his citation of Bill Robinson and his quoting of "Dinah"—help to bury his Jewishness by veiling his slave performance in allusions to Black culture, thus revealing the ways in which Cantor is White, rather than another Other. Cantor's gamut of protean transformations throughout all three of the films I discuss in this chapter do this work and speak to the number of layers involved in instances of covert minstrelsy.

In *Whoopee!* Henry Williams (Cantor) plays the part of an effeminate hypochondriac who fears strong women and struggles with sexual advances. While Williams thinks he is just giving Sally Morgan (Eleanor Hunt) a ride out of town, Morgan has in fact used Williams to help her escape her fast-approaching wedding to Western sheriff Bob Wells (Jack Rutherford) because she is actually in love with part-American Indian Wanenis (Paul Gregory) whose race is an obstacle. Unbeknownst to Williams, Morgan leaves a note to members of her hometown that she and Williams have eloped. The remaining plot revolves around the chase and capture of Henry Williams. Williams's circumstance requires that he befriend anyone with whom he comes into contact, including the local "Indians" Black Eagle (Chief Caupolican) and Matafay (Lou-Scha-Enya). The plot also offers several opportunities for narratively cohesive disguises, like his performance in blackface and his stint as an American Indian.

Cantor goes through a succession of transformations over the course of the film. He begins as his character, Henry Williams, and then transforms into a series of different personalities while traveling "West." On arriving at Jerome Underwood's (Spencer Charters) ranch, Cantor changes his name to Henry Ford and identifies his new "wife" (Sally Morgan) as Mrs. Ford: "She's one of those new Fords, you know?"[23] The manager of the ranch's restaurant falls for Cantor's façade and quickly recruits him to be the ranch's new chef. Cantor quickly changes into a cook's uniform and begins making (inedible

84   BEHIND THE SCREEN

Epsom salt) waffles. Amid his waffle-making and veneer as a Greek cook with a thick accent, the groom-to-be sheriff walks in with his entourage. Cantor swiftly jumps into the oven. The sheriff rallies his men: "Don't let a White man get by you, you hear me. Don't let a White man get by you." The restaurant manager sees the bowl of waffle batter on the stove and lights a burner. The whole stove combusts. Out of the oven climbs a blackened Eddie Cantor, yet somehow the smoke and ashes have only covered his face and the front sides of his hands. His clothing is untarnished; the interior of his palms are still completely white, and white minstrel lips have appeared on his coal-black face in the process. The black-faced Cantor scurries out of the kitchen as all the sheriffs stare him down. Sally does not recognize him at first, so he turns over his palms and asks, "Don't you recognize me? It's Henry?" Sally stares blankly. "Well, who am I," he asks again, "Amos 'n' Andy?" It all clicks for Sally: "Wow! your disguise is perfect. How did you ever think of it?" "You mean the black?" asks Cantor "I didn't. I got in the stove and someone else thought of it."

Cantor's performance in *Whoopee!* marks a live action example of the *protean guise*. The protean guise acts as a distinct subset of covert minstrelsy precisely in the way that it presents itself as something in a new form. This form can change multiple times over the course of a film, as in Cantor's shift from effeminate hypochondriac to a more masculine Greek cook, or even more rapidly within the same scene, as in Cantor's quick transformations on the *Roman Scandals'* auction block between Black female jazz singer, Jewish immigrant, Black male tap dancer ad infinitum during the slave auction. The protean itself relies most heavily on the performance's visual content, but in the case of Cantor, the protean takes on a sonic and citational dimension as well.

Cantor notoriously appeared as a range of characters within a single film, but the roles he took on always served a narrative function. Because he constructed scenarios where he was usually on the run, the plots of these films often necessitated a disguise. While the protean does not necessarily insinuate metamorphosis *qua* disguise—as will be the case when we look at protean variations in animated films—Cantor's quick transformations utilize the disguise mechanism as a means of becoming "Other." While not always an ethnic or racial Other, the practicality and accidental nature of Cantor's concealments allow him to become ethnically and racially Other in a fashion that is permissible within the parameters of early Code. Furthermore, because his character morphs so frequently within a single film, an audience is

OPTICAL ILLUSION AND DESIGN   85

forced to reconcile more offensive mutations (e.g., blackface) as par for the course.

Cantor's Visual and Verbal Ventriloquism

Cantor always used blackface as one of his disguises in these films. In the case of *Whoopee!* he strategically sets up his disguise as a complete accident: "I got in the stove and someone else thought of it." Henry is not responsible for the blackening of his face; the stove combusts and naturally he absorbs the charcoal. In this sense, Cantor's protean transformation into blackface appears seamless. The fact that Cantor (or his character) can "black up" re-affirms his Whiteness and helps to qualify the White heterosexual male underneath the mask of all his disguises. Cantor diminishes his own (ethnic) Otherness off the screen through his onscreen racial masquerade in blackface. But Cantor's disguises go beyond makeup, costume, and title change. His protean makeovers always involve a corporeal and aural component, most often in the form of citations.

After convincing Sally that he is in fact Henry Williams and not Amos 'n' Andy, Cantor physically expresses the caricatured gait of famed typecast actor Stepin Fetchit, known for playing to the Jim Crow and Zip Coon stereotypes. He proceeds to perform this reference to "the Laziest Man in the World" (i.e., Jamaican/Bahamian comedian Lincoln Theodore Monroe Andrew Perry) for the remainder of his blackface disguise. This embodied quotation reveals several things, not least of which is the transformation of Lincoln Perry from human to the "hollowed-out savage scarecrow with only the appearance and not the substance of the human," one of many examples these films offer in terms of a "symbolic evisceration" of Black people when the Jim Crow and Zip Coon stereotypes are evoked.[24] Cantor's gait and posture also produce our first example of the *citational guise*, another subset of covert minstrelsy actions, which in the case of Cantor usually accompany the protean. While any mention of a person, performer, or practice with a well-known connection to blackface constitutes a citation, I reserve the subset of a "citational guise" for those instances which are less overt.

Cantor's question, "Well, who am I, Amos 'n' Andy?" constitutes a citation because he states a verbal referent that cannot be misidentified. The citational guise, however, requires a more covert performance. This is usually

86 BEHIND THE SCREEN

expressed physically (through the body) or aurally (through song, dialect, or intonation)—or as a combination of the two. The most common examples of citational guises in the 1930s and 1940s appear as references to Al Jolson (and specifically his performance of "Mammy") as we saw in chapter 1 and allusions to Bill Robinson (and specifically his stair dance) as we will see in chapter 3.

Something similar happens in *Whoopee!* when Cantor physically quotes Stepin Fetchit. Citing Fetchit was less common than references to Jolson and Robinson, but his characteristic shuffle walk would have been widely recognized by audiences of the era; Fetchit peaked in popularity between 1929 and 1934.[25] The subtle yet unmistakable nature of these corporeal re-embodiments make materially evident what Barbara Lewis has described as the "excommunication of the Black body outside humanity's gates."[26] Because references still left Fetchit "fractionally human," they were permissible under the guidelines of the 1930's Production Code and an effective means of bolstering the caricature aspect of Cantor's blackface within a framework of disguise, both in *Whoopee!* and in *Roman Scandals*.

Cantor continues to go through a series of transformations in *Whoopee!*, yet these changes become more rapid when, as in *Roman Scandals*, the sonic layer enters the picture. Bob Wells hastens the corked performer over to a crowd of spectators: "What's your name?" the sheriff asks. Cantor changes his voice, "Rudy . . . Vallée (a comical decision considering that he is trying to masquerade in blackface and ironic in light of Vallée's "crooner" label)," he says.[27] The sheriff holds a gun to Cantor's stomach and asks him to sing. Without pause, he breaks into "My Baby Just Cares for Me," the somewhat obligatory song and dance performed by Cantor in blackface.[28] The blackface mask here is once again offered within a frequently changing framework of disguise, making Cantor's outdated racial masquerade "acceptable" within Code parameters. But it also operates as a citation of self, since Cantor had spent the better part of the previous decade building his reputation as *the* blackface comedian. A song and dance performed in burnt cork was almost expected of him by 1930; he was, so to speak, doing nothing out of the ordinary. As he finishes his number, some strange voices are heard in the distance. Cantor acts swiftly: "I throw my voice in different directions; I'm a contortionist. Didn't you know it?" Cantor frequently used his ability to quickly transmogrify his vocals to comedic effect in these films, which adds an entirely different ease to his ability to morph rapidly from one character to the next. Taking on several different forms (vocal and physical), he could play up to three characters within the same scene.

Following another spectacle-heavy Busby Berkeley routine, Cantor's Whiteness is "discovered." He conceals himself as a cowboy—though struggles with the phallic nature of his newly acquired gun—and then flees to a nearby American Indian reservation run by Chief Black Eagle. Here Cantor's performance of blackface continues, but this time without makeup.

Already the chief's title references Blackness overtly, but his connections to blackface evolve in more discreet ways over the course of this scene. The first is a purely sonic reference to minstrelsy while Chief Black Eagle lectures Wanenis on why the White man is bad: "You must *MAARRY* Matafay," he exclaims. His voice changes when he utters the word "marry." For a brief second, he cites Al Jolson's famous "mammy" phrase. He changes nothing in his body; his citation is intimated purely through sound. Mendi Obadike has discussed how sound may in fact summon the presence of Blackness even in its absence. I would like to extend her concept of acousmatic Blackness to include *performances* of Blackness arguing that Chief Black Eagle's citation of Jolson's "Mammy" mobilizes the presence of caricatures of Blackness even in their absence.[29] Because Black Eagle's citation is stripped of its visible signifiers, spectators' attention may be drawn toward sound traits that would normally be imperceptible, including Black Eagle's vocal register and the accentuation of certain syllables, both of which resemble the aural qualities of Jolson's famous performance.

When Cantor (as Henry Williams) arrives on the reservation, he is determined to make friends with Chief Black Eagle. Part of Cantor's comedic formula was to form some sort of partnership with characters of different races and ethnicities to satirize racial and ethnic prejudice. However, this often resulted in constructing his Whiteness as distinct from an essentialized notion of Blackness or American Indian-ness. In this scene Cantor breaks the ice between himself and the three "Natives" with a series of jokes. The chief laughs: "You want be friend with Indian?" "I'm friend with everybody," replies Cantor, "even my broker." Cantor's quick retort gets at the heart of his Depression-era humor: he both befriends the Other—possibly aided by his passing reference to Jewish stereotypes around Jews and money—while also critiquing the economy. But his attempt to befriend the Chief and the community of "Indians" turns out to serve an even deeper function than speaking to Depression-era fears.

88 BEHIND THE SCREEN

As will continue to unfold, the efficacy of blackface as a covert minstrel form generally relies on its entanglement with at least one other ethnic or racial masquerade. In *Whoopee!* Cantor's blackface becomes embroiled with a sonic and protean form of (American Indian) redface. Despite Cantor's removal of the blackface mask on the ranch, he has taken his burnt cork routine to the reservation as well. While sitting around a fire smoking a peace pipe, Cantor asks Black Eagle some questions about Pocahontas who is rumored to have saved John Smith. "But why didn't she do something for his brother Al?" Chief Black Eagle looks confused: "His brother Al?" Cantor continues, "Yes, and I don't mean Jolson. . . . Mammy!" Once again, we get a reference to Jolson, this time directly. Even though Cantor uses no visible redface or blackface makeup, this interaction between himself and Chief Black Eagle exemplifies a key facet of covert minstrelsy. One benefit to incorporating American Indians living on some unidentified Western land was that American Indians made up no part of Hollywood's economy and were not in a position of power to object. Goldwyn could embrace redface stereotypes without fear of backlash from either American Indians or the MPPDA.

The above scene demonstrates one way that stereotypes of redness were mixed up with those of Blackness; their entangled nature says something more powerful about the bodies of each than an isolated caricature of Blackness or American Indian-ness could accomplish on its own. Like blackface, redface caricatures most commonly involved visible indications, like coloring the skin of the colonized red or brown when the image was drawn. When live, they more often included a set of stereotypical props— e.g., drums, elaborate headdresses, and peace pipes—that could be worn or used by characters to enhance their "Native-ness" or used on their own to signify a part of the whole; *Whoopee!* utilizes the latter. However, the muddying of caricatures surfaces first in Chief Black Eagle's audible citation of Al Jolson, a comedian known for his blackface. As is the case in all examples of the protean guise, this presentation, or acousmatic change, happens so quickly that the audience watching has no time to register the overlay.

This practice of presenting blackface caricatures through a redfaced vessel becomes most prominent in animated films of the mid-late 1930s, but the number of protean collocations in live action films are not insignificant. Note that Black Eagle's citation is almost imperceptible, yet it allows for a seamless (and unquestioned) moment later in the dialogue when

Cantor also cites Jolson's "Mammy." Thus, Chief Black Eagle's almost undetectable sonic suggestion of blackface in fact narratively substantiates and excuses Cantor's later quotation of "Mammy" and allows the two (i.e., Chief Black Eagle and Cantor's character) to bond over blackface humor. This instant protean transformation in the form of a citation not only conflates notions of Otherness but also takes the blame for blatantly racist representation away from the White man by placing the stereotype in the hands of the Other. Moreover, "Black" Eagle comes to stand in as a synecdoche for Cantor's now invisible blackface. Put differently, the protean guise is what allows Cantor to take on different forms—to be both White, and "red," and "black" simultaneously—so fast that the audience barely has time for these new configurations to resonate on a conscious level. The citation is what allows for the collapsing of racial categories, thus opening up the possibility for these forms to be substitutable: Black Eagle stands in for Cantor's blackface while performing Al Jolson and Cantor will soon "play Indian." In other words, visible redface surrogates blackface, and sonic blackface becomes part of Cantor's American Indian masquerade, each of which diffuses and further obscures the other. I have examined some of the ways in which references to Black culture—both real and imagined—have offered Cantor a means of redirecting his audience away from his Jewish identity onto his more assimilated, secular self. In what follows, I track the ways in which redface becomes the predominant mode of ethnic entanglement for Cantor in 1930, all while standing in as a surrogate for blackface and racial caricature.

Redface caricature was fashionable on the screen in the early 1930s. Its popularity and excusability stemmed from the language used by federal commissioners of the Bureau of Indian Affairs (BIA) who believed that "Indians—like children—often did not know what was best for themselves."[30] The fictions these commissioners professed were designed to convince the (non-Native) American public that too much federal support for Native peoples would lead to their laziness and dependency (among other things). Writing on this history, Scott Vickers notes, "Commissioners of the BIA became both the spokesmen for the national conscience regarding the treatment of Indians and also the designers of a racial ideology with which to justify westward expansion of Manifest Destiny. The language used by these commissioners laid the foundation and language for the construction of and reinforcement of Indian stereotypes."[31] The BIA also claimed that the only solution to "deal" with these "Others" was to either exterminate or assimilate them: "The goal, until the administration of John Collier in 1933, was consistent and unrelenting: 'to impress American civilization upon the Indian, to whiten the red man,' whether by political, religious, or military might."[32] This attitude was summed up in the Dawes Act (1887–1933), which aimed to assimilate American Indians into the American mainstream.[33] The 1934 Indian Reorganization Act (IRA), or Indian New Deal, banned the (further) sale of American Indian land, required that un-allotted land be returned to tribal control, and granted judicial autonomy to certain Indian communities.[34] Despite American Indians' uphill struggle to become equal citizens of the United States, the screen remained an acceptable outlet for rehashing age-old stereotypes about the "red" body. This struggle overlaps most directly with the period in which Cantor was most successful, 1930–1934.[35]

But for Cantor, the "red" body did more than stand in for his blackface on screen; it also helped to create a viable Jewish identity for himself off screen. Michael Rogin has noted that immigrants, especially Jews, "Americanized themselves by crossing and recrossing the racial line."[36] We see this in the following scene where Cantor starts integrating his Jewish identity with his Indian masquerade. Shortly after Cantor bonds with Black Eagle over Jolson's blackface, the chief decides that he likes Cantor. "Come. I make you belong tribe," he says. The camera cuts to Cantor dressed up as an Indian chief (no makeup, just costume). It is here that Cantor begins to "play Indian" although his performance, as usual, is confused with other ethnic and racial caricatures. He begins to bargain like a hackneyed Italian immigrant—"Me no capeesh"—and then refashions his dialect, this time bargaining like a stereotypical Jewish immigrant—"Such a *chutzpah* (slapping Mr. Underwood's *punum*)!"—and then performs a brief hybrid Jewish folk/cliché American Indian dance. His use of Yiddish begs the question of whether "*chutzpah*" (nerve) and "*punum*" (face) serve to signify difference, "an attempt to present the qualities of the Jew . . . as separate from the referent group," as a form of self-hatred as Sander Gilman would posit,[37] or whether this very quick linguistic code switching is in fact more motivated by the part of the protean guise that uses such verbal alacrity as yet another means of distracting audiences from seeing the depth of caricature present. Cantor's humor becomes speedily inter-ethnic and intra-racial, blurring the line so quickly that it becomes difficult to keep track of his many impersonations. Many Jewish scholars have written about the "wild west" as a vaudeville stage, "a performative space open to Jewish appropriation as a vehicle for inclusion."[38] It is through the Western mythos and through redface that Jewish performers often Americanize themselves. Like so many forms of caricature, the Jewish identity is established through the simultaneous identifying with and distancing from another oppressed group. Both redface and blackface ultimately helped to mark the Jewish performer's Otherness as illusory—"It's me, Henry. Who did you think it was, Amos 'n' Andy?"—easily taken off as costume or mask. But the key difference between redface (and as future films will show, brownface) for someone Jewish like Cantor was that he was transforming racial difference—that is, the difference between Black and White—into ethnic difference, thereby staking a claim on his ability to assimilate and thus acquire a "true" American identity. Even when Cantor is not playing up his Jewishness as he does in the redface scenes, his performance marks a type of imperfect assimilation, demonstrating his Otherness in relation to a constructed hegemonic Whiteness. His ability to live on the fringe in this sense helps him form alliances with other racial and ethnic groups only to ultimately encourage a certain kind of exceptionalism by "denying that identification and claiming a higher social status for the Jew as the 'white' person underneath the mask."[39]

But as seamless as are Cantor's physical and aural transformations throughout the film, one further layer assists in his ability to cover up his use of racial masquerade vis à vis the protean guise. The three big Busby Berkeley numbers in *Whoopee!* require an audience's complete immersion in the visual and bookend the film in such a way as to redirect viewers from seeing the specifics of Cantor's protean transformations. Berkeley's unique camera angles and ordering of the female body into machine-like configurations create the optical illusions necessary for audiences' incomplete viewing of the show as a whole.

Form Follows Function

Busby Berkeley excelled at perceptible conformity. This included a simple yet calculated production process of combining camera work, choreography, and casting. Additionally, new lighting and camera technology allowed Berkeley novel methods for producing and reproducing synchronous images onscreen. The first step in Berkeley's process was to select his women performers in such a way that they all conformed to the same White Western beauty standards. Often the first cut was made based on the attractiveness of a girl's face and her ankles, and then the selection was further whittled down by an assessment of the attractiveness of her knees[40] [FIG.I.3, bottom] Berkeley also favored blonde women, even if the color was manufactured: "With the new lighting for talkies, peroxide hair stands out on the screen and enables girls to steal scenes."[41] But hair was not the only thing he looked for in a woman. While incredibly subjective, this selection process was to Berkeley, an optical investment. He felt that this kind of scrutiny was necessary to offer Americans satisfaction with the extreme close-ups for which he became known.[42] Yet, at the same time he sought uniformity, he also wanted a group of women diverse enough that most White audience members could identify with at least one of his girls. Of course, he subscribed to strictly White, Western, non-Jewish standards of beauty, but he felt this economically sufficient for his *intended* audience. For Berkeley, the woman's body had to be center stage, but it was clear that the camera rather than the performer was the star.

Camerawork was the focus of Berkeley's choreography, and both his musical numbers and the way he filmed them stand liberated from the demands of the film's overarching narrative. Martin Rubin describes Berkeley's camera technique as "freed from the constraints of realistic, narrativized, cause-and-effect discourse and [embracing] liberated elements of play and display."[43] Many have described his work as pure display for the sake of spectacle because of the ways he creates abstract images that often make viewers forget the human basis of his geometric designs. Particularly notable is the Berkeleyesque exhibition of extravagance and overindulgence amid the country's most impoverished period. While these numbers serve no obligation to the film's plot or character development on the surface, I dispute the commonly held belief that Berkeley's optical grandeur does not serve a larger, more covert function in the greater scheme of the movie, even if this is unconscious.[44]

Whoopee! opens with "The Cowboy Song," Berkeley's first-ever dance for the camera. Unlike most of his future numbers, this dance includes a group of uniformly dressed cowgirls and identically garbed cowboys. Berkeley's dances usually featured female dancers with maybe one or two men who appeared in the final minutes. This dance, however, establishes a clear divide between the sexes, where men offer a "supporting" role, lifting women, and assisting in characteristic Berkeley choreography. The flirtatious child's play that fills "The Cowboy Song," seeks to restore order in an America where gender dynamics have been turned upside down. The Goldwyn Girls not only promised the heterosexual men in the audience an escape from reality, but as

Ziegfeld taught Goldwyn during the making of this film, "women enjoyed looking at beautiful women in beautiful clothes, the glorification of their gender," or so that is what they told each other.[45] These Berkeley numbers seem to be more in line with the contradiction written into cinematic images of the woman. As Mary Ann-Doane has argued, Berkeley's presentations were "a writing in images of the woman, but not *for* her."[46] Everything from the signature Berkeley wave—i.e., girls in quick succession "bending downward to the waist and up again"—to the medium close-up of each girl hiding her face with a prop before revealing her big smile, with the camera showing the girls rapidly one after the other in single file, helped to define the Berkeley aesthetic, one that foregrounded the reification of women as things and as commodities, thus offering the male gaze a distraction from the growing economic and social power of women.[47]

These routines also helped to conceal many of the ethnic and racial caricatures present on Cantor's screen by offering visual distraction during the application and removal of burnt cork (as we see in the "Stetson" number) or by normalizing—and sexualizing—the act of appropriating the culture of Others (as apparent in "The Song of the Setting Sun" at the culmination of *Whoopee!*). These large ensemble dances provide "interludes" that are completely superfluous to the plot and act as a form of hypnosis apart from what has gone right before or right after. The "Stetson" number strategically bookends Cantor's big blackface number "My Baby Just Cares for Me" and the removal of his burnt cork. The various elements involved in one of Berkeley's kaleidoscopic dreamscapes helps move the audience's focus away from the novelty of Cantor's blackface and toward the sparkle (and sexuality) of Berkeley's attractive shapes and young women. This phenomenon is, as Doane has pointed out, a product of the image orchestrating "a gaze, a limit, and its pleasurable transgression. The woman's beauty, her very desirability, becomes a function of certain practices of imaging—framing, lighting, camera movement, angle."[48] As Berkeley became more seasoned these numbers became increasingly elaborate. The final number in *Whoopee!*, however, offers a taste of the extravagance and complexity of Berkeley's future spectacles. Like other examples we have seen of the female body embroiled in a web of race and cultural capital, Berkeley stages the female body as ornament and object of capitalist desire in the context of ethnic caricature in "The Song of the Setting Sun."

With a seven-figure budget in the midst of the Great Depression, the Goldwyn/Ziegfeld team did not shy away from spectacle; this final dance evidences the excessive amounts of money that were poured into costuming

94 BEHIND THE SCREEN

FIGURE 2.2 Three photos from *Whoopee!* (1930). Directed by Thornton Freeland: (*Top left*) Close-up of Goldwyn Girl Christine Maple in "Song of the Setting Sun" costume. (United Artists/Photofest); (*Top right*) Top Shot of Goldwyn Girls in "Setting Sun." (Private collection); (*Bottom*) Long shot of Goldwyn Girls in "Setting Sun." (Private collection)

for this film. The visual pageant of this ersatz ceremonial dance-turned American Indian fashion show revels in Berkeley's classic top shots and geometric constructions. Yet the elaborate headdresses add an optical dimension that surpasses anything the unadorned body could accomplish on its own. Here the mesmerizing patterns distract viewers from an appropriation of American Indian textiles. The dance breaks off into a passing parade of girls coming down the mountainside. Darker-skinned men carry these White, almost naked women down the hill on horseback. The extravagance of this scene covers up the ways this exotic fashion show presents a social hierarchy by placing the "red" man in a subordinate position to the regal White woman while at the same time maintaining that women are objects up for public consumption. The bikini-wearing women in 1930s Hollywood would have been scorned (and would not have passed even the soft guidelines of the Code) in almost any other milieu, but their feather headdresses protect their sexuality by placing them within an exotic context. These Indian wares are not only at the White man's disposal in this scene, but they create a safe space for presenting the White female body as sexual because they are cloaked in redface, masked by the safer sexuality of exotic pleasure. Furthermore, by rendering a fashion show on this fictional reservation, the film stages a type of illusory assimilation, thereby promoting the work of the Dawes Act while also offering an escape from the industrial world through its disingenuous engagement with "authentic" craftsmanship.

Berkeley's dance numbers—such as "The Song of the Setting Sun"—sold *Whoopee!*, and Cantor received a contract for three additional films with Goldwyn, the "Ziegfeld of the Pacific."[49] With the success of *Palmy Days* (1931), Goldwyn committed to five more films with Cantor. *The Kid from Spain* was the first of these, followed by *Roman Scandals*. Even though the Production Code was in place, by 1932 directors had discovered ways they could circumvent many of the "rules" that the Studio Relations Committee (SRC) and the Producers Appeal Board (PAB) tried to administer. Goldwyn and others knew very well that there was a hierarchy of guidelines, and put in the proper context, the boundaries of racial and sexual representation could be tested. During these years it was much more scandalous to portray scenes that showed any sort of acceptance of communist ideals or anything that went against the laws of prohibition. Thus, shown in the right light and within the proper context, Goldwyn could do what he wanted.[50]

Bracketing Brownface in the Mythical Kingdom

Although many leaders in the industry claimed that films were "depression proof," 1931 marked the beginning of a grim downturn for box office sales.

96 BEHIND THE SCREEN

Less than a year after the release of *Whoopee!*, attendance in American theaters had plummeted, with 30 million fewer viewers attending movies each week. Directors used spectacle to try to entice the public; Berkeley, unlike so many film creatives, would continue to see great triumph.[51] But often spectacle was not enough to ensure his box-office success. The MPPDA was under great scrutiny from the Catholic Church, and the church seemed to care less about representations of ethnicity and race than it did about portrayals of sex and crime. If the screen was to "promote 'social spirit' and 'patriotism' and not confuse audiences with a cynical contempt for conventions'" then directors like Samuel Goldwyn just needed to find methods for appealing to (White) Catholic American values and ways not to offend those groups that had the biggest impact on box-office sales.[52]

By placing his films off American soil, Goldwyn narratively excused things like redface and brownface; as such, the international settings of his films usually allowed for more liberty with scant clothing and mixed-race marriages. But the way these films were received internationally was just as important. The industry had to "convince foreign censors and trade representatives that its output was culturally inoffensive and ideologically neutral."[53] Mexico was a big market for American movies, so finding ways to cast Mexicans in a positive light would ensure a better profit margin for directors. Already in place was a resolution to do everything in a film's power to avoid " 'present[ing] the Mexican character in a derogatory or objectionable manner,' which was designed to overcome a boycott of Hollywood films by the Mexican Government."[54] As a result, many studios avoided overt representation of actual countries (like Mexico) and instead utilized the "mythical kingdom." In *Spain*, Goldwyn chooses to make Mexico the primary setting, but then strategically has the main character Eddie (Cantor) disguise himself as a Spanish bullfighter. In this way he protects himself from presenting any of the Mexican characters in an objectionable manner and is likely safe from Spaniards taking offense since Cantor's character is disguised as a Spanish hero.

To avoid censorship from the SRC and PAB in this period, Goldwyn mostly had his characters inhabit ancient or fictional lands. In *Roman Scandals*, Goldwyn begins the film in West Rome, Oklahoma, itself a made-up city and comically filmed in the San Fernando Valley and West Hollywood. Eddie (Cantor), the lead, falls asleep and finds himself transported to ancient Rome, which at times resembles ancient Greece and at others suggests Babylonia. The unit of money used at the slave auction is a "dinar," or دينار

(*dīnār*), which although etymologically derived from ancient Rome's silver coin (from the Latin *dēnārius*) was in fact introduced to Iraq (replacing the Indian rupee) in 1932, just before this film was made. Through accents, costumes, or landscapes, "mythical" settings such as these would suggest an actual location but never overtly name it, and very often one nation would be conflated with another. While these mythical places contained a full range of stereotypes, they generally "avoided direct protest through the nominally fictional nature of the locale." It was an audience's responsibility to draw its own conclusions.[55]

Placing most of the plot in *Spain* on Mexican soil and that of *Scandals* in a pastiche of ancient lands allowed Goldwyn to present the more sexualized body in the context of exoticism and Cantor's blackface beside other performances of brownface, even where no makeup was used. Nobody used brownface makeup in *Spain* or *Scandals*, yet the Orientalist approach to conflating all Latin and Hispanic cultures in the former film and several ancient civilizations in the latter aids in its own form of masking, even if only for economic gain. Furthermore, such "cultural pastiche"—that is when "two or more cultural terrains normally considered distinct, or even antithetical" come together for comic effect—was a favorite comic conceit in 1930s Hollywood cinema.[56]

The dance the Goldwyn Girls perform during Cantor's blackface routine in *Spain* that opened this chapter opens might best be summed up as a Charleston-infused tap dance with hints of commercialized rumba, popular in American nightclubs and Mexican rumbera films of the era. Decorating this tap dance with two additional Africanist forms offers a semiotic effect similar to the blurring of blackface and redface that occurred in *Whoopee!*. Here, however, the distortion surfaces in the tension between blackface and a composite brownface.[57] [FIG. 2.1]

The composite brownface utilized in *Spain* coincides with the birth of a musical genre that Gustavo Pérez Firmat has labeled "Latunes," or a "tune with a Latin beat and an English language lyric," that would prevail in Hollywood for the next thirty years.[58] While they comprise a variety of genres, latunes of the 1930s and 1940s were dominated by Cuban rhythms, specifically the "rhumba" that "included up-tempo *sones* and guarachas as well as languid boleros." I place "rhumba" in quotes because the term itself carries a loaded history; that is, even what most recognize in the United States as a "rhumba" has a much more nuanced identity and bears little resemblance (if any) to the Afro-Cuban rumba.[59] Firmat describes these tunes as "'so near' to and

98   BEHIND THE SCREEN

yet 'so far' from Indigenous Cuban music," and yet "gracefully poised on the cultural border of Anglo and Latin America, somewhere between Tin Pan Alley and El Malecón."[60] Their in-betweenness makes these songs perfect candidates for covert minstrelsy as they help to construct a "Latin American" identity while they obscure a strong Africanist aesthetic.

Rumba evolved in the poor Black communities of Havana and Matanzas in the mid-nineteenth century. The three subgenres of rumba (yambú, guaguancó, and columbia) "drew heavily on dance traditions imported by slaves from Africa, although hybridization of dances from distant African tribes and their reformulation as rumba was a uniquely Cuban phenomenon."[61] During the Harlem Renaissance, Cubans began reinventing Afro-Cuban culture to suit Western fantasy and presented extremely hybridized forms of the rumba to American audiences on teatro vernáculo (vernacular theater) stages.[62] During the 1920s and '30s, publishers and performers in the United States and Europe appropriated the term "rumba" for any generic Latin American–influenced rhythm. By the time *Spain* was made in 1932, this crossbred style had become increasingly popular in Parisian and American nightclubs. It was a distinctively hybrid variety characterized by a predominantly Africanist musical style infused with European commercial elements and then performed by White bodies as a means of distancing it from its Black roots. In Havana, however, this dance was still predominantly performed by Black and mulatto performers. Juliet McMains describes this phenomenon: "By exporting *son* under the name rumba, white Cubans could profit from rumba's exotic appeal without 'dirtying' themselves with what they considered the crude vulgarity of Cuba's black underclass rumba." Mexican *rumbera* films from the 1930s have preserved a version of this cabaret rumba style. In the rumbera films, dance scenes "feature almost exclusively white actresses playing sexually alluring, but morally reprehensible, mulatta rumba dancers."[63] The White Goldwyn Girls perform a version of the Whitened cabaret rhumba during the big dance sequence at Café Sevilla in *Spain*.

Firmat has grouped latunes into three classes, the first of which parallels Hollywood's ubiquitous culture-blurring/geography-bending in the 1930s/ '40s. Like "La Paloma" in *Spain*, the "Carioca" rhumba in *Flying Down to Rio* (1933), and Carmen Miranda's Portuguese "Mamãe Eu Quero" in *Down Argentine Way* (1940), these "Latinoid" films full of latunes dissolve national differences in favor of borderless, history-less, brown space places with "contours rather than coordinates."[64] Those Others who exist somewhere *down* there make "possible acquaintance without contact" and keep the "appropriated object at a distance."[65] These songs' lyrics and film's titles help to create a Latinoid atmosphere; their (predominantly Cuban) Latin beats (generally a rhumba in the 1930s/'40s and a mambo in the 1950s/'60s) provide these films an opportunity to move more seamlessly between an Africanist aesthetic and a "Latin" one. Dances like those performed by the Goldwyn Girls in *Spain* not only blur the lines between Black culture and an elusive brown culture but also gain the ability to move more freely within the Code's recommendations.

Already the café's Spanish reference creates an ironic obfuscation of the film's actual locale. This is further mystified by the White dancers who perform three profoundly diasporic forms (tap, Charleston, and rumba) to jazz music. The film's setting in Mexico makes the dancers' performing more hip-centered movement agreeable under Code guidelines—after all, these women are supposed to be "locals"—while accentuating the sexuality of Berkeley's dancers. The dance they perform at once references a number of "African retentions and transformations" while establishing Berkeley's classic Hollywood style of tap dancing.[66] That is, within the movements that these women perform is written a diasporic process and condition, yet their Whiteness ascribes new meaning to these movements, further removing Africanist roots from the dances and assisting in a larger project (even if unconscious) to reallocate movements historically marked as Black to the White vernacular. The spectacle created by these women's conglomerate "brown" bodies and Berkeley's camera techniques distract viewers from the routine's blatant references to blackface.[67] They in effect become, as Laura Mulvey has suggested, "more closely associated with the surface of the image than its illusory depths, its constructed 3-dimensional space which the man is destined to inhabit and hence control."[68] But their spectacle goes beyond the illusory depths of male dominance and at the same time works to further conceal the ways in which Whiteness operates underneath their "brown" bodies. Thus, their most visible layers—their brownface and the way that Berkeley frames their female sexuality—repress their references to blackface while disguising a much more complex pattern of appropriating an Africanist aesthetic [FIG 2.1, bottom]

The protean guise in this context becomes a reconfiguration and successive substitution of the body that performs, allowing for the concealment of everything else going on in the production. To understand the full effect of the protean here, however, we must look back at the circumstances that led

100 BEHIND THE SCREEN

Cantor to wear blackface in the first place. Once again on the run, Cantor as "Eddie," pretending to be the famous Spanish bullfighter Don Sebastian II, gets himself into a bit of trouble. He hides under a table in a Mexican nightclub to avoid getting caught by Pancho and Pedro, two enemies. But Pancho and Pedro end up taking their personal beef to the same table under which Eddie is hiding. Pancho, thinking he is aiming his gun at Pedro's stomach under the table, and Pedro thinking that he is aiming his gun at Pancho's stomach, inadvertently hold Eddie at double gunpoint. Knowing he must act fast to avoid getting shot Eddie turns around so that his back side is now the object sandwiched between the two pistols. But a wine cork from a nearby table flies under the table and hits Eddie on the behind. Realizing what has just happened, Eddie turns around to pick up the flying object and quickly determines that this cork could be useful for his next disguise. He takes a lighter to the cork and tests the residue on the back side of his hand like lipstick. Seconds later, Eddie has painted on a full blackface disguise using a polished knife blade as a mirror, including white lips and darkened dorsals. He then quickly crawls out from underneath the table. When he gets caught, he slowly stands and explains in a "Negro dialect" that he is "just a table-looka unda."

Cantor's decision to use this particular dialect helps discern for the audience that he is in fact trying to be an African American server as opposed to a Black local or even Caribbean American working in Mexico. This depends on what Jennifer Stoever has deemed the sonic color line: Cantor's decision to use the dialect that he does is part of a larger process of "racializing sound" and determining a hierarchy of sound production, the "how and why certain bodies are expected to produce, desire, and live amongst particular sounds."[69] Cantor's transformation from Black local to African American is thus marked purely by an aural register.

The conversation is interrupted by the first few bars of "What a Perfect Combination" coming from the dance floor. "Oh, excuse me," Eddie exclaims, "Here's my act, oohoo!"[70] Eddie scurries over to the stage where two (uncredited) Black tap dancers perform in blackface.[71] Once again the sonic assists in distinguishing Cantor's new disguise as African American, as these two Black tap dancers are performing an (Africanist) American dance form to an (Africanist) American style of music. Michael North has argued that the "black mask is less important than the process of masking," and that the American personality is free insofar as he may "don and change masks at will."[72] Cantor's fundamental identity as a White male allows him access to all these protean transformations. Each mask he dons throughout the course of the film further establishes him as White and thus free to identify as he wishes when he wants. In this nightclub scene, Cantor's "inauthenticity and mutability measures itself against the presence of the authentic" Black performer in blackface. Or as North puts it, whereas "blackface declares itself openly as a mask, unfixes identity, and frees the author in a world of self-creation," "the black persona carries all the connotations of natural, unspoiled authenticity."[73] Eddie's mask as juxtaposed to the two Black tap dancers in blackface magnifies the disguise and inauthenticity of his costume for spectators of the film while trying to fit in to the film's diegesis.

I highlight Eddie's transition from being disguised as the Spanish Don Sebastian II to masking as an African American because this metamorphosis also marks an evolution from the ethnic to the racial. Up until now the ethnic has been envisaged as a composite brownface, one comprised of a fluidness between Mexican, Spanish, and Cuban. Cantor's transition into blackface marks an end to that fluidness, as defined by his sonic suggestions of blackface as patently African American. While his disguises up until this moment have marked a certain unstableness, the boundaries of African American-ness have been clearly defined. After seeing Eddie dance with the two Black dancers, the joke, grounded in essentialism, is further defined when he tries—and fails—to keep up with these more seasoned tap dancers. Even if he looks like them, his dancing sets him apart as White. When the Black tap dancers exit, Eddie has no trouble taking center stage and performing his customary blackface song and dance. The song for a small ensemble of instruments and solo crooner transitions into more big-band jazz.

The Goldwyn Girls masking as Latin (whether Mexican, Cuban, or some mix of the two) and Cantor camouflaging as Black while pretending to be Spanish are primed for the secondary and tertiary layer of masking that surfaces at the end of "What a Perfect Combination." As in Cantor's blackface routine in *Whoopee!*, his several disguises leading up to the blackface performance in *Spain* not only frame the current imitation as just another masquerade but also necessitate the mask as disguise. Eddie, masquerading as Don Sebastian II, must wear blackface in order to deceive Pancho and Pedro into thinking he is an African American restaurant server. Part of the joke here is that this disguise does not work at a fancy Mexican nightclub because the servers are all "brown," each of either Mexican, Cuban, Latin, Spanish,

102 BEHIND THE SCREEN

or Puerto Rican origin. When Pancho and Pedro question Cantor's mask, he quickly joins the only true African American people in the room: he runs over to perform alongside the artificially blackened Black performers performing a tap dance onstage. Here the intended joke runs much deeper than irony. To see Black performers in blackface in films during this era was rare.[74] Several conclusions can be drawn from this directorial decision to include African Americans in blackface, but a few are particularly relevant. Given the comedic context of this scene, it seems that a piece of the joke is that Cantor's disguise as an African American servant does not work in the first place because the Café Sevilla has no African American employees. For his disguise to be successful, Cantor must find two Black men whom he can classify and conceptualize as African American. When he cannot find them working as servants he turns to the performing arts. His disguise would have continued to fail if the two tap dancers with whom he sought refuge were White. Had his disguise failed yet again, he would have been forced to remove his disguise before completing his reputed performance in cork. The blackface utilized by Black performers thus narratively excuses Cantor's blackface while also reinforcing certain paired associations between Black people and specified occupations.

The mask strips the Black dancers of their individual identities; this makes it not only easier to omit their names from the credits but also contributes to a larger set of assumptions about the fungibility of the Black dancing body, a topic I will explore more in chapter 3. This scene presents what James Snead has described as mass-media "codes" or "private conversations," wherein stereotypes of Blackness are entangled in such complex symbolic webs that "the pleasure of recognizing codes displaces the necessity for a viewer to verify them."[75] Here Cantor's joke both relies on this private conversation and perpetuates it.

As the Black dancers exit the stage, Cantor slips into his solo performance as if he is part of the slated act, further masking the fact that there is something strangely unnatural about him performing in blackface. That is, he transitions smoothly from one disguise to the next; also, the politics of representation behind the two blackfaced Black tap dancers goes unquestioned, and they, stripped of an identity, dissolve. This at once assists in Cantor's seamless protean transformation and recalls a nineteenth-century minstrel stage where blackface reigned regardless of natural skin color. Like the re-framing that took place with Jolson's "Mammy" in 1927, so too does

Hollywood attempt to incite both tap dance and blackface performance as a modern practice, not just something steeped in slavery. It is an attempt to rewrite history while gesturing at a nostalgic past.

Cantor's song flows seamlessly into the film's final Goldwyn Girls number, which, like the redface fashion show in *Whoopee!*, attempts to bookend a long series of disguises within the context of highly sexualized brownface. Again, the women simultaneously signal ethnicity and a cultural capital steeped in sexuality vis-à-vis "brown" exoticism. As such they are in a position to smoothly transition from ethnic objects to more racialized ones. Berkeley's top shot captures the convergence of race and cultural capital when the women remove their hats and tilt their heads to expose the minstrel caricatures. The man known for close-ups and intimate vantage points anonymizes the particular women of his ensemble. The multiplicity of breasts and minstrel faces strips the Goldwyn Girls of their individuality, capitalizing on the visual effect of fetishized female parts and racial stereotypes, a "sensory plentitude (there is 'so much to see') and yet haunted by the absence of those very objects which are there to be seen."[76] This image of mass production indicates an abundance of cultural capital which cannot be compromised, even during the Great Depression. Out of this image emerges Cantor in blackface.

Up until this blackface bit (beginning with Cantor's blacking up under the table), the comedian has established his character as both gender fluid and ethnically flexible. I have explored the ways in which he has established ethnic mutability, but as in all of his films, Cantor plays a more effeminate man with "a high-pitched tenor voice" and is "characterized in [his] films as weak, anemic, nervous, and a coward, his inadequate physicality emphasized early in each film."[77] His disguises—usually roles perceived as more masculine—offer an ironic contrast to this effeminate character. Thus, his plan to disguise himself as a bullfighter is made funnier as *Spain* opens with Eddie hiding in the girls' dormitory of an American college reciting "I'm a Naughty Girl" until he is caught by the headmistress.[78] What this film accomplishes aurally in the opening number with "I'm a Naughty Girl," the dance at the Café Sevilla achieves visually, especially through its closing image of Cantor in blackface surrounded by a sea of Goldwyn Girls. Cantor's diminutive size in relation to the tall women, amplified by Berkeley's camerawork, and Cantor's lack of interest in their sex appeal both work to further emasculate him.

104 BEHIND THE SCREEN

Cantor's troubled gender performance was a revival of the "pansy craze" of the 1910s and 1920s, which took on new meaning in the crisis of masculinity that occurred during the Great Depression. Speaking to men's fear of emasculation as well as a more widespread concern that women were becoming too powerful in the workforce (as we see in his 1931 film *Palmy Days*) and colleges (as we see in this opening scene of *Spain*), Cantor's roles sought to turn this dynamic on its head.[79] Here his performance of effeminacy marks a type of imperfect assimilation, as it does in *Whoopee!*, making it easier for him to ally himself with Mexicans and Spaniards at different points throughout the film. The final dance sequence, "What a Perfect Combination," not only underpins race as fixed but re-asserts a more "normative" relationship between the sexes. The second stanza of the song reads: *"She has charms and perfect taste; I have arms that fit her waist; What a perfect combination, No wonder we're in love!*[80]

While cloaked in blackface, Cantor shows that although gender might be supple and ethnicity fluid, race and the relationship between the sexes is still fixed. That is, while some might read his effeminate performances as queer, his fluid shifts between two normative gender identities are, more exactly, aimed at normalizing the country's temporary rupture in the hegemonic order. As Cantor engages this fissure beneath the surface, Berkeley's choreography and camera work create an optical distraction that blurs how Cantor arrives at these conclusions. Here escapism, grounded in female sexuality and fashion, covers up the more deeply embedded messages this number has to offer regarding sex and race. These messages become even more layered and further veiled in Cantor's next rendezvous with blackface in *Roman Scandals* the following year.

Cantor's troubled gender performance also doubles representation, allowing him more ease to pursue his various masquerades. Doane has argued that sexual mobility is a distinguishing feature of femininity. That is, while the male is "locked into sexual identity, the female can at least pretend that she is other."[81] The ways in which Cantor unfixes his sexual identity in all these films allows him greater leverage in identity swapping. Furthermore, the coupling of Cantor's racial masquerade alongside the signs (i.e., the Goldwyn Girls) of sexual desire might complicate the film's more overt masks, "a false promise of the visible as an epistemological guarantee."[82] Which is to say, the most visible elements of these dances merely obscure the truth in order to justify their own means of representation. The juxtaposition of such simultaneous masquerades is equally complicated in *Scandals*.

FIGURE 2.3 Two photos from *Roman Scandals* (1933): (*Top*) Eddie Cantor challenging normative gender roles through humor; (*Bottom*) White "slaves" fawning over the Ethiopian doctor (Cantor) while the Black slave watches awkwardly in "Keep Young and Beautiful." (Private collection)

Bathing in Blackface

A scantily dressed Oedipus/Eddie-pus (Cantor) walks in on Princess Sylvia (Gloria Stuart) during a mud facial. She screams, shocked to see a man in the ladies' bathing area. When she runs away from shock, he climbs in her bed and waits for the facialist to come back with a pot of fresh mud. "Oh yes! This mud is absolutely wonderful," exclaims the facialist, "Take this little girl, right here (referring to Eddie under the sheets) why she's only had two treatments and already you wouldn't recognize her." She slathers Eddie. His face, now completely covered in mud, resembles the burnt cork of blackface but lacks the white lips and full body makeup that Cantor's disguises usually entail. The camera cuts away and then shifts back to Eddie who now sits up in bed, patting down the still exposed surfaces of his body with the remaining mud. When the camera cuts back to his face, his lips have been exaggerated in white. The female supervisor of the baths approaches Eddie. At first disturbed by the presence of a man, Eddie quickly clarifies: "You mean you don't know who I am! Well, am I glad (to meet you)!" he exclaims reaching out his hand for a formal introduction. "Ooh are you the Ethiopian beauty specialist?" inquires the supervisor. Eddie contorts his voice and switches into his "Negro dialect" mode. "You sho—guessed it!" His voice takes on an Uncle Remus tone, "That's what I is! Yah Yah Yah Yah. An empry sent me down here to kind of look after the princess, Sylvia."[83] "Ah, I see," says the supervisor, "Slave, (she says to the Black woman standing behind her) show the doctor to the princess Sylvia's compartment." Eddie tips his head and then shuffles behind the "slave" with his oft-cited Stepin Fetchit walk.

In what translates to just roughly over a minute of screen time, Eddie has gone through a full protean transformation, from posing as a visiting White slave (Oedipus/*Eddie-pus*) in Imperial Rome to becoming the "Ethiopian beauty specialist." The mud has allowed him to go through the *accidental* physical transformation of wearing black makeup, but his less accidental completion of the mask (i.e., he blackens his remaining bare skin and adds white lips) proclaims the details of Eddie's masquerade. Eddie-pus poses as "Ethiopian," which takes on two meanings. Eddie first identifies his place of origin—he comes from Ethiopia, a location that makes a lot of sense considering he is inhabiting ancient Rome, and as we have come to learn, a Rome confused with all parts of the Middle East. The second implication of "Ethiopia" surfaces as a form of what historian Barbara Savage has labeled "aural blackface," or performing what might be recognized as Black dialect when Cantor "contorts" his voice and takes on a "Negro dialect," complete with a shift in tonal quality.[84] Through this sonic layer he complicates his ethnicity, turning "Ethiopian" into a depreciating label for anyone Black. This label at once evokes a reference to earlier minstrel performances and yields the same flattening effect that was achieved with earlier uses of the term.

Eddie-pus's disguise as specifically Ethiopian, and not a more generic African, acts as a marker of both ethnicity and race. Throughout the nineteenth and early twentieth centuries, Black Americans and Europeans were often labeled "Ethiopian" regardless of their unique heritage. This was especially prominent in the performing arts, as in Black minstrel troupes that identified their members as "Ethiopian Serenaders" or tried to increase their "authenticity" by advertising their use of "authentic Ethiopians."[85] The minstrel reference within Cantor's beauty specialist sequence is bolstered when the actor cites Stepin Fetchit through his posture and gait. Quoting Fetchit not only educes the Jim Crow and Zip Coon archetypes but also completes the cyclical lie that minstrel archetypes are real and Ethiopian origins in fact tie such realism to authentic origins.

As we have seen, Cantor's blackface transformations are always coupled with a Berkeley song and dance that tells some story of normative gender roles and female comportment. His otherwise effeminate persona gets flipped on its head when he dons the blackface mask, while his blackness becomes further obscured by overt female sexuality in the form of risqué tap dancing and optical reverie. [FIG. 2.3] By offering a critique of female behavior, and how this normative female behavior lends itself to the promise of healthy heterosexual relationships, "Keep Young and Beautiful" helps disguise Cantor's otherwise blatant appraisal of race and helps to restore the disruption in America's (vis-à-vis ancient Rome) perceived ideological and social order.

When the girls catch sight of the Ethiopian doctor, they immediately ask for some beauty tips; Cantor offers these instructions in the form of a song: "*Keep young and beautiful; It's your duty to be beautiful. . . . If you wanta be loved, dah-dah-dah-dah.*"[86]

As Eddie sings the lines of this song, he makes his rounds through the bath house. White women with long bleached blonde hair ogle at the doctor and listen avidly to all of his beauty tips while they are simultaneously being groomed by the Black slave girls. The camera cuts to a series of close-ups: the camera zooms in on singing White women being groomed by Black slaves. We

108 BEHIND THE SCREEN

get nice close-ups of the White women's faces and intimate views of the Black women's hands rubbing, scrubbing, and shaving the White women's bodies. A series of sensual images follows, including a close-up of White legs in two-inch heels all being patted down by Black forearms and hands. The sequence morphs into a variation of patty cake, which concludes with the Black women's heads peeking through the slim space between each woman's White knees. The mood changes as the Black women disappear behind a rotating backdrop. Ten White women dressed in bras and iridescent hula skirts emerge from the paneling; they perform a kick line tap routine. The camera then trucks right as ten Black dancers emerge from the rotating backdrop; they appear performing a lindy/Charleston variation. The camera trucks left as ten more White dancers join the Rockette variation. The camera trucks right again as ten more Black dancers join the Black variation, this time breaking into a syncopated rhythm tap sequence. Eddie-pus accidentally lifts his skirt and two Black dancers give him a wide-eyed glance before scaring him away with their "Voodoo" arm motion. Chaos ensues and the wall separating the White and Black dancers disappears. While the White dancers stay in one line and the Black dancers stay in another, the two differently raced groups begin trading stages, upstairs then downstairs. While this is clearly organized chaos, the two differently-raced lines never blend. Finally, the two lines trap Eddie-pus in the shower and one of the Black performers turns on the steam. Everyone watches as Eddie-pus's body starts to shrink, once again replicating the image of a diminutively sized Cantor in a sea of enlarged female bodies. The blackface mask seems to offer a temporary defense from his frequent emasculation. He emerges from the shower an even more shrunken version of himself, still in blackface. He sprints away falling into an adjacent pool. The camera zooms in as a full-size Cantor emerges from the pool with his mask completely gone. He submerges himself in shame. Scene end.[87]

This dance is one of very few mixed-race, large ensemble dances of the era. In many ways it demonstrates the great strides that had been made since United Artists made *Puttin' on the Ritz*, and in other ways it shows how far the industry still had to go before offering a truly integrated song and dance on the silver screen. Closely examining those strides and failures, however, allows us insight into the ways the camera work in these films directly impacted how certain bodies would be interpreted by the Production Code and how the visual assists in a larger system of distraction and display.

OPTICAL ILLUSION AND DESIGN   109

Before the dance even begins, the script clearly delineates the differences between the Black slaves and White, where the Black slaves constitute "the help" and the White slaves serve a more sexual function. Already the plot has hyper-sexualized the White women. The clearest example comes in the form of the first big Berkeley number, "No More Love," sung by Ruth Etting. Female (White) slaves who appear to be completely nude with only long peroxided wigs display themselves on a multi-tiered ionic-style pedestal.[88] These women can be sexualized to the degree that they are in this scene because of their exoticized and fictionalized existence in ancient Rome. More fashion show than dance, this number establishes the White women as eye candy, first and foremost. By the time we get to the bath house scene, these women's characters have been fully developed as sexual objects and the women are treated in a way so as to enhance their beauty. The White women, even though "slaves," are pampered with facials and steam baths. The Black slaves, on the other hand, must wait on the White slaves; one of these Black slaves is shown awkwardly watching the White slaves fawn over the blackened Eddie Cantor. [FIG.2.3, bottom]

But the work of the camera to develop these characters is even more telling. While Berkeley is known for his close-ups of the Goldwyn Girls' faces, he makes a point in "Keep Young and Beautiful" to show close-ups of only the parts of the Black women that toil. For example, in the same frame that we get a medium shot of a White woman's body, we get a close-up of a Black forearm lathering a White woman with lotion. In a subsequent frame we get an extreme closeup of a single Goldwyn Girl's face and an equally close shot of an indistinctive Black hand brushing her hair. While there is nothing inherently wrong with showing an extreme close-up of a hand or forearm, the juxtaposition of these Black hands' anonymous labor alongside the individuating shot of White leisure reinforces a long-standing master-slave relationship.

Transformed from the completely apportioned Black and White stages of the last chapter, the segregation of Black and White bodies in "Keep Young and Beautiful" is still apparent. The White women show off their sparkly bras and skirts, while the Black women are dressed in drab brown fabric. [FIG. 2.3] The two dances they each perform are clearly differentiated in style and sound (again a distinction of the quiet verticality of the White performance and a more polycentric, playful, raucous performance by the Black dancers). This dance makes it appear as though the style of tap dance that the Goldwyn Girls perform is purely a White phenomenon, while the more "wild and hot" Charleston-infused rhythm tap dance performed by the Black dancers is not. Though seemingly more mixed than the "integrated" stage in "Puttin on the Ritz," the filing of each race into two distinct lines and then taking care that they do not mingle still sends a clear message about integration. Not only are the bodies kept visibly distinct, but unruly Black motion stands in stark contrast to the order and stability represented by the White women. Even as "slaves" whose work is purely sexual, the White women in *Scandals* have been marshaled into an ideal order as factory girls and busy worker bees. Furthermore, as in Cantor's blackface performance at the Café Sevilla, Cantor's most overt emasculation occurs only while he is cloaked in blackface. His shrunken blackened body appears at the mercy of an ensemble of full-size White women. Only after his mask has been removed can Cantor return to his normal proportions.

***

It would be less than a year before the MPPDA adopted an amendment to the Code, obliging it to become "enforced." Thomas Doherty attributes the timing of this amendment to a combination of factors including the New Deal in Washington (which insinuated federal censorship) and a series of reports published by the reformist educational group called the Motion Picture Research Council proclaiming a link between bad behavior and bad movies.[89] The SRC and PAB were then replaced by the Production Code Administration (PCA) which would answer directly to the MPPDA. Will H. Hayes appointed the former newspaperman and "influential Roman Catholic layman," Joseph I. Breen to spearhead the PCA from 1934 until 1954. By the time Cantor made his next Goldwyn film (*Kid Millions*), his blackface would look quite different, and the various guises would take on even more covert configurations. As much as Breen worked to censor the work of these 1930s directors, however, he could only control so much. Doherty writes of the censor's primary concern: "The job of the motion picture censor is to patrol the diegesis, keeping an eye and ear out for images, languages, and meanings that should be banished from the world of the film . . . to connect the dots and detect what is visually and verbally forbidden by name."[90] The more challenging task would be to uncover—through textual and sociological analysis—the hidden lessons, meanings, and interpretations lurking beneath the surface.

Despite Cantor's blatant use of black face paint in *Whoopee!*, *The Kid from Spain*, and *Roman Scandals*, the culture of façades created around these more overt performances carries more insidious messages. Something as simple as the Goldwyn Girls' peroxided hair or superficial focus on diet and exercise literally and metaphorically cast light on the female physique in ways that distract from more obvious forms of body modification at play in these films. The escapism grounded in female sexuality and fashion that Busby Berkeley creates through his optical distractions further blinds viewers from seeing the encoded messages these women offer through their dancing. Their geometrically transfixing choreography, combined with Eddie Cantor's quick-witted humor, physical comedy, and song, also creates another layer of disguise that masks the threats of economic chaos, gender instability, and upward mobility for Black people in the States. Berkeley funnels the Goldwyn Girls' tap dancing, Charleston rhythms, and attributes of rhumba into massive spectacles of order that not only commodify the Other in the process but also erode the link between Blackness, Latin-ness, and an Africanist aesthetic. That is, the latunes themselves, which favor an Afro-Cuban beat, rarely if ever reference Black people and instead rely on the vague brown body and countries "down there" to act as intermediaries between Blackness and Whiteness. I complicate the use of brownface in later chapters where I discuss the ways in which Hollywood further mystified what constituted these intermediary Others vis-à-vis the conflating of Latin countries with tropical islands.

Both the protean and citational guises further mask these messages. Cantor's protean transformations not only conflate notions of Otherness but also take the blame away from the White man by placing the stereotype in the hands of the Other, as seen for example with Chief Black Eagle. The protean in many ways normalizes or justifies the use of more blatant forms of minstrelsy, such as blacking up, playing Indian, or straddling different performances of gender. Often this protean guise is accompanied by sonic or physical citations that comment on a past moment when minstrelsy has been directly referenced (e.g., Jolson and "Mammy") or quote a caricature of someone known for playing archetypal roles tied to racial subordination (e.g., Stepin Fetchit's shuffle). As the rules surrounding censorship tightened, so too did the layers obscuring controlled material thicken. For the duration of Joseph Breen's tenure, these coverings would make the MPPDA's job of expurgating all the more complex.

112   BEHIND THE SCREEN

Notes

1. Jeffrey Spivak, *Berkeley: The Life and Art of Busby Berkeley*, Screen Classics (Lexington: University Press of Kentucky, 2011), 63–64.
2. Steve Vineberg, "Busby Berkeley: Dance Director," *Threepenny Review*, no. 128 (2012): 23.
3. Ruth Vasey, "Beyond Sex and Violence," in Matthew Bernstein, *Controlling Hollywood: Censorship and Regulation in the Studio Era* (New Brunswick, NJ: Rutgers University Press, 1999), 112.
4. Here I intend two uses of the word "bracketing": the more colloquial use as well as the photographic term that refers to the action of capturing the same shot using different exposure values to ensure that a whole scene is exposed properly.
5. Other notable Busby Berkeley films that take up these themes but are not being explored include *Golddiggers of 1933, Footlight Parade* (1933), and *42nd Street* (1933). See Vineberg's "Busby Berkeley: Dance Director," 23–24, for plot synopses of these films.
6. Margaret T McFadden, "'Yoo-Hoo, Prosperity!': Eddie Cantor and the Great Depression, 1929–36," *Studies in American Humor* 1, no. 2 (2015): 256–57, for an analysis of the ways Cantor's films addressed Depression-era anxieties.
7. Gustavo Pérez Firmat, "Latunes: An Introduction," *Latin American Studies Association* 43, no. 2 (2008): 184.
8. Quoting the famous jazz standard from 1931 with words and Music by Seymour Simons. It was first recognized by the public when Belle Baker's recording was broadcast on radio. Ruth Etting recorded a version that same year and also appears as Olga in *Scandals*.
9. Woody Herman and The New Third Herd were the first to record this rhythm, which they named "Buck Dance," in 1953. The Copacetics (est. 1949) unanimously decided to perform their famous chair dance to this tune in 1953–1954 because they liked the rhythm (author's phone conversation with Reggio McLaughlin, April 27, 2020). However, this "buck dance" rhythm likely goes back to the late teens, early twenties. It appears to have been a common rhythm used by hoofers on the vaudeville circuit, which is why it was then given the name "Buck Dance" when Herman recorded it— early tap dancers were known as buck dancers and early tap dancing was known as bucking—and why Cantor would have been familiar with the tune in 1933. I have also found evidence that both Herman and Cantor worked with Gus Arnheim. It is possible that they might both have been exposed to the rhythm here if not on the vaudeville circuit. While the "Buck Dance" as recorded by Herman is certainly bluesy, it bears no relation to the bluegrass song that goes by the same name (email correspondence with Nic Gareiss, April 7, 2020). The fact that this song much preceded the 1953 recording speaks to what music scholar Matthew Morrison has identified as the commercial aspect of blacksound. He writes, "Blacksound also accounts for the legacy of violence that is embedded in the commercialization of popular music out of blackface performance, as black people have experienced, and continue to experience, systemic racism, while white (and other nonblack) people freely express themselves

through the consumption and performance of commodified black aesthetics without carrying the burden of being black under white supremacist structures." See Matthew Morrison, "Race, Blacksound, and the (Re)Making of Musicological Discourse," *Journal of the American Musicological Society* 72, no. 3 (2019): 791. See also Saidiya V. Hartman, *Scenes of Subjection: Terror, Slavery, and Self-Making in Nineteenth-Century America* (New York: Oxford University Press, 1997), 23.

10. Music written by Harry Akst and lyrics by Sam M. Lewis. Ethel Waters introduced the song in 1925 at the Plantation Club and it was later integrated into the film *Kid Boots* (1926), in which Eddie Cantor starred. It has widely been covered and re-recorded. Some notable recordings include Josephine Baker's in 1926, Cab Calloway's in 1932, and Duke Ellington's also in 1932. Dozens of other notable recordings exist but the aforementioned were recorded before *Roman Scandals* was made.

11. Henry Bial, *Acting Jewish: Negotiating Ethnicity on the American Stage and Screen* (Ann Arbor: University of Michigan Press, 2005), 4.

12. Ibid., 18–20. "Goyish" is a Yiddush word for "not-Jewish."

13. Ibid., 20.

14. Herbert G. Goldman, *Banjo Eyes: Eddie Cantor and the Birth of Modern Stardom* (New York: Oxford University Press, 1997), 3–35, 71–72, 100–1.

15. Cantor had done work in film prior to *Whoopee!* Cantor made his first film in 1911 in a test talking picture. In *Widow at the Races* (directed by Thomas Edison) he starred with his friend George Jessel. *Kid Boots* (1926) was his first major picture performance, and his career took off with *Whoopee!* in 1930. See Goldman, *Banjo Eyes*.

16. Cantor published three bestselling books between 1929 and 1931 which satirized the current political and economic crisis. These were *Caught Short* (1929), *Between the Acts* (1930), and *Yoo-Hoo Prosperity!* (1931). His familiar comic persona comes through in the writing, and each of these books opens with a short one-liner that accompanies a caricature of Cantor in blackface. The heading for this section is a reference to Cantor's book *Yoo-Hoo Prosperity!* from 1931. The blackface cartoon located on the first page represents the widespread mockery of President Hoover's claim that prosperity was "just around the corner."

17. McFadden, "Yoo-Hoo," 267.

18. *Whoopee!* was based on Owen Davis's play *The Nervous Wreck* about a hypochondriac who goes west for his health. Florenz Ziegfeld produced and Cantor starred in this smash hit during Ziegfeld's 1928–1929 season. Then the stock market crashed, and Ziegfeld lost everything. He hated Hollywood but when Samuel Goldwyn (and Paramount) asked to buy the rights to *Whoopee*, he was left with no choice. See Scott A. Berg's *Goldwyn: A Biography* (New York: Knopf, 1989), 195–203.

19. McFadden, "'Yoo-Hoo," 272.

20. Rebecca Rossen, "The Jewish Man and His Dancing Shtick: Stock Characterization and Jewish Masculinity in Postmodern Dance," in *You Should See Yourself: Jewish Identity in Postmodern Culture*, ed. Vincent Brooks (New Brunswick, NJ: Rutgers University Press, 2006), 139.

21. I credit Rebecca Rossen for making this connection between Eddie-pus and Eddie-putz.

114   BEHIND THE SCREEN

22. Sander Gilman, *The Jew's Body* (New York: Routledge, 1991), 6. See also Charles Musser, "Ethnicity, Role-Playing, and American Film Comedy: From *Chinese Laundry Scene* to *Whoopee* (1894–1930)," in *Unspeakable Images: Ethnicity and the American Cinema*, ed. Lester D. Friedman (Urbana: University of Illinois Press, 1991), 39–81.

23. This is likely an acknowledgment of Ford's blatant anti-Semitism that culturally informed subjects would read as such, but non-Jews might read this as a goyish reference.

24. Barbara Lewis, "Daddy Blue: The Evolution of the Dark Dandy," in *Inside the Minstrel Mask*, ed. Annemarie Bean (Middletown, CT: Wesleyan University Press, 1996), 267.

25. Donald Bogle describes Fetchit's character as being the "lanky, slow-witted, simple-minded, obtuse, synthetic, confused humbug." See Donald Bogle, *Toms Coons, Mulattoes, Mammies, and Bucks: An Interpretive History of Blacks in American Films* (New York: Viking Press, 1973), 38–44.

26. Lewis "Daddy Blue," 267.

27. Rudy Valée was classified as a "crooner" throughout his career. The term "crooner" when assigned to White male singers without blackface was first intended as an insult since the term "crooner" had historically been reserved for minstrel performers and "mammy" singers. See Allison McCracken's "God's Gift to Us Girls: Crooning, Gender, and the Re-Creation of American Popular Song, 1928–1933," *American Music* 17, no. 4 (Winter, 1999): 365–395. There is another citation embedded in this transformation: a reference to Cantor's cameo alongside Valée in Florenz Ziegfeld's pre-Code musical comedy film *Glorifying the American Girl* (1929).

28. Music by Walter Donaldson and lyrics by Gus Kahn.

29. Mendi Lewis Obadike, "Low Fidelity: Stereotyped Blackness in the Field of Sound" (PhD diss., Duke University, 2005).

30. This federal agency was established in 1824 to try to "control" the Indians and their territory. See Scott B. Vickers's *Native American Identities: From Stereotype to Archetype in Art and Literature* (Albuquerque: University of New Mexico Press, 1998), 16.

31. Ibid.

32. Ibid., 18.

33. Federal policy invented several things about American Indian culture that reinforced earlier stereotypes while creating others. Vickers notes the following about William Medill, commissioner from 1845 to 1849, who "assumed Indians to be 'ignorant, degraded, lazy, and [in possession of] no worthwhile cultural traits.' Medill possessed no prior knowledge of Indian affairs, yet was able to say, with great persuasion, that too much federal support of impoverished tribal welfare led to 'the means of living for a time, independent of industry and exertion, in idleness and profligacy, until the disposition to labor for the habit of impermanence become so strong, that [the Indian] degenerates into a wretched outcast,'" ibid., 16–17.

34. The act was enforced too late to save the 100,000 landless Indians who had been transferred off tribal land following the General Allotment Act of 1887. This Act allotted parcels of land to individual American Indians (in sizes of 40, 80, or 160 acres) on reservations and on public lands. This attempt to assimilate American Indians

OPTICAL ILLUSION AND DESIGN 115

backfired, mainly because few American Indians could sustain themselves economically, and the BIA's budget was not large enough to provide these American Indians with adequate health and educational facilities. World War II further exacerbated the financial problems of the BIA, and as a result, American Indians lost another million acres of land—not to mention the war's impact on American Indian attitudes. Of approximately 350,000 American Indians in the United States in 1941, 25,000 served in the armed forces. This was a higher proportion than from any other non-White minority, including African Americans. In the years following, efforts were made to relocate American Indians to parts of the country where jobs were more available. But, like African Americans who had fought for their country and still received an onslaught of hurtful representations on the screen, many of the country's "Native" stereotypes would not budge. See "Act of June 18, 1934 (Indian Reorganization Act)" accessible through the US Department of the Interior's Bureau of Indian Affairs (BIA), https://www.govinfo.gov/content/pkg/COMPS-5299/pdf/COMPS-5299.pdf, accessed October 27, 2022.

35. Another reason that the American Indians were used as a target of White satire was precisely because they were seen as less threatening than African Americans at this time. Americans often viewed Indigenous people as figures of nostalgia, "supposedly absent and buried in the past." See, for example, Peter Antelyes's "'Haim Afen Range': The Jewish Indian and the Redface Western," *Melus* 34, no. 3 (2009): 26.

36. Michael Rogin, *Blackface, White Noise: Jewish Immigrants in the Hollywood Melting Pot* (Berkeley: University of California Press, 1996), 56.

37. Gilman, *Jew's Body*, 12. See also Gilman's *Jewish Self-Hatred: Anti-Semitism and the Hidden Language of the Jews* (Baltimore: Johns Hopkins University Press, 1986).

38. See, for example, Antelyes, "'Haim Afen Range,'" 16.

39. Ibid., 21–22 and Rogin, *Blackface White Noise*, 73–120.

40. Spivak, *Berkeley*, 66.

41. Spivak, *Berkeley*, 55.

42. Ibid., 51. Berkeley's biographer Jeffrey Spivak writes, "On a 1930 theater screen, it was a revelation of sorts to view glamorous film dancers desirably up close and almost obtainable."

43. Martin Rubin, "Busby Berkeley and the Backstage Musical," in *Hollywood Musicals, the Film Reader*, ed. Steven Cohan (London: Routledge, 2002), 60.

44. One example of this commonly held belief is articulated by film-scholar Jean-Louis Comolli who writes that "cinema that resolves itself totally into spectacle, these images, these shots, these scenes . . . have no other function, no other meaning and no other existence but visual beauty." See Comolli, "Dancing Images: Busby Berkeley's Kaleidoscope," *Cahiers du Cinéma* 174 (January 1966), reprinted in *Cahiers du Cinéma in English* no. 2 (1966): 24.

45. Berg, *Goldwyn*, 201.

46. Mary Ann Doane, "Film and the Masquerade: Theorizing the Female Spectator," *Film and Theory: An Anthology* / S. [495]–509 (2000), 132.

47. Given its name because of its similarity to a sine wave on an oscilloscope (Spivak, *Berkeley*, 49). Also William D. Routt and Richard L. Thompson, "'Keep Young and

116   BEHIND THE SCREEN

Beautiful': Surplus and Subversion in Roman Scandals," *Journal of Film and Video* 42, no. 1 (1990): 27.

48. Doane, "Film and the Masquerade," 133.

49. Goldwyn was given this name immediately following the success of *Whoopee!* See Berg, *Goldwyn*, 206.

50. Goldwyn famously said, "If you want to send a message, call Western Union." Quoted in Thomas Doherty, *Pre-Code Hollywood: Sex, Immorality, and Insurrection in American Cinema, 1930–1934*, Film and Culture (New York: Columbia University Press, 1999), 46.

51. See "Who Controls What We See: Censorship and the Attack on Hollywood 'Immortality,'" in *Movies and American Society*, ed. Steven Joseph Ross. Wiley Blackwell Readers in American Social and Cultural History (Hoboken, NJ: Wiley-Blackwell, 2014), 109.

52. Ibid., 114.

53. Vasey, "Beyond Sex and Violence," 112.

54. Ibid.

55. Ibid., 121.

56. Esther Romeyn, *Street Scenes: Staging the Self in Immigrant New York, 1880–1924* (Minneapolis: University of Minnesota Press, 2008), 193.

57. By brownface I am referring to a range of practices performers use to seem more "ethnic."

58. Pérez Firmat, "Latunes," 180.

59. Ibid., 181. See also John Storm Roberts, *The Latin Tinge: The Impact of Latin American Music in the United States* (New York: Oxford University Press, 1979), 77.

60. Pérez Firmat, "Latunes," 183.

61. Juliet McMains, *Glamour Addiction: Inside the American Ballroom Dance Industry* (Middletown, CT: Wesleyan University Press, 2006), 118.

62. Ibid., 119. See also Robin Moore, *Nationalizing Blackness: Afrocubanismo and Artistic Revolution in Havana, 1920–1940*. Pitt Latin American Series (Pittsburgh, PA: University of Pittsburgh Press, 1997), 57.

63. McMains, *Glamour Addiction*, 120.

64. Pérez Firmat, "Latunes," 189.

65. Ibid., 187.

66. I am borrowing this phrase from Anthea Kraut's description of Josephine Baker's dancing in "Between Primitivism and Diaspora: The Dance Performances of Josephine Baker, Zora Neale Hurston, and Katherine Dunham," *Theatre Journal* 55, no. 3 (2003): 440.

67. Regarding the spectacle of this production, Sam Goldwyn borrowed $1 million to produce this film, the first seven-figure loan given by Bank of America for a motion picture.

68. Laura Mulvey, "Visual Pleasure and Narrative Cinema," *Screen* 16, no. 3 (Autumn 1975): 12–13.

69. Jennifer Lynn Stoever, *The Sonic Color Line: Race and the Cultural Politics of Listening* (New York: New York University Press, 2016), 18.

OPTICAL ILLUSION AND DESIGN   117

70. Music and lyrics by Harry Ruby and Bert Kalmar, the same team that wrote music for the Marx Brothers.
71. It was incredibly common for Black performers to go uncredited in films where they only danced bit parts. No record exists of who these tap dancers are.
72. Michael North, *The Dialect of Modernism: Race, Language, and Twentieth-Century Literature*, Race and American Culture (New York: Oxford University Press, 1994), 6–7.
73. Romeyn, *Street Scenes*, 190, and North, *Dialect of Modernism*, 6–7.
74. While Black artists were still performing in blackface on Broadway (e.g., Florence Mills in *Dixie to Broadway* (1924) or Josephine Baker in *The Chocolate Dandies* (1925), very few (credited) onscreen Black performers utilized such makeup during this era. Films featuring Mantan Moreland utilized blackface for comic effect and Oscar Micheaux sometimes used blackface as a form of satire.
75. James Snead, *White Screens, Black Images: Hollywood from the Dark Side* (New York: Routledge, 1994), 141.
76. Doane, "Film and Masquerade," 135, and Christian Metz, "The Imaginary Signifier," *Screen* 16, no. 2 (Summer 1975): 60 and 61.
77. McFadden, "'Yoo-Hoo,'" 269.
78. For a detailed description of the camera work implemented and "invented" by Berkeley during this scene, see Spivak, *Berkeley*, 63–64.
79. Ibid., 270. See also George Chauncey, *Gay New York: Gender, Urban Culture, and the Making of a Gay Male World, 1890–1940* (New York: Basic Books, 1994), 310–35, 354–55; Nancy Cott, *The Grounding of Modern Feminism* (New Haven, CT: Yale University Press, 1987), 179–211; Lynn Y. Weiner, *From Working Girl to Working Mother: The Female Labor Force in the United States, 1829–1980* (Chapel Hill: University of North Carolina Press, 1985), 83–95, 98–110.
80. This is one of many stanzas that do this work. Cantor makes another reference to Rudy Valée in the second half of this song: "Once she liked crooning; used to go for Rudy Valée; Ewe started spooning; Now her radio is in the alley."
81. Doane, "Film and Masquerade," 138.
82. Amy Robinson, "It Takes One to Know One: Passing and Communities of Common Interest," *Critical Inquiry* 20, no. 4 (1994): 716.
83. Here I am offering an example of the tonal qualities that Eddie co-opts during his Negro dialect lines. While this was a common tonal quality in Hollywood films of the 1930s that sought to caricature a Black way of speaking, James Baskett's voice in the role of Uncle Remus in Disney's *Song of the South* is a good comparison.
84. Barbara Savage discusses the concept of "aural blackface" in *Broadcasting Freedom: Radio, War, and the Politics of Race, 1938–1948* (Chapel Hill: University of North Carolina Press).
85. For most African Americans, such qualifiers were in fact marketing tactics. David Krasner has highlighted this phenomenon specifically in relation to Bert Williams and George and Aida Overton Walker where the real was used as a commercial device as a means of transgressing the color barrier on stage. He writes, "The real enticed white audiences because realism was in vogue." See David Krasner, "The Real Thing,"

118   BEHIND THE SCREEN

in *Beyond Blackface: African Americans and the Creation of American Popular Culture, 1890–1930*, ed. W. Fitzhugh Brundage (Chapel Hill: University of North Carolina Press, 2011), 99.

86. This is an abridged version. The full song was written by Harry Warren (music) and Al Dubin (lyrics). Of note, the melody of this song is virtually identical to "Bend Down Sister" from *Palmy Days* (1931).

87. Berkeley's actual regimen for "keeping young and beautiful" was not far off from the song. According to Jeffrey Spivak, Berkeley had nine commandments for chorus girls for keeping young and beautiful enough to appear in his films: Chorus girls were "handed a copy of Berkeley's Beauty Commandments: (1) three square meals a day, with a steak or chop once a day when working; (2) one quart of milk and one glass of orange juice daily; (3) cold showers every morning; (4) daily sunbath when not working; (5) open-air exercise—golf, tennis, or swimming, daily; (6) a minimum of makeup, except for screen work, and no mascara; (7) no high-heeled shoes while working or exercising; (8) eight hours of sleep a night starting before midnight; and (9) one late date a week, when working. Berkeley . . . observed: 'Dancing is strenuous work, as strenuous as playing football. Strict observance of these rules will result in better health for the girls, better dancing, and it will help them to preserve their beauty and freshness.'" Also interesting to note is that the scene in the slave market as well as "Keep Young and Beautiful" "made *Roman Scandals* the most expensive musical ever produced to that date. . . . Goldwyn made more than $1 million profit on the film." Spivak, *Berkeley*, 95 and 96.

88. According to Spivak, Berkeley chose fifty women for the slave-girl scene after viewing several thousand screen tests. These women were in fact filmed in the nude. Spivak writes, "Berkeley really didn't think he could pull off the nudity, long hair or not. He thought a flesh-colored body suit (a 'fleshling') would be needed. . . . The body suit would surely be visible, so he asked the girls outright if they wouldn't mind being undressed. He stressed the fact that everything would be shot tastefully, and the hair would cover breasts and other regions. The girls . . . demanded a closed set and that filming be done at night to avoid the nuisance of dealing with visitors. Berkeley shifted his schedule with Warner Bros. to film the slave auction. At night, only he, cinematographer Gregg Toland, and the girls were on the set. Berkeley completed his work with the knowledge that he had pulled a fast one. Nobody would ever guess the girls were completely nude except for the long blond wigs." Spivak, *Berkeley*, 94.

89. Doherty *Pre-Code Hollywood*, 8–9.

90. Ibid., 10.

FIGURE 2.4 Three moments from Disney's Silly Symphony, *The Three Little Pigs*, 1933: (*Top*) The Fuller Brosh Man visits in jewface; (*Middle*) Practical Pig prepares to slap the Wolf with a Fuller Brush; (*Bottom*) The Fuller Brosh Man's mask temporarily transforms into that of Groucho Marx. (Private collection)

♪♫ An Excerpted Silly Symphony: Walt Disney's *Three Little Pigs* (1933) ♪♫

The Practical Pig, with oversized white gloves on his tiny hoof-hands, scolds his brothers.

He sits down at the piano and begins to jam.
Fifer and Fiddler begin to sing and dance with flute and violin:

"Who's afraid of the big, bad wolf,
Big, bad wolf, big, bad wolf?
Who's afraid of the big, bad wolf?
Tra la la la la-a-a-a!"

A knock at the door interrupts the fun and Fifer and Fiddler dive back under the bed.
"Who's there?"
The camera cuts to the other side of the door where the wolf, posing as a very large peddler with the same white minstrel-like gloves as the three little pigs, awaits. He is dressed in an oversized coat wearing thick-rimmed glasses with protruding green eyes, a gigantic hook nose, and an Orthodox beard. He recites his script with a thick Yiddish accent: "I'm de Fuller-brosh man. I'm giving away free semples."

Is that you? Practical Pig grabs a Fuller brush from the peddler's stash and using it as a club, whacks the wolf's paw.

"Now I got you!" (the wolf disguised as a Fuller Brush man struggles as Practical Pig jams him in the door). The wolf jumps back. Practical Pig locks the door and reaches through the window, continuing to clobber the wolf until his Jew disguise falls off. First the hat fades away and then what appears to be a mask of eyes, nose, and beard follows. Through a series of quick protean transformations the Fuller Brush man becomes Der ewige Jude (The Eternal Jew),[i] the generic American peddler wearing an Orthodox hat, a wolf masquerading as Groucho Marx (see Figure 2.4), a wolf wearing an oversized coat and minstrel gloves, and finally just a wolf.

"By the hair of my chinny-chin-chin,
I'll huff and I'll puff,
And I'll blow your house in!"

---

i. German for "The Eternal Jew." The Eternal Jew was originally the name of an anti-Semitic exhibit sponsored by Joseph Goebbels and displayed in Munich's German Museum from November 8, 1937 to January 31, 1938. A few years later this became the title of Fritz Hippler's propaganda film (1940) which depicted Jews in such a perverse way that the film was a flop even for German audiences. See Galit Hasan-Rokem and Alan Dundes, *The Wandering Jew: Essays in the Interpretation of a Christian Legend* (Indiana: Indiana University Press, 1986).

FIGURE 3.1 The Three Eddies (Tiny [Earle] Ray, Chick [Layburn] Horsey, and Charles Woody), stars of *Blackbirds of 1926,* perform in Paris, 1926. (Mary Evans Picture Library/Jazz Age Club Collection)

3

Public Works and Accolades

Race Film, Southern Repossession, and the Rise of Bill Robinson, 1929–1935

Three Black men dressed in white spats, dark suits with white vests, white gloves, blackface with accentuated white lips, white rimmed glasses, and bowler hats make an energetic entrance. The man in center begins a furious flash tap solo with hints of legomania[1] while the two men on his side keep the beat with a basic crossover step, calling and responding to his syncopations with pantomime and barely audible murmurs. As the energy picks up, the three men join in song, gradually synchronizing their tap dancing into a series of high-kneed runs, culminating this ecstatic 8-bar rhythm with a shave-and-a-haircut break. They proceed to take turns soloing: the first 16 bars feature trench-heavy flash dancing, the second, a 16-bar solo of single-legged wings, over-the-tops, and eccentric glides performed to an extremely upbeat version of Jimmy McHugh's recent composition "Doin' the New Lowdown."[2] The final performer takes his 16 bars half time, strutting, gliding, and then finally speeding up for a series of smooth trenches. The first performer, Chick Horsey, solos again, gradually increasing the virtuosity of his movements. After 28 bars, the other two dancers join him in a series of trenches to complete the chorus before grabbing one another's torsos. Like upright dominoes, they perform a popular "one man" dance in perfect synchrony.[3]

This short routine performed by the Three Eddies—Tiny (Earle) Ray (b. New Jersey 1897), Chick (Layburn) Horsey (b. Chester, Pennsylvania, 1903), and Charles Woody (place and date of birth unknown)[4]—opened the British musical revue film *Elstree Calling* (directed by Alfred Hitchcock) in 1930.[5] While the revue received mixed publicity from the British press and was largely canned by Americans, the two performances by the Three Eddies (this and " 'Tain't No Sin") seem to have stood out for England theatergoers. The *Manchester Guardian* wrote of their performance, "The Three Eddies rather

---

Behind the Screen. Brynn W. Shiovitz, Oxford University Press. © Oxford University Press 2023.
DOI: 10.1093/oso/9780197553091.003.0004

124 BEHIND THE SCREEN

staggered us with their exuberant energy and their dexterity of foot."[6] But the significance of this footage goes well beyond their talent. That they—and their co-star Anna May Wong—received significant accolades in the British press during a time when their talents were being overlooked in America says something about the publicity of color in Hollywood at this time and helps explain the expatriation so many Black and Chinese Americans were forced to endure in the late 1920s and early 1930s.

The Three Eddies began their theatrical careers in American vaudeville. The leader of the act, Tiny Ray, began his professional career as a "pick" for Gussie Francis and then later Belle Davis. He formed the class-and-flash act sometime around 1918.[7] The three began as a pantomime act, noted for their comic ability even in the absence of sound. By 1919, White newspapers noted not only the act's pantomimic abilities but also each of the dancer's acrobatic talents and expertise in burlesque.[8] The Eddies appeared all over the country between 1918 and 1924 performing a variety of acts including their "comedy keystone cops" and "pantomimic novelties." The Eddies then seem to have settled more in New York City, appearing at the Club Alabam in 1924 and at the Plantation in 1925. But the three did not receive wide recognition until joining American jazz pianist Sam Wooding and his European run of *Chocolate Kiddies* in 1925 alongside Adelaide Hall.[9] Their big break came in 1926 when they performed in the all-Black revue *Blackbirds of 1926* alongside Florence Mills and Johnny Hudgins. The show opened in Paris and the Three Eddies remained in the show through most of its British run from September 1926 into March of 1927. While the treatment of Black performers during this time was more favorable in Europe, White journalism was still rife with stereotypes. *The Times* in London writes of *Blackbirds*: "A colored review, however, has one disadvantage as compared with the other exotic productions. It cannot in these days claim novelty. At the London Pavilion on Saturday night we were prepared for an orgy of jazz, not only by the programme, but by the appearance in the orchestra. . . . The Three Eddies in 'A Lot of Nonsense' provided a good deal of real fun."[10] And the press took great advantage of Chick Horsey's violent run-in with fellow cast member Johnny Hudgins over dating a White woman: "Following the unfortunate melee," writes the *Pittsburgh Courier*, "the Eddies resigned from the show after the other actors refused to further appear with Horsey. They are on their way back to the States."[11] They then returned to Britain for *Elstree Calling* in 1930.[12] Covert minstrelsy looked different when commissioned for Black performers; racial stereotyping occurred between the lines and behind the scenes, as it did for the Eddies in these reviews of *Blackbirds* and in those of *Elstree Calling*.

Most striking is the Three Eddies' use of blackface within a citational context. While the Three Eddies in *Blackbirds of 1926*, *Blackbirds of 1927*, and *Elstree Calling* are clearly caricaturing Eddie Cantor and his use of burnt cork—their name, their blackface, and their rimmed glasses are dead giveaways—it is unclear as to whether this is how their act began. The timeline matches up—Eddie Cantor began performing in vaudeville in 1907, changed his name to Eddie (from Izzy) Cantor in 1914, and began performing in Ziegfeld's *Follies* in 1917. But given the fact that Eddie did not become a household name until 1923 when he starred in *Kid Boots* on Broadway, the Eddies likely would not have named their act after him. Furthermore, until 1924, the Three Eddies were billed as pantomimists and burlesque performers, making it unlikely that blackface and tap dance were part of their routine. Generally, blackface was the first characteristic to be highlighted next to a performer's name. The first instance of billing them as blackface performers appears in the *Boston Globe* in November 1924 and the first mention of their tap dancing capabilities is printed a month later by the *Times Union*.[13]

Three semi-successful performers began wearing blackface and immediately became highly successful in Europe as blackface minstrels pretending to be the White American legend (Cantor) known for his blackface. This is curious for many reasons and yet we will never know their exact intentions. But their decision to "black up"—and maybe more appropriately "white up" in blackface—*does* point to the fact that covert minstrelsy does not discriminate and that, as with other forms of minstrelsy, ambivalence is a central tenet. Even if their act constituted an overt use of the blackface mask, the Eddies' performances from 1924 to 1930 exhibit a version of covert minstrelsy in the form of a citation. Their masks, regardless of intent, point to the limitations of Cantor's colonial discourse and offer a counter-reading of his blackface performance. The Eddies, like so many visibly Black minstrels, embody a critical pitfall of relying on visibility as a primary means of seeing. Race "wields its claim most forcefully and destructively in the realm of the visible, yet it designates and relies on the unseen."[14] This chapter explores covert minstrelsy from a different perspective by taking into account the ways that covert minstrelsy surfaced through Black artistry in the early years of the Code. Everything from the types of roles assigned to Black performers to the lens through which Black performers retold histories of the enslaved

126　BEHIND THE SCREEN

constitutes a counter-narrative to covert minstrelsy and speaks to the fundamental ambivalence of all racial masquerades. Their performance also complicates notions of realism by highlighting the "real" as a cultural signifier and marketing tool.[15]

The Three Rs: A History and an Introduction

In the decade between the Great Depression and the start of World War II, the United States experienced the biggest social and economic changes the country had seen since the Civil War. The infamous stock market crash known as "Black Tuesday" set off a period of darkness for the American workforce, leaving one quarter of previously employed workers without a job by 1933 and a staggering number of families homeless. President Hoover's attempts to remedy the situation proved fruitless, and not until Franklin Roosevelt was elected president in 1932 did the United States see any glimmer of hope. Yet despite the nation's state of fiscal darkness and waning optimism, artistic and technological breakthroughs helped the film industry see the dawning of a Golden Age.

Mainstream cinema provided immediate relief from the stress of unemployment and increasing poverty for many White Americans, and race films produced by independent studios attempted to do the same for Black Americans. Finances permitting, both populations flocked to their respective movie houses hoping to find distractions from everyday problems. Smaller, Black-run studios and distributors, however, were hard hit by the Depression and by the growing implementation of expensive synchronized sound equipment. Larger White production houses capitalized on this and cultivated the African American market to recoup some of the money lost by the closure of foreign markets during World War II.[16] Consequently there was a major disparity in the quality of films these two markets could produce; most all-Black cast films fell in the hands of large studios telling a history of the Black experience through a White consciousness.

This reform in Hollywood narratives and casting coincided with a larger restructuring on the national level: Roosevelt's "New Deal" of relief, recovery, and reform created unprecedented legislative shifts and changed the racial and ethnic makeup of the workforce.[17] Running parallel to Roosevelt's reorganization on the national level were smaller, regional restructurings. Unemployment in the South, for example, exceeded the national average as farm incomes fell and manufacturing plummeted.[18] As a result of the South's economic despair, a surge in Klan activity and membership sparked a stronger progressive undercurrent (e.g., the Commission on Interracial Cooperation) that challenged "overt racial logics of Jim Crow." As Tara McPherson notes, more "covert strategies of racism and racial representation gradually came to replace these more overt logics associated with Jim Crow and the KKK, partially because of the hopefulness of the progressive era but largely because the South began to recognize the need for an image makeover."[19] Images of the South would not disappear from the screen, but lynching scenes and explicit racial violence would be replaced by what I am terming "southern repossession." Reframing the South within a covert context was one way that Hollywood could avoid the stakes of racial visibility while also slipping in the blackface mask under the Code.

While strongly motivated by the changing Code, the onscreen "reform" of this era changed the way class, gender, and racial stereotyping unfolded on the screen even so, it still conveyed potent messages about what it meant to be a person of color, a woman, or a member of the wealthy class. In this chapter I offer an overlapping set of three R's which developed out of the competing representation of Black artists and sound as mediated by the Code: race film, southern repossession, and the rise of Bill Robinson all ran parallel to Roosevelt's attempts at restoration and offered targeted groups a means of coping with the shifting social dynamics that came along with reorganizing the economy, the workforce, and the arts.

Beginning with an analysis of race film, I demonstrate four directions that depictions of Blackness took on the screen between the years 1929 and 1934. Race film might be viewed on a continuum of consciousness: on one end of this spectrum is blackface performed by Black artists (historically referred to as black-on-Black minstrelsy) who capitalized on a successful White performer's use of the blackface mask as do the Three Eddies. Situated beside Black performers' use of the citational guise is Black representation depicted through a White consciousness. These are all-Black films made by all-White creative teams that utilize a range of overt and covert masks to uphold a set of imaginary beliefs about Black life and the visibly Black body. While many of these films spotlight Black artistry, many do so at the expense of reinforcing old stereotypes. Some of these depictions included blatant uses of blackface makeup that the Production Code allegedly excused due to a series of narrative interventions and covert guises. The "minstrel show-within-a-show" and "southern repossession" formulas—variations of the citational

128   BEHIND THE SCREEN

guise—were common frameworks that allowed flagrant uses of burnt cork in mainstream Hollywood pictures. When cork was absent, the roles Black actors played and the songs to which they danced often stood in for blatant blackface, sending encrypted messages about Black people. Somewhere in the middle of this race film continuum is the material realized through the work of Oscar Micheaux and other Black writers and filmmakers who linked themselves to White consciousness only insofar as it impacted the funding of films that were otherwise made by Black people for Black people.

The remainder of this chapter examines the concealed ways in which films intended for a White audience utilized covert masks through a handful of exceptional Black artists, the most popular of which was Bill Robinson's.[20] Highlighting both Robinson's strengths and his quirks, I demonstrate the tap dancer's complicated relationship to blackface minstrelsy, including the ways in which certain idiosyncrasies and song choices became stand-ins for more obvious masquerades. Robinson's aesthetic captures what Ashon Crawley defines as the "choreosonic"; as Crawley writes, The "portmanteau underscoring that choreography and sonicity, movement and sound, are inextricably linked and have to be thought together."[21] Robinson's aesthetic utilizes sound and movement to embody certain minstrel tropes without alluding to them through obvious visual markers. Hollywood then created its own narrative of Robinson's body through its amplification and repeated use of the dancer's more discreet signs. As the positioning of Black and White people in previous chapters has shown us, the ways in which Blackness is juxtaposed tells a story all its own. While Robinson never donned burnt cork himself, his physical relationship to others wearing blackface mediated the visible absence of his mask. Robinson's most concealed use of covert minstrelsy, however, in fact manifests sonically when his rhythms are underlaid by those of Shirley Temple's: on the surface Black and White dancers had, for the first time in Hollywood, fully commingled, yet their underlying aurality tells a different story. That is, juxtaposing Robinson and Temple invisibly codes and repeats old ways of seeing when integrated with sound.

Robinson pioneered an era on screen for Black actors, often making sacrifices through casting, song choice, choreography, and reputation. In fact, the dancer was recognized as being so remarkable, that his image (like that of Cantor in blackface) became more famous than the man himself. This chapter concludes with an analysis of the Bill Robinson effect through which romanticized portrayals of an individual allow audiences access to a nostalgic and unquestioned slave-owning past while shielding them from the shameful parts of this narrative.

Bill Robinson's unique status in live action film made between 1930 and 1936 simultaneously extends and contains Black subjectivity in Hollywood, relegating the Black artist to certain roles, particular modes of being, and a restrictive vocabulary of movement. While the "real" Bill Robinson was both an icon of upward mobility and a marker of perceived social progressiveness for many White moviegoers, his "exceptional" status would in fact *promote* Hollywood's logic of erasure under the guise of racial progress. His likeness, and certain sounds associated with his persona, became so popular that other performers in Hollywood began collapsing and repurposing fragments of Robinson's image, serving up what Miles Orvell calls a "tension between imitation and authenticity."[22] In effect, this tension minimized his individual experiences and authored a repertoire of subtle gestures that both created and fed racial difference and its borders onscreen.

Reform: Race Film and Chromatic Aberrations

The talkie era brought about many changes in Hollywood, including a greater demand for Black performers.[23] Fox Pictures and MGM embraced this change with two feature-length Black musical films, *Hearts in Dixie* and *Hallelujah!*, respectively in 1929.[24] *Hearts in Dixie* (released first) takes place on a southern plantation and features "contented slaves" laboring all day singing melancholic spirituals like "Massa's in the Cold Cold Ground." The advent of sound might have been new but representing the "happy-go-lucky slave" was not. Donald Bogle captures the spirit of these false representations poignantly when he writes, "Instead of suffering or misery, they seemed to be floating on some euphoric high brought on, one would assume, by cotton fields and spirituals." Integrating song and dance into folk communities paired Black people with this notion that they held some "spontaneous and authentic culture that allowed for collective, emotional expressions of musicality."[25] Unlike narratives of ethnically marginal White groups that offered social mobility plots—for example, Jolson in *The Jazz Singer* or Cantor films of this era—these Black musicals emphasized a rural past and, as such, "denied the black presence in urban spaces of the modern era."[26] This problem would plague most Black actors until the 1960s.[27] The all-Black or predominantly Black films that Hollywood produced were not Black life as told through a

130 BEHIND THE SCREEN

Black consciousness; instead they were Black life as told by White producers, White directors, and White writers, but Black actors.

King Vidor, the director of *Hallelujah!* and many all-Black ensemble films to come, realized his longtime dream of "filming a story of real Negro folk culture" with this 1929 film. The way he dealt with Black characters—as "sentimental idealists" or "highly emotional animals," and more generally, Black life as realized through a White consciousness became models for subsequent all-Black musicals in Hollywood.[28] Vidor, like so many White filmmakers of the era, believed that his position afforded him both "privileged access to profound ontological questions" and an ability to explore the ontological contours of 'the Negro,'" and a kind of "specialized knowledge of African American life, acquired through his own empowered position as a white male observer."[29]

Yet despite the White press's—albeit racist—praise, neither *Hearts in Dixie* nor *Hallelujah!* (nor the year's other big all-Black musical *St. Louis Blues*) saw any box office success.[30] American audiences were still ill-prepared to see persons of color featured on the screen, especially in the South. Alain Locke and Sterling Brown took an "accommodationist" standpoint, supporting these two films on the grounds that they held the potential to model "spiritual revelations of some fundamentals of Negro folk character," where the "folk" is a representation of "black spontaneity in the hands of Black actors, the depiction of a cross-section of characters and emotions, and the sense of a shared identity rooted in a common experience."[31] That is, Locke and Brown saw progress in the development of Black song united with Black people and hoped this would pave the way for even greater successes in cinema.

Over the next eight years few feature films with all-Black ensembles were made. Four directions for Black screen performers ensued: first, shorter pictures called "race films" made by Black creative teams with tiny budgets and little time were made and shown in Black theaters.[32] Second, some of the larger studios produced all-Black shorts that would play in both Black and White theaters as preambles to feature-length White musicals.[33] They had larger budgets than those films made by Black creative teams, but these were generally told through a White consciousness and thus included both blatant and covert forms of minstrelsy. Third, Black performers could be cast in bit parts in White musicals but then "go missing" from the credits (as was the case with the two Black tap dancers in *The Kid from Spain*). Finally, a handful of "exceptional" Black performers were cast as domestics: Stepin Fetchit often played the porter or janitor, Bill "Bojangles" Robinson usually a servant,

PUBLIC WORKS AND ACCOLADES   131

Hattie McDaniel a maid or cook, and Thelma "Butterfly" McQueen a maid.[34] As the country headed into the Great Depression, studio owners saw Black people as an increasing threat in the workplace. These new roles offered, to use the words of Jon Cruz, a "countersensibility to a modernity that constantly threatens increasingly fragile notions of identity and authenticity."[35]

Race films allowed Black creatives to tell a different story of Black life than those told by the White-run Hollywood studios. The booking agent for the Lincoln Motion Picture Company (a comparatively tiny, Black-run studio) counted more than fifty race film companies operating between 1916 and 1924 alone.[36] Filmmakers like Oscar Micheaux and Richard Norman sought to create "an alternate set of cultural referents and establishing new Black character types and situations, particularly those that reflected postwar social changes."[37] These films were largely unseen by White audiences and offered Black viewers a utopian vision of an all-Black world. This was particularly important in helping to define Black identity in a White world and assisting in the smooth transition into a modern urban America. Race film companies emphasized visual self-determination when marketing their products to Black communities as they knew the demand for "authentic" representations of Blackness was high among their target audience.[38]

Many of these films are unknown to the general public and are worthy of study. I look at a sampling of these films made between the years 1929 and 1934 which stand out in their reworking of Black identity through the staging of the tap dance numbers. I then compare these stagings to a handful of all-Black musicals made during the same years but produced by big Hollywood studios, namely, Warner Bros. and RKO, to highlight the differences between Black life as told through a Black versus a White consciousness. Through the repeated representation of Black stereotypes Hollywood creates a larger symbolic complex, one that relies on marking and mythifying Black people, where Blackness exists only in relation to a White norm.[39]

Some race films, like Micheaux's *Darktown Revue* (1931), contain blatant instances of blackface. In this recreation of a classic nineteenth-century minstrel show, Amon Davis (himself a turn-of-the-century minstrel performer) performs his "Hard Shell Sermon" routine: Davis, in full blackface, impersonates an outlandish minister giving a satirical sermon of gibberish. This is not covert minstrelsy but instead a use of the blackface mask as historical document.[40] Other race films, like Warner Bros.' *King for a Day* (1934),[41] recreate the nineteenth-century minstrel show within a citational framework, thus making the film—and particularly its featured tap dance routine starring Bill Robinson—a prime example of covert minstrelsy; I return to the "recreated minstrel show" variation later in the chapter.

Race films made and distributed by Black creative teams[42] tended to borrow genre and characterizations from White films, but they set these films in a Black milieu, thus infusing them with "black sensibility that changed the dynamics of the film's receptive structure."[43] For example, Evelyn Preer's leading role as Jonquil Williams in Al Christie's *The Melancholy Dame* (1929) reveals a strong Black female role.[44] Aristo Films' *Georgia Rose* (1930) demonstrates the diasporic reality of Black life rather than presenting migration as allegory.[45] Taking up the impact of diaspora on the family structure, *Georgia Rose* "negotiates rural and urban space in a nuanced fashion, depicting both positive and negative character types in each."[46] In addition to recuperating Black identity through narrative, these films provide excellent documentation of Black tap dancers playing respectable roles. During a nightclub scene in *The Exile* (1931), a long set of unrestrictive couples dancing to "Doin' the New Lowdown" is followed by an announcement from the emcee: "Ladies and gentleman, the next performer for your approval is Roland Holder, recently of the Hot Chocolate Productions, Roland Holder."[47] In addition to getting fully acknowledged by name, Holder freely executes a superb example of solo hoofing in a classy suit and top hat. He wears no blackface, exhibits no eye-rolling, and performs to a stop-time heavy song of his choosing. In Lincoln Motion Picture Company's *Harlem Is Heaven* (1932),[48] Bill Robinson plays a decorous dance director. The big chorus line routine he choreographs for the film's show-within-a-show resembles the kind of dancing we witness by the (White) Goldwyn Girls performing around the same time in shows like *Footlight Parade* and *42nd Street*. Unlike the "wild" and "hot" dancing these Black women are forced to perform in White musicals of the era, the chorus dancers in *Harlem Is Heaven* perform in a manner that is at times highly syncopated, flexible, and groovy, and at others perfectly synchronized, even, complete with Rockette-style kick lines and waist-held bombershays in unison. This film allows them the freedom to perform all aesthetics and not just a stereotypically "hot and dangerous" one. The film might also offer a subtext about the kinds of performances Harlem performers curated for their White audiences.[49] During rehearsal we see these women do more of a smooth jazz tap style dance to a scatted and accented jazz tune. On the stage during their performance, which we later learn is presented to a White audience, their style has shifted drastically. Robinson also performs his famous stair dance to a Stephen Foster medley for this White audience in Harlem.

FIGURE 3.2 (*Top*) Bill Robinson performs atop a bar counter to Black patrons, backstage after performing his famous stair dance to a White audience in *Harlem Is Heaven*, 1932. (Private collection); (*Bottom*) Bill Robinson and uncredited chorines rehearse the "Bill Robinson Stomp" in *King for a Day*, 1934. (Pictorial Press Ltd./Alamy Stock Photo)

134 BEHIND THE SCREEN

In contrast to the films that utilized an all-Black creative team and directed the films according to a Black sensibility, the short films with an all-Black cast that were made by the big, White-run production houses used Black artists to construct and uphold *stereotypes* about Black behavior. In Warner Bros.' short *That's the Spirit* (1933) we see a shift in narrative, casting, and the presence of covert minstrelsy.[50] Mantan Moreland's first movie role offers a good dose of blackface (along with his partner Flournoy E. Miller) and a rehashing of various trickster tropes as "comic relief."[51] Noble Sissle and his band provide the accompaniment for Cora LaRedd's show-stopping song and tap dance solo "Jig Time."[52] Yet despite the force of LaRedd's voice and the power of her lightning-fast swinging feet—which truly are extraordinary—her frequent eye-rolling and head bobbling do something to diminish her power. Even though these were now emblems of some very famous contemporary Black performers—like Josephine Baker and Bill Robinson, for example—they also reinforce the Jim Crow and Zip Coon archetypes of the nineteenth-century minstrel stage. Another subtle yet powerful statement of covert minstrelsy appears in Warner Bros.' *An All-Colored Vaudeville Show* (1934/5) when in the background of Adelaide Hall's performance of "To Have You, To Hold You" are a series of one-eyed blackface minstrel caricatures painted on the set's life-size sheet music.[53] [FIG. C.3, middle left] While these caricatures are merely painted in the background, they haunt Hall's stage in a manner akin to the Chewy Gooey Gum ad in *Puttin' on the Ritz* [FIG. 1.2] and the Goldwyn Girls' decorated skullcaps in *The Kid from Spain*. [FIG. 2.1, bottom] This citational disruption and reference to minstrelsy is further muddled by the Nicholas Brothers extremely high-energy, smiling tap duet that immediately follows Hall's song and dance.[54] Here the virtuosity of the Nicholas Brothers' routine acts in a manner akin to the kaleidoscopic effects of the Goldwyn Girls' dancing, offering viewers both visual and aural distraction.

Several all-Black shorts made by these large movie studios produce a covert effect through erasure. Often the big music and dance scenes in these otherwise mediocre-written screenplays omit the names of their jazz musicians and tap dancers. A remarkable illustration of "one man" tap dancing can be seen in RKO's *Black and Tan Fantasy* (1929).[55] Yet the names of the "Five Hot Shots"/"Five Dancing Blazers" featured in the dance scene remain completely absent from the credits. Three Black tap dancers in RKO's *The Sport Parade* (1932) go uncredited in a nightclub scene, and the jump-roping *coup de maître* tap dance and the culminating rubber-leg sensation in Warner Bros.' *Smash Your Baggage* (1932) have also gone without identification.[56]

PUBLIC WORKS AND ACCOLADES 135

Only closely documented oral histories and scrupulous research have brought these legendary performers back to life: the jump roping dancer is most likely Danny Alexander but could also be James "Hutch" Hudson, two tap dancers known for their jump rope feats while tap dancing;[57] the rubber leg dancer has retrospectively been identified as Henry "Rubberlegs" Williams, also known as Butterbeans.[58] This phenomenon lasts well into the 1940s: in Paramount's *Hi De Ho* (1947) the names of the Peters Sisters disappears as well as those of Danny Miller, George Miller, and Lois Bright, who go mostly unacknowledged for one of the flashiest and riskiest tap dance performances captured on film during this era.[59] Other than a pedestal that appears midway through this perilous flash dance and reads "Miller," and a barely audible announcement of their entrance, the film excludes the Miller Brothers and Lois from the credits.[60]

Most of this book looks at White films that have erased the presence of Black artistry. We have already seen this phenomenon evidenced in the omission of Black dancers' names in the credits of *Ritz*, *Spain*, *Scandals*, and the films mentioned above.[61] Some Black performers, like the Three Eddies, found more prominence in Europe. But counterintuitively, another important way that Black artists disappeared was with Hollywood's new tendency to cast Black performers as domestics. This new visibility that emerged around 1930 and peaked in the mid-1930s, shortly after the MPPDA began enforcing the Code, in fact contributed to another trend in Hollywood: soon many Black performers—especially those cast as singers and dancers in White films—would be culled into a handful of exceptional Black performers. I turn now to the way this shift involved Hollywood's *most* exceptional Black tap dancer and how simulacra of Robinson's image would inform the era's future presentations of the tap dance form.

"And now, ladies and gentleman, it is my proud privilege to present to you America's foremost tap dancer, Bill 'Bojangles' Robinson."

The camera awkwardly cuts to Bill Robinson standing at the foot of a portable staircase in his iconic bowler hat and suit. An orchestra member plays the first few notes of Stephen Foster's "Swanee River" on an old ragtime piano and Robinson's classic stair dance commences. His sounds are crisp and light and make use of the wood as percussive filler for the pianist's accents. Robinson remains focused on his dance, barely acknowledging the presence of an audience except for an occasional tipping of his hat. Robinson begins changing up his tone by trading off the sounds of his taps with those of his hand knocking and patting the stairs. His choreography has up until this point only taken him as far as the third step, but as the song transitions into a stop-time heavy version of "Old Black Joe," Robinson passes the third and makes it all the way down the five steps of the reverse side with his syncopated tapping. The light now hits his dancing body in such a way that Robinson's shadow along with the silhouette of his staircase becomes a prominent part of the optics of this dance. The camera then cuts to a shot of the audience. Dozens of White patrons converse with one another, almost oblivious of Robinson's rhythms. This is Harlem, 1932. Robinson continues his dance, eventually making his way down the original side of the staircase. He rhythm-turns to reverse and then shoots right back up the stairs as the pianist once again alters the tune, now offering Robinson a slightly more upbeat rendition of "My Old Kentucky Home." The energy shifts drastically as the musician takes a back seat, muting his piano tones so that Robinson's sounds dominate the room. Robinson performs the remaining part of the dance on the top step with a series of crisp paddle-and-roll variations, wings, and his classic time step. The camera zooms in on his feet, accentuating the fact that his dance surface is only a few inches bigger than his dancing feet. The pianist increases his volume, making his classic ragging more audible. Robinson frantically scurries up and down each side of his stairs, adding in occasional eighth and sixteenth notes to make it more interesting before scurrying off the stage with high-kneed runs. He never acknowledges the audience directly.

Relief: The Rise of Bill Robinson

Bill Robinson was born on May 25, 1878, in Richmond, Virginia. Like Eddie Cantor, Robinson's parents died when he was very young. He was raised by his grandmother, Bedilia Robinson, who was formerly enslaved. Around the age of five Robinson ran away to Washington, DC, and supported himself by dancing in the street for pennies. He soon joined a vaudeville circuit. While Robinson did not himself don burnt cork, he and his friend and dance partner Eggie started boot-blacking, imitating the famous White minstrel George Primrose whenever Primrose and West came to town. Eggie mastered the soft-shoe and Robinson, the buck-and-wing.[62] As we saw with the Three Eddies, it was not uncommon for Black performers to imitate White entertainers either as a form of mimicry or for pure comic effect.

Between 1909 and 1915 Robinson and friend George Cooper played the (White) Keith and Orpheum circuits (headlined as "Cooper and Robinson").[63] By 1912, the two had become very well established in theater, because of a combination of their talent and the fact that they were "real Ethiopians."[64] Cooper's frequent use of the blackface mask secured even more approval from White audiences. Moreover, it was not unusual for the media to play up Black "foul play" as we saw with Chick Horsey's violent run-in with fellow *Blackbirds* cast member Johnny Hudgins. The media's negative attention ended the Eddies' run in *Blackbirds* and was similarly responsible for the breakup of Cooper and Robinson. Ultimately the reporting of one of Robinson's mishaps with the law led to the demise of their act around 1914, but Robinson's exceptional status granted him a pass.

This split ended Cooper's career and marked the beginning of Robinson's stint as a solo performer. While Robinson still refused to wear blackface, talent was enough to keep him performing on the White stage. Along with the split up of "Cooper and Robinson" came Robinson's second major contribution to the Black image on stage. Within three years of this separation, Robinson had worked his way up to the Keith Circuit becoming the first Black man to perform solo (and without blackface) on the White circuit.[65]

In 1918, Robinson introduced his signature stair dance routine at the Palace Theater in New York. Robinson was one among three total Black acts that performed at the Palace: During the First World War, Bert Williams, Greenlee and Drayton, and Robinson were the only performers of color to grace its stage.[66] According to one story, Robinson caught sight of some friends in the house and so he danced down the four steps that lined the outskirts of stage right and left. He unexpectedly received a round of applause for his moves and so he decided to work the stairs into his solo act.[67] Finding theaters equipped with stairs was difficult and consequently the stairs did not become a consistent part of Robinson's act until roughly 1924.[68] While many performers might have included stairs in their acts prior to 1918, Robinson's stair routine became so popular that he even tried to secure a US patent on the routine around 1921. His request was denied, but soon his name was so tied to the stairs that nobody dared to copy his act.[69] While Robinson did not have a large tap vocabulary, his light-on-the-feet style, happy disposition, and role as "authentic Ethiopian" gave him premiere status on the national stage.

In addition to his famous stair routine, Robinson had a collection of signature steps he could execute better than any of his contemporaries.[70] Stearns and Stearns write, "Robinson might use . . . a cross-over tap which looked

138 BEHIND THE SCREEN

like a jig; hands on hip, one arm extended, with eyes blinking, head shaking, and derby cocked . . . or a broken-legged or old man's dance, one leg short and wobbling with the beat; or an exit step, tapping with a Chaplainesque waddle.[71] Robinson had found the perfect balance between fulfilling White expectations of Black corporeality as "safe" yet exotic while not sacrificing the quality of his dancing. His lack of makeup and perpetual smile assured his audiences that he was both of African origins *and* happy. Robinson's gaze gestured at subservience while hinting at forgiveness; his Black face alluding to the control White America had over Black people, while reminding its spectators that slavery was extinct.[72] That is, while his tap dancing went uncompromised, Robinson's performances contained some trademark idiosyncrasies that alluded to the minstrel stage, and the roles Hollywood assigned him often reinforced White stereotypes about Black life. Although the NAACP would take issue with some of these movie roles, he gained favoritism among White and Black audiences alike.

Robinson's willingness to straddle this fine line allowed him to succeed on Broadway and in Hollywood. In May 1928, Robinson joined the (all-Black) cast of *Blackbirds of 1928*. Note that *Blackbirds of 1928* was the American production of Europe's highly successful *Blackbirds of 1926* and *1927*, both of which had made a star of Florence Mills and featured the Three Eddies overseas. This 1928 production is significant for several reasons: it marked the first time that Robinson would work alongside his ex-vaudeville partner, George Cooper, since their split-up. Second, while the show still included a large number of gross caricatures (e.g., children eating watermelon) referencing Black people, this production also "discovered" Robinson and Earl "Snakehips" Tucker, among others, on a main stage. Third, the first act finale includes a staging choice that will become pivotal in a high percentage of Hollywood tap dance sequences for the next two decades: taking a cue from DuBose Heyward's 1925 novel, *Porgy*, Lew Leslie staged a tribute to the author in *Blackbirds* featuring "a huge black screen on which were reflected the magnified shadows of the performers."[73] A similar stage effect can be seen in Robinson's stair dance in *Harlem Is Heaven* (1932), in the Gershwin opera *Porgy and Bess*, and in several future "tributes" to Bill Robinson. [FIG. 4.3, for example] Finally, I highlight this show because one can attribute its success largely to Robinson's dancing in the second act, which, according to reviews, "electrified" the production. Here Robinson introduced his famous routine, "Doin' the New Lowdown," where he tapped up and down five steps. While programs and advertisements for the show continued to represent Blackness as a series of stereotypes, this was the first show where White journalists began talking about Robinson's dancing without the highly critical minstrel narrative; this show would be directly responsible for his imminent success.[74]

While Robinson never donned burnt cork himself, he played stereotypically Black roles in most of the White films in which he danced. Robinson made his first film debut in 1930 with RKO's *Dixiana*, a Wheeler and Woolsey musical comedy that takes place in the Old South.[75] Robinson plays a very tiny part—that of a male maid who shows up merely to feather-dust and perform a specialty tap dance. Two years later he played a much bigger role in the all-Black film, *Harlem Is Heaven* (1932).

Harlem Is Heaven was a far cry from the films mainstream (White) Hollywood was producing about the Black experience and marks one of the earliest examples of the use of what Paula J. Massood has termed the "Harlem chronotope." Massood describes Black-produced race films that used the trope of Harlem as a catalyst for social uplift as the Harlem chronotope, or "a contemporary, although often symbolic, city space connoting African American modernity."[76] However, the difference between this 1932 vision of Harlem and the one that becomes a central trope for race films made after 1935 is that the city in *Heaven* is still one steeped in Locke's "New Negro" and the Harlem Renaissance. Despite the economic devastation the country was facing between the years 1929 and 1933, White patronage allowed select Harlem artists and clubs to stay afloat. The presentation of Robinson's stair dance in *Heaven* to a completely White audience offers a small glimpse into this dynamic. The plot seeks to recuperate urban Black life vis-à-vis individualism and ambition. [FIG. 3.2, top] It speaks to middle-class ideology and specifically that of the hard-working performer. But the film also captures the reality of Harlem artists at this time who curated their output for a White upper-class sensibility. Small gestures of this reality surface in Robinson's *Heaven* rendition of the stair dance, including director Irwin Franklyn's camera supervision, as well as Robinson's choice of music.

One small clue occurs midway through Robinson's stair dance performance when the camera quickly cuts to the film's diegetic audience, a White upper-middle-class crowd, slightly disinterested in the performance itself. Jane Feuer has described the specific camera direction given in backstage musicals as "progress[ing] from showing the diegetic audience to aligning that audience's gaze as a 'conservative' reflexivity, a move that firmly secures the film viewer's alignment with the (conservative, utopian, reconciliatory) ideology of the musical text rather than one that reveals the spectacle by distancing the viewer."[77] In *Heaven*, the choice to align the viewer's gaze in this way reminds the Black audience for which the film was intended that Black people entertain White people with money, and those paying customers may or may not take an interest in the performance itself, but they are paying customers nonetheless. For those unlikely White spectators who saw this film, a White diegetic audience ensures an alignment of spectatorship.[78] Such curated output surfaces at the level of this scene's soundtrack.

Little footage of Robinson's early-stage performances of his celebrated stair dance exists. We do know, however, that Robinson performed the stair dance to "Doin' the New Lowdown" in Lew Leslie's *Blackbirds of 1928*. While it is not unfathomable that Robinson could have performed to Stephen Foster's pseudo spirituals onstage, his use of them on an all-Black stage in an all-Black film made during the height of the Harlem Renaissance is notable.

The similarity between Foster's music and many Negro spirituals gave Foster's music extra credibility; its similitude presumed "authenticity" with regard to the "Black experience." Often spectators could not distinguish between blackface (the caricature) and Black music (the real), and these minstrel shows featuring Foster's music taught White spectators everything they knew about Black culture. As Karl Hagstrom Miller has posited, minstrelsy taught White spectators that authenticity was in fact performative; this pairing taught that "genuine black music emerged from White bodies."[79] Non-minstrel performances that utilized Foster's music thus lent authority to minstrel shows, as the line between the real and the pseudo became blurred through Black performers' use of these tunes.[80]

Foster's music held a high commercial value, not only in the nineteenth century but also in the early twentieth when connections to the plantation-owning South promised a certain White satisfaction; White films made during this era offer the strongest evidence. Interestingly, prominent Black thinkers who condoned the work of Foster claimed that he made African American music more accessible to the general public. According to W. E. B. Du Bois, Foster's music was neither an imitation nor a debasement of the Black man. It spread the message of the slaves to the world.[81] Robinson performed to Foster's tunes in *Heaven* only a few years following Alain Locke's publication of a similar opinion in *The New Negro*. Locke believed Foster was "the Joel Chandler Harris of Negro music, breaking its dialect bonds and smoothing it out palatably for the general American ear."[82] It is thus no wonder that Robinson would have performed his stair dance to a Foster medley in a film that sought to speak directly to his fellow "Black

PUBLIC WORKS AND ACCOLADES   141

folk" at the same time it viewed Black performance through a lens of White spectatorship in Harlem. But it was not until 1934 when Robinson started landing big roles in White films that his nods at minstrelsy became more prevalent.[83]

A marquee reads: "Abe Lincoln Theater—Green's Black Orchids—Opening Night"

The camera cuts to a curtain on which are painted four men in tuxedoes and top hats gazing out through the exaggerated white eyes of their minstrel masks. The curtain parts, revealing a tiered stage lined with an extremely fair-skinned Black chorus of female tap dancers. Hattie Noel and Muriel Rahn belt the lyrics to "Harlem Honeymoon" while an emcee announces "Eddie Matthews; Mr. Dusty Fletcher; Mr. Limehouse Brown."[84] Each of the three performers struts onstage in some version of a suit, top hat, and full blackface. The emcee pauses and then announces the last guest, "Mr. Bill Green." Bill Robinson makes a grand entrance but with a simpler suit and no makeup. Everyone takes their place. "Ladieeees and Gentleman. Beeee Seated." Dusty Fletcher begins asking Mr. Green a series of questions in a thick, exaggerated Negro dialect: "Did you evuh live in the Black seas?" Green responds: "Brutha, I bathed in the Black sea." Without pause Mr. Fletcher responds: "And you forgot to dry off." Matthews and Brown provide the laugh track. After more jokes from the end men and a performance of "Love Locked Out" by Miss Muriel Rahn, Mr. Green and Mr. Fletcher begin to gamble, a pervasive trope in this film and many films caricaturing Black life during this period. The interlocuter interrupts their round of poker: "Mr. Bill Green and his famous tap dance." The recognizable first notes of "Swanee River" begin as Mr. Green makes his way to center stage. He breaks into his famous syncopated time step, accenting the pickups of his second four bars with small eye-rolls. He exaggerates these eye-rolls more in the second section, this time adding his vocal "yah" syncopations between heels and toes. The music shifts to a sophisticated arrangement of Foster's "Old Black Joe." Robinson (as Green) soon adds in vocals, singing softly between tap notes. He looks up occasionally, syncopating his sweet voice with the whites of his eyes before offering the camera a glimpse of his infectious smile during a classic Robinson crossover step. He begins countering the stop time of the musicians with his own vocals muttering select lyrics of "Old Black Joe" in between his syncopated back flaps. The pace picks up considerably as the music shifts into "Love's Old Sweet Song."[85] The camera pans across the stage capturing the facial and body

142 BEHIND THE SCREEN

reactions of the other performers onstage. The song shifts once more into the foxtrot rhythm "Smiles."[86] Green sings the lyrics as he heads into the grand finale: Wing wing. Pull back. He scats and taps: "Yah, hoo—hoo—hoo." Tap-tap. "Ohh. Hah." Jump Jump, Jump-jump. Jump Jump, Jump-jump. Green springs erect into a comedy step as if on a pogo stick. The energy stays high until he makes his classic exit: right hand on hip; left arm flapping, feet tapping. Upright. He grabs his bowler hat; smiles; and struts off the stage. Wild applause.

Now You Roll Your Eyes Bill Robinson Style

The show-within-a-show or "integrated musical" format was a common Hollywood trope throughout the 1930s and 1940s. This formula takes several different forms: the first version can happen in any film, not just musicals. Characters visit a nightclub or the theater and watch a show along with the off-camera audience. The film's lead characters do not participate in the show. This is common in many of the White films I discuss earlier in the chapter where Black dancers and singers are employed in bit parts and then vanish; no further trace of them exists in the film or its credits. A reworking of this invisibilization can be seen in a film whose plot takes one or several of the leads to a nightclub or the theater and they purposely or inadvertently perform in the nightclub or theater scene. Performers like Cantor and Fred Astaire notoriously played this role. For Cantor, the inadvertent performer is often part of his narratively driven blackface disguise, as we saw in *Spain*, for example. Familiar to many 1930s and 1940s musicals are the narratives whose plots revolve around the making of a show or use a showbiz background, as seen in *Ritz* and *Heaven*. The show-within-a-show was also a Busby Berkeley trademark in 1933 with films such as *Footlight Parade*, *Golddiggers of 1933*, and *42nd Street*, all of which were about the making of a show and its final production within a Depression-era economy. Revue films (e.g., *George White's Scandals* and *Ziegfeld Follies*) were especially popular in the 1930s, and backyard musicals (e.g., *Strike up the Band* and *Babes on Broadway*) were equally popular in the 1940s. These latter variations constituted the perfect platform for narratively excused blackface minstrelsy. Dozens of these integrated musicals, especially of the "backyard" type, used the plot to their advantage. In *Everybody Sing* (1938),[87] for example, Judy Garland escapes being sent off to Europe by trying out for a musical show as a blackface singer. We

PUBLIC WORKS AND ACCOLADES   143

might view Jolson's character in *The Jazz Singer* as one of the earliest instances of "blacking up" within the integrated musical. But the most convenient way to sidestep the more rigid parameters of a Breen-era Code was the minstrel show-within-a-show variation, a subtype of the citational guise.

While there is nothing covert about the way in which blackface makeup appears in these films, the fact that these scenes featuring burnt cork are narratively diffused gives them great leverage in presentation, even when the Code was at its most stringent between 1934 and 1954. The minstrel show-within-a-show in the talkie era occurs as early as 1929 in films such as *Happy Days* and extends well into the 1970s, but its use was most common between 1934 and the end of World War II.[88] In chapter 2, I examined the ways in which the citational guise involves individual performers associated with the minstrel stage. The same set of standards applies to the minstrel show-within-a-show variation, but in these examples, the citational guise happens on a bigger scale and becomes "justified" by the film's plot. The citation is in fact so obvious that it cannot be mis-identified, but it still constitutes a form of "covert" minstrelsy because it requires narrative justification to exist and must follow the minstrel formula, which includes a particular stage setup, a roster of minstrel characters (e.g., an interlocutor and some version of tambo and bones), and a format, including comedy, song, and dance. The minstrel show-within-a-show will include both embodied quotations (expressed physically through the performers' bodies) *and* aural ones through song, dialect, and intonation.

Despite the large number of these citations that exist in Hollywood films of this era, only a handful of these minstrel shows feature Black performers; *King for a Day* is an exception. The whole plot revolves around gambling, a trope that was all too common in films made about Black life in the 1930s and 1940s, and an addiction for which Robinson was widely known. In the film, the character Mr. Brown (Ernest Whitman) refuses to let Bill Green (Robinson) audition for his vaudeville show "Brown's Black Orchids." Green challenges Brown to a long game of dice until Brown has nothing to offer Green but his vaudeville show. The show is renamed "Green's Black Orchids" and Robinson becomes the featured performer of the minstrel show-within-a-show. The production follows a typical minstrel show format of song, *olio* (variety), and tap dance and also includes the traditional roster of parts: the interlocuter and four end men (one of whom is Robinson) as well as a chorus. The thing that sets this minstrel show apart from "real" minstrel shows is Robinson's lack of blackface. I have discussed previously that Robinson

144 BEHIND THE SCREEN

refused to don burnt cork both on the vaudeville stage and in Hollywood. But I offer his performance in *King* as exemplary of the kind of racial caricature for which he became known.

Robinson's performance in this film includes both aural and physical references to the minstrel stage. While these allusions exist within a minstrel narrative and thus might be viewed as more admissible by the censors, Robinson incorporated these embodiments for the duration of his Hollywood career regardless of the film's plot. Since no evidence exists that Robinson performed to Stephen Foster's music prior to his career in film (c. 1932), his use of a Foster medley for the stair dance acts as his most prominent sonic reference to minstrelsy in *King*. Frequent eye-rolling and the exposure of eye whites were already signature moves of Robinson—so much so that Eddie Cantor references them when he cites Bill Robinson on the auction block in *Scandals*. However, Robinson debuts a song and dance called the "Bill Robinson Stomp" earlier in this film.[89] [FIG. 3.2, bottom] Its recurring phrase, "Now you roll your eyes, Bill Robinson style," frames his performance on the minstrel stage as part of *his* style rather than as a reference to minstrelsy.

These famous eye-rolls come to stand in for Robinson's lack of blackface. Not only is the minstrel show-within-a-show variation a justification for blackface, but it also validates some of Robinson's more covert evocations of minstrelsy while helping to establish these movements as part of the more widely recognized "Bill Robinson repertoire." Thus, while Robinson may never have donned blackface, his repertory included several aural and embodied signifiers of such makeup. Robinson's disguise in *King* may be invisible, but the minstrel mask still operates effectively in this film.

Robinson's relationship to the minstrel show-within-a-show is not a common illustration of this variation but instead an example of the ways the various offshoots of covert minstrelsy often overlap. Generally, the minstrel show-within-a-show utilized blatant blackface and was allowed to be seen onscreen because of its narrative framing. This variation, like all the subtypes discussed in this book, does not discriminate between live action film and animation. The earliest instance of the animated type can be found in Walt Disney's *Mickey's Mellerdrammer* (1933) in which Mickey and the gang stage a production of *Uncle Tom's Cabin*. [FIG. I.2] Other animated minstrel shows-within-shows appear in *Toyland Broadcast* (1934), *Mississippi Swing* (1939), and *Fresh Hare* (1942).[90] In all of these cartoons the minstrel show formula is used to narratively justify blatant blackface, play music often associated with the nineteenth-century minstrel stage, mask the vocal talents of Black musical groups like the 4 Blackbirds, and further reinforce a relationship between tap dancing and Negro caricatures. In the case of *Mellerdrammer* and *Swing*, the plot also glorifies the old South, something easily defensible when cute characters perform in Kentucky or Mississippi.

Recovery: Southern Repossession

Another way in which these integrated musicals and cartoons of the era justified the use of blatant blackface was to create a show that glorified the old South. By placing a routine on a southern plantation, these Hollywood revues or shows about showbiz could justify the use of certain dialects, songs, imagery, and the use of burnt cork all while attempting to "glorify" the institution of slavery. Performances that fall under the category of southern repossession tend to rely on the protean guise as a primary means of sidestepping Code.

Soundtracks played an important role in southern repossession films' depictions of the Civil War era. The pairing of Foster's canon along with songs like Daniel Emmett's "Dixie's Land" and "Turkey in the Straw" function in a performative manner similar to the way Hagstrom Miller proposes this music operates for nineteenth-century minstrelsy. That is, the images of carefree Black people laboring paired with these Black-inspired and/or minstrel tunes helped cement the way audiences came to "hear the South."[91] Musicals that sought to glorify the old South thus relied on these tunes to establish certain clichéd southern expectations for White moviegoers.

In *Going Hollywood* (1933),[92] Sylvia Bruce (Marion Davies), follows Bill Williams (Bing Crosby), a popular crooner, to Hollywood where he is to make a picture with his fiancée, the French actress Lili Yvonne (Fifi D'Orsay). Bruce's fluency in French, combined with a series of disguises, allows her not only to break into showbiz but also to win over Williams. Midway through the film, Bruce sneaks onto a southern plantation set. She disguises herself in black makeup and then grabs the hand of one of the Black child actors. She sits down beside Williams and, in a full Negro dialect, offers to read his palm. The temporariness of her mask is revealed at the end of the scene when Williams realizes what Bruce is doing (he only realizes when she purposefully breaks her dialect). He rubs the Black child's face to make sure he has not been doubly duped: "Who is this here," he asks.

146 BEHIND THE SCREEN

The little boy responds: "Massa Williams, I is *real*." In this pre-Code iteration of black makeup used within the integrated musical, Davies's performance is one of disguise, not unlike Cantor's use of the blackface mask. It is her series of protean transformations throughout the film culminating in her blatant use of the mask that constitutes her guise; her dialect provides a second, sonic layer. Davies's voice utilizes what Roshanak Kheshti describes as "the cultural logic of intelligibility." That is, her dialect takes on a "process of subjectification in which sounds are gendered and racialized, the means through which sound, and in particular its reception—aurality—figures as a site in the production of difference."[93] In co-opting this way of speaking, Davies can better distinguish her real self from her disguise. Because the removal of the mask marks an important part of this distinction and transformation, the audience is fully privy to her "dressing" and "undressing." It begins when she shifts her dialect back to "normal" and is exaggerated by the Black child's distinguishing remark "I is real." In case this were not transparent enough, the scene ends when she kisses the picture's producer Ernest Pratt Baker (Stuart Irwin) and leaves residue from her mask all over his face.

George White's Scandals (1934) offers another pre-Code example of glorifying the old South within the integrated musical.[94] This film, which has no real plot, was released in March of 1934, just months before most of the revue's numbers would have been cut for lewd conduct. The blackface number appears as a show-within-a-show: Happy McGillicuddy (Jimmy Durante) is seen backstage with his co-producer Tommy. McGillicuddy shares his concern that "Eddie" has not shown up yet despite it being time for his song. "That's what I came up to tell you," Tommy responds, "he won't be here. Our mammy singer has a bad case of water on the knee." This, of course, is a reference to Eddie Cantor, who by this point was known as THE blackface comedian. "Who's gonna do his song," asks McGillicuddy. "You are," says Tommy, "here, blacken up." "Me, ruin this schoolgirl complexion? Me, put that dirty black cork on this lily-white epidermis? Who's the quitter? Where's that Mississippi mud? The show must go on," says McGillicuddy. He proceeds to cork his face. Like all blackface citations performed by White people, the audience is privy to the blacking up and/or removal process.

The camera cuts to a clichéd cotton field—comically a much more complicated set than anything that could be set on stage—where McGillicuddy in blackface breaks into the song "Cabin in the Cotton and the Cotton in the Cabin."[95] As he completes the final phrase "That's why 'darkies' were born," an ensemble of White women in full body brownface and dressed in Haitian-inspired Karabelas with matching headbands run on to the stage, each with a mannequin of a Black male cotton-picker attached to her waist. Although the women are the ones tap dancing, their costumes create the illusion that the cotton pickers are dancing with the women on their backs. McGillicuddy returns for the grand finale where he, dressed in a black-faced Mother Ginger costume, lifts his skirt to reveal three pickaninnies. This revue number would have been cut had it been released just a few months later. And yet, some artistic decisions still seem to have been motivated by potential censorship. Female chorus dancers rarely wore blackface in Hollywood so the decision to use a fainter brownface without exaggerated lips offers a "softened" usage of the blackface mask while also sending a message about the perceived relation between female beauty and fairer skin. The fact that the men in this number are nearly mannequins functions similarly to some of the painted references to minstrelsy we have explored. [FIG. C.3] The gum ad in *Ritz*, the animated minstrel caricatures in Adelaide Hall's performance, and the Goldwyn Girls' painted hairdo in *Spain* probably did not violate Code because they were not viewed as masks but as "illustrations."

As censorship tightened and as the South became more vocal about solidifying its reputation as one stuck in the past, such cotton parades would also be tempered. The theme of glorifying the old South would continue to pervade the screen, but uses of blackface would become increasingly more covert. To be clear, the Code did not challenge tradition at its core. A precursor to MGM's *Gone with the Wind* (1939), James A. FitzPatrick's (with MGM) Technicolor short *Memories and Melodies* (1935) traces the life of Stephen Foster.[96] This short biopic narratively justifies its southern setting and the use of eight of Foster's tunes, including those with questionable lyrics. While no blackface is used in this film, it draws on every stereotype of Blackness (ante and post-bellum) imaginable and once again erases its Black artistry by omitting certain performers from the credits. A Los Angeles-based quartet, the 4 Blackbirds (Geraldine Harris, David Patillo, LeRoy Hurte, and Richard Davis) for example, sings a medley of "Old Uncle Ned," "Old Folks at Home," "Ring de Banjo," and "Massa's in the Cold, Cold Ground" as plantation entertainment. Very little is known about this Black musical group since they do not appear in the credits of any of their film "appearances," but according to a few news sources, they were "The Mills Brothers Equals."[97] Thus, even

148 BEHIND THE SCREEN

if Code challenged blatant racial caricatures, many types of representations easily slipped through the cracks, not least of which were the names of many of the industry's most employed Black artists. Hollywood produced a record-breaking number of Civil War–era films in the year 1935 alone. Three of these featured Bill Robinson: *In Old Kentucky*, *The Littlest Rebel*, and *The Little Colonel*.[98]

Like so many Black performers of his time, Bill Robinson faced a double standard. In order to be "seen" or recognized by White society, Robinson had to subscribe to the racist rules of Hollywood on set. While the context in which Robinson danced was contingent on the plot of Hollywood films, he generally played the role of a butler/servant and utilized excerpts from "Doin' the New Lowdown" and the stair dance he made famous. Everything from his musical pairings to his partner contributed to the covert nature of his life on screen, one dictated by a double standard yet bearing the fruits of success like few of his Black contemporaries.

(a) Synchronous Southern Repossession

I went to the market
for to get some meat.
And the meat so tough
and I couldn't get none.
I paid five dollars
for a great big hog.
And the hog so fat
and I couldn't get back.[99]

Walker (Robinson) recites these words while performing an upright buck dance for Lloyd Sherman (Shirley Temple) in *The Little Colonel*'s (1935) famous stair dance sequence. The young Temple watches attentively while her servant, played by Robinson, shuffles up and down the main flight of stairs in her grandfather's Civil War–era plantation home. His rhythms and steps increase in complexity as the dance progresses until he reaches a climactic sand dance finish at the top of the staircase and then leaps down (tapping all the while) to offer Lloyd (nicknamed the honorary "Little Colonel") his hand. She grins, giggles, and then utters the words, "I want to do that too!"

PUBLIC WORKS AND ACCOLADES   149

Hollywood had come a long way since the completely segregated dance space of the silent film era and the apportioned stage of the pre-Code era. As social relations shifted out in the world, so too did they change on the screen. Black actors slowly started transitioning from domestic roles (like servants) to confidants and/or playmates.[100] Often these two would be rolled into one as in the relationship between Robinson and Temple; Robinson played both the domestic and the companion. But more important, their bond marked the transition between an integrated and apportioned stage and one on which Black and White artists could make real physical contact.[101]

Audible tap dances such as those found in *Colonel* and *The Littlest Rebel* (1935) utilize the mask of southern repossession to conceal an aural matrix of difference. By placing Robinson alongside Temple, these films simultaneously herald a new way of seeing how Black and White artists *can* relate on screen—that is, Temple and Robinson demonstrate that physical contact is not only possible but potentially desirable—and creates a divide between these two bodies by exposing the space that exists between their relationship: Black and White, man and child, master and servant, teacher and novice. In pairing the ruse of integration alongside such opposites Hollywood reinforces the imagined difference between the two.

In many ways the juxtaposition of these two bodies echoes the sentiment proposed in Hollywood's first "integrated" song and dance just five years prior. Physical proximity can be traced from a completely apportioned stage in *Ritz* to a shared but separate stage in "Keep Young and Beautiful" in *Scandals*, to finally the hand-holding of Robinson and Temple. Unlike the highly visible distinction made between Black dancing and White in these pre-Code musicals, Hollywood covertly obscures the differences between Temple and Robinson.

In both *Colonel* and *Rebel* the physical contact between the two dancers, gives a superficial image of equality. Yet on closer examination of their sounds, their seemingly synchronal bodies diverge. In the stair dance described above, Robinson simplifies his choreography: for every two sounds uttered by Temple's body, Robinson works to produce four.[102] The sonic guise intervenes to conceal Robinson's double labor, for which he receives only half as much credit as Temple. The visual also distracts from the sonic reality in *Rebel*: In the *Hollywood Reporter*'s review of the film, the

150 BEHIND THE SCREEN

critic applauds the film for being "well produced and with an appeal that is practically universal in Miss Temple," while describing Robinson's performance as "the other steady attraction" whose sole contributions were noted as "some amusing negro dialect and humor" instead of his tap dancing or choreography.[103] Thus the sonic guise works along two registers within these films: first, Robinson's choreography appeals to a double consciousness whereby he compromises his own artistry in order to augment that of Shirley Temple. By doubling his own choreographic labor, Robinson's dancing makes it seem as though his sounds emanate from her body. At the same time Robinson's feet utilize the sonic guise, so too does his voice work to obscure his Black artistic labor and augment Temple's White image. It is in this way that Robinson's audibility resonates with Matthew Morrison's notion of "blacksound," which refers to both the real and imagined legacies of African American bodies.[104] Robinson's sound is a combination of an Africanist rhythmic sensibility—both in his tap dancing and in his vocal rhyme—as well as a prescribed Negro dialect, both of which are negotiated by Whiteness vis-à-vis Temple, the directors, and the intended audience for these films. Southern repossession writes off Robinson's role as the family slave in both films and also excuses his use of a Negro dialect; this latter use of the sonic guise further accentuates the visibility of racial difference by creating a visual scenario where blacksound is not restricted to Black bodies but instead is mediated by White bodies.

These early pairings between Temple and Robinson demonstrate Hollywood's transition from representing blacksound as emanating solely from the Black body to seeing tap dance as part of broader American narrative, one tied to Black enslavement and the continued marginalization of Black people, through the enfranchisement of White people. Not only does this film's plot offer an overarching glorification of the old South, but the plot re-creates the dynamic between confederate slave owners and their enslaved by turning the master/slave dynamic on its head. In *Rebel*, Virgie Cary's (Temple) "Uncle Billy" (Robinson) means more to her than her own mother. At one point, one of the enslaved children (Sally Ann) offers Virgie a pickaninny doll (in blackface) for her birthday. Virgie announces that this is her "very nicest birthday present," emphasizing approval over minstrel objects. Later on, Sally Ann suggests to Temple that she use the blackface mask as a disguise from the Yankee soldiers, making it seem desirable to fit in with the rest of her father's enslaved. The Confederates become the "good guys" and the enslaved who work for the "most dangerous" confederate Herbert

Cary (John Boles) seem to advocate the upholding of slavery. Here it is the interactions rather than the segregation between Black and White that reveal the social hierarchy.

Even though *Rebel* applies an overt display of blackface justified as a form of fitting in, or disguise, the deeper-seated messages of these Robinson/ Temple films lay in their sonic manifestations. In the opening scene of *Rebel*, a dozen Black servants wait on fifty children between the ages of six and eight. Once all of Virgie's guests have finished their cake and ice cream, she gathers their attention: "How would you all like to see Uncle Billy dance?" "Oh boy," everyone cheers. One of the other enslaved men takes out his harmonica and Uncle Billy heads to the center of the banquet room. The "smiling slave" performs a spritely tap dance to "Turkey in the Straw" or "Zip Coon," arguably the most popular song among White circles of the mid-nineteenth century and the one that closed almost all minstrel performances.[105] Thus, even without blackface makeup or lyrics, Robinson's use of minstrel music combined with this routine's narrative context recreates the minstrel space. In other words, by placing Black people in closer proximity to White, Hollywood defines their differences.[106] More telling than Robinson's role as a servant in this film is that Temple, his less skilled junior, is his master.

Such sonic manifestations happen to an even more covert degree in the tap dance sequences that Robinson and Temple share. The stair dance shared by Robinson and Temple offers a commodified resource for pleasure. Bill Robinson—a kind of magical Negro when placed alongside his significantly younger White dancing partner Shirley Temple—transforms the amateur tap dancer into a highly competent partner. On the surface these dance sequences masquerade under the guise of progressive Black-White screen relations, when in fact they exploit fantasies about the Other "in a manner that reinscribes and maintains the status quo."[107] It appears that Robinson has the power to transform Temple into a tap dancing prodigy. However, their sonic interdependence offers a different perspective. Here Hollywood expects its White audience to find pleasure in Robinson and Temple's visible differences, but it is in fact through their sonic disparities that we may see the ways in which this relationship marginalizes Black agency while empowering and normalizing the hegemonic forms of Whiteness that Temple's character represents.[108]

The tap dancing that one hears—the syncopated beats against a wooden staircase—will, moving forward, no longer signify the Black or blackfaced

152 BEHIND THE SCREEN

body. Instead, the tap dancing that one hears onscreen will signify an American aesthetic that includes audible Africanisms disguised by the White bodies who perform them. Here the aural and the visual "stand before one another," and as Fred Moten writes, "Then the aural emerges as that which is given in its fullest possibility by the visual: you hear . . . most clearly in seeing . . . the visual emerges as that which is given in its fullest possibility by the aural: you see . . . most clearly in hearing the space and silence."[109] Placing the sonic in line with the visual, Hollywood allows its White audience to hear unity at the same time it sees difference. Through their synchronicity Temple and Robinson cover up tap's historical connotations and transition it into the present moment.

This new method of presenting tap dance on the Hollywood stage breaks the *ocular-sonic* relation between sign, signifier, and signified. The new sound one hears resists reification; it survives acousmatically, independent of its object. For example, we get a clear sense of Robinson's capabilities during his "Turkey in the Straw" solo in *Rebel* and in his solo for Temple in *Colonel*. He consistently executes complex rhythms while continually changing his weight as he leaps from one step to the next. His facings change at the same time he plays with tempo and stylization of the steps. In both films Robinson's use of rhythmic complexity and stylistic nuance is attenuated as soon as he grabs hands with Temple: the flow of the dance becomes stagnant; no more syncopated buck-and-wing steps; no more effortless flights through space. The whole routine from this point forward becomes a series of cramp rolls, flaps, and toe knocks with the performers' backs to the camera. The camera zooms in on Temple's feet executing standard cramp rolls, a step that, in its most basic form, makes only four sounds. Viewing Temple's feet in isolation does not account for the sonic discrepancy the viewer hears when six beats are uttered. For a moment the camera zooms out and one can see that Robinson's basic cramp roll includes two extra (syncopated) heel drops. Something similar happens when Temple's single flap is accented by her partner's *hop flap*, the effect of which is a seamless sonic *pick-up*. Neither Robinson's complex tapping, nor Temple's simple steps, are signified by the sound one hears in these films. The image of Robinson and Temple dancing side by side gave White audiences the impression that onscreen integration was occurring when in fact such pictures only masked the ways in which their acoustics reinforced old ways of seeing Black people. I do not want to downplay the significance of Robinson and Temple's relationship for viewers who had previously only seen Black and White dancers perform on separate circuits and stages. But inasmuch as Robinson made great strides for the visibility of Black artistry onscreen, his distinction was not without sacrifice.

The Bill Robinson Effect

A White man in full blackface shuffles onstage in a bellhop's uniform and begins tap dancing to a stop-time-heavy tune played by the adjacent White jazz orchestra. Some of his steps vaguely resemble steps from Bill Robinson's vocabulary but are sloppy in their execution. The performer keeps his gaze on the floor and slaps his feet, barely acknowledging the orchestra's groove and without any sense of musical texture. The stage is full of contradictions: the five-tiered staircase upstage, the persistent stop time, and the vocabulary all scream Robinson, yet this performer's bellhop costume, blackface, and complete lack of facial and vocal engagement send a different message. However, on performing a particular alternating hop brush tap en route to the staircase, it is clear that this performer is imitating the work of Robinson. The choreography he performs on the stairs is a rearranging of Robinson's choreography in a manner that is entirely unflattering both as it concerns stereotypes of Black representation and Robinson's flawless rhythmic articulations. A failed copy of the exceptional Black dancer.

Beginning with the minstrel stage, "imitating black performance became a constituent component of white identity."[110] Temple's simplified reproduction of Robinson's material in *Colonel* characterizes one version of this imitation and the above description from *The Musical Beauty Shop* (1930) denotes another, an early example of the citational guise taken to an extreme.[111] The next two decades would be full of these sorts of quotations and imitations. Following Robinson's success in *Blackbirds of 1928*, replicas of his image would appear in live action film, animation, puppetry, and a slew of other visual media. In fact, Robinson's image, like that of Cantor in blackface, became more famous than the man himself.[112]

154 BEHIND THE SCREEN

The Bill Robinson effect occurs when society latches on to an iconic dancer of color and begins to see other dancers of color working within the same genre/discipline as mere replicas of the original. Under this model, the individual's unique looks and stylistic qualities dissolve and get re-presented under the guise of a caricatured version of the former. The Bill Robinson effect takes two forms: the first, more common iteration reveals itself visually as an archetypal snapshot of disjointed elements of the icon's step vocabulary, wardrobe, or props and caricatures or exaggerations of elements of his face or body. We see this form of the Bill Robinson effect in the above imitation where the White man in blackface in no way attempts to duplicate Robinson's stylistic qualities or demeanor, but it also includes certain signature steps and a staircase—citations of Robinson's performance. Often the cited vocabulary is collapsed into something as general as tap dance. The second form of the Bill Robinson effect takes shape as a narrative revision in which authors evoke a historical figure through a biased lens. By omitting crucial details of the historical figure's biography, the subject of this re-telling becomes the *exceptional* Black man capable of transcending time and thus the social stigmas he endured while alive. In this chapter I explore examples of the first order. Exceptionalism and synecdochization set the Bill Robinson effect apart from strict imitation; its pervasiveness in the 1930s and 1940s makes it a special case of the citational guise.

We might view the reproduction of Robinson's image as a symptom of modernity and shifting social codes, especially as these codes involve race and representation. Robinson's image became a site of "both the formation and the revelation of ideology and value consciousness."[113] By adding to parts of his image that never existed, his reproductions embody socially significant values around Blackness yet, like the caricatures created for the minstrel stage, remain far from the truth of what Robinson (the man) sought to represent.

Bill Robinson was an *exceptional* Black dancer for whom American employers made special allowances. Robinson, for example, was one of the only Black dancers performing before 1930 who was allowed to perform as a soloist without blackface makeup. This does not mean that his performances were unbound from allusions to the minstrel stage, but they were free from the obvious forms of caricature that some of his contemporaries implemented. Robinson also never went uncredited, even when he held smaller bit parts as he did in *Dixiana* and *In Old Kentucky*. As Robinson became more and more famous, his reputation took on a life of its own, and

PUBLIC WORKS AND ACCOLADES 155

this acted both in service and to the detriment of other Black tap dancers working at this time.[114]

However, some reproductions of his image were vehicles for deep-seated racial narratives, as was the case in the unidentified tap dancer's imitation of Robinson's stair dance in *Beauty Shop*. The dancer's citation contains enough (accurate) references to Robinson that the association cannot be mistaken. However, he ad libs in areas that are potentially damaging to Robinson's image. We will see more and more of these types of imitations toward the end of the decade. In fact, they become most popular as Robinson's physical body starts to fade in Hollywood. That is, as the "real" Robinson disappeared, more and more tap dancers began producing mockups of his image. Many of these duplicates surface in live action films under the tribute guise—the topic of chapter 5—but the Bill Robinson effect becomes much more prevalent in cartoons of the late 1930s and early 1940s. I explore the turn toward animation that covert minstrelsy takes in later chapters, but here I offer one of the earliest animated examples of the Bill Robinson effect to show just how complex these fabrications could become with the new medium.

Throughout the 1930s, animators would insert a caricatured version of Robinson in places where they needed a Black tap dancer. We see an obtrusive example of this in a Harman-Ising "Happy Harmonies" Production (distributed by Lowe's and MGM), *Old Mill Pond* (1936), which seemingly tries to replicate Robinson and Fats Waller's "Livin' in a Great Big Way" in *Hooray for Love* (1935).[115] [FIG. 3.3] A fish, frogs, and toads gather at a pond to listen to a jazz concert. The jazz narrative lends itself to a Robinson cameo and the frogs offer a convenient vehicle for minstrelsy's stereotypically large-mouthed performers. Dressed in a bowler hat and suit, the Robinson toad stands atop a staircase pursing his giant amphibian lips to mirror the kind of harmonica sounds Robinson would produce while tap dancing. The toad's lips go from big to giant as he begins to tap dance up and down the staircase. He also rolls his eyes Bill Robinson style, but this quickly devolves into a bucking of them, followed by a crazy kind of rolling that sometimes took place on the nineteenth-century minstrel stage. He engages the nearby frog pianist (a cartoon resembling Fats Waller) in some call-and-response and refers to himself as Mr. Sippi. Even if this toad executes some impressive tap dancing for a cartoon, minstrel references ensnare the Robinson citation.

FIGURE 3.3 (*Top*) Bill Robinson and Fats Waller perform "I'm Living in a Great Big Way," in *Hooray for Love*, 1935. (Private collection); (*Bottom*) Amphibianized caricatures of Bill Robinson and Fats Waller perform "Mista Sippy" in *Old Mill Pond*, 1936. (Private collection)

PUBLIC WORKS AND ACCOLADES   157

Representing Robinson's image through an animated toad takes on a Sartrean "detotalized totality" or "synechdochic fragmentedness."[116] Citations of this nature adopt totemic properties and take on a life of their own in the way that Jean Baudrillard has described the fetish as taking a deconstructive turn. Read in light of covert minstrelsy and specifically the ways in which the citational guise can be taken to totemic extremes, reducing Robinson's dancing to rolling eyes, minstrel lips, or even a bowler hat says much about those who "use it" and, as Baudrillard notes, actually "expose[s] their own magical thinking."[117] In other words, Robinson's reproduced image says more about the fantasies of those creating these simulacra than about Robinson himself.

While these reproductions might have begun as simple nods to the famous tap dancer, they became a combination of real and imagined attributes, creating a much more complicated effect. Examples such as the reproduction of Robinson's stair dance in *Beauty Shop* not only show clearly the fabricated nature of these sorts of simulacra but also get at the heart of Walter Benjamin's notion of replica realism. For Benjamin, art—and in this case performance—must be based on the praxis of politics: "for aura is tied to his presence; there can be no replica of it."[118] Adding in blackface, the White performer fabricates parts of Robinson's character and in the process loses not only the aura of Robinson's representational politic but also the whole quality of his dancing as if somehow blackface and a staircase can stand in for the man. As these caricatures multiplied, Robinson's commodity value increased, but his legacy morphed. In the overproduction and misrepresentation of Robinson, we lose his Black individuality: this includes the kind of loss of labor involved in a Marxist commodity fetishism and a reconfiguration of aura in the Benjaminian sense; his body is valued insofar as he can sustain certain beliefs surrounding the Black man dancing and his ties to the minstrel stage.

***

The evolution of Robinson's image is similar to Eddie Cantor's blackface persona: the reproduction (caricatures of Robinson and the image of Cantor in blackface) began holding more credence than the original; however, these two masks operate differently on the level of fetish. Cantor's Whiteness assures that his real image suffers no real consequence. In the case of Cantor, the thing being reproduced is his masquerade, not his race or even his ethnicity, leaving his real image untarnished. The Three Eddies imitated Cantor's

158 BEHIND THE SCREEN

façade, not Cantor, and because the costume was so clearly a costume, it was always very apparent that there was someone beneath the makeup.

As Cantor's image in blackface became more and more reproduced, the mask became an accessory that was almost expected of him. We see this in Jimmy Durante's blackface bit in *George White's Scandals* where his joke makes clear that Eddie Cantor is synonymous with blackface. In this way, Cantor's blackface mask functions more as fetish in the Freudian sense than as a commodity detached from labor or aura. His Whiteness, combined with the way the audience is always privy to his process of "blacking up," offers his mask as specular mimesis. This phenomenon becomes even more clear in the Three Eddies' schtick. Their espousal of Cantor's blackface (which included his famous spectacles) is a testament to the success of the comedian's mask; even without the name "Eddie," these Black performers could summon the reference. The fact that they as Black men can cite Cantor's blackface mask as entirely performative offers Cantor's mask as a kind of Freudian fetishism; their masking as comedic citation exists in an "ambiguous state that demystifies and falsifies at the same time, or that reveals its own techniques of masquerade while putting into doubt any fixed referent."[119]

The Bill Robinson effect, on the other hand, generates a copy "for an original that never was there in the first place."[120] With the Bill Robinson effect, imitators were reproducing a version of Robinson that he crafted for the White gaze, arguably a performance that stemmed from his own double consciousness of performing on a White stage as a Black man. Furthermore, because Robinson's mask was covert, unlike Cantor's, it was easier to see all extrapolations of his image as being based on some primary source. For the most part, reproductions of Eddie Cantor's blackface stayed stagnant in their appearance. Copies of Bill Robinson, on the other hand, straddled a fine line between imitation and racial caricature.

Bill Robinson marks an interesting deployment of the citational guise since he was known by many as the man who bore no relation to the minstrel stage because of his adamant refusal to wear burnt cork. As we have seen, however, Robinson carried many ties to minstrelsy; they just manifested in covert ways. Everything from rolling his eyes to using Foster's tunes in White films were physical and sonic ties to the blackface mask. He was generally cast in menial roles or meant to portray the happy-go-lucky Black man who dances for White enjoyment. His performances were often situated in minstrel shows-within-shows and glorified southern plantations; therefore, his connections to blackface manifest narratively by means of juxtaposition. Furthermore,

PUBLIC WORKS AND ACCOLADES   159

while several sources document that the relationship he shared with Shirley Temple was genuine, Hollywood's pairing of the two is complicated: although seemingly integrated, Robinson sacrificed the technical virtuosity and authorship associated with his own image to uplift that of Temple. The image of a Black man holding hands with a White girl covers up their aural discrepancies while their ostensibly synchronous tapping masks the vast distance that still separates White from Black politically, socially, and economically.

As Robinson gained more and more public visibility, his image took on a life of its own. Two trends ensued: first his image became a surrogate for all Black tap dancers of this era, with the public often conflating Black tap dancing with Robinson's stair dance. Like the White films that omitted the names of their Black jazz musicians and tap dancers, the Bill Robinson effect in this way assisted in a practice of erasing Black individuality. At the same time, these Robinson reproductions added elements to his body that not only undermined the sophistication of his tap dancing but also made explicit his ties to minstrelsy. That is, additions like the burnt cork used in *Beauty Shop* and the exaggerated amphibian lips in *Old Mill Pond*, combined with subpar artistry, minimized Robinson's talent in favor of making associations between his Black artistry and long-standing stereotypes of Blackness as primitive, grotesque, and dangerous. Thus, if Robinson's career in Hollywood included covert references to minstrelsy's stereotypes, citations of his work—fashioned as poor imitations—overtly announced a connection between his Blackness, tap dance, and the alleged truth of these stereotypes.

While the Bill Robinson effect would pervade the screen for the next decade, the changing Code would alter the way Hollywood offered the image of Robinson and others. The narrative framing took on an even greater significance during the Breen era as directors had less leverage with representation. Rather than slipping in citations to Robinson or his contemporaries, films would frame their references as tributes to their respective legacies, at times adopting a blackface mask where one was never present.

Notes

1. A kind of eccentric dancing that features high kicks and especially loose leg movement.
2. Jimmy McHugh wrote the music and Dorothy Fields the lyrics for this popular jazz tune composed in 1928 for the Broadway revue, *Blackbirds of 1928*. Bill Robinson was the first to perform this song live on May 9, 1928.

160 BEHIND THE SCREEN

3. Constance Valis Hill has written about the "one man" dance in the context of the "Five Hot Shots"/ "Five Dancing Blazers" in the film *Black and Tan* (1929). See *Tap Dancing America: A Cultural History* (New York: Oxford University Press, 2010), 94.

4. Charles Woody replaced the original member Shakey (Clarence) Beasly (b. Orange, NJ 1898) between the European run of *Chocolate Kiddies* and the opening of *Blackbirds of 1926* in Paris.

5. André Charlot and Jack Hulbert, *Elstree Calling* (September 29, 1930; UK: British Imperial Pictures), Film. Hitchcock's role in this has been largely debated, but he at least oversaw the making of the film. The film presented a series of nineteen musical and comedy vaudeville sketches, presented by Tommy Hadley. Two of these sketches were performed by the Three Eddies.

6. "Review" in *Manchester Guardian*, published August 28, 1928.

7. See billing as the "Three Eddies—Pantomimists" in *Nashville Banner* July 14, 1918.

8. Noted as a "Pantomimic Novelty" in *The Allentown Democrat* (Allentown, PA) September 26, 1918. The *Tribune* (Scranton, PA) also writes of the Three Eddies: "The Three Eddies have been billed. They present a comedy pantomimic aero acrobatic act that will undoubtedly prove to be one of the funniest things on the program. All are clever acrobats and their burlesque is up to the minute." See "Big Draping Act One of the Features at Popular Vaudeville House" in the *Tribune*, January 6, 1919.

9. Hall was an American-born jazz singer who garnered much attention in the United Kingdom, but he also saw great success in the United States and was considered a major figure in the Harlem Renaissance.

10. "Blackbirds: A 'Coloured Review' at the London Pavilion," in the *Times*, published September 13, 1926.

11. "Three Eddies Coming Home from England Following Horsey's Attack on Hudgins," in the *Pittsburgh Courier* (Pittsburgh, PA) March 26, 1927.

12. Howard Rye, "Three Eddies," in *The New Grove Dictionary of Jazz*, 2nd ed., Grove Music Online (New York: Oxford University Press, 2013), Encyclopedia Article 2002.

13. "Three Eddies Blackface" at Waldron's Casino in *Boston Globe* (Boston, MA), November 25, 1924, and advertisement in the *Times Union* (Brooklyn, NY), December 21, 1924: "The Three Eddies are colored youths whose forte is syncopated stepping."

14. Anne A. Cheng, *Second Skin: Josephine Baker and the Modern Surface* (New York: Oxford University Press, 2011), 13.

15. David Krasner, "The Real Thing," in *Beyond Blackface: African Americans and the Creation of American Popular Culture, 1890–1930*, ed. W. Fitzhugh Brundage, 99 (Chapel Hill: University of North Carolina Press, 2011.

16. Lillian Johnson, "Light and Shadow," *Baltimore Afro-American*, January 13, 1940, 13.

17. Known as Franklin Roosevelt's "Three R's," his response to the Great Depression was to create domestic programs aimed at recovery (helping the economy bounce back), relief (providing assistance to those recently unemployed), and reform (targeting the causes of the Depression with the goal of preventing future stock market crashes).

18. Patricia Sullivan, *Days of Hope: Race and Democracy in the New Deal Era* (Chapel Hill: University of North Carolina Press, 1996), 20–22.

19. Tara McPherson, *Reconstructing Dixie: Race, Gender, and Nostalgia in the Imagined South* (Durham, NC: Duke University Press, 2003), 62–63.

20. By exceptional I mean those bodies who marked an exception as determined by White filmmakers as opposed to "exceptional" in Du Bois's notion of a "talented tenth." While this was first and foremost a superlative marked by talent, other factors went into this designation. This chapter explores many of these.

21. Ashon Crawley, "That There Might Be Black Thought: Nothing Music and the Hammond B-3," *New Centennial Review* 16, no. 2 (2016): 12.

22. Miles Orvell, *The Real Thing: Imitation and Authenticity in American Culture, 1880–1940* (Chapel Hill: University of North Carolina Press, 1989), xvi, 34.

23. In photography, "chromatic aberration" or "color fringing" is a lens problem caused by dispersion so that a lens is unable to bring all wavelengths of color to a single focal plane and/or when wavelengths of color are focused at different positions in the focal plane. Chromatic aberration results in a blurring of color especially in high contrast situations. Here I intend both this meaning and the more metaphoric meaning, as related to the social and representational disparities between Black and White performers in Hollywood, especially when Black actors are placed in a film directed by a White creative team.

24. Paul Sloane, *Hearts in Dixie* (May 1929; USA: Fox Film Corporation), Film; King Vidor, *Hallelujah!* (August 20, 1929; USA: Metro-Goldwyn-Mayer), Film.

25. Desirée J. Garcia, *The Migration of Musical Film: From Ethnic Margins to American Mainstream* (New Brunswick, NJ: Rutgers University Press, 2014), 46.

26. Ibid.

27. Donald Bogle, *Toms, Coons, Mulattoes, Mammies, and Bucks: An Interpretive History of Blacks in American Films* (New York: Viking Press, 1973), 27.

28. Ibid., 28–31.

29. Judith Weisenfeld, *Hollywood Be Thy Name: African American Religion in American Film, 1929–1949* (Berkeley: University of California Press, 2007), 22.

30. See, for example, reviews from the *New York Times* and *Variety* as cited in Bogle's *Toms, Coons*, 30. *Variety* reads: "Apparently in the massed ensemble groups, Vidor had a mighty tough job holding that bunch down, yet he held them under remarkable restraint and still brought out the effects desired."

31. "'Hearts of Dixie' Cast Entertained," *Chicago Defender*, March 23, 1929, 6; Alain Locke and Sterling A. Brown, "Folk Values in a New Medium," in *Black Films and Film-Makers: A Comprehensive Anthology from Stereotype to Superhero*, ed. Lindsay Patterson, 25–26 (New York: Dodd, Mead, 1975). See also Garcia's *Migration of Musical Film*, 57–58.

32. According to Desirée Garcia, "Entrepreneurs like E. C. Brown created their own films and built theaters in which to watch them free from discrimination. An advertisement recounted Brown's personal experience of being denied a seat at the Forrest Theater in Philadelphia. 'Disgusted, disheartened, and embittered,' he decided to erect 'a place of amusement where his people could have equal accommodation—a place where any respectable person could get what he paid for—a thing that legislation in the North, as well as the South, could not, or rather, would not enact.' " See "Douglas Amusement

162   BEHIND THE SCREEN

Corporation," in Johnson Negro Film Collection, Charles E. Young Research Library, University of California, Los Angeles.

33. Budgets were so sparse for these films that filming often was wrapped in ten days. Oscar Micheaux went so far as to recycle footage. I have located an example of Micheaux's using the exact same dance footage in *Ten Minutes to Live* (1932) and *The Girl from Chicago* (1932–33). In both films we see an awkward splicing of Arnold Wiley performing a tap dance solo with a Black chorus during a nightclub scene.

34. "Bojangles" was the name by which most Americans knew Robinson. While many stories exist for why he acquired the moniker, it likely was a reference to his reputation as a gambler as well as for the color of his skin.

35. Jon Cruz, *Culture on the Margins: The Black Spiritual and the Rise of American Cultural Interpretation*, Princeton Paperbacks (Princeton, NJ: Princeton University Press, 1999), 32.

36. "A Partial list of White and Negro individuals and corporations organized to produce Negro films," in Johnson Negro Film Collection, box 53, folder 32, Charles E. Young Research Library, University of California, Los Angeles.

37. Barbara Tepa Lupack, *Richard E. Norman and Race Filmmaking* (Bloomington: Indiana University Press, 2014), 10.

38. Cara Caddoo, *Envisioning Freedom: Cinema and the Building of Modern Black Life* (Cambridge, MA: Harvard University Press, 2014), 183.

39. James A. Snead, *White Screens, Black Images* (New York: Routledge, 1994).

40. Oscar Micheaux, *Darktown Revue* (1931; USA: Micheaux Film), Film. Micheaux's work often drew criticism from both the White and African American middle classes for its controversial material.

41. Roy Mack, *King for a Day* (June 30, 1934; USA: Warner Bros.), Film.

42. Sometimes White directors or producers were involved for financial, technical, or distribution backing. Another way these Black films distinguish themselves is that they are small production companies, unlike the major motion picture studios. See Paula J. Massood, *Black City Cinema: African American Urban Experiences in Film*, Culture and the Moving Image (Philadelphia: Temple University Press, 2003), 47.

43. Gerald R. Butters, *Black Manhood on the Silent Screen*, Culture America (Lawrence: University Press of Kansas, 2002), 124.

44. Arvid Gillstrom, *The Melancholy Dame* (February 2, 1929; USA: Christie Film Company), Film.

45. Harry A. Gant, *Georgia Rose* (September 20, 1930; USA: Aristo Films), Film.

46. Garcia, *Migration of Musical Film*, 70.

47. Oscar Micheaux, *The Exile* (May 16, 1931; USA: Micheaux Film), Film.

48. Irwyn Franklin, *Harlem Is Heaven* (May 27, 1932; USA: Lincoln Motion Picture Company), Film.

49. A subtext regarding the idea of the lighter-skinned chorus dancer is also embedded in these films. Jayna Brown reads these light-skinned showgirls as "ambivalently rendered figure[s]" who at once reference "urban pleasures and freedoms" and also stand in as symbols of White privilege, "of access and immoral desire and for African Americans' collusion in their own cultural contamination." See Jayna Brown, *Babylon*

PUBLIC WORKS AND ACCOLADES   163

Girls: Black Women Performers and the Shaping of the Modern (Durham, NC: Duke University Press, 2008), 195.

50. Roy Mack, *That's the Spirit* (April 15, 1933; USA: Warner Bros.), Film.

51. Moreland replaced Aubrey Lyles in the famous vaudeville act Miller and Lyles. The two of them transitioned from the Black stereotype of comic routines to a trickster idiom. Constance Valis Hill describes their characters as "a scheming city slicker and a feisty but gullible underdog. Constance Valis Hill, *Tap Dancing America: A Cultural History*. New York: Oxford University Press, 2010), 73.

52. For an excellent biography of LaRedd, see Valis Hill, *Tap Dancing America*, 92–93.

53. *An All-Colored Vaudeville Show* (June 22, 1935; USA: Warner Bros.), Film. Music by Harry Revel; lyrics by Mack Gordon; sung and tap danced by Adelaide Hall.

54. Another example of covert minstrelsy but not directly related to tap dancing appears in sonic form in RKO's short *Bubbling Over* (1934), where Ethel Waters sings Harold Spina's "Darkies Never Dream."

    Sometimes the references were not so covert: Skibo Productions (a studio known for producing "educational" films created *Slow Poke* (1933) featuring Stepin Fetchit in his typical role and the tap dancing of "Bunny and the Cotton Girls" ("Bunny" is referring to Bunny Briggs and the Cotton Girls go with individual credits). While I am not sure what is didactic about this plantation short, it certainly reinforces all kinds of stereotypes about Blackness and perpetuates the allegory of migration and contented rural slaves.

55. Dudley Murphy, *Black and Tan Fantasy* (December 8, 1929; USA: RKO Radio Pictures), Film.

56. Dudley Murphy, *The Sport Parade* (November 11, 1932; USA: RKO Radio Pictures), Film; Roy Mack, *Smash Your Baggage* (October 29, 1932; USA: Warner Bros.), Film.

57. I credit Brian Seibert for this astute observation in *What the Eye Hears: A History of Tap Dancing* (New York: Farrar, Straus and Giroux, 2015), 200–201.

58. Henry "Rubberlegs" Williams was an American blues and jazz singer, female impersonator, and dancer known for the rubber-like quality of his lower body. He was popular on the TOBA (Theater Owners Booking Association) vaudeville circuit and later became a regular at the Cotton Club performing with the Count Basie Orchestra, Fletcher Henderson, Chick Webb, and Charlie Parker. He achieved international fame after recording the vocals on Dizzy Gillespie's first recording of "Hot House" in 1945.

59. Josh Binney, *Hi De Ho* (May 9, 1947; USA: All American), Film.

60. There seems to be one consistent exception to this "rule" of omission, and this pertains to all-Black films made by large White studios that were strictly about music and dance. I am thinking specifically of films like Paramount's *A Bundle of Blues* (1933), which features the tap dancing of Florence Hill and Bessie Dudley, and Warner Bros.' *The Mills Rhythm Blue Band* (1934), which features the Three Dukes. Though not identified by name (Leslie "Bubba" Gaines, Arthur "Pye" Russell, and James "Hutch" Hudson), their act was listed in the credits.

61. Other examples include the lack of individuation in *On with the Show* (1929) which collectively names the Four Covans but does not identify each of them separately.

164 BEHIND THE SCREEN

They are Willie Covan, his wife Florence, his brother Dewey, and his brother's wife Carita Harbert. Another example of this is the omission of Johnny Taylor's and Clark Rutledge's names when they perform a spectacularly synchronized rhythm tap dance on stairs in Paramount's *Many Happy Returns* (1934). The same omission occurs a year later for their performance in *Music Is Magic* (1935).

62. Around 1890, Bill Robinson formed a street partnership with Al Jolson. Around 1892, Robinson became a pick, or pickaninnie for Mayme Remington, a famous French burlesque dancer who employed as many as fifteen picks per show including Eddie Rector and Toots Davis, to name just two. See James Haskins and N. R. Mitgang, *Mr. Bojangles: The Biography of Bill Robinson* (New York: William Morrow, 1988), 44.

63. The Keith and Orpheum circuits played the leading theaters highlighting White performers in blackface makeup and in special cases, "real" Black acts (Williams and Walker and Cooper and Robinson being two of the most famous couples). In 1914, Sherman Dudley established TOBA (Theater Owners Booking Association or "Tough on Black Asses") as an all-Black vaudeville union. While White vaudeville primarily toured the northern states and the west coast, TOBA performers played the racist southern states and were paid on a much lower pay scale than performers who found work within the White circuits. See Rusty Frank, *Tap!: The Greatest Tap Dance Stars and Their Stories, 1900–1955*, rev. ed. (New York: Da Capo Press, 1994), 37–38. Additionally, artists who toured with TOBA would have to conform to the racist rules of their patrons, which included entering through the service doors of the venues that booked them. While the establishment of a Black vaudeville circuit meant that more people of color could perform on the American stage, it also placed a serious divide between Black talent and White. Black performers who graced the White stage were the exception and even those exceptions had stringent rules. At this time the country had a "two-colored" rule, which stated that Black people were allowed to perform on the vaudeville stage only in pairs. See Haskins and Mitgang, *Bojangles*, 91.

64. *Denver Tribune* article published May 14, 1912.

65. To build up his client's visibility on the stage, Marty Forkins arranged to have him teach dance to a chorister of one of Chicago's top theaters. Thus, in addition to winning the audience over with his solo acts on smaller stages, Robinson made a name for himself with the Marigold Gardens choristers (two of whom were Ruth Etting and Joan Crawford) as dance instructor. He worked with these chorus girls for a year and continued performing on small Chicago stages and later other small stages across the Midwest.

Robinson gained more exposure when he started performing for the troops in 1917 when the United States entered World War I. Over the next year, Robinson continued to entertain both Black and White troops regardless of how he was treated. He accepted the poor treatment he received without complaint in the name of patriotism and in exchange for stage time and public recognition. See Haskins and Mitgang, *Bojangles*, 96–97.

66. The Palace Theater was one of the Keith Circuit's major venues, the "undisputed crown jewel of vaudeville theaters (one at which few Black performers appeared, and certainly not as singles)." Ibid, 99.

PUBLIC WORKS AND ACCOLADES   165

67. Marshall Winslow Stearns and Jean Stearns, *Jazz Dance: The Story of American Vernacular Dance* (New York: Da Capo Press, 1994), 179.

68. Some contention exists among tap historians and the origins of this stair dance. King Rastus Brown claims that he was utilizing stairs long before Robinson. Haskins notes that some vaudeville historians credit Al Leach and his Rosebuds as being the first to use stairs, while others cite the Whitney Brothers as the originators at Hyde Behman's theater in 1899. He also notes that Mack and Williams had three versions of a stair dance in 1915 and that Paul Morton and his wife Naomi Glass did a stair routine around the same year. Haskins and Mitgang, *Bojangles*, 100. Frances Nealy, who often performed the stair routine with Robinson claims to have learned the dance from Eddie Redmond. See Constance Valis Hill, Performing Arts Encyclopedia, Library of Congress, "Nealy, Francis," http://www.loc.gov/performingarts Tap Dance America, http://lcweb2.loc.gov/diglib/ihas/html/tda/tda-home.html,   accessed   October 27, 2022.

69. According to Haskins's account of this routine, a dancer by the name of Fred Stone borrowed the stair routine idea and sent Robinson a check for $1,500 along with an apology for impinging on his territory. Haskins and Mitgang, 101.

70. His bag of tricks included a signature skating step to stop-time, a scoot step, a jig-like crossover step, and a special Bojangles' Time Step.

71. Stearns and Stearns, *Jazz Dance*, 187.

72. Numerous Newspapers make such implications. One example from the *Pittsburgh Sun* reads: "Bill Robinson, not as black as the ace of spades, but a gentleman of color nevertheless" (*Pittsburgh Sun*, October 18, 1921). Another example can be seen in *The Rockford* (Illinois) *Republic*, which reads: "Bill Robinson does as many monkey shines as any colored performer" (*Republic*, November 29, 1921).

73. Haskins and Mitgang, *Bojangles*, 187.

74. Richard Watts for the *Herald Tribune* remarked, "This veteran tap dancer is one of the great artists of the modern stage and is worth in his unostentatious way several dozen of the Mary Wigmans, Charles Weidmans, Martha Grahams . . . who are more pompous in their determination to be Artists." Stearns and Stearns, *Jazz Dance*, 183.

75. Luther Reed, *Dixiana* (July 22, 1930; USA: RKO Radio Pictures), Film.

76. Massood, *Black City Cinema*, 46.

77. Arthur Knight, *Disintegrating the Musical* (Durham, NC: Duke University Press, 2002), 187, and Jane Feuer, *The Hollywood Musical*, 2nd ed. (Bloomington: Indiana University Press, 1982), 22–47.

78. Gerald Mast notes that this filming technique presents a problem for an all-Black cast backstage musical like *Stormy Weather*. He writes, "In the theatres where black acts perform, the camera deliberately avoids that previously unavoidable image of backstage musicals—shots of the audience enjoying the show, to remind us that we are in a theatre and the show is a success." This, he argues, would expose a major problem: Is this show intended for a Black audience, a White audience, or an integrated audience (and the integrated audience did not exist in 1943)? See Gerald Mast, *Can't Help Singin': The American Musical on Stage and Screen* (Woodstock, NY: Overlook, 1987), 232.

166 BEHIND THE SCREEN

79. Karl Hagstrom Miller, *Segregating Sound: Inventing Folk and Pop Music in the Age of Jim Crow*. Refiguring American Music (Durham, NC: Duke University Press, 2010) 5.

80. Many members of the Black community then began incorporating Foster's music into their repertoire. The Fisk Jubilee singers, for example, integrated several of his tunes beginning in the 1870s.

81. Du Bois writes, "The first is African music, the second Afro-American, while the third is a blending of Negro music with the music heard in the Foster land. The result is still distinctively Negro and the method of blending original, but the elements are both Negro and Caucasian. One might go further and find a fourth step in this development, where the songs of White America have been distinctively influenced by the slave songs or have incorporated whole phrases of Negro melody, as 'Swannee River' and 'Old Black Joe.' Side by side, too, with the growth has gone the debasements and imitations—the Negro 'minstrel' songs, many of the 'gospel' hymns, and some of the popular tunes labeled 'coon' songs,—a mass of music in which the novice may easily lose himself and never find the real Negro melodies." See W.E.B. Du Bois, *The Souls of Black Folk* (Cambridge, MA: Harvard University Press, 1903), 256.

82. Quoted in William W. Austin, *"Susanna," "Jeanie," and "The Old Folks at Home": The Songs of Stephen C. Foster from His Time to Ours* (New York: Macmillan, 1975), 300.

83. One form of proof we have that Robinson was not performing to these tunes earlier comes from an interview with his boyhood friend Lemmeul Eggleston; "Eggie" recalls some of the flak he received for dancing in blackface: "I was criticized so much about that play 'cause I used 'Old Black Joe.'" Haskins and Mitgang, *Bojangles*, 33.

84. Limehouse here is likely a reference to the district located in London's East End once associated with squalor.

85. Also known as "Just a Song at Twilight" composed by J. L. Molloy in 1884 with lyrics by G. Clifton Bingham.

86. Composed in 1917 by Lee S. Roberts with lyrics by Will J. Callahan. See Lee S. Roberts and J. Will Callahan, "Smiles" (1918). *Historic Sheet Music Collection*, 1684, https://digitalcommons.conncoll.edu/sheetmusic/1684.

87. Edwin L. Marin, *Everybody Sing* (February 4, 1938; USA: Metro-Goldwyn Mayer), Film.

88. Spike Lee's satire of minstrelsy, *Bamboozled* (2001), would be a more contemporary example of a minstrel show-within-a-show.

89. Cliff Hess wrote this song specifically for *King for a Day*.

90. Rudolf Ising, *Toyland Broadcast* (December 22, 1934; USA: Harman-Ising Productions), Film; Connie Rasinski, *Mississippi Swing* (February 7, 1939; USA: Terrytoons), Film; Friz Freleng, *Fresh Hare* (August 22, 1942; USA: Leon Schlesinger Studios), Film.

91. Robyn Stillwell, "Black Voices, White Women's Tears, and the Civil War in Classical Hollywood Movies," *19th Century Music* 40, no. 1 (2016): 60.

92. Raoul Walsh, *Going Hollywood* (December 22, 1933; USA: Metro Goldwyn-Mayer), Film.

93. Roshanak Khesthi, *Modernity's Ear: Listening to Race and Gender in World Music* (New York: New York University Press, 2016), 86.

PUBLIC WORKS AND ACCOLADES 167

94. *George White's Scandals* (March 16, 1934; USA: Fox Film Corporation), Film.
95. Music and lyrics by Irving Caesar.
96. Victor Fleming and George Cukor, *Gone with the Wind* (January 17, 1940; USA: Metro Goldwyn-Mayer), Film; James Fitzpatrick, *Memories and Melodies* (February 16, 1935; USA: Metro Goldwyn-Mayer), Film.
97. Marv Goldberg, R&B Notebooks—4 BLACKBIRDS, http://www.uncamarvy.com/RedCaps/redcaps.html, accessed January 23, 2021.
98. George Marshall, *In Old Kentucky* (November 28, 1935; USA: Fox Film Corporation), Film; David Butler, *The Littlest Rebel* (December 27, 1935; USA: Twentieth Century Fox), Film; David Butler *The Little Colonel* (February 22, 1935; USA: Fox Film Corporation), Film.
99. Azizi Powell, "Bill 'Bojangles' Robinson–His Nickname and His Stair Dance," *Pancocojams*, January 10, 2013.
100. Bogle, *Toms, Coons*, 45.
101. Patricia Turner argues that White filmmakers scripted all parts of these films and that the relationship between Temple and Robinson was modeled after the Little Eva/Uncle Tom team, which the public adored. (Bogle cites Robinson as a "cool-eyed Tom"). Turner writes, "With laws against miscegenation on the books in many states, the match between Shirley Temple and Bill Robinson was the only one that would be tolerated." See Turner's *Ceramic Uncles and Celluloid Mammies: Black Images and Their Influence on Culture* (New York: Anchor Books, 1994), 83.
102. Directors of *The Little Colonel* wrote Robinson's famed stair dance into the script; it was Robinson's responsibility to figure out how to get Temple involved. He realized that to teach her how to tap well in just a few short days would be impossible, so he taught her how to make the "necessary extra-tapper-step sound" by teaching her how to kick the staircase. Temple had to keep her tap steps small and precise and "must always tap the riser instead of trying to get the same effect on the step itself." See Haskins and Mitgang, *Bojangles*, 225–26.

    The resulting sound was that of two tappers working together to create a complex rhythm. Temple believed that she was mastering everything Robinson gave her. In her autobiography she writes, "We made an unusual couple. A raggedy urchin with tousled curls paired with a regal black man . . . every sound matched, every gesture, the scuffle, the staccato tap . . . the smile on my face was not acting." She saw herself in stark physical contrast to Bill Robinson, but also as his dancing equal. See Shirley Temple Black, *Child Star: An Autobiography* (New York: McGraw-Hill, 1988), 92.
103. "Shirley Temple at Best; Robinson Big Help," *Hollywood Reporter* (Hollywood, CA), November 19, 1935.
104. Matthew Morrison, "The Sound(s) of Subjection: Constructing American Popular Music and Racial Identity through Blacksound," *Women & Performance: A Journal of Feminist Theory* 27, no. 1 (2017): 18.
105. Christopher Lehman, *The Colored Cartoon: Black Representation in American Animated Short Films, 1907-1954* (Amherst: University of Massachusetts Press, 2007), 16–17.
106. When Hollywood cast Robinson it was well aware of what was at stake: Winfield Sheehan of Fox said, "There is nothing, absolutely nothing, calculated to raise the

168   BEHIND THE SCREEN

gooseflesh on the back of an audience more than that of a White girl in relation to Negroes"; this was known as the "gooseflesh" theory. Hollywood in effect, grafts the "sub" onto Robinson. See Black, *Child Star*, 90.

107. bell hooks, "Eating the Other: Desire and Resistance," in *Eating Culture*, ed. Ron Scapp and Brian Seitz, 182 (Albany: State University of New York Press, 1998).

108. Interesting to note here are the racial distinctions made by Temple in her autobiography. Even though she claims that she and Robinson were the best of friends, her description of Robinson is notable: "The first thing I noted was the way his arms and legs moved with a silky muscular grace. He was square-jawed and shiny cheeked, his great round eyes showing whites all around. I was instantly attracted." See Frank, *Tap!*, 90. Though ultimately describing an attraction, Temple chronicles it in terms of the ways she notices their physical differences, somehow proving that opposites attract—or at least provide something attractive for their audience.

109. Fred Moten, *In the Break: The Aesthetics of the Black Radical Tradition* (Minnesota: Minnesota University Press, 2003), 172–73.

110. Hagstrom Miller, *Segregating Sound*, 11.

111. Monty Banks, *The Musical Beauty Shop* (June 1, 1930; UK/USA: Andre Charlot Productions), Film.

112. While I am isolating Bill Robinson, a similar phenomenon can be traced in the previous century with William Henry Lane, while Savion Glover operates similarly in the twenty-first century.

113. William Pietz, "The Problem of the Fetish I." *Res*, no. 9 (Spring 1985): 13.

114. Robinson himself became a commodity. Dance manuals would sell their tap lessons by explaining that you could get feet as fast as Bill Robinson and would often insert his caricatured image on their covers.

115. Hugh Harman, *Old Mill Pond* (March 7, 1936; USA: Harman-Ising Productions), Film; Walter Lang, *Hooray for Love* (June 14, 1935; USA: RKO Radio Pictures), Film.

116. Pietz, "The Problem of the Fetish I," 5–17.

117. Jean Baudrillard, *For a Critique of the Political Economy of the Sign*, trans. Charles Levin (St. Louis: Telos Press, 1981), 90.

118. Walter Benjamin and J. A Underwood, *The Work of Art in the Age of Mechanical Reproduction* (London: Penguin, 2008).

119. Ibid.

120. Emily Apter, *Feminizing the Fetish: Psychoanalysis and Narrative Obsession in Turn-of-the-Century France* (Ithaca, NY: Cornell University Press, 1991), 14.

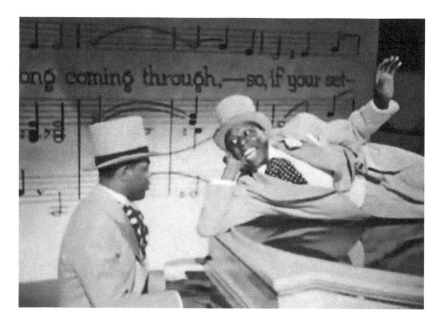

FIGURE 3.4 Ford Lee "Buck" Washington and John "Bubbles" Sublett perform a song and dance medley in *Varsity Show*, 1937. (Private collection)

PUBLIC WORKS AND ACCOLADES   171

HAVE YOU GOT ANY CASTLES?

From the Warner Bros. Production
"VARSITY SHOW"

Lyrics by
Johnny Mercer

Music by
Richard A. Whiting

Moderato (not too slowly)

Two men peek out from behind an oversized sheet of music singing the same lyrics that appear on the page: "Love is on the air to-night . . ." The taller of the two then appears at the top of the stage, one leg stretched in the air, arms out like wings. The brass and woodwinds of the orchestra beneath accompany John Bubbles's slide down the winding ramp, descending the scale,

as the dancer gradually makes his way to stage level, punctuating his journey with a dive onto the piano where his longtime partner Buck, on keys, is playing and awaiting his arrival. As Bubbles sings "Have you got any castles you want me to build?," Buck promptly scats in response to each line of the song. Bubbles leaps off the piano and steadily carries on with the song as he adds his

rhythmically full tap dancing, first standing, and then from a seated position alongside Buck. Bubbles then energetically springs up and continues his signature rhythm tap dancing while taking up an impressive portion of the stage. The two performers vocally harmonize for a few bars before Bubbles, once again, climbs onto the piano's surface which has been coated in

the synthetic plastic, polyoxybenzylmethylenglycolanhydride for an extra spectacular shine. The next thirty-two bars of stop time that follow allow Bubbles to show off a series of unique time steps. His reflection in the shiny Bakelite floor adds a layer of glamour, but when the camera zooms in for an extreme close-up of Buck percussively shining Bubbles's tap shoes, one

gets a glimpse of just how easily this covering tarnishes. "On with the dance, let the melody be mellow, Let me put a spell over you, and meeee." *The two performers switch places—Bubbles on piano and Buck now upright doing an eccentric tap dance, offering contrast to the style of his partner. In an oversized suit and a series of pendulum-like slides, Buck recites a rubber leg*

style popular to comedy acts of the era. Bubbles jumps up for the final 16 bars of this musical medley and the two dance in an almost spooning-like position, singing and dancing in perfect unison.

Copyright MCMXXXVII by HARMS Inc. New York

9-741-4   *International Copyright Secured*   *Made in USA*

FIGURE 4.1 Ann Sothern, George Murphy, Ethel Merman, and Eddie Cantor sing "Mandy" with the Goldwyn Girls (including a very young Lucille Ball) in *Kid Millions*, 1934. (Photo by United Artists/Getty Images)

4

Bon Homage

Female Figures, the Tribute Guise, and Pre-War Departures, 1934–1939

I want to be a minstrel man

. . .

I want to dance just like a dandy[1]

A thirteen-year-old Harold Nicholas dressed in a white top hat and tails opens the S.S. Luxor's "Minstrel Night" en route to Egypt. The well-known tap dancer's smile is so infectious that it is hard not to take his words at face value. Soon after Harold greets his audience, four Goldwyn Girls appear dressed in sparkling top hats and the 1930s feminine version of a sequined tuxedo. An extreme close-up of the four reveals uniformly flawless red lipstick, perfect white teeth, pristine sausage curls, and a very young Lucille Ball. The girls sing a slightly revised version of Harold's lyrics: "The way he dances sure is dandy, and sings a song about his sugar candy," modifying Harold's romanticizing of blackface into a narrative of romance. The subsequent long shot reveals the risqué nature of this 1934 wardrobe, an interesting juxtaposition to the adolescent Nicholas brother who performs a jazz tap solo downstage. The women flirt with their eyes and Harold with his feet. In many ways, this intro is an inversion of the Shirley Temple/Bill Robinson dynamic, with the highly visible age discrepancy quietly justifying the shared performance space of Black and White dancers, something neither the Nicholas Brothers nor the Goldwyn Girls have done to date. The choreography picks up as do the number of references to the minstrel stage. A cutaway shot reveals another close-up of a Goldwyn Girl masking her face with a tambourine. The screen "cracks" and reveals the whole ensemble assembled on bleachers typical of the twentieth-century minstrel stage. The Girls incorporate their tambourines into the choreography as they continue to sing "We've always loved a minstrel man." The music slows. Two Goldwyn Girls come to center stage and synchronously announce: "Ladies and Gentleman: Introducing our interlocuter, Mr. Jerry Lane." Jerry Lane (George Murphy) enters at the top of the bleachers, removes

Behind the Screen. Brynn W. Shiovitz, Oxford University Press. © Oxford University Press 2023.
DOI: 10.1093/oso/9780197553091.003.0005

his top hat and introduces the next entertainer without pause: "Presenting Mrs. Edward Wilson Sr." Ethel Merman enters stage left in a bright white tuxedo. "Mr. Edward Wilson Jr." Eddie Cantor in a bright white tuxedo and blackface enters stage right. The Girls rattle their tambourines like a drumroll. "Ladies and Gentleman, Beeeeeee Seated."

Despite the industry's enforcement of the Code beginning in 1934, it became common for Hollywood to recreate the minstrel show-within-a-show; this reenactment from *Kid Millions* (1934) is just one example. Restaging the minstrel show served several functions: first, it was an obvious solution to continuing the tradition of blackface performance despite the Code's rules surrounding the representation of other "races and creeds." It also reiterated old formulas within a modern context. Situating the male interlocuter amid a "troupe" of sexualized women took the focus off minstrelsy's racial implications and instead made the female body the focus. It protected the idea that Black men were a "powerful cultural sign of sexuality" as nineteenth-century minstrel skits and songs preached.[2] But rather than presenting lyrics and phallic imagery through caricatures of the Black male—for example, the use of coat tails, sticks, or poles that were "strategically placed near the groin"[3]—White male spectators were encouraged to indulge in White heteronormative fantasies of female sexuality through the Goldwyn Girls' proximity to Blackness vis-à-vis the minstrel show-within-a-show. In many ways it echoes what the gum ad did in "Puttin' on the Ritz" but does so with real human flesh and overt expressions of masking. Furthermore, in following the minstrel show format of popular song, *olio* (variety), and *afterpiece* (which usually included slapstick and tap dancing)—a structure established by the Christy Minstrels almost 100 years earlier—the minstrel show-within-a-show reminded audiences of America's roots, prompting them to continue associating things like tap dance with the blackface mask.

The Production Code changed little between 1934 and 1954, but it was more strictly enforced during this period than in previous years or years following. The remainder of this book looks closely at films produced during this *enforced* period. This chapter specifically examines the covert practices that surfaced in the late 1930s as a consequence of the authoritative measures that emerged around the time *Millions* was made. We can ascribe some of the shifts in content that occurred in the late 1930s to the broader historical context out of which these films were produced. In some cases, particular causes and/or organizations protested non-White actors taking certain belittling roles. Civil rights organizations, for example, objected to Bill Robinson playing the servant and Hattie McDaniel playing the mammy figure. By World War II, groups such as the National Association for the Advancement of Colored People (NAACP) began fighting for less racist roles. Some White people with high visibility (e.g., the 1940 Republican nominee for president, Wendell Willkie) also helped to influence these shifts by arguing that racial stereotypes were not only demeaning but that they were oppositional to the war effort.[4] But the few years between the Code's adoption and the beginning of World War II mark for Hollywood a meaningful relationship to Blackness.

As fewer Black entertainers signed on to play racialized archetypes, narratives began to shift. Rather than a Black character breaking into song or dance (e.g., Robinson as the butler spontaneously performing a stair dance), it became more popular to see jazz and nightclub scenes featuring cameos by lesser-known Black artists performing solos, duos, and trios.[5] These short sketches by Black artists in otherwise White films were fairly popular in 1936 and 1937. By 1938 most of these small acts found the majority of their work in Harlem at the Apollo,[6] and we do not see their Hollywood return until roughly 1941.[7] Moreover, these performers often went uncredited. As these novelty acts started to fade from the screen, a noticeable rise in the presence of White tap dancers using blackface emerged. Such blackface tap dance routines took on bit parts in a manner similar to those performed by Black dancers in that they served no narrative function; furthermore their blackface required that audiences see the tap dance as a walk-on—or "dance-on"—inserted as auxiliary and for sheer entertainment. One reason for this auxiliary status might be attributable to changing race relations between the Harlem Riot in 1935 and the time America entered the Second World War.[8] The tribute narrative allowed Hollywood to make this transition more covertly by shifting the definition of "interracial" on set through a series of narrative and visible references to Blackness.

Between 1936 and 1939 we see a rise and peak of the *tribute guise* as the dominant mode of covert minstrelsy in screen performance. The tribute guise involves someone using the "tribute" label in conjunction with burnt cork and various stereotypes within an integrated backstage musical to convince the audience that their makeup merely acknowledges a historical moment or honors a particular individual; it is central to this chapter as well as to Hollywood's steadfast desire to preserve century-old ties between the blackface mask and tap dancing. Not only did tributes provide an exemption from the Code in matters of blatant blackface, but they also gave directors and animators carte blanche to display themes that threatened to "lower moral

176 BEHIND THE SCREEN

standards." By presenting racial caricature under the pretext of a "tribute," Hollywood invited audiences to read blackface as something unifying and patriotic rather than differentiating and shameful.

Whether or not the purpose of the tribute was to obscure Hollywood's use of blackface is less important than the idea that such a behavior supports: using blackface to pay tribute implies that the *only* way to honor a Black dancer is to highlight race as his most discernible—and interesting—feature, even when the honored performer boasts a surplus of mannerisms, idiosyncrasies, and props that could easily stand in for his person. This chapter unpacks the role that tributes play within a larger framework of covert minstrelsy while also locating the ways in which race figured into Hollywood's narrative of tap dance. The tribute guise not only aided in sneaking blackface past the censor; perhaps more important, it assisted in the general remapping of Africanist sensibilities onto White bodies.

Finally, tribute performances often occur "in-transit." The so-called transit narrative will surface from this point forward, both in relation to the tribute guise and the Bill Robinson effect, and it will figure prominently in films that utilize brownface as a gradation of blackface. While the intrinsic liminality of tribute performances is by no means the focus of this chapter, I chart those performances that occur between "here" and "there." At this juncture Powell's "passage," between the American mainland and the Hawaiian Island in *Honolulu* serves a crucial function in the appropriation of Black aesthetics. Her "Tribute to Bill Robinson" performed en route at once removes a Black presence from the mainland and strategically situates her blackface nowhere. Performing blackface while passing from one place to another suspends America's dominant values and disturbs—albeit temporarily—the very structure of the Production Code.

> *"Mr. Interlocuter, there's a little somethin' I wanna ask you,"*
> *announces Cantor, the end man.*
> *"If you insult me just once more, I'll have you taken right ashore."*
> *"Oh you make a prose, don't you?"*
> *"Prose, why don't even know the difference between prose, and poetry."*
> *"Who don't?"*
> *"You don't. Look I'll show you . . . if I said to you, poor little Annette she Fell in the water and got all wet, that would be poetry. But if I said to you poor little Annette she fell in the water and got soaked, that would be prose, do you see?"*
> *"Oh that's easy, I can do that."*

"You can?"

*"Well of course, look.: poor little Annette fell down the well, she got to the bottom
and went straight to—-. What do you want? Prose or poetry?"*

Ensemble on cue: "A ha ha ha ha ha ha ha ha ha."

In typical minstrel fashion, this minstrel show-within-a-show proceeds with the evening's *olio*, a variety of comedy and song. Because there was nothing audibly vulgar about Eddie Cantor's retorts in the above dialogue—after all, he omitted the word "hell," which according to the Catholic church at this time would have been a profane use of the word—this segment passed Code regulations. The hyper-visibility of Cantor's blackface seems to be justified by the context. Since this is more of a *citation* of minstrelsy—as we saw in chapter 3—rather than a real minstrel production, the MPPA turned a blind eye. But this performance becomes even more complex in the next scene when Cantor breaks into song. "Mandy," perhaps the film's most well-known song and dance number, bears a set of complicated ties to the minstrel stage.

Irving Berlin originally wrote "Mandy" for the army-themed musical revue *Yip Yip Yaphank* (1918), which followed the format of a traditional minstrel show and offers some clues as to why the MPPA may have vindicated Cantor's blackface *in Kid Millions*. The song was designed as a cakewalking marriage proposal to be performed in blackface by hairy-chested men in drag. "Mandy" did not become a hit, however, until a year later as part of a ten-minute minstrel segment of the *Ziegfeld Follies of 1919*. Cantor and Bert Williams in blackface opened the segment (as end men), Gus Van and Joe Schenck (Van and Schenck) then sang "Mandy" as part of the first act finale—known as "The Follies Minstrel"—alongside forty-five shimmying choristers known as "The Follies Pickaninnies." Marilyn Miller simultaneously performed a tribute tap dance to the famous Irish soft- shoe dancer George Primrose.[9] The song resurfaced fifteen years later in *Kid Millions* and then nine years after that in a World War II film, *This is the Army*.[10] The performance was similar to its original staging in *Yip Yip Yaphank*, but the blatant use of blackface was removed.[11] The number made its final appearance in Michael Curtiz's *White Christmas* (1954). The tuxedoes and tambourines remained in this version, but the blackface did not make the cut. With or without the use of blackface however, "Mandy's" very aurality signifies the minstrel stage. I return to this song's sonic guising in *This is the Army* and

178   BEHIND THE SCREEN

White Christmas at a later point, but the hyper-visible ties "Mandy" has to the blackface mask are what interest me here.

As I explored in chapter 2, Cantor's image in the 1930s was indelibly tied to the blackface mask. In fact, very rarely did Cantor perform without the use of burnt cork and many movie theater-goers at this time might have found it alienating to see the comedian onstage sans makeup. It was as if blackface had been written into his stage and screen persona and wearing the mask was him "being himself." A good example of this can be seen in *The Great Ziegfeld* (1936) wherein the actor (Buddy Doyle) playing Cantor in one of the film's shows-within-a-show sings the song "If You Knew Susie" in blackface.[12] "If You Knew Susie" was one of Cantor's signature songs, but there is no evidence to suggest that he performed this number in blackface. The original sheet music for the song has Cantor without blackface on the cover. Publishers made sure to include Cantor's blackfaced image on the covers of signature songs he performed with cork. Furthermore, Cantor performed this very song in a 1948 film by the same name without the use of blackface, suggesting that this was one routine he did without makeup. That Buddy Doyle performs this song in blackface in *The Great Ziegfeld* is significant in that it demonstrates just how tied the performance of Cantor was to the minstrel mask.

Doyle's tribute to Cantor as an illustration of the tribute guise captures a few key elements of the tribute phenomenon that distinguish it from the citational guise: first, the use of a song that is inextricably linked to the performer being honored; second, the use of physical mannerisms and choreography that are recognizable as belonging to the honoree, third, utilizing particular costume and makeup that ostensibly say something about the tributee's character; finally an announcement by name of the performer being indicated, either verbally or as text. All four of these must be present to constitute a tribute, in contrast to the citational guise which only requires one of the first three from this list. In the above example Doyle's blackface mask reinforces the fact that this is a tribute to Cantor and not someone else who might have, at some point, performed this song. Yet, I would classify the blackface mask as an auxiliary element because despite Cantor's relationship to the mask, all these other elements (as well as some other textual and narrative clues not mentioned here) signify un-mistakenly that *Ziegfeld's* intended tribute (vis-à-vis director Leonard) is to *the* Eddie Cantor. We see this event repeat itself verbatim in *The Eddie Cantor Story* which Warner Bros. released in 1953. Tributes to Cantor such as these emphasize the performer's intrinsic relationship to the blackface mask and offer insight into the strategies which Goldwyn, and other studios of the early-mid 1930s, used to justify Cantor's continued use of blackface during the Code years. Thus, Cantor's blackface makes an appearance in *The Great Ziegfeld* and *The Eddie Cantor Story* even when no makeup was necessitated, underscoring this performance as not merely one of citation but in fact one that reinforces the idea that race—and, in this instance, Cantor's Whiteness accentuated by his relationship to blackface—is his most iconic feature.

> *The pace of the S.S. Luxor's minstrel show picks up during the grand finale of "Mandy." George Murphy, Ann Sothern, and Ethel Merman exit the stage making room for Cantor's tap solo. The Nicholas Brothers quickly rescue the amateur hoofer, offering flashy over-the-tops to distract the audience from Cantor's double basic time step. Harold then steals the stage for 8 bars while Cantor keeps time with his right foot. Harold's hand signals in his brother Fayard, but Cantor misinterprets this gesture as a sign to begin his double basic time step again. Harold scolds Cantor, putting his hand on Cantor's arm to stop. Fayard ends his show-stopping solo with a split and a gesture similar to Harold's; once again Cantor misinterprets the cue and Fayard places his hand on Cantor's abdomen to keep him from moving. Harold picks up his next 8 bars with a series of trenches and slides and this time resorts to grabbing Cantor by both legs and squeezing them to prevent Cantor from tap dancing. This level of physical contact between Black and White performers is astounding. When Fayard completes his 8 bars, the Brothers gesture at Cantor, who then takes this as his exit cue. The Brothers finish off their routine with an impressive series of toe stands before finally making their exit. The all-female chorus continues singing on the bleachers, slowly moving into the final formation. They all, in unison, cover their faces with tambourines. The four leads emerge from the clump of percussive masks and the final shot is a close-up of Eddie Cantor in his blackface. He rolls his eyes and accentuates his lips. Audiences will not forget this image: Cantor's identity dissolves, allowing the skin of America's past to re-emerge under the auspices of modern celluloid expression.*

While I would in no way classify Eddie Cantor's performance alongside the Nicholas Brothers in *Kid Millions* (1934) as an example of the tribute guise, a few elements of this trio demonstrate an overarching shift in racial representation—and specifically that of physical contact between Black and

180 BEHIND THE SCREEN

White dancers—that occurred between 1934 and 1936, the year in which the tribute guise surfaces. However, this "mixed race" performance also models several elements that remain constants in the tribute formula; these are worth discussing. One of the most visible shifts between Cantor's performance alongside the Nicholas Brothers and performances like Fred Astaire's "Bojangles of Harlem" (1936) and Powell's "Tribute to Bill Robinson" (1939), which I discuss at length, is the former's juxtaposition of Black artists alongside corked White performers. As discussed in chapter 3, this shift begins with the rise of Robinson, his refusal to wear burnt cork, and the interracial pairing of him and Shirley Temple. Robinson and Temple's relationship represents something much more complicated than a kind of surface level race mixing that was important for the White American narrative in 1934–1935. Their onscreen relationship acts as a stepping stone between the kind of race mixing we see in Cantor films of the *pre-enforced* Code era (1930–1934) and the tributes we see between 1936 and 1939.

Tap dance of this latter period saw a decline in popularity of Black actors on the White stage and a peak in White tap dancers performing a rhythm tap style popular among African American hoofers of this era. This is not to say that strong Black rhythm tap dancers disappeared from the screen altogether but instead to note that their "appearances" were sparse and often surrogated.[13] Thus, with the disappearance of Bill Robinson (the person) on the screen came a rise in rhythm tap, rarely executed by the people who "invented" and refined the style performed by these dancers' White protégés in so-called tributes.[14] Through this evolution from White men in blackface dancing alongside Black tap dancers to White rhythm tap dancers "paying tribute" to Black tap vis-à-vis rhythm tap performances dedicated to Robinson, we see how the Bill Robinson effect plays out in tap dance performances of the late 1930s. We also observe how such performances qualify the use of blackface as narratively and theatrically necessary. The tribute label in effect distracts White audiences from seeing the ways in which Hollywood separated a complex rhythmic aesthetic from Black people by re-introducing certain rhythmic sensibilities through White people in blackface.

The Tribute Guise Exposed

Understanding how the blackface mask is used in these tributes is crucial to considering the mechanisms at play in covert minstrelsy and in seeing that it dates back to Cantor's application in *Millions*. The performance is only part of the tribute. How the dance is framed through its *mise-en-place* and *mise-en-scène* are crucial to the tribute's success as a covert means of concealing a much more entrenched narrative of appropriation. The visible act of "putting in place" the blackface makeup as well as an allusion to its removal is something that all tribute performances share. Prior to "Mandy," the camera cuts "behind the scenes" where a Black butler holds a dish of black paint while Cantor smears it on his face. "This is tough to put on," Cantor says, "and take off." (*Pause*) "You know, you're lucky," he continues. Framing his performance this way emphasizes the costume-like nature of his Blackness, which stands in contrast to the permanence of the butler's racialized subjectivity. We will see a similar move leading up to Fred Astaire's tribute to Bill Robinson in *Swing Time* (1936) where he hums the "Bojangles of Harlem" tune while masking his face. Eleanor Powell, too, dons blackface in a backstage mirror before her big tribute in *Honolulu*.[15] In front of her sits a black mannequin head, foreshadowing the doppelgänger that will soon be her own corked face. In all three of these performances (and countless others), a certain level of transparency about the makeup itself serves an important function. Michael Rogin has noted a common thread in almost all blackface musicals wherein the camera or stage exposes the performer putting on blackface, an event he refers to as the "primal scene." Transparency consequently helps to define the act of "becoming" Black, where the act of masking itself becomes a spectacle.[16] This explains why films that contain blackface performed by Black actors rarely, if ever, show the performers donning makeup; this would risk rupturing the fallacy of "Black" authenticity.[17] By showing White performers applying the blackening agent, by exposing the fiction behind the mask, the makeup acts as a fetish.[18] The blackface performance, when stripped down and presented as costume, makes it clear that the person donning this mask is still in control. A White person who chooses to "become Black" in the context of a performance distinguishes the person who must perform in blackface to find work from the person who chooses to "black up" for fun. To show the process of "blacking up" is to deny the existence of (real) Black people and to avow Blackness as a role that can be played by others; the Black person as character fashions it as substitutable. Thus, when a tribute begins with the performance of blacking up, the performance that follows necessarily disavows the subjectivity of the one it seeks to honor. In the process, as in all facets of covert minstrelsy, what is really being masked is a conflation of blackface with real lived Black experience and the alleged fungibility of the Black body.

182   BEHIND THE SCREEN

Such narrative framing also serves an important role in the efficacy of covert forms like the tribute guise. Both the introduction—whether as visible or verbal announcement—and the performance's location help to distinguish the tribute guise from other forms of blackface performance. Like the sign that introduces the big minstrel show-within-a-show as part of the S.S. *Luxor*'s "Minstrel Night," or even Harold Nicholas's preamble to "I Want to Be a Minstrel Man," Fred Astaire's and Eleanor Powell's performances are framed by very strategic announcements. Furthermore, most of these performances take place "in transit" and specifically on a ship transporting American mainlanders to "exotic" locations. In the case of *Millions*, Cantor performs in transit to Egypt, and in *Honolulu*, Powell performs in transit to Hawaii. That these performances occur between "here" and "there" is not coincidental.[19] Blackface performances that exist in this liminal space gesture at Hollywood's ambivalence around such racial representation but also raise the question of whether it was easier for blackface to bypass the Code when its use occurred off American soil. Performing such routines in transit is similar to being in the mythical kingdom where certain events occur "nowhere"—that is, nowhere real—and it liberates Hollywood from some of the Code's restrictions. But the transit narrative is not the only mode of distraction that operates in tandem with the tribute guise. To better understand this facet of covert minstrelsy it would be helpful to further distinguish the tribute from other guises.

Several things distinguish the "tribute" from typical performances of blackface and all other iterations of these forms. While all sorts of homages to famous singers and dancers exist in Hollywood films of this era, not all tributes are examples of the tribute guise, even if they do constitute examples of racial masquerading. The narrative within which these tributes exist is primary: all of my examples of tributes exist within an *integrated* backstage musical. That is, these shows are all about producing a final show/showcase, and/or about the life of someone in showbiz. These shows are *integrated* insofar as their blackface routines are auxiliary to the plot's overarching narrative. The mask is neither necessary nor ancillary; it just exists. Because the mask ostensibly pays homage to Black (or "Native") culture, its use is "appropriate" and satisfies the bounds of the Code. Such framing allows the blackface mask to be used to *incorporate* Black culture at the same time it appropriates its contributions to American entertainment. In doing so, it justifies the disappearance of "real" Black people in favor of a *representation* of Blackness.

The use of tap dance within these narratives is also significant in that tap dance as an art form was built on a premise of "stealing and sharing."[20] While numerous concert works have been inspired by a Western modern dance canon—and perhaps even labeled "tributes"—it is the classification of tap dance as a Black vernacular tradition that makes it more vulnerable to copyright infringement/appropriation. As Anthea Kraut has noted, because such traditions are "not only collectively created, orally transmitted, and improvisational," and also "make regular use of 'signifyin'" or intertextual techniques," their form conflicts with American copyright.[21] This is not to say that Black vernacular dancers in America had no rules surrounding theft in the early twentieth century. Many clubs had uncodified or "unofficial" rules by which dancers were expected to abide. As Marshall and Jean Stearns recount, the Hoofer's club—a major hangout on Seventh Avenue (between 131st and 132nd) in Harlem for tap dancers in the 1920s and 1930s—had an unwritten law: "Thou Shalt Not Copy Another's Steps—Exactly." The Stearns write, "You could imitate anyone inside the club, and it was taken as a compliment. But you must not do so professionally, that is in public and for pay. If and when your act appeared on the stage . . . your routine must be notably different."[22] Thus, while the tap tradition might not have lent itself naturally to official copyright laws, these dancers were acutely aware of intellectual property and had alternative systems in place.[23] Ironically, Bill Robinson was one of the few tap dancers of this era who "developed unofficial ways of licensing their material."[24] His (Black) contemporaries knew his stair dance belonged to him and made sure to secure his consent through either a handshake or by monetary means before performing it.[25] I suggest that this unofficial licensure necessitated a combination of labeling future renditions of Robinson's stair dance "tributes" *and* wearing a blackface mask. Robinson's rendition of the stair dance performed by White tap dancers in blackface would surface in several Hollywood films over the next decade under the guise of a tribute.

Bojangles, the King of Harlem

Fred Astaire's "Bojangles of Harlem" in the film *Swing Time* (1936) is the earliest example of the tribute guise I have been able to locate. It is the only routine in the film that serves no narrative function; all of the other songs/ dances are duly motivated by the plot. As previously mentioned, the performance begins backstage with Astaire blacking up; the notion that Astaire is merely "trying on" Blackness is unmistakable from the beginning. Because scholars have already written exhaustively on this particular performance—generally in the context of excusing the blackface component in virtue of the era and the fact that this number was exemplary in choreography and film technology—I highlight the elements that exemplify the Bill Robinson effect and the tribute guise.[26]

While the title alone indicates a flattering reference to the famous Bill Robinson, the song's lyrics—sung by twenty-four White chorus dancers—announce Robinson as the president of Harlem and then proceed to frame Harlem as the center of "hot" music, gambling, and truancy.[27] Harlemites, according to the song, know Bojangles's beat better than they know the president of the United States. In fact, they are ready to gamble on him, his beat is so infectious.

> *Brother, you go and bet all your dough!*
> · · ·
> *Tough guys rumba out of poolrooms*
> *And kids start "truckin'" out of schoolrooms!*
> · · ·

Few historians have commented on the lyric aspect of this song, but the narrative these lyrics tell offers an important scaffold for my analysis and is one of the many layers of masking involved in this performance of covert minstrelsy.

This song stands in stark contrast to the soundtrack for the rest of the film. Despite the picture's title, the *swing* rhythm rarely surfaces. It appears briefly during syncopated sections of the "Waltz in Swing Time" wherein phrases in double meter are laid over the waltz's natural triple meter, but beyond that, "Bojangles of Harlem" is the only decidedly syncopated number. The generally energetic tune is accentuated by jazz-oriented countermelodies and cyclic vamps that modulate chromatically.[28] This gives the song an overall syncopated feel while still satisfying Jerome Kern's older sensibilities. According to John Mueller, Astaire convinced Hal Borne to compose these vamps during rehearsal without consulting Kern. He notated them in the sheet music as "Jig Piano Dance," implying a desire to communicate a certain "Black music" feel during Astaire's solo dance sections.[29]

The lyrics further establish this *feel* by association—*Bojangles of Harlem; You dance such hot stuff!*—the "hot" in this context referring to swung rhythms. Music scholar Todd Decker has analyzed the significance of the code words "hot," "swing," and "jazz," in Astaire films of the 1930s and early 1940s, a lexicon he claims insinuated "improvised, highly syncopated music, and music making" which carried connotations of a Black musical aesthetic.[30] He writes, "*hot* meant fast tempos and improvised virtuoso solos; it was the opposite of sweet arranged music of a more sedate kind, slower in tempo, lower in volume, and without standout soloists."[31] The "hot rhythms" in "Bojangles of Harlem" are further underscored by mentioning the "*Young folks*" and "*kids*" who particularly like Bojangles's beat. But the final few lines imply the mayhem caused by Bojangles's dancing: "*The whole town's at your heels. . . . Going astray, throw those long legs away!*"

Kids "truckin'" out of schoolrooms is only the beginning. The real danger is in Bojangles's long legs, the vehicles responsible for his jazzy "hot" rhythms. This narrative might help to explain why Astaire's first appearance on stage begins with a larger-than-life amputated and caricatured black body and the choristers removing the giant legs from the stage in order to make way for Astaire's "normal" yet remarkable dancing legs and feet.

The first image we get of "Bill Robinson" is that of a towering three-dimensional pair of black tap shoe soles adorned in a bowler hat, exaggerated red lips, and what appears to be a spotted suit and matching bowtie. A key facet of the Bill Robinson effect is the way the reproduction reveals itself visually as "an archetypal snapshot of disjointed elements of the icon's step vocabulary, wardrobe, or props and caricatures or exaggerations of elements of his face or body." While the bowler hat in conjunction with tap shoes is a common synechdochic pairing for Robinson, the suit's "polka dots" and the blackface implied by the exaggerated red lips atop a cork-black surface should arouse some suspicion about the contents of this so-called tribute. Bojangles's bowtie was never spotted, and the dancer adamantly refused to wear blackface. Some close-ups of Astaire's costume, however, add symbolic complexity to the dance. [FIG. 4.2] What appear to just be dots onscreen are in fact dice, highlighting the White press's coverage of Bojangles's proclivity for gambling. Astaire's costume thus reinforces the stereotypical linkages between gambling, Harlem night life, Black personhood, and illegal economic activity. Furthermore, Astaire's brightly patterned textiles allude to those worn by minstrel performers in the early twentieth century. Thus, despite this song's lyrics and labeling, and the use of a bowler hat (which was worn by many Black dancers of this decade), nothing else about this performance signifies the real Bill Robinson; this "tribute" instead collapses several stereotypes of Blackness into one proverbial image.

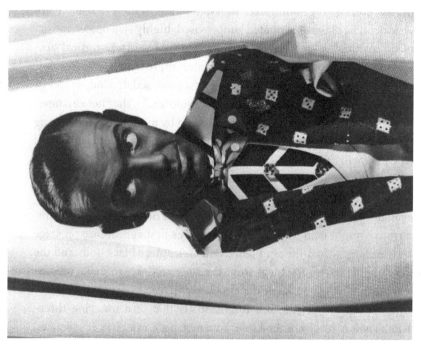

FIGURE 4.2 Close-ups of Fred Astaire as John "Lucky" Garnett in "Bojangles of Harlem" from *Swing Time*, 1936. (*Left*) Full body shot including bowler hat, spats, and white minstrel gloves in front of "Harlem." (Private collection); (*Right*) Detail shot of polka-dotted bowtie and die-patterned blazer. (RKO Radio Pictures Inc./Photofest)

Thus, as we have seen, the backdrop alone can reduce the Other to metonym. The monstrous buildings and the Chewy Gooey Gum ad in "Ritz" re-schematize the minstrel stage by reducing the mask to a series of parts (i.e., black façade, shifty eyes, exaggerated lips) and then rearrange those parts in a Picasso-esque fashion for (re)presentation on a set of modern surfaces. In the case of "Bojangles of Harlem," the number first reduces Black tap dance to Robinson's dancing image and paired association with "dangerous rhythms," further exaggerated by the costume's gambling motif. The number then synecdochizes his image and re-mounts attributes of Robinson's person on the modern stage and through Astaire's body, now the modern "skin" of both blackface and tap dance. Eleanor Powell's body acts as a similar vessel in 1939 when key aspects of Robinson's famous stair dance are exhibited in her modern styling of his dance.

But this subrogation becomes even more complicated when we consider the soundtrack for all these tributes. The film's soundtrack assists in this substitution of Astaire's White body for Black artistic innovation because of the inaudibility it achieves when coupled with image and embedded within a complex narrative structure. Jeff Smith explains this phenomenon in terms of film music's "inaudibility and abstraction." Smith contends that despite a soundtrack's crucial narrational and structural functions, these functions are " 'unheard' by the spectator, who is too immersed in the film's fiction to attend to the interplay of image and sound, music and narrative."[32] Pairing images of Black people with sound "binds" the spectator to this fictional world. Just as blackface minstrelsy allowed White performers to imitate Black people regardless of whether these renditions had a basis in reality, the tribute guise allowed performers to pay tribute to a continuum of real and imagined elements of Black culture, where the real itself was often entangled in a web of "imaginative and constructive employment of cultural paradigms," which Black artists sometimes manipulated to both pander to and manipulate structures of White power.[33]

The soundtrack in "Bojangles of Harlem" attends to this inaudibility and abstraction in two ways: first it harkens back to a specific moment in American history when Harlem was the cultural center of all things syncopated and allegedly "hot." Situating Bojangles in this past at once calls attention to Harlem as the old, but also the primitive.[34] It is through Astaire's tribute that we see a now familiar pairing of primitivity and modernity, here displayed through Astaire's ability to honor those who have

188   BEHIND THE SCREEN

gone before him. We are not only reminded of Harlem's glory days but are also asked to see Astaire as the new face (and body) of tap dance.[35] Accordingly, the music does its part to *abstract* the narrative and reassign certain artistic roles in 1936, yet the *inaudibility* is in fact achieved through Astaire's tap dancing.

On the surface, Astaire's performance acknowledges Robinson, but his tonal quality and distinct sense of rhythm confirm that a citation lies underneath this mask: if not a candid homage to his Black mentor John Sublett ("Bubbles"), this choreography openly cites Astaire's training with Bubbles.[36] Even if Astaire's rhythmic references are made inaudible through the triple masking at play here (i.e., Astaire masquerading as a Black tap dancer; John Bubbles disguised as Bill Robinson; blackface hiding from censors as a tribute), his costume should provide some clues. The costume the audience is asked to read as Bojangles-like at the beginning of the performance becomes more and more a reference to Bubbles's costume from *Porgy and Bess* (1935). The bowler hat, slacks, and black and white spats are references to the wardrobe of Sportin' Life (the opera's drug dealer associated with Harlem night life)—clothes that Bubbles wore the previous year. Again, the close-up image offers further evidence. The suit pockets are also adorned with dollar signs, which in combination with the dice could be read as references to Bubbles. [FIG. 4.2, right] Two jewel-encrusted letter Bs also decorate the shirt creating another layer of symbolic ambiguity about whether this dance refers to Bojangles or Bubbles. Thus, the interplay of narrative, soundtrack, and tap dancing—together with the Bill Robinson effect—create a certain inaudibility for the audience. The "Bojangles" narrative in effect mutes Bubbles's contributions to rhythm tap dancing. When the soundtrack is combined with all the other elements in the "signifying chain"—to use Lacan's phrase—it allows spectators to see (or not to see) something other than what Hollywood presents.[37]

A series of metonymic reductions and sonic displacements therefore dissolve the distinctiveness of Black individuals so that tap dance becomes more about its ties to dangerous Black Harlem than about its rhythm and artistry. But at the same time that this dance minimizes particular rhythmic contributions and conflates all Black tap dancers, these dance performances by White artists such as Astaire also expand definitions of Blackness by abstracting what is real and what is caricature. Astaire's gloves, for example, suggest a reference to blackface practices dating back to the nineteenth century. They cite a past steeped in caricature and an equally distorted history of racial representation of the twentieth century. As so many Hollywood performers of this era did, the gloves might also allude to Al Jolson's standard blackface attire. If this is the case, then they help to highlight one point during the performance where Astaire appears to cite the famous Jolson "Mammy" moment with his hands while mouthing something which resembles the word "Mammy."

Covert minstrelsy is all of these metonymic *dis*articulations working in synch to reinforce racial masquerades of the past and establish racial paradigms of the present. Classifying this performance—and others—a "tribute" helps to justify this layered charade. What is important here is not honoring Robinson but instead authenticating this 1936 tap dance as "the real" hot swing that comes from Harlem.[38] In chapter 1, I discussed how the public became obsessed with Harlem's authenticity and, until 1935, would migrate uptown just to feel as though they were experiencing jazz-hot rhythms in their element. As Harlem became "unsafe" and Black artists disappeared from the screen, White tap dancers would need to prove themselves worthy of such a transfer of goods. Thus, when the "tribute" label is combined with a series of sonic displacements in the context of Astaire's "Bojangles of Harlem" and Powell's "Tribute to Bill Robinson," its role is to transition viewers from seeing Black tap dancers as the most qualified and to then capitalize on White surrogates who can offer tap dance and a Black sensibility in an unthreatening manner.

Honolulu Bound

Like Astaire's performance in *Swing Time*, Eleanor Powell's performance in *Honolulu* further exemplifies how the tribute guise extends far beyond the façade of its "tribute" label. Powell's "Tribute to Bill Robinson" entails a complex choreography leading up to the tribute performance as well as certain sonic features (perceptible in both the routine's soundtrack and Powell's tap dancing), Powell's specific use of props, her gaze, and of course her blatant use of black face paint. The covert minstrelsy present in MGM's *Honolulu* will become increasingly more layered in chapter 5, with its elements of brownface playing a significant role in the production's use of synchronous masking.[39] Here, however, I will concentrate on the ways one routine in particular utilizes simultaneous masks for full effect, a process even more complicated than the one involved in Astaire's performance three years earlier.

190 BEHIND THE SCREEN

Because the film's overarching narrative frames Powell's tribute performance, I begin with a bit of background on the film's characters and cast.

Honolulu boasted a stellar cast of Robert Young, George Burns, Gracie Allen, and the "Queen of the Taps" herself, Eleanor Powell, when it previewed at the Fox theater in Westwood, California, in February 1939.[40] By the time Powell took this role she had already received public approval for her lightning-fast feet and for her charm, which she had recently shown off in the musicals, *Born to Dance* and *Rosalie*.[41] I note her reputation because her status as "Queen of the Taps" makes her one of few subjects capable of executing moves as complicated as those of her subject, Robinson. Because Robinson held "exceptional" status on the screen as the most gifted Black dancer of his era, only a handful of White dancers could pull off a comparable rhythmic feat: Astaire and Powell are two such examples. This is why these "tributes" tended to fall in the hands of a limited number of White performers. While the tribute motif pervades film of this era, we see a high recurrence of its use within a small circle of dancers. Furthermore, not all White performers of the era were comfortable donning blackface by this point, which further limited the range of talent Hollywood could use for these sorts of performances. While one cannot know the degree to which Powell was *comfortable* wearing such a mask, this was not the first time she had been involved with outdated racialized content. MGM had abandoned her last project *Gentleman Be Seated* because it would not have passed censorship guidelines of the time.[42]

While likely not a conscious move on the part of the film's writers, the doppelgänger narrative present in this film offers an interesting parallel to the idea of masking and adds yet another layer of distraction from the seemingly less complicated identity Powell "tries on" during her tribute number.[43] George Smith (played by Robert Young) owns a pineapple plantation in Honolulu and is the spitting image of Hollywood movie star, Brooks Mason (also played by Robert Young). While George Smith is visiting Hollywood, the obsessed and star-struck moviegoing public mistakes him for Brooks Mason and mauls the plantation owner. When the two lookalikes finally meet and not even Mason's Black butler of ten years can tell the two apart, Mason convinces Smith to take his place on his upcoming New York City publicity tour. Smith agrees to swap lives mainly because he believes some time in New York will "culture" him as his fiancé Cecelia (played by Rita Johnson) requests of him before tying the knot. The two men agree to keep

BON HOMAGE   191

this swap a complete secret. As the film progresses George Smith's stint as Brooks Mason results in a comedy of errors with most of the comedy coming from Mason's agent Joe Duffy (George Burns) and much of the error a result of the doppelgänger effect. All of this serves as a great distraction from some of the film's more complicated subtexts.

The big opening dance number on board the ship to Honolulu also frames Powell's tribute performance providing a complete contrast to many of the performative elements in her later dance sequences standing in as Robinson and as a "Native" Hawaiian. Like the extreme spatial and social contrasts United Artist producers set up between the Black dancers and White dancers in "Puttin' on the Ritz," Powell's three tap dance performances, when juxtaposed, offer the brown body as a kind of safe exoticism as compared to the "homely" White dancer and its opposite, Powell's "uncanny" performance *as* Bill Robinson.[44]

In just a few short frames, MGM places what will be Powell's onscreen dancing debut—and the only tap dance performance where Powell is dressed as her very White feminine self—in the midst of clichéd White American upper-middle-class leisure: Millicent de Grasse (played by Gracie Allen) has just spotted who she thinks is Brooks Mason and runs to tell her best friend Dorothy March (played by Eleanor Powell) the news. Miss March is unimpressed and leaves de Grasse to her childish fandom. Shortly after this interaction between the two women, the camera cuts to the main deck of the ship where men play a game resembling water polo and women giggle while jumping rope on the swimming pool's perimeter. March reads peacefully on a deck chair off to the side while de Grasse strums her ukulele and plays the meddlesome character for which she, Gracie Allen, is known. De Grasse's rhythms inspire March and within a few seconds Powell begins to taunt the audience with her syncopated rhythms. Powell's decision to tap dance from a seated position likely comes from the African American community; Black dancers would have been performing a version of this in Harlem's Hoofer's Club for a few years now.[45] Powell and Allen then rise and dance together for the first few bars—a unique combination of rhythm tap and subtle hula gestures of the hips and arms. Powell then ditches her friend and begins to do more of her signature choreography: she starts traveling through space with more complex rhythms, and props. Powell executes a virtuosic bit with one of the jump ropes on set. She then finishes out of breath but camera-ready and seemingly unaffected. In addition to positioning Eleanor Powell among the White leisure-class wherein she dances for fun—as opposed to occupation— this dance sequence helps to integrate an Africanist vocabulary into what had already become the style of tap typical of 1930s Hollywood.[46]

Gentleman Be Seated

The dance that Powell performs on the ship's main deck reinforces a set of social norms regarding the performance of gender, race, and tap dance. Powell's dance on board the ship bound for Honolulu exemplifies the style of tap dancing that quickly became synonymous with the Golden Age of film. For example, taking up space did not faze Powell: in *Honolulu* she performs in the round, utilizing all dimensions of her body as well as the vertical and horizontal planes of the ship. Since Astaire and Hermes Pan's recent (1934) discovery that a dancing camera opened up new possibilities for filming the body in motion, Hollywood had been obsessed with dances that moved through and around space.[47] Powell's sound is light, the mood whimsical. She wears a flowing form-fitting dress that falls to the mid-shin. Her shoes are white, more substantial than the heels worn by choristers throughout the first three decades of the twentieth century, but still very different from the Oxford flat tap shoes worn by men at this time. These shoes allowed her more pliability and offered a stronger sound than the higher-heeled, lighter-weight shoes worn by many of her contemporaries. Even though much of her lower body form—loose legs, heavy feet, stationary hips—exhibits similarities to the technique taught and executed by male tap dancers, her upper body carriage and style remains visibly feminine and the coy nature of her character in this scene aligns with a 1930's attitude of what it means to be a White woman; Powell is goofy, playful, and utterly feminine.

Her *ballon*, suspension, and effortless turns evidence her ballet training, while the firm command of her feet, weighted rhythms, and ability to switch her center of gravity into her hips almost immediately following a sustained *soutenu*, demonstrate that she has also spent a great deal of time hoofing with the men. This dance, while showcasing Powell's impressive breadth of vocabulary, remains humble with regard to rhythmic choices, giving Powell an opportunity to prioritize the visual spectacle of "flash" dancing over the routine's aural components.[48] That is, the camera helps to direct the audience's focus toward Powell's (very feminine) body and visible skill set as well as her very precise and intentional use of facial expressions and hand gestures.

In the film's first big dance sequence, Powell can tap dance in a more masculine style so long as she maintains a feminine appearance while doing so; this includes a specific set of costume, movement, and sound choices, as well as a list of facial expressions and defined angles at which her body must be shot. By the end of the number, Powell has established herself as a good female tap dancer, capable of using space, unique props, all while staying in character.

The dance performed at home stands in stark contrast to the choreography, costume, and camera work in her two succeeding tributes by establishing a clear distinction between the feminine and the masculine in tap dance and defining White tap dance as something distinct so it may later be differentiated from her tribute to Black tap dancer Bill Robinson and homage to Native Hawaiian dancers, the latter of which I discuss in chapter 5. Additionally, when juxtaposed with her "Tribute to Bill Robinson," the performance helps transition viewers into a 1940s way of seeing the White female body while requiring its audience to re-think the role of tap dance in relation to national identity.[49]

As discussed in the previous chapter, an escalating fear of Black corporeality—in part due to its association with rioting and crime—and consequent decline in the popularity of the Black image for White spectators led Hollywood to begin employing a number of White dancers who had been trained by Black tap masters. Astaire marked a prime example in the onscreen shift from Black to White dancers performing an Africanist rhythmic sensibility, but not until Powell's debut on the big screen did America see women as capable of executing tap dance with the same rhythmic rigor as their male contemporaries. Powell's success at replicating Robinson's stair dance in the second act of *Honolulu* helped establish a new era of White female tap soloists. If Powell could perform her highly skilled yet visually gratifying and feminine tap dance aboard the ship *and* the rhythmic complexity of Robinson's stair dance, then White audiences might perceive her as possessing at least as much talent as her Black male counterpart; Powell could dance *as* a man, *like* a woman. While not the first woman to manipulate the social and artistic conventions of this era, her ability to subvert rigid concepts of masculine/feminine tap dancing, male/female dress, and Black/White rhythmic sensibilities gave her more visibility.[50] With this scaffolding

194   BEHIND THE SCREEN

established, Powell could effectively perform a tribute to America's greatest living tap dancer.

The Tribute Guise in *Honolulu*

Powell's tribute performance is neither imperative nor subsidiary to the plot and exists for the sheer purpose of entertainment. It is an excuse to showcase Powell's talents as much as it is an excuse to wear blackface in a show about doppelgänger mix-ups and Hawaiian pineapple plantations. As such, her performance is embedded within the ship's costume ball, another pattern we will see repeated throughout the duration of World War II:

> *The camera zooms in on a poster that reads: "Tonight, Costume Ball; Seaman's Fund, Come as Your Favorite Movie Star, Tonight" as Tony Martin serenades viewers with "This Night Will Be My Souvenir."[51] The camera cuts to a close-up of Powell donning blackface in a backstage mirror. Already we see how the narrative—in this case a costume ball—frames and superficially excuses the use of makeup. That is, the event itself justifies Powell's "costume," and the tribute label shields Powell from possible Code violation and even conceivable claims of copyright infringement from Twentieth Century Fox, which essentially "owned" Bill Robinson at the time MGM was filming Honolulu.[52]*
>
> *The performance is further framed by an unprecedented number of self-referential Hollywood citations. The camera cuts to the ballroom where the ship's passengers delight in seeing each other's costumes: Gracie Allen, dressed in a garish Mae West–inspired evening gown, scolds seven passengers dressed as Snow White's Dwarfs; Charlie Chaplin picks up a bite to eat at the buffet while Gene Autry converses with some other passengers dressed as cowboys; the camera then pans to Douglas McPhail impersonating the up-and-coming Bing Crosby. The camera pans the room and rests when it reaches Brooks Mason who is standing front and center, disguised as George Smith but impersonating Beethoven. Within the first few bars of Mason's conducting, Miss de Grasse plucks a couple of off-key notes on the harp, further frustrating the already irritable Beethoven-impersonator; Mason exits the stage, and de Grasse moves center. We then witness a series of Marx Brothers*

citations: a Harpo Marx impersonator (played by Budd Linn) sits behind the piano; Groucho Marx (played by Ken Darby) is on cello; a second Groucho Marx (played by Rad Robinson) is on piccolo; and finally Chico Marx (played by Jon Dodson) is on harp. The Four King's Men disguised as the Marx Brothers join Allen in singing "The Leader Doesn't Like Music."[53] The King's Men do a short Duck Soup routine eventually leaving Allen on stage alone with their instruments.[54] Clapping on the screen subsides slowly as de Grasse's performance continues with "Would You Like to Buy My Violins," until The King's Men join her once again for an even more slapstick routine than the one previously performed. And then, Brooks Mason's announcement: "And now Ladies and Gentlemen, Miss Dorothy March, in her impersonation of Bill Robinson. The King of Harlem!" These abundant citations underscore the nature of the event; the diegetic applause reminds viewers that this is a backstage musical, that is, a show-within-a-show and therefore twice removed; and finally, the interlocuter's announcement emphasizes Bill Robinson's standing as "The King of Harlem." Aside from the unlikely fact that people traveling for leisure would pack their best movie-star lookalike costume in their trunks, costume balls generally do not feature long performances.

A slim, five foot six Powell enters from a wing off house left dressed in Robinson's famous wardrobe. The resemblance is uncanny. Applause fills the room as the band starts playing a version of "Swanee River". The camera reveals a slight Powell disguised as Robinson; she is dressed in "Bojangles'" standard white shirt, plaid vest, suit jacket, bow tie, white gloves, pleated pants, bowler hat, and suede oxford shoes. She tips her bowler hat, acknowledging the audience, before entering a glossy stage. When she reaches the center of the performance space, a small cube-shaped podium rises from a trapdoor, providing Powell with a second surface for making sound. As she nods her head, the camera catches a glimpse of the stark contrast created between her white sclera and the thick burnt cork of her face paint.

She clicks her toes on the cube, then shuffles left, click, shuffles right, click. Gradually more cubes of varying height emerge from the floor, forming a five-step staircase that resembles Robinson's. The camera zooms in on Powell's face: she blinks, revealing long eyelashes and delicate cheekbones. She smiles almost as if flirting with the camera. But in fact, there is more to her gaze than pure flirtation. Buried beneath Powell's mask sit several layers of meaning, each one contributing to a long theatrical history and disguise of the Other.[55]

FIGURE 4.3 (*Left*) Bill Robinson performing his famous stair dance in his classic suit and bowler hat, c. early 1930s. (Photofest); (*Right*) Eleanor Powell performs her "Tribute to Bill Robinson" in *Honolulu*, 1939. (Alamy Stock Photo)

The visible parts of Powell's interpretation of Robinson's stair dance offer more exaggeration than replication. Although her costume captures the quintessence of Robinson's wardrobe much better than the one Astaire used in his rendition, her use of white gloves creates an odd contrast. Robinson never performed the stair dance in white gloves and rarely performed any role with white gloves.[56] Rather, white gloves allude to Astaire's "tribute," minstrel shows and to Jolson while also accentuating certain hand gestures performed throughout the two pieces. Furthermore, as much as Powell might have been trying to look *like* Robinson, her use of burnt cork undermines the essence of Robinson's character; Robinson absolutely refused to perform in burnt cork. In addition to viewing the blackface mask as racial fetish, I want to suggest the blackface mask here as a means of skirting copyright laws.

Earlier I proposed that Robinson's unofficial licensing process necessitated both the "tribute" label and the use of a blackface mask. While the "tribute" designation seems like an obvious move to avoid criticism, Hollywood's use of blackface is more than a simple fixation on reinforcing racial caricature. Eva Cherniavsky has discussed Whiteness as it relates to a certain kind of "possessive individualism." She argues that within a modern context, race "signifies the body's improper relation to capital."[57] Moreover, if the colonizer "claims an inalienable property in the body . . . the bodies of the colonized are made in varying degrees susceptible to abstraction and exchange."[58] Distinguishing White from Black in these tributes plays a critical role in both the protection against and demarcation from the "potential threat of commodification."[59] Moreover, that Astaire and Powell can reduce Robinson's performances to a handful of abstractions, including a mask that Robinson never wore, suggests that Hollywood saw Blackness and blackface as interchangeable.

If Powell possesses an "inalienable property in the body," her use of the blackface mask clearly delineates her Whiteness from Robinson's Blackness.[60] The mask then in a way overwrites Robinson's unofficial laws surrounding the use and appropriation of his stair dance. In wearing the mask, Powell not only draws a line between her Whiteness and Robinson's Blackness, but she also evokes the trafficking of Black bodies associated with the act of performing Blackness; her burnt cork evokes a subject/object distinction that dates back to chattel slavery—not to mention the ways in which blackface itself evokes a type of second skin for Powell. As we saw in chapter 1, the Hollywood stage of the 1930s became a site of transfiguration where not only was the Blackness reduced to flesh, but it was in fact "evacuated of an interior" such that Powell's "costume"—or shell—marks Spillers's "signifying property plus." In this way, Robinson's body becomes a "salable body in which others may traffic," thus relinquishing Powell's (and MGM's) responsibility to protect his intellectual property.[61] That is, the blackface mask in the context of a tribute asserts, by making Black *flesh* hyper-visible, that the person to whom the performer pays tribute has no rights and thus ownership over his/her dance.

Powell's gaze makes the blackface mask even more visible and this delineation between White and Black intellectual property rights more legible. Her facial expressions and movements are slight: she either directs her gaze straight in front of her, or intentionally diverts her eyes to the audience with a precise turn of the head. While her face remains motionless, due to the exaggerated lips that she has painted on herself, it appears that she smiles throughout the duration of the dance. Only when the camera zooms in for a close-up can one see the static nature of her painted lips and the shocking glazed-over look that results from the outline of the thick white makeup she has used to accentuate her eyes. In other words, her gaze heightens the effect of the minstrel mask insofar as it draws attention to the mask-like properties of her face and thus the objectifying process of her masquerade.

Powell also embellishes the movement itself. While she captures the essence of Robinson's "light-on-your-feet" style, her gestures are more pronounced than anything ever gesticulated by Robinson. Within the first minute of choreography, Powell places her hands on the waist of her trousers and continues to hold the fabric in suspension as she glances down at her feet. While Robinson on occasion pulled his trouser fabric out of the way, such a gesture served a utilitarian function; he had to ensure that nothing got in the way of his sounds. Still, such a movement lasted only a split second. Something similar happens when Powell places her hands on her stomach or in her pockets. No filmed performances of Robinson using such gestures/movements exists. Powell's very intentional exaggeration may serve two purposes: first, the exaggerated gestures reinforce certain character traits: all three of these movement choices signify insouciance, characteristic of Robinson's attitude. He not only tended to play it "cool" but was also known for his "Everything will be, everything will be, copacetic" adage. While this might have been Robinson's social performance, it nonetheless reinforced the "happy slave" archetype in circulation since the mid-1800s.[62]

Powell's exaggeration also reinforced certain racialized roles: this can be seen in the very literal translation of some of Powell's movements that gesture at everything from Black man qua servant . . . *hands offer a serving platter* to various animal dances that Robinson never performed . . . *head jerks back and forth like a wild turkey, a version of Peckin'.* This dance pretends to make the tap dance stage of the 1930s Hollywood screen one of community when, in fact, it portends a new chapter in the art of covering up racist caricature, collapsing Robinson's dancing into a finite number of "roles."[63]

Utilizing the set, she performs several attention-grabbing steps. But these stylized acrobatics and turns are not the focus of this dance. In true Bojangles manner, the rhythm is paramount to the movement. The staircase is a nice gimmick, and although its primary function is to provide the feet and hands with yet another dance surface on which to produce sound, its material, height, and weight diversify the list of possible dynamics her body can produce: *hollow; muted; high.* Powell-as-Robinson does not assert her relationship with the camera through coy expressions or flirtatious gestures. Instead, she uses her Whiteness, signified by her ability to dance in blackface, as well as her role on the ship as being one of passenger rather than servant, to establish her power on the screen. Powell thus gains acceptance from her White audience insofar as she can demonstrate her ability to dance *like* a black man but *as* a White woman. The mystery of what lies behind the mask (i.e., elegance, Whiteness, female-ness) is confirmed by the irony of what presents itself visibly (i.e., rhythmic precision, Blackness, masculinity). While Powell's Whiteness is signaled visibly through her ability to dance in blackface and in her gestures, which suggest servitude, the sonic guise also works to highlight racial difference.

Foregrounding Background Music

What one hears is as important as what one does not hear, and what one hears in two pivotal medleys, or "tributes," in *Honolulu* is a testament to the ways that covert minstrelsy functions at both the perceptible *and* subceptional levels. While MGM commissioned composers Harry Warren and Gus Kahn to write most of the film's score, exceptions were made for *Honolulu's* two "tributes." The first "tribute medley" accompanies Powell's tribute to Robinson.[64] The score for this piece comprises four different works: Stephen Foster's "The Old Folks at Home" or "Swanee River" (1851), followed by Richard Milburn's "Listen to the Mockingbird" (1855), Foster's "Old Black Joe" (1861), and finally, "The Darktown Strutters' Ball," written by Shelton Brooks (1917). While each song is significant, the extent of aural masks in this soundtrack presents itself when we listen to these four songs as a compilation. Because the musical arrangement blurs the beginnings and endings of each of these four songs, the audience has no clear understanding of which songs belong to whom and receives no clue regarding where one song begins and another one ends. These four songs, two written by Black men and two written by a White man pretending to write from the perspective of all Black men are supposed to signify "authentic" Blackness. Hence, Brooks and Milburn's music attempts to qualify Foster's music as "true" to the life of Black folk.

Blackface performers and Stephen Foster approached the subject of race differently, but both modes had a lasting impact on how America perceived people of color. Visible blackface tended to tease out a perceived distinction between Whiteness and Blackness, creating artificial distance between self and Other. Foster, on the other hand, sought to collapse this binary of human experience into something universal; he worked to find similarities between White folk and Black in order to unite the nation. In trying to universalize human experience and conflate a mentality of the enslaved with that of a master, Foster normalized plantation life and reified various linguistic and behavioral traits of Black people.[65] Furthermore, Foster sold most of his early sheet music to minstrel troupes, in effect undermining his work to "universalize" human experience and contributing to the very institution that worked so hard to delineate humans based on the color of their skin.

In the three years that lapsed between the time Foster wrote "Old Folks at Home" and "Old Black Joe," he modified his language to make the song less offensive.[66] This is not dissimilar to the lyric manipulations Irving Berlin made between his first publication of "Ritz" (1929) and the revised version he published in 1946 for *Blue Skies*. The replacement of "Lenox" with "Park" Avenue or the omission of "Lulu Belle" and "High Brown" designations were quantitatively small adjustments that changed the song's whole meaning. Foster, too, renamed his characters in future iterations in the song, supplanting one derogatory slur for another.[67] An example of this is changing "Massa" to "Grandpa" or some other substitute.[68] These alterations did not change the meaning of the songs but instead lessened the public backlash the songwriter received in future years. Changing certain lyrics in many ways disguised some of the songs' original meaning, or at least made it "legal" to publish Foster's tunes in the twentieth century in a manner that is similar to the small-manipulations composers had to make in the 1930s to satisfy the maturing Code. By the time both successful composers changed their lyrics, the tunes themselves—just like that of Berlin's "Mandy"—carried a trace of the minstrel stage; the tunes themselves needed no lyrics to convey a narrative of racial difference.

In the case of Foster's musical works, even without the songs' lyrics, Americans had tied a minstrel message to the tunes. Foster had severed his ties to Christy's Minstrels and had omitted blatantly racist words, but (White) American consumers had already developed associations between Foster's music and the Black or blackfaced body. Even though lyric substitutions helped the composer's music sell, new words could not completely break the underlying melodic relationship with racial ideas. The tunes themselves could carry racial implications without directly referring to Black people and Black behavior. The lyrics' apparent meaning possessed much less power than the tunes' covert implications. The underlying meaning of Foster's songs becomes important in Powell's tribute precisely because MGM commissioned a score devoid of lyrics, a pattern we will see repeated throughout the Production Code's reign, especially in animated sequences.

Not only did these tunes' historical ties to Black life make them a likely musical source for Hollywood, but the image of Powell in blackface affects the audience's perception of the music itself. The soundtrack chosen for Powell's "tribute" works on a subliminal level to further substantiate Powell's performance. Here the music "encourages narrative comprehension."[69] Powell's black makeup summons up in viewers the memory of a Negro dialect and other audible elements of minstrelsy. Foster's melodies arouse nostalgia for a slave-owning past while simultaneously uniting its viewers as Americans. The audience is thus forced to reconcile the sound and the image regardless of whether they are in synch. As Jeff Smith argues, "Film music does not so much displace the importance of narrative in engaging the process of suture, but rather makes narrative a more efficient means of implementing the identification on which the text's positioning of the subject depends."[70] Robinson's famous stair dance and his artistry get lost in this "quasi-magical" process whereby Powell, a White female performer, suddenly becomes the new face of tap dance. His choreography becomes America's choreography in the same way that Negro spirituals become America's vernacular music, and the White man or woman becomes the arbiter of such national identifiers. The

202   BEHIND THE SCREEN

music therefore had meaning at both the perceptible and subceptional levels simultaneously while also erasing Black presence from America's narrative.

According to Claudia Gorbman, film music signifies according to pure musical codes, cultural codes, and cinematic codes.[71] Foster's music signifies according to both musical cultural codes: long ties to the minstrel stage result in a permanent signification of Black caricatures and perform southern repossession. The music itself further signifies American vernacular culture because of the ways in which musical codes have intersected with cultural codes over time. Let us focus, however, on the cinematic significance of Foster's music—specifically "Old Black Joe" and "Old Folks at Home"—as presented in Powell's dance solo.

In the case of cinematic codes, the filmic context itself helps to codify the music.[72] The very placement of the music within the film is crucial to its signification. In Powell's solo, the music is presented as a medley with Foster's songs "Joe" and "Kentucky" sandwiched between the (African American street composer) Richard Milburn's "Listen to the Mockingbird" and (Black Canadian jazz composer) Shelton Brooks's "The Darktown Strutter's Ball." In positioning Foster's music with that of two Black composers, MGM is in some way qualifying Foster's music as "authentically" Black, that is, written by a Black composer about the real experiences of the Black enslaved. Because the musical arrangement blurs the beginnings and endings of each of these four songs, there is no clear understanding of which songs belong to whom and no immediately perceptible moment marking the end of Foster's interpretation and that which he seeks to interpret. Four perspectives seemingly tell one fluid narrative, one that boasts real lived experience. This soundtrack, in other words, mediates the Black experience in America through White logic and a White lens.

Generally, according to the German composer Richard Wagner's theory of motifs and leitmotifs, musical themes become associated with people, places, and/or situations.[73] In the case of Powell's tribute to Robinson, Hollywood relies on Powell's costume and the four songs of this routine's medley to signify Blackness. As we saw in the previous chapter, Robinson, danced his famous stair routine to Foster's "Kentucky" and "Joe" beginning in 1932. This is important for several reasons: first, the fact that Robinson was dancing to Foster's tunes shows how much a part of the vernacular Foster's music had become. It also hints at a level of double consciousness that Robinson may have experienced as a Black man on the White stage. Second, given the meaning behind these two tunes, the use of "Kentucky" and "Joe" demonstrates a double consciousness intrinsic to Robinson's dancing. There also arises the disparity in song choice between those songs to which Robinson danced and those to which Powell danced when imitating Robinson. Whether or not Powell is paying tribute to Robinson is not nearly as important as that she seeks to signify Blackness as a general concept through costume, song, and dance. Accordingly, Foster's music becomes a temporally fluid leitmotif of Blackness. One Foster tune becomes metonymic for Blackness in a way that is similar to the impacts of the Bill Robinson effect. Here "Joe" represents all Black people (both as objects and as an ontology) across all space and time.

Over the course of a century, American entertainment turned Foster's Black-inspired vernacular music, which sought to represent ALL bodies, into a catch-all musical phrase that ostensibly signified Blackness. With or without lyrics, Foster's tunes could instantly conjure up an image of Blackness in all its contrived variations. One musical phrase could instantly evoke everything ever signified by a particular dialect, makeup, costume, class, or aesthetic without trying anything on or even coming into contact with Black people. Thus, when blackface makeup became outdated and Hollywood did not want to employ real Black artists, it could achieve all these things, and more, with a simple score written by someone White. Hence the music in *Honolulu* contributes to a general remapping of an Africanist aesthetic onto White bodies under the ruse of national unity.

This musical medley puts Foster's voice in dialogue with two African American voices so that the Black voice and the White voice become fused. On a perceptible level this song marks "Blackness" as something codifiable. On a subceptional level, this song simultaneously "Whitens" Brooks's and Milburn's voices and offers credibility to Foster's, thereby blurring the line between what constitutes the Black experience and what makes up its White narration. The medley's lack of lyrics opens up a space onto which its audience can project meaning, while the song's aural depth collapses into a two-dimensional image of Powell in blackface. That is, what one hears as one sees the burnt cork emerge is no longer a fluid notion of aesthetics or race but is instead flat and fixed. While the music masks what lies beneath, the mask seemingly stands in for Black flesh.[74]

Her Dance in His Shadow

Powell's tap dancing augments the meaning of *Honolulu*'s soundtrack: at the same time the tribute guise obscures parts of Powell's dance, the dance—and

204 BEHIND THE SCREEN

specifically its audible parts—further problematizes the layers of disguise within the soundtrack, if one listens. Within the first eight bars of choreography, Powell's "tribute" distinguishes itself from her last routine on the ship's deck: she is dressed like a man—a Black man—complete with black makeup and a man's suit. Second, her use of space is primarily vertical—accentuated by the use of a five-level staircase—and contained; she takes up no more space than is absolutely necessary for producing certain sounds. This stands in complete contrast to her use of space in the first dance, possibly offering her viewers a subversive message about Blackness; White dancers have command over the space in a way that Black dancers do not. Though it could just as easily comment on Robinson's upright and minimalist style characteristic of a certain "cool" aesthetic.

Although Powell held a remarkable reputation as a tap dancer, having her pay "tribute" to Robinson as the second major dance sequence in *Honolulu* helped Hollywood shift a presumed association between tap dance and the Black male body to that of an "American" dance form and the slim, White, female body. Such a narrative conveyed a broader message of national identity as it concerned public image and power. Though women were never explicitly banned from performing tap, it was rare to see a female tap soloist. Of the handful of female tap soloists, most were African American, and many performed in drag. By the 1930s White female tap soloists had become more popular, especially on the big screen, due in part to the popularity of tap dance in America, a Deco-inspired obsession with the female body, and Hollywood's declining interest in Black dancers.[75]

Yet in addition to providing a narrative purpose, Hollywood's decision likely served the practical function of drawing Powell's audience's attention toward her visible dance rather than to her performance's sonic dimensions. Robinson was known for his clarity and speed and all surviving footage of him doing his stair dance shows that about a third of the way through his routine, the tempo would speed up about 5 to 10 percent. By the time he got to the last quarter of the dance, the musicians often stopped playing to allow Robinson the opportunity to speed up the tempo by as much as 40 percent. At the same time, the last third of his dance was usually full of more intricate rhythms and even more taps per measure of music. Powell's tempo never speeds up and at times it even slows down to allow her more time to exaggerate her visible motion. She relied on the visual to mask the fact that she could not, or at least chose not to, execute as many beats per second as her honoree. To summon the words of Fred Moten, "The aural emerges as that which is given in its fullest possibility by the visual: you hear . . . most clearly in seeing."[76] In keeping with the way in which covert minstrelsy tends to rely on one phenomenological experience to distract from another, Powell's lack of sound is invisibilized by the parts of her performance that are highly visible, such as her makeup and facial expressions.

If one carefully analyzes the sonic elements of her stair dance in relation to Robinson's, one will notice that rhythmically, Powell's piece is significantly less complex than Robinson's. In certain parts, Bojangles's dance includes almost twice as many audible beats as Powell's. Also, the way that Robinson uses space is completely different from Powell's movement about the stage. This is not to say that Powell was not an extremely skilled performer in her own right, nor is this to say that one needs to perfectly replicate her "master" to pay tribute. What I do hope to suggest is that this "tribute" was in fact more variation than replication, especially when one considers the song choice for this routine in addition to Powell's makeup, costume, and choreography. Each of these elements acts as a layer that contributes to disguising the integrity of Robinson's Black personhood resulting in a dancing body that signifies not Bill Robinson but a caricature of Blackness.

Citing Citations

While not all citations are tributes, tributes, like those performed by Astaire and Powell, are always exemplary of the citational guise, of which a primary function is to be able to rewrite a semiotics of race and gender, especially as these markers of identity relate to entertainment. Sometimes, however, a citation appears embedded within a tribute. Citations of a person, performer, or practice who/that has a well-known connection to blackface (like Al Jolson or Eddie Cantor) surface within tributes in details as small as the white gloves that Astaire and Powell wear in their blackface routines. Almost undetectable, Astaire's gloves combined with a specific gesture and mouthing of "Mammy" in the middle of his tribute reflect on Jolson's 1927 performance.

But as we have seen in previous chapters, citations surface even where no tributes exist; Hollywood films were full of citations from the early 1930s to mid-1950s. In *Santa's Workshop* (1932) an animated pickaninny doll goes through quality control and blurts out "Mammy" on its knees, arms outstretched with white gloves toward Santa. Since the doll functions—and is funny in Santa's eyes—he receives an "OK" stamp; he is ready to be gifted.[77]

206 BEHIND THE SCREEN

Mickey Rooney belts out "Mammy" at the beginning of *Boys Town* (1938) perhaps as a way of justifying the blackface he dons later in the film but also as a way of situating his performance within a broader narrative of American entertainment.[78] Jolson and Cantor were the subjects of such citations from 1928 onward, but Astaire and Powell also became popular sources of citation following their appearances in blackface in 1936 and 1939, respectively.

Following the blackface debuts of Astaire and Powell, Hollywood dancers began citing their performances, though these citations were unique in that they did not contain the use of blackface. Understanding how the citational guise has been used in reference to Astaire and Powell's bodies elucidates the general remapping of Robinson and other Black dancers' talent onto Astaire and Powell's White bodies. Lorraine Krueger's "imitation" of Robinson's "stair" dance in the film *Career Girl* (1944) illustrates the relocation of value that occurs between 1936 and the end of World War II from the onscreen privileging of the Black male tap dancer as the expert to showcasing White tap dance soloists like Astaire and Powell as the hoofing authorities.[79] While the Code may have played some part in Krueger's performance, her decision to perform a Robinson solo without blackface and without Foster's tunes attests to the success of Powell's 1939 performance as an act of transfer. Krueger's "impression" of Robinson is a tribute to Powell, further qualifying Powell as an adequate replacement for the Black tap dancer.

Krueger introduces her performance as an "impression of our greatest colored tap dancer," reminding her audience (without mentioning names) that Robinson was the greatest *Black* tap dancer. Her outfit, a white suit in the style of Powell, clearly suggests a reference not only to Powell but specifically to Powell's tribute to Robinson in *Honolulu*. Thus, while presumably impersonating Robinson, Krueger in effect cites Powell's rendition of the stair dance helping to reinforce Powell's reputation as the "Queen of Taps," while slowly erasing the contributions of Black dancers like Robinson from the Hollywood narrative. Put differently, Krueger's performance, read as a tribute to Powell masquerading as an impersonation of Robinson, demonstrates how in addition to acknowledging Robinson in her 1939 tribute, Powell also checkmates him, replacing his Black body with that of her own seductive White female body, a transaction made more successful in light of her commodified sexuality. We continue to see similar impressions or imitations of Powell until 1945, when Powell's image began to fade in favor of other White female tap soloists such as Ann Miller and Vera-Ellen.[80]

These internal references, which help to reinforce new semiotics of race and gender, sometimes reference cinematic moments rather than people. Through technology, for example, Powell's tribute could allude to how far camera work had come over the last decade. Powell's stair dance quotes Astaire and Hermes Pan's use of Bojangles's shadow in *Swing Time*'s own rendition of a tribute to Robinson by replicating the way the still camera captured Astaire's shadow. In both Astaire's and Powell's tributes, the dancer's big black silhouette provides a two-dimensional backdrop against which his/her three-dimensional image may be filmed. Whether or not *Honolulu*'s technology was the same as that used in *Swing Time*, the reference to Astaire's tribute within Powell's tribute draws attention to new modes of projection, both technologically on the screen and psychologically onto the White body.[81] Furthermore, calling on a previous Hollywood tribute that was performed by one of Hollywood's leading men helps to legitimize Powell's act, both choreographically, in terms of gender, and as it regards Hollywood's legitimization of visible blackface in the middle of the twentieth century. Furthermore, embedding Powell's tribute within the on-ship costume ball full of references, helps justify Powell's "costume" within the context of a tribute. That is, one must dress *as* the person to whom he or she refers because tributes seem to rely on visible similitude and sonic semblance.[82]

Powell's performance simultaneously reiterates social codes while attempting to challenge them. One can view this disparity (i.e., reiterating versus challenging) in terms of dance scholar Susan Foster's distinction between choreography and performance. Foster defines choreography as the "tradition of codes and conventions through which meaning is constructed in dance" as opposed to performance which is merely the execution of such codes.[83] "Choreography" manifests in Powell's first dance on the ship's deck and in Robinson's Stair dance. The first makes a statement about the "codes and conventions" typical of 1930s American culture as they pertain to ideas of femininity. The second (Robinson's choreography executed by a White woman in blackface) speaks to the values and limitations America had prescribed for Black male entertainers in the 1920s and '30s. Robinson can share the White stage and refrain from using burnt cork, but his movement choices are heavily influenced by the roles Black men were allowed to play on the early twentieth century stage and screen. Furthermore, Robinson's facial expressions and gaze reiterate nineteenth-century caricatures and confirm the conviction that the Black man is meant to perform *for* the White. Thus,

208 BEHIND THE SCREEN

Powell's and Robinson's choreographies offer a framework for understanding the social codes present at the time *Honolulu* was made.

At the same time, however, the performance's narrative (i.e., the film as a whole and specifically the "tribute" thread throughout) asks viewers to re-think Black representation. The unspoken social norm at the time *Honolulu* was conceived was that the use of burnt cork was outdated. Powell's tribute speculates that blackface is acceptable in the context of a tribute. The tribute guise is thus the act of one using the "tribute" label in conjunction with burnt cork and various "Negro" stereotypes and convincing the audience that the makeup merely acknowledges a historical moment. Here the mask is part of the choreography; the narrative that MGM tells, however, is specific to this particular performance. Yet the onscreen validation that moviegoers ex-perience (e.g., the applause on screen that follows Powell's tribute, a happy care-free atmosphere captured by great big smiles from performer and audi-ence members alike, and Powell's "safe" body, to name a few) only encourages the ethical soundness and viability of blackface. Furthermore, like Stephen Foster's vernacular music, Powell's engagement in traditions of old reminds her nostalgic White audience of happy times past. Through this specific per-formance, Powell re-frames blackface performance as glamorous precisely through her White, highly feminine body, carving out a space for women on the tap dance stage.

Performing this routine in blackface and drag allows Powell to be seen in a new light. Performing this dance as a Black man "authenticates" her steps and allows her audience to hear her tap dancing for what it is rhythmically, free from the visual distractions of watching a White, hyper-feminine body per-form. Performing this dance as a "tribute" paradoxically creates distance be-tween herself and Black corporeality while, at the same time, diminishing the space that prevents her, as a female dancer, from being taken seriously on the tap dance stage. Nothing about Powell's tribute number resembles—visually or aurally—the choreography of the first number. But each movement and every sound executed by Powell in the first dance affects the meaning of her second routine. Only when one views these two dances side by side do the dynamics of gender and race as performance become clear.

The tribute guise not only allows Powell to perform in blackface, but it collapses—like the Bill Robinson effect—individual Black performers into a fixed set of properties that all point back to the nineteenth-century min-strel stage. Individual labor is erased, stylistic qualities dissolve, and White performers are sanctioned into new roles onscreen. From 1940 onward,

Hollywood would prioritize White dancers performing Black affect and Africanist sensibilities over Black artistry.

Powell's "Tribute" to Robinson waves goodbye to the Black male body—which for the last twenty years has dominated the tap dance stage—and welcomes the White female body to take its place. The ship (on which Powell dances) that leaves the mainland and heads for the "exotic" Hawaiian Islands mirrors this corporeal gesture. These two moving vessels—that is, Powell's White female body and the ship bound for Honolulu—stand in for the film's overarching message regarding (White) American national identity: if America can incorporate an Africanist aesthetic into the national narrative and "clean up" any remaining trace of Blackness, it can just as easily annex Hawaii and capitalize on its "Native" culture.

Notes

1. Written for Goldwyn in 1934. Music by Burton Lane and Lyrics by Harold Adamson. Lyricist Adamson later went on to write the lyrics to the *I Love Lucy* theme song.
2. Eric Lott, "The Seeming Counterfeit: Racial Politics and Early Blackface Minstrelsy," *American Quarterly* 43, no. 2 (1991): 232.
3. Sam Dennison, *Scandalize My Name: Black Imagery in American Popular Music* (New York: Garland, 1982), 61.
4. Clayton R. Koppes and Gregory D. Black, "Blacks, Loyalty, and Motion Picture Propaganda in World War II," in *Controlling Hollywood: Censorship and Regulation in the Studio Era*, ed. Matthew Bernstein, 138–39 (New Brunswick, NJ: Rutgers University Press, 1999).
5. I am thinking specifically here of the Berry Brothers' "dance-ons" in *San Francisco* (1936) and *The Music Goes Round* (1936), Bill Bailey's bit in *Going Native* (1936), Stringbean Williams's solo in *Underworld* (1937), the Three Chocolateers in *The New Faces of 1937*, and Tip, Tap, and Toe in *You Can't Have Everything* (1937).
6. See Cheryl Willis, *Tappin' at the Apollo: The African American Female Tap Dance Duo Salt and Pepper* (Jefferson, NC: McFarland, 2016) for an exhaustive list of these Apollo stars.
7. This claim is based purely on my viewing of hundreds of films from this era.
8. The Harlem Riot of 1935 resulted from years of escalating tension due to unemployment and police brutality. One event in particular set off 4000 rioters in Harlem in March of 1935. A Black Puerto Rican boy named Lino Rivera stole a penknife from the Kress Five and Ten store on 125th street (across the street from the Apollo). A police officer was called to the scene, but neither the store manager nor assistant manager wanted to press charges. The officer led Rivera out the back so that he could avoid the crowds. Rumors started to spread that the officer had killed Rivera. The

210 BEHIND THE SCREEN

Young Communist League and the Young Liberators led a demonstration that drew in thousands of people. Then one aroused individual threw a rock through the Five and Ten store's window, kicking off a series of destructive behaviors and arrests.

9. Berlin wrote this during his recruit time at Camp Upton in Yaphank, New York. Even though this song was cut, there were several others in the revue that required the use of blackface, including the popular song with derogatory lyrics "Ragtime Razor Brigade." See Don Tyler, *Hit Songs, 1900–1955: American Popular Music of the Pre-Rock Era* (Jefferson, NC: McFarland, 2007), 104–5; Seymore Stark, *Men in Blackface: True Stories of the Minstrel Show* (Bloomington, IN: Xlibris, 2000), 75; and David Jasen and Gene Jones, *Spreadin' Rhythm Around: Black Popular Songwriters, 1880–1930* (New York: Routledge, 2005), 71.

10. Michael Curtiz, *This Is the Army* (August 14, 1943; USA: Warner Bros.), Film.

11. I examine the not-so-blatant uses of blackface in this performance in the coming chapters.

12. Song written by Buddy DeSylva and Joseph Meyer and published in 1925 by Shapiro, Bernstein, & Co. While the song was originally written for Jolson, it became a staple for Cantor.

13. *Varsity Show* is one instance where John Bubbles performs a rhythm tap dance sequence as the janitor in an all-White mens' locker room, for example. In that same year, Bubbles also appears in the British film, *Calling All Stars*.

14. John Bubbles is credited for inventing his own "new style" in 1922 that soon became known as rhythm tap. According to the Stearns, Bubbles "changed from two-to-a-bar to four-to-a-bar, cutting the tempo in half and giving himself twice as much time to add new inventions. . . . [F]or the jazz-oriented, the switch in rhythmic accenting may be described as the difference between Dixieland and the swing beat." Marshall Winslow Stearns and Jean Stearns, *Jazz Dance: The Story of American Vernacular Dance* (New York: Da Capo Press, 1994), 215.

15. George Stevens, *Swing Time* (August 27, 1936; USA: RKO Radio Pictures), Film; Edward Buzzell, *Honolulu* (February 3, 1939; USA: Metro Goldwyn-Mayer), Film.

16. Rogin writes, "There is a primal scene in every blackface musical: it shows the performer Blacking up. The scene lets viewers in on the secret of the fetish: I know I'm not, but all the same. The fetish condenses the unanalyzed magical significance assigned to blacks, functioning like the . . . commodity in Marx's [theory]. Signifying transvestite masquerade and the expropriation of black labor, burnt cork fetishized not only blackness but sexual difference and the commodity form as well." See Michael Rogin, "New Deal Blackface," in *Hollywood Musicals, the Film Reader*, ed. Steven Cohan (London: Routledge, 2002), 176.

17. For a particularly excellent analysis of the film's blackface routine performed by Miller and Lee, see, Arthur Knight, *Disintegrating the Musical* (Durham, NC: Duke University Press, 2002), 110–19.

18. In an earlier version of the *Honolulu* script, Mason insists that Dorothy remove her makeup before he escorts her to the deck. Something similar happens in *If You Knew Susie* (1948) when the big blackface scene is followed by a blackface removal bit. Protagonist Joan Davis goes on about the relief she feels when she removes her *Black* face.

19. See, for example, Arpad Szakolczai, "Liminality and Experience: Structuring Transitory Situations and Transformative Events," in *Breaking Boundaries: Varieties of Liminality* 2 (2015): 141, and Victor Turner, "Betwixt and Between: The Liminal Period in Rites of Passage," in his *The Forest of Symbols* (Ithaca, NY: Cornell University Press, 1967).

20. Constance Valis Hill, "Stepping, Stealing, Sharing, and Daring: Improvisation and the Tap Dance Challenge," in *Taken by Surprise: A Dance Improvisation Reader*, ed. Ann C. Albright and David Gere (Middletown, CT: Wesleyan University Press, 2003).

21. Anthea Kraut, "Stealing Steps and Signature Moves: Embodied Theories of Dance as Intellectual Property," *Theater Journal* 62, no. 2 (May 2010): 175–76 and Siva Vaidhyanathan, *Copyrights and Copywrongs: The Rise of Intellectual Property and How It Threatens Creativity* (New York: New York University Press, 2001), 126.

22. Stearns and Stearns, *Jazz Dance*, 338.

23. Anthea Kraut, *Choreographing Copyright: Race, Gender, and Intellectual Property Rights in American Dance* (New York: Oxford University Press, 2016), 141.

24. Ibid. See also Cholly Atkins and Jacqui Malone, *Class Act: The Jazz Life of Choreographer Cholly Atkins* (New York: Columbia University Press, 2001), 27.

25. James Haskins and N. R. Mitgang, *Mr. Bojangles: The Biography of Bill Robinson* (New York: William Morrow, 1988), 101.

26. See, for example, Arlene Croce, *The Fred Astaire and Ginger Rogers Book* (New York: Dutton, 1987).

27. Music by Jerome Kern and Dorothy Fields. See John Mueller, *Astaire Dancing: The Musical Films* (New York: Knopf, 1985).

28. Ibid., 107 and 109.

29. Ibid., footnote 12, p. 109.

30. Todd Decker, *Music Makes Me: Fred Astaire and Jazz* (Berkeley: University of California Press, 2011), 116.

31. Ibid., 117.

32. Jeff Smith, "Unheard Melodies? A Critique of Psychoanalytic Theories of Film Music," in *Post-theory: Reconstructing Film Studies*, ed. David Bordwell and Noël Carroll (Madison: University of Wisconsin Press, 1996), 230.

33. David Krasner offers an excellent analysis of realism as such. See David Krasner, "The Real Thing," in *Beyond Blackface*, ed. W. Fitzhugh Brundage (Chapel Hill: University of North Carolina Press, 2011), 100–02.

34. Astaire shared these stereotypical sentiments in a text he published in 1936 entitled "Hot Dance." He writes, " 'Hot dance' is not a very attractive term but it is the only one I can use to describe dances like the Lindy Hop and the Shim Sham Shimmy, which were originated by the coloured people. And incidentally, how I do love to watch coloured people dance." He later writes that the " 'hot dance' " is the Fox Trot gone mad. It's an expression of bubbling over spirits and exuberant vitality. It's a combination of the primitive and the ultra-modern. Savages did their 'hot dance' to the sound of the tom-tom. Jungle rhythm still strikes a responsive chord in our beings after many hundreds of years of civilization." Quoted in Decker, *Music Makes Me*, 118.

35. Note the similarity here to what will happen in *Blue Skies* a decade later. See chapter 1.

212 BEHIND THE SCREEN

36. Rhythm Tap is a style of tap dancing developed by John Bubbles in 1922. Bubbles's unique style was a highly syncopated version of the day's popular tap dancing and required that he slow the tempo of his musical accompaniment by half, which allowed him to squeeze in more sounds per note. This style revolutionized tap dancing and was the basis for Powell's style. See Jerry Ames and Jim Siegelman, *The Book of Tap: Recovering America's Long-Lost Past* (New York: D. McKay, 1976), 43.

37. According to Lacan, "What this structure of the signifying chain discloses is the possibility I have . . . to use it in order to signify *something quite other* than what it says." See Jacques Lacan, "The Agency of the Letter in the Unconscious or Reason since Freud," in *Écrits: A Selection*, trans. Alan Sheridan (London: Tavistock, 1977), 155.

38. Todd Decker notes that RKO's interest in "hot bands" and "hot music," the explosion of Benny Goodman's band, and a "shift in popular music taste initiated by White teenagers listening to network radio, [all indicated] swing . . . [as] a musical marker which quickly became a marketing tool." "Swing" as a word and a concept quickly emerged as the new "hot," hence the musical's title, *Swing Time*. I will return to the popularity of swing in the coming chapters. Decker, *Music Makes Me*, 119. See also Kenneth Bindas, *Swing. That Modern Sound* (Jackson: University Press of Mississippi, 2001.

39. *Honolulu* previewed at the Westwood Village Theater in Los Angeles, California, on February 4, 1939, before moving to New York City's Capitol Theater on February 22 that same year.

40. A title Powell received after her performance in *Broadway Melody of 1936*. See Alice Levin, *Eleanor Powell: First Lady of Dance* (Potomac, MD: A. B. Levin, 1997), 49.

41. *Born to Dance*, perhaps one of Powell's most well-known works, was released on November 27, 1936, and *Rosalie* was released December 24, 1937,

42. In 1938, MGM announced that Powell would be performing alongside George Murphy in *Gentleman Be Seated*, a musical adapted from Daly Parkman and Sigmund Spaeth's minstrel stories. I was able to get a copy of this show's soundtrack, and the lyrics reveal that the show was blatantly racist and would not have passed the censorship guidelines of the Hays Code that the MPAA began enforcing in 1934. See Margie Schultz, *Eleanor Powell: A Bio-Bibliography* (Westport, CT: Greenwood Press, 1994), 15.

43. The doppelgänger narrative was very popular during this moment in American cinema. It was common in German expressionist films of the 1920s, but *Honolulu* marks the beginning of such a tradition in America. For a more in-depth description of this history, see Jan-Christopher Horak's essay, "German Exile Cinema, 1933–1950," *Film History* 8, no. 4 (December 1996): 373–89.

44. At the risk of a complete digression, this performance aboard the ship prior to its departure from the mainland could even be considered "homely" to some. That is, its target White, middle-class audience might consider it comfortable in the way Sigmund Freud has analyzed *Heimlich*, where Powell's cozy performance is both familiar and yet so proverbial that it remains hidden to those outside her guarded (White) space. Lying within the bounds of this intimate presentation yet positioned "in transit" is Powell's tribute to Bill Robinson, which she performs in transit between

"home" and the Hawaiian Islands. Juxtaposed to Powell's homely dance performed on the ship's deck (prior to departure), her attempt to portray an uncanny likeness to Robinson produces a performance of the *Unheimlich* (in the true sense of the German translation) wherein the subject (Powell as a Black man) "arouse[s] dread and horror" and "coincide[s] with what excites fear in general," but also lies within the realm of the familiar. Before leaving the mainland, Powell's Africanist influence is concealed and kept out of sight. It is through her performance as Robinson that the familiar surfaces through the uncanny. Her mask provides a diversion from White America's comfort with appropriating a Black aesthetic. Reading Powell's performance in this way—seeing through the veil of covert minstrelsy—exposes what Hollywood tried to conceal. Through the tribute guise the performer both masks and must reveal the homeliness of the Other. For a deeper explanation of *Heimlich* and *Das Unheimlich* see "The Uncanny" in James Strachey, Anna Freud, Carrie Lee Rothgeb, and Angela Richards, *The Standard Edition of the Complete Psychological Works of Sigmund Freud/Translated from the German under the General Editorship of James Strachey, in Collaboration with Anna Freud, assisted by Alix Strachey and Alan Tyson* (London: Hogarth Press, 1953).

45. The Hoofer's Club was the back room of one of Harlem's most popular gambling houses (*The Comedy Club* located on 131st Street and Seventh Avenue). It was where prominent African American tap dancers of the 1920s, '30s, and '40s would exchange steps and challenge one another. See Ames and Siegelman, *The Book of Tap*, 50. While the Copacetics choreographed the Copacetic Chair Dance around 1949, the idea stemmed from their years at the Hoofer's Club. Reggio McLaughlin has relayed the story to me as the following: young men without a home would often try and sleep at the club despite not being allowed to do so; they developed a series of tap dances they could do while seated so if caught napping in the chairs, they could pretend it was part of the choreography (Author's interview with Reggio McLaughlin, February 27, 2015).

46. Brynn Shiovitz, *Masks in Disguise: Exposing Minstrelsy and Racial Representation within American Tap Dance Performances of the Stage, Screen, and Sound Cartoon, 1900–1950* (PhD diss., University of California, Los Angeles, 2016).

47. *The Gay Divorcee* (1934) was the first film in which Astaire and Pan explored this new technique of using the camera across the screen to film dance rather than coming straight down the middle. This was different from the Busby Berkeley technique and changed dance for camera forever. See John Franceschina, *Hermes Pan: The Man Who Danced with Fred Astaire* (Oxford: Oxford University Press, 2012), 55–57.

48. "Flash" here refers to a style of tap dance that was popular in the late teens, 1920s, and 1930s. It included "flashy" acrobatic steps like Over the Top and Through the Trenches, steps that were influenced by World War I and ways of moving through the battlefield. See Stearns and Stearns, *Jazz Dance*, and Constance Valis Hill, *Brotherhood in Rhythm: The Jazz Tap Dancing of the Nicholas Brothers*, New York: Oxford University Press, 2000) for more on Flash Dance.

49. In "Choreographies of Gender," Susan Foster contends that if one views gender as a performance (as the post-essentialist thinkers do), then one should also be able to resist and re-think routinized behavior. This requires understanding the dynamics at

214 BEHIND THE SCREEN

play between categories of race, gender, and sex that impact the behavior or performance of one another. See Susan Foster, "Choreographies of Gender," *Signs* 24, no. 1 (1998): 3.

50. I am thinking specifically of other women who were subverting gender, race, and sexual conventions during this time, such as Bessie Smith, Gertrude "Ma" Rainey, and Gladys Bentley. Bentley in particular was known for being an "avowed 'bulldagger' []famous for her suggestive songs and masculine appearance." See James F. Wilson, *Bulldaggers, Pansies, and Chocolate Babies: Performance, Race, and Sexuality in the Harlem Renaissance* (Ann Arbor: University of Michigan Press, 2010), 155–57.

51. Written in 1938 by Harry Warren and Gus Kahn for *Honolulu*.

52. While this opens up a completely different discussion, I am thinking more in terms of copyright infringement here as it applies to the various Hollywood studios and their individual "rights" to performers once a performer had signed a contract with the studio rather than in the context of a "racial project" as Anthea Kraut discusses in terms of the trafficking of African American bodies in *Choreographing Copyright*, 91–95. See also Eva Cherniavsky, *Incorporations: Race, Nation, and the Body Politics of Capital* (Minneapolis: University of Minnesota Press, 2006). Robinson made his first film debut in 1930 with RKO's *Dixiana* where he did a "specialty number" within an all-White film and signed with Twentieth Century Fox a few years later so that he could perform his famous stair dance alongside Shirley Temple. See Haskins and Mitgang, *Bojangles*, 205. In 1938, Twentieth Century-Fox revoked his contract due to the decline in popularity and thus need for Black performers. I will return to the issue of copyright in a racial context at a later point in the chapter.

53. The King's Men was a musical quartet that formed in 1929 and had a successful career in Hollywood Films and Radio. One of their more notable performances was as select Munchkins in *The Wizard of Oz* (1939). Ken Darby went on to be a successful vocal arranger and supervisor, working in the Music Department for Walt Disney for the duration of the 1940s (*Bambi, Song of the South, So Dear to My Heart, Make Mine Music*, and *Pinocchio*) and winning three academy awards (*The King and I, Camelot*, and *Porgy and Bess*) in the 1950s and '60s.

54. *Duck Soup* was a Marx Brothers comedy from 1933.

55. Shiovitz, *Masks in Disguise*.

56. An exception would be his dance in *Rebecca of Sunnybrook Farm* (1937) where he and Shirley Temple are dressed as soldiers.

57. Cherniavsky, *Incorporations*, 84.

58. Ibid., 84.

59. Cheryl Harris, "Whiteness as Property," *Harvard Law Review* 106, no. 8 (1993): 1707–93

60. Cherniavsky, *Incorporations*, </INT>84.

61. Ibid., 85.

62. I in no way intend to assign blame to Robinson. I just want to note the complexity of his performance. While he made many strides for his race, some people have taken issue with the roles he agreed to play on-screen.

BON HOMAGE 215

63. This surfaces most visibly in two striking gestures: at one point when Powell dances down the staircase, she holds her palms out as if offering a serving platter, insinuating that servitude, or at least the role of servant, is an important part of Robinson's persona.

64. A term I will be using throughout this and future sections to denote a mix of songs written by composers other than Harry Warren and Gus Kahn that also happen to offer the music for tribute dances.

65. I cannot infer whether this was Foster's intent, especially since the most convincing evidence of his music's social impacts can be seen in the history of American theater which transpires apart from and outside of Foster's control. The Tom show, for example, began as something positive, as did Foster's desire to convey the message of Stowe's *Uncle Tom's Cabin*. By granting permission for his songs to be used in the theatrical space, Foster signed off on the possibility that his music would be used for ulterior motives; the life of the Tom show became the life of his music.

66. William Austin identifies three types of Foster songs: comic, poetic, and pathetic; "Old Folks at Home," "Massa's in de Cold Ground," and "Old Black Joe" he considers to be of the "pathetic" type. Here "pathetic" simply means that these songs invoke pathos. See William Austin's *"Susanna," "Jeanie," and "The Old Folks at Home": The Songs of Stephen C. Foster from His Time to Ours* (New York: Macmillan, 1975), ix–xi.

67. For example, using the word "Darkey" instead of "N[*sic*]." Harold Vincent Milligan, *Stephen Collins Foster: A Biography of America's Folk-Song Composer* (New York: G. Schirmer, 1920), 69.

68. Examples of such lyrics can be seen in Ken Emerson, *Doo-dah!: Stephen Foster and the Rise of American Popular Culture* (New York: Da Capo, 1998), 186.

69. Smith, "Unheard Melodies?," 237.

70. Ibid., 234.

71. Claudia Gorbman, *Unheard Melodies: Narrative Film Music* (London: BFI Publishers, 1987), 2–3.

72. Ibid., 3.

73. Ibid.

74. As an aside, Jolson starred in a film by the name of *Swanee River* this same year. The whole film is a "tribute" to Stephen Foster (his life and music) and one big excuse for Jolson to perform several numbers in blackface as Mr. Christy. Not only do we see Jolson perform in burnt cork (e.g., his big tap dance during "Camptown Races"), but we also see intentional juxtapositions of blackface archetypes and slang. One example of this can be seen in the timed placement of a gruesome yet smiling blackface cartoon (perfectly framed behind Jolson backstage) alongside the line "while all the darkies are gay" in the soundtrack.

75. The Art Deco period celebrated the slim and slightly androgynous female figure. According to Katharine McClinton, we can examine Art Deco from two angles: "On the one hand, there was the 'masculine' geometric pole in which 'curves gave way to angularity and motifs of design tended to be more dynamic.' On the other hand, there was the 'feminine' curvilinear mode that favored such sentimental imagery 'rose[s] . . . garlands and baskets of flowers, fountains and jets of water, doves, female

216 BEHIND THE SCREEN

deer and nudes' (quoted in Fischer, "Designing Women," 298). Powell exhibited the slim-hipped female ideal of this period. See Lucy Fischer, "Designing Women: Art Deco, the Musical, and the Female Body," in *Music and Cinema*, ed. James Buhler, Caryl Flinn, and David Neumeyer, 295–315 (Hanover, NH: University Press of New England, 2000).

76. Fred Moten, *In the Break: The Aesthetics of the Black Radical Tradition* (Minnesota: Minnesota University Press, 2003), 172.

77. Wilfred Jackson, Santa's Workshop (December 26, 1932; USA: Walt Disney Productions), Film.

78. Norman Taurog, *Boys Town* (September 9, 1938; USA: Metro-Goldwyn-Mayer), Film.

79. Wallace Fox, *Career Girl* (January 11, 1944; USA: Producers Releasing Corporation [PRC]), Film. Krueger does not perform Robinson's traditional stair dance but instead performs a light-on-your-feet tap solo with the same syncopations and pervasive use of stop time that Robinson used in his solos. She performs the entire routine at the base of a staircase resembling the one used in *The Little Colonel*. She also exits the stage with a caricatured version of one of Robinson's signature moves.

80. Another clear example can be seen in *Top of the Town* (1937) where a young Peggy Ryan imitates Powell—not Robinson—as an audition to tap dance on a ship. Ryan begins her routine by saying, "I'm 10 years old and I imitate Eleanor Powell." Ralph Murphy and Walter Lang, *Top of the Town* (April 18, 1937; USA: Universal Pictures), Film.

81. According to Franceschina, the shadow dance portion of "Bojangles of Harlem" was a last-minute addition that delayed the projected shooting schedule of *Swing Time* by nine full days. The story is relayed as follows: "Hermes got the idea while he and Hal Borne were on the sound stage waiting for Astaire to arrive for rehearsal. He noticed three lights at the top of the stage that cast three shadows as he moved around. The idea amused him so when Astaire arrived he pointed to the shadows suggesting . . . If it could be done, it will be interesting. You could dance with your shadows. . . . Vernon Walker, RKO camera-effects specialist, jumped on board immediately. 'All you do is get Astaire in front of a screen and photograph his shadow first. Then we take those shadows and make a split screen, and then we photograph Astaire doing the same routine in front of them.' . . . Hermes Pan never ignored the opportunity to mention afterward that 'Bojangles of Harlem' is one of the few musical clips in the collection of the Museum of Modern Art in New York City." See Franceschina *Hermes Pan*, 80–81.

82. Inasmuch as this tactic overtly flaunts the triumphs of American art and science vis-à-vis the cinema, this subtle gesture also hints at the potentially inescapable fact that no matter how good these White dancers are, they will always be dancing in Robinson's (Black) shadow. For both Blackness and blackface have cast shadows on the ways in which the public perceives tap dance; its association to Blackness, whether real or fictitious, will always compromise the art form's ability to capture national representation without a racialized subtext.

83. Susan Foster, "Gender," *Signs* 24, no. 1(1998): 5.

FIGURE 4.4 (*Center*) Eleanor Powell performs a "tribute to the Islands" alongside Andy Iona's Orchestra (uncredited) and ensemble in *Honolulu*, 1939. (Private collection); Various clippings (The New York Public Library for the Performing Arts).

Skirting Censorship: Brownface and Technology in Transit

"Ladies and gentleman, for our first presentation, Miss Dorothy March, as a tribute to the islands, will do a Native drum dance, a hula, and her version of a Native dance done with taps."

A revolving orchestral platform spins 180 degrees covering up the Fiesta Room's White musicians to expose an orchestra of dark-skinned "Native" musicians sitting on the other side. These shirtless "Natives" begin playing "traditional" instruments: ukuleles, drums, and a bass. The onscreen audience sits engrossed in this sight. They resume their applause as they witness dozens of scantily clad, bare-midriffed female dancers putting a Hollywood touch on Hawaiian performance. The camera cuts to Eleanor Powell, who gracefully makes her way to center stage positioning herself in the spotlight. The chorus dancers slowly form a circle around her, executing a series of moves that acknowledge a 1930s syncretism: Ruth St. Denis's Orientalist influence on modern dance, Busby Berkeley's innovations in Hollywood, and a classic Patty Cake.[i] Meanwhile Powell's strength, precision, and pleasant face captivate her audience, her White body distracting spectators from seeing in her style elements of Horton,[ii] early Dunham,[iii] and West African body percussion. The high-energy dance then morphs into a seductive solo by Powell encapsulated by an image reminiscent of Busby Berkeley's kaleidoscopic top shots. Two dozen made-up "Native" dancers fan Powell from all angles as she continues to perform an allegedly "authentic" hula. The music

---

i. Ruth St. Denis (b. 1879) was a modern dancer known for creating works largely based on Hindu and Egyptian mythology, as well as broader themes inspired by the "Orient." Denis co-founded the American Denishawn School of Dance in 1915 with fellow modern dancer and husband, Ted Shawn. This school relied heavily on Delsarte gymnastics, Dalcroze eurhythmics, and "ethnic" dancing and trained a large number of notable modern dancers including Graham, Weidman, and Humphrey. Patty cake is one of the oldest surviving English nursery rhymes, with written record dating back to Thomas D'Urfay's *The Campaigners* from 1698. The rhyme often accompanies a clapping game between two people with alternating individual and two-handed claps with a partner. Powell mimics this clapping routine. See Opie and Opie, *The Oxford Dictionary of Nursery Rhymes* (New York: Oxford University Press, 1951), 341–42.

ii. Lester Horton (b. 1906) was an American modern dancer and choreographer best known for incorporating American Indian dance and modern jazz into his technique.

iii. Katherine Dunham (b. 1909) was an American dancer, choreographer, and anthropologist known for her writings on dances of the African diaspora, innovations in African American modern dance, and contributions to American modern dance.

220 BEHIND THE SCREEN

picks up. Drummers interrupt the soothing music and flow of Powell's hula. As the time signature shifts and the filming technique changes, the camera introduces extreme close-ups of Powell's ethereal white hands which stand in stark contrast to the extreme close-ups of the dark-skinned drummers' strong and powerful hands, beating out the rhythms of this Hawaiian drum chant. The camera and music cut immediately to the metallic toe taps of Powell's glistening shoes; the camera zooms in and then proceeds to accentuate each muscle in her powerful legs. The camera comes to a halt when it reaches the small opening in the dancer's revealing ti leaf skirt and quickly zooms out in time with the music. This bare-midriff dance is quite risqué for its time. Powell spins effortlessly on the glossy floor alternating between Maxie Ford and flap heel turns. She travels through space with a distinctive elasticity—left, right, up, down—stretching like a rubber band from one level to the next and punctuating the dominant ukulele beats with her hips. She executes flawless rhythm tap with her feet while maintaining a smooth, calm, cool upper body. The ensemble suddenly appears and the shot wavers between showing Powell in the center of a circle of hypermasculine dark-skinned drummers and hyperfeminine fair-skinned American hula dancers. The piece ends with all the females lined up vertically in an inverted passing parade, again using Berkeley optics in a new way. Powell chaîné turns straight down a center aisle composed of their seated bodies. She picks up speed with each turn until she lands in a seated cross-legged position right in front of the camera, hands framing her face, smiling.

Brownface thrived in Hollywood between 1934 and the bombing of Pearl Harbor. Dance films made during this period tended to take place "in transit," especially between the American mainland and its territories. During the period 1933–1941—coincidentally the time it took America to decide whether to enter World War II—Hollywood took an interest in Hawaiian-themed films and transit narratives.[iv] The imperialist relationship America had toward surrounding islands allowed Hollywood to present the "brown" body within a mythical kingdom that was both American and not American. By

---

iv. Examples include *Flame of the Pacific* (1934), *Honolulu* (1938), *Typhoon* (1940), *Honolulu Lu* (1941), *Moonlight in Hawaii* (1941), and *Hawaii* (1941). In most of these films about Polynesian Islands, regardless of the narrative, filmmakers could write off their inclusion of the "brown" or "brown-faced" body as a tribute to this colonized land and "Native" culture.

creating plots centered around an imagined Hawaiian community off mainland soil Hollywood could simultaneously "annex" the parts of Hawaiian culture toward which it was drawn (and for which it saw economic benefit), and also fabricate cultural intimacy between the mainland and its surrounding Islands while still keeping the Other at a distance.

Hawaii's idyllic landscape made the islands a popular site for films that sought to provide a "safe" getaway for their audiences while the body read as brown mediated between the perceived threat of the Black body and a professed lack of exoticism offered by White bodies. Eleanor Powell's "Hula Tap" performance, described above, marks the choreographic resolution of a four-part arc in *Honolulu* where her engagement with a Native form overseas allows Powell to certify her identity as a strong rhythm tap soloist who can maintain tap dance's Africanist qualities without burnt cork, exert her White privilege over a US Territory and its dance forms, and safely accentuate her female sexuality through her gestures at Native culture. Because of the ways the film strategically sets up her encounter with Nativeness, narratively, Powell could achieve all these things at the height of the Hays Code. That is, her identification with the Hawaiian Islands and "mastery" of Native Hawaiian material allowed for more liberal camerawork and wardrobe selections. Because brownface could be achieved without a literal mask, she could signify the "brown" body without making herself up to look like one.

The film exaggerates a binary between Nativeness and Whiteness by deemphasizing White female sexuality and White masculinity. While it is conceivable that accentuating Otherness through corporeal and performative markers was at play, Production Code files from *Honolulu* (known earlier as *Lucky Star*) offer a logistical explanation: early correspondence between Joseph Breen and Louis Mayer (of Metro-Goldwyn-Mayer) demonstrate a fixation on the way White characters were portrayed. Breen writes, "Political censor boards may delete the showing of Robert [Young] in underwear" and remarks that "Robert should be wearing both trunks and a shirt, to avoid deletion," pointing to the abundance of care taken with the "indecent" exposure of White men. The "Native" men, on the other hand, are never shown wearing shirts. Similarly, Breen warns the creative team to exercise caution with the White dancers. The White dancers "should not execute any suggestive or 'bump' movements," while no such advice existed for the dancers portrayed as Native in this film or elsewhere. Furthermore, the censors were clear that any suggestive scenes between White performers and so-called Natives should be eliminated, as was cautioned with regard to an early take of scene

222　BEHIND THE SCREEN

117. Breen advises, "Care should be taken with the business and dialogue between Millie [Gracie Allen] and the Kanaka boy to avoid offense. Physical contact should be avoided."[v] The film expects viewers to read Powell's body as White while on the mainland and while in transit and "brown" once she arrives in Honolulu.

Once on the Island, Powell's body becomes a sign of Nativeness, carrying a distinctive pleasure that satiates her audience's need for escape from the mainland through a "safe" encounter with the exotic. For this reason, brownface situated within this Island context not only helped to shift the tap dancing body away from the practice of "blacking up," but in fact capitalized on Powell's often-censored sexuality as key to the maintenance of White America's national identity. Furthermore, this shift in color from blackface to brownface allowed parts of the *mise en scène* (i.e., setting, costume, sound, and movement) to stand in for blackface, the brownface an intermediary on the color spectrum, "Nativeness" an intercessor of exoticism. When the "Native" female "brown" body was presented in conjunction with the transit narrative, its liminality further obscured the relationship between an Africanist aesthetic and Blackness so that White bodies could covertly perform minstrelsy while openly performing tap dance and jazz.

Powell's hula tap dance is not the only dance of its kind.[vi] The Peters Sisters perform an embedded hula tap dance routine, "Broadway's Gone Hawaii," in *Love and Hisses*;[vii] Johnny Downs also performs a tap dance in *Hawaiian Nights* (1939); a year later Alice Faye and Betty Grable perform a hula tap dance in the film *Tin Pan Alley*;[viii] and Powell performs another hula tap dance during the opening of *Ship Ahoy*.[ix] Furthermore, hula in the 1920s and '30s had become so popular and the market for it so strong that iconic entertainers began publishing dance manuals and articles on the hula, promising mainland women from all classes and backgrounds that they too could

---

v. Edward Buzzell, *Honolulu* (February 3, 1939; USA: Metro-Goldwyn-Mayer), Film. MS Hollywood, Censorship, and the Motion Picture Production Code, 1927–1968: History of Cinema, Series 1, Hollywood and Production Code Administration, Margaret Herrick Library, Beverly Hills, California.

vi. The tap dance performed by Johnnie Downs and Sunnie O'Dea in *Moonlight in Hawaii* (1941) might be another example, but I have not been able to access the footage.

vii. Words and Music by Mack Gordon and Harry Revel, Copyright 1937 by Leo. Feist Inc.

viii. "K-K-K-Katy," which goes through several lyric revisions throughout the course of the film, was written by Geoffrey O'Hara in 1918. Sung and danced by Alice Faye and Betty Grable as the Blane Sisters. See Albert S. Rogell, *Hawaiian Nights* (September 8, 1939; USA: Universal Pictures), Film; Walter Lang, *Tin Pan Alley* (November 29, 1940; USA: Twentieth Century Fox), Film.

ix. Edward Buzzell, *Ship Ahoy* (May 1942; USA: Metro Goldwyn-Mayer), Film.

experience the exotic without ever leaving home.[x] These choreographies shared no relation to the actual hula but alternatively enacted a sexy female body. According to dance theorist Jane Desmond, the phrase "South Sea Dance" came to include a variety of "exotic" dances, all of which resembled one another and fell under an amorphous category of "Oriental dance." The shimmy and the Charleston, despite their Africanist origins, were frequent movements in the "South Sea" vocabulary. Such hula dance manuals showed no attempt to deliver an authentic hula but instead increased an interest in Hawaii as a tourist destination and kept money flowing into the (then) American territory. Such aspects of "song and dance tourism" solidified the act of difference-making in the imagination and, as Desmond argues, "underline[d] the centrality of the performing body, binding notions of 'facticity,' presence, naturalism, and authenticity together under the sign of spectacular corporeality."[xi]

Aside from skin color, "spectacular" hula performances like these underscored two mainlander stereotypes: Native Hawaiian women must be graceful and sexy, and Native Hawaiian men must be strong and look "savage." According to Jane Desmond, men in these Native contexts tended to provide a contrast for the women's soft-primitivism.[xii] In Powell's performance at the "Fiesta Club," the women dancing perform feminine codes of behavior: the choreography emphasizes female sexuality: shimmying of the shoulders attracts attention to the breasts, and shimmying of the hips brings attention to her erogenous zones. Likewise, the grass skirts are long, but revealing, giving the audience a peek, but not exposing too much; the metallic bras draw attention to the breasts, but do not reveal anything but slight cleavage; finally, the long hair, dark eye makeup and bright lipstick bring attention to the face.

The camera further emphasizes a coexistence of sexiness and feminine grace through its filming technique, at times fragmenting the female body into parts: cutting to the hips or the legs, veiling the audience from the whole body. Thanks to Berkeley's optic technology, dance on camera changed the way the body could signify. In addition to being able to export "Nativeness" to the mainland, the camera made fragmentation of the female body possible. The camera uses only a panoramic shot to showcase the women against

---

x. Jane Desmond, *Staging Tourism: Bodies on Display from Waikiki to Sea World* (Chicago: University of Chicago Press, 1999), 72–75.

xi. Ibid., xv.

xii. Ibid., 25.

the muscular bare-chested drummers. The camera rarely puts the men's faces in the viewfinder; instead, it zooms in on their veiny hands beating their solid drums or the infinitesimal movement of minute musculature across their broad backs. The drums they strike in unison further amplify the strength behind their masculinity. The men move very little, but their wide stance combined with a broad upright posture conveys their power to the audience. In this way, the technology of large-scale, dance-for-camera numbers like this one helped to redirect viewers' gazes to focus on the parts rather than the whole. Furthermore, the camera allowed for geographic/scenic flexibility: one could add or subtract various elements of Hawaii's land/atmosphere in order to realize aspects of viewers' imaginations.

While the signifying components of Powell's performance carry little resemblance to the performance repertoire's purported signified, they do fall in line with a White Western notion of the "ideal Native": "Nationalism, figured as White, troubled by Blackness, grappled with the challenges of encoding Hawaii's racial polemics and complexity within a model of nationalism that could barely contain them."[xiii] In an attempt to erase a complex Hawaiian demographic and suture the fragmented concept of the American mainland, 1930s national discourse surrounding Hawaii collapsed all islanders into one Euro-American imaginary, playing the part of the noble and the romantic savage simultaneously. Publicity for the dance goes so far as to call Powell's hula tap a conga as if her hula stemmed from Cuba. Viewing the Native Hawaiian body as a composite "brown," as opposed to Black or White, allowed the tourist to escape the complicated racial binaries of the mainland while conflating many islands into a mysterious composite ideal, full of "tropical richness and splendor." [FIG. 4.4] It allowed for exotic bodily difference while maintaining distance from the Black body. The "brown" hula dancer thus provided the tourist with a "safe" encounter, enabling colonial expansion by figuring ownership of an exotic who was better than the mainland's Black Other. It is here that the significance of transit narratives to the larger goal of skirting Production Code guidelines emerges. Powell's body acts as the equivalent of the increasingly popular *hapa-haole*[xiv] who, through performances like her hula tap, creates a discourse of ambivalence, "continually producing its slippage, its excess, its difference," marking "soft" difference in order to preserve the idea of a diverse national whole.[xv]

xiii. Ibid., 7.

xiv. A half-White, half-Native Hawaiian body.

xv. Homi Bhabha, "Of Mimicry and Man: The Ambivalence of Colonial Discourse," in his *The Location of Culture* (London: Routledge, 1994).

FIGURE 5.1 Rex Ingram as De Lawd in *The Green Pastures*, 1936. (Private collection)

5

With a Glory Be

The Gabriel Variation, Jazz, and Everything In-Between, 1934–1942

"Ever since I was a little Pickanniny . . ." A blackened Al Wonder (Jolson) dressed as a sharecropper croons to a young child also in full blackface. He cradles her and sings: "When I pass away, on that judgment day, I'm goin' to heaven on a mule. . . . Ma-mmy waits, at those pearly gates . . ." As he finishes his song, a choir begins humming the tune and Wonder slowly shuffles to his mule, Zeke. The camera takes some liberties and transports viewers into a dreamscape of silhouetted women and the pearly gates of heaven, which look shockingly similar to the Wizard of Oz's depiction of Emerald City five years later. As Wonder makes his way through the doors of this Art Deco heaven, Saint Peter and Gabriel in blackface greet him. Three cherubim also in full blackface sing Cab Calloway's famous Hi-de-ho scat. As Wonder gets fitted for his angelic paraphernalia, Peter and Gabriel send the misbehaving folk down the "chute to hell." Viewers get a glimpse of imaginary southern locations such as Pork Chop Orchard and Possum Pie Grove as well as "Old Black Joe playing a banjo-o" and that "Old Uncle Tom that I used to know-ow. I'm so glad that he landed up here with his cabin showww." The camera cuts to chickens in cages and then jump cuts again to a plucking machine and chicken rotisserie, and then again to Wonder eating fried chicken. Wonder is soon greeted by the Milky Way/Lenox Express trolley that transports him to an idyllic city of swing-dancing seraphs, barber shops, and even a watermelon palace. Wonder stops for a shoe-shine and then very deliberately peeks out over his Yiddish newspaper, the "Garden of Eden Star." A series of racial mockeries in rapid succession follow: Emperor Jones; drinking; gambling (including an extreme close-up of the now-clichéd Black hand rolling dice); and finally, a watermelon caricature taken to the extreme—a giant watermelon unfolds its slices to reveal a tap dancing Hal Le Roy in full body blackface. A close-up of his tack Annie reveals that the creative team did such a thorough job applying makeup to his legs that whether this is a White or Black performer in blackface is unclear. A chorus of blackfaced chorus

Behind the Screen. Brynn W. Shiovitz, Oxford University Press. © Oxford University Press 2023.
DOI: 10.1093/oso/9780197553091.003.0006

228   BEHIND THE SCREEN

girls remain mostly hidden behind the swaying melon slices but occasionally show their legs. As Le Roy completes this 32-bar chorus of sprightly rhythm tap, the chorus reconfigures the melon. The camera pans out to reveal the Big Dipper Cabaret's entire ensemble. What appears to be hundreds of performers in black-face join in praise hands, swaying from side to side as they sing about judgment day. The final shot centers in on Jolson citing his famous "Mammy" moment. "With a 'Glory be,' I'll be glad to see, Abe Lincoln like he used to be, the man who set me free; Yes, I'm goin' up to heaven . . ."

Four months before Joseph Breen assumed command of the newly established Production Code Administration, Warner Bros. released *Wonder Bar* (1934),[1] an overtly racist film starring all of Hollywood's big names and stars-to-be: Al Jolson, Kay Francis, Hal Le Roy, Ricardo Cortez, Dolores Del Rio, Guy Kibbee, Dick Powell, and many others participated in a picture full of forbidden subjects. In addition to the big blackface number "Goin' to Heaven on a Mule" described above, the story is teeming with blackmail, adultery, debauchery, and murder.[2] In fact, the film was so "immoral" that its release catalyzed Breen's exacting iteration of the Code as well as the establishment of the Production Code Administration (PCA) that would have to give its final approval before a film could be released. In addition to drastically altering the narratives Hollywood was telling, such changes would directly impact Busby Berkeley's choreography. Naughtiness and racial slurs would have to be implied rather than explicit in these large-ensemble numbers.

In spite of *Wonder Bar's* disturbing deviations from the Motion Picture Association's (MPA) "guidelines," the film turned out to be one of the year's top-grossing pictures. Most of the complaints from White people about this film's immoral plot line came from the Catholic Church and the NAACP, not the moviegoing public.[3] Mordaunt Hall's review in the *New York Times* remarked on this film's "several amusing features" but neglected to say anything about its inherent racism.[4] Yet despite *Wonder's* widespread success, approval from the church and the NAACP would be crucial to the industry's long-term financial stability. Thus, storylines that relied on racialized tropes of gambling, watermelon, and fried chicken—as in the kind of overblown racial caricature one sees in *Wonder*—mostly disappear by the end of 1934. What remains, however, is a strong use of the citational guise in the form of "Black heaven," a subset of covert minstrelsy I refer to as the Gabriel variation, which helps to justify the use of dangerous rhythms in otherwise "morally

FIGURE 5.2 Hal Le Roy performs in "Goin' to Heaven on a Mule" from *Wonder Bar*, 1934. (Warner Bros./Photofest)

230 BEHIND THE SCREEN

decent" motion pictures. "Goin' to Heaven on a Mule," like Jolson's original "Mammy" becomes yet another cinematic foundation on which films of the new Breen era will build.

Returning to both the sonic and citational guises as well as racial caricature in the form of brownface, this chapter examines a general shift in attitude toward syncopated rhythms and the significance of blacksound when offered in a "holy" context. Beginning in 1934, Hollywood's White stars flirted with an increasingly popular swing aesthetic, one that had hitherto been tied to the devil and subject to unforgiving censorship laws, even during the Code's most permissive years. To circumvent the Code, directors utilized two primary strategies. The first was to cast Black actors and White actors in blackface within a White conception of Black heaven—caricatured to the point of Black dystopia—which not only housed dozens of minstrel caricatures but also foregrounded these fictions in a swing aesthetic. The Gabriel variation presented as such allowed Hollywood to sidestep many of the rules surrounding racial representation while simultaneously pulling "hot" rhythms out of the depths of hell. Films such as *The Green Pastures* (1936), *A Day at the Races* (1937), and *The Singing Kid* (1936) offer Whiteness as the arbiter between the sin of syncopation and salvation as granted by the White savior.[5] If the Gabriel variation was not present, a swing-inspired scene or film might work to encode a classic primitivist framework—often utilizing a generalized "brownface"—into its overarching narrative, as do the films *New Faces of 1937* and *Ali Baba Goes to Town* (1937). The blackface sequences in these two films are presented in transit—in space and time, respectively—demarcating swing's journey from Black to White but also expressing a certain ambivalence around the use of burnt cork in the film present. That is, in addition to establishing racial in-between-ness or "safe" exoticism, the transit narrative assists in the passage of swing from the audibly Black to the visibly White.

Hollywood's presentation of swingin' Black vernacular forms such as peckin', truckin', and the popular Suzy-Q acknowledge how such hot music gained popular momentum in 1936–1937 despite its motion in some circles as early as 1920. The divide between the existence of a Black aesthetic as a subculture and its acceptance into the White mainstream is partially accounted for in David Stowe's claim that swing was a musical expression of the New Deal, "accessible, inclusive, distinctively democratic, and thus distinctly American," mirroring Franklin Roosevelt's politics.[6] Also, swing was widely accessible because of modern technologies such as the radio and sound film. Joel Dinerstein's conception of the techno-dialogic, or "an artistic bridge between self-expression and the technological soundscape," offers this chapter a technologically and historically motivated nuance of the sonic guise.[7]

Beyond a handful of exceptions, big movie studios would align themselves with a small number of White stars, offering performers like Fred Astaire and Eleanor Powell mega contracts that would guarantee them each a few pictures a year. Even the visibility of Bill Robinson and Cab Calloway would fade as their appearances were soon relegated to either all-Black films or caricatures designed in their images. As we have begun to see, Astaire and Powell's mastery of rhythm tap—and arguably a swing aesthetic—assists in the strange fading of Black dancing onscreen between 1939 and March 1941. It is also this process vis-à-vis covert minstrelsy that obscures the relationship between an Africanist aesthetic and Blackness, making hot rhythms and hoofers Whiter and thus more acceptable vehicles for representing American identity on the national level.

Finally, the period from 1934 to 1941 is marked by distinct passages: jazz underwent a "Whitening" due in part to key "crossover" figures, like Cab Calloway, who double coded their performances to garner a racially diverse audience, and due in part to Benny Goodman's version of swing that enjoyed mass circulation; the Harlem Riot of 1935 and the subsequent relocation of the Cotton Club from Harlem down to Broadway and 48th Street no doubt aided in the Whitening of jazz; the concurrent "rhumba craze"—resulting from the abundance of the dance's appearance in Hollywood musicals and nightclubs—offered curious Americans a way of bridging swing's dangerous Black rhythms and "squaresville" with the slightly safer and amorphous brown bodies from the Middle East, Latin America, and the nation's surrounding islands; the Production Code experienced its biggest ever shift in administration and thus law enforcement, greatly affecting the kinds of narratives that could be told and how; a number of economic shifts occurred that were directly correlated to Roosevelt's presidency; and finally, the country experienced a multi-year debate of when the United States should enter World War II. These many changes disrupted notions of national identity, helping to explain the in-between-ness of covert minstrelsy's various iterations.[8]

Specifically, these passages manifest both literally and figuratively through the pervasive use of transit narratives: the White Jewish body as intercessor between Black heaven and hell, and the brown body as a mediator between Black and White appear during these social and economic transitions and

232   BEHIND THE SCREEN

define covert minstrelsy of this unique pre-war era. I conclude this chapter with yet another iteration of the transit narrative. Eleanor Powell's morse code tap dance in *Ship Ahoy* (1942) signals the dawning of a new era in covert minstrelsy, one defined entirely by its in-between-ness and the thickened application of covert masks despite a waning trend in visible blackface.

***

"Going to Heaven on a Mule" contains obvious racial caricatures seen in the hyper-visible use of blackface as well as clichéd references to watermelon, fried chicken, and gambling. The number also makes use of several less visible forms of masking: the dialect—"Yes you is and da chickens am free"—makes use of racial caricature through the aural register as does the interweaving of "real" and newly written Negro spirituals. The sonic meets the citational guise in moments when the cherubim in blackface scat Calloway's famous *Hi-di-ho* lyrics as well as in the number's final shot, which centers on Jolson citing his famous "Mammy" moment. Narratively, the naming of "Uncle Tom" and "Ol' Black Joe" internally reference Black archetypes of the stage and screen while the Milky Way/Lenox Express names a geographic divide between Whiteness and Blackness. The production number exhibits traits of southern repossession in its labeling of "Pork Chop Orchard" and "Possum Pie Grove" within this "heavenly" plot line but also in glorifications of Abe Lincoln—"like he used to be, the man who set me free." An Africanist presence is undeniable in the number's references to tap dancing, lindy hop, and swing, and it is rife with the sort of double-coding for which Jolson was so well known, seen in his frequent references to the Old Testament and in his several-second freeze behind a Yiddish newspaper. The set design operates on an even more covert level through the *mis-en-scène's* juxtaposition of pseudo portrayals of Black life and Art Deco architecture similar to that in *Ritz* as well as through Busby Berkeley's newest offerings in optical technology.

The mirror science that Berkeley utilizes in *Wonder Bar* changed what could be possible for large-ensemble numbers in Hollywood. Such eye-trickery was more economical and more distracting than anything used earlier. Not only could the studio hire fewer bodies, but the sheer scale overstimulated an audience, making less cognitive space for other disguises at play. According to Jeffrey Spivak, Berkeley asked Warner Bros.' property department head Albert Whitey for twelve revolving mirrors, each to be twenty feet high and sixteen feet wide and arranged octagonally. While the ensemble at the end of "Mule" appears to include hundreds of dancers in blackface, only a few dozen were on set. By using an unseen camera, Berkeley was able to play with the laws of reflective physics to create the effect of hundreds of performers. Spivak explains Berkeley's science: Per Berkeley: "'We finally had to dig a hole through the stage floor, and we put the camera on the piece of pipe. The operator laid flat on his stomach underneath the stage and crawled and moved around slowly with the turning of the camera.'"[9]

While optical illusions such as Berkeley's mirror science might not have negatively impacted anyone on set and likely had no emotional bearing on its viewers, it speaks to a more general "smoke and mirrors" ethos similar to what we saw in chapter 1. If Berkeley's optical science was sound enough to fool the majority of viewers, then what else was the *Wonder* creative team slipping in without an audience's conscious knowledge? Jolson's performance of "Mammy" in *The Jazz Singer* helped to broaden the spectrum of aural signifiers that White American audiences came to recognize as definite ties to the minstrel stage. Similarly, the various modes of covert minstrelsy in "Mule" thickened the layers of sonic, narrative, and visual imagery American audiences came to comprehend as recognizable ties to minstrelsy. Consequently, future onscreen pairings of the Gabriel variation/projections of Black heaven and a swing aesthetic would project Africanist rhythmic sensibilities through a White lens while simultaneously reinforcing a connection between modern "hot" music and the nineteenth-century minstrel stage.

The Gabriel variation enters Hollywood roughly four years after writer Marc Connelly adapts Roark Bradford's collection of short stories (1928) for the stage.[10] Connelly's Pulitzer Prize–winning play *The Green Pastures* (1930) saw huge success with White audiences, but Black audiences and writers tended to be more critical of the White author's depiction of the Bible as seen through a Black consciousness. Zora Neale Hurston, for one, wrote, "If there is anything that is not in the Negro's conception of Heaven, it is work. . . . This is the White man's idea of Heaven palmed off to perpetuate the belief that the Negro's status, even in eternity, will be that of menial."[11] Connelly felt strongly that his "research" in the deep South lent a certain credibility to the way Black life, and specifically religion, "really" was, yet his "characterization of African American Protestant theology as simplistic, unchanging, and oriented exclusively toward future benefits" downplayed the complexity of Black theology during this period.[12] In 1936, Connelly partnered with director William Jackson Keighly to create a film version of *Pastures*. Although the film was one of six all-Black cast films made during Hollywood's studio

234 BEHIND THE SCREEN

era, its depictions of African American life, to use G. S. Morris's words, "satisf[ied] his spiritual needs while affirming his own white liberal racism and defending the white, middle-class status quo."[13] While the Gabriel variation tends to be more prevalent in films with White casts, the fact that *Pastures* utilized such a form of covert minstrelsy—the opening number likely a citation of "Mule"—should say something about the fallacy inherent in Connelly's supposed anti-racist sentiment as well as the insidiousness of Gabriel and other variations of the citational guise.

Who Dat Man? It's Gabriel . . .

The Gabriel variation emerges as a way of combating the ever-increasing popularity of a swing aesthetic. As an approach to music and dance that was very situated in an Africanist aesthetic and therefore tied to Blackness, Hollywood seems to justify its incorporation of a swing aesthetic into mainstream media by juxtaposing its presentations with notions of salvation, and specifically Black liberation as tied to the devil integral to syncopation's temptations. These scenes tend to feature a White (often Jewish) performer as the savior—as God, as angel, or as king—who leads those "infected" by the swing aesthetic on a path to redemption. Sonically these depictions of Black heaven will incorporate Negro spirituals—both traditional and contrived—as well as a handful of Negro dialect catchphrases such as "who dat," "de lawd," and "chillun." Finally, suggestions of Cab Calloway—both his real body and caricatures designed in his image—exist as pervasively as do references to Bill Robinson during this period. These mentions generally offer a visual component to these scenes' overarching soundscapes, with Calloway's wild hair—popularly identified as the "conk"—metaphorically standing in both for swing's out-of-control-ness and Calloway's in-between-ness. Audible markers of Calloway's presence include phrases like "*Hi-di-ho*" and "*Zah-zu-zaz*" sprinkled throughout the dialogue and song lyrics. The "Who Dat Man (Gabriel)" number from the Marx Brothers' 1937 film *A Day at the Races* supports the use of the Gabriel variation as justifying the incorporation of a swing number and blackface in a film narratively unrelated (though the leading horse is named "High Hat") and otherwise (and perhaps intentionally) devoid of Black performers.

This scene featuring Whitey's Lindy Hoppers, Ivie Anderson (from Duke Ellington's orchestra), and the uncredited Three Chocolateers makes no narrative sense: Harpo Marx literally appears out of nowhere in a Black quarter of town adjacent to the horse stables playing a tin flute. Hearing "Gabriel's" sounds, a group of Black children flock behind him and sing "Who dat man?" The answer is Gabriel and as such, Harpo leads these Black children (and later teenagers and adults) on his path to salvation. This musical montage features "Nobody Knows the Trouble I've Seen," a large-scale singing and Lindy number performed to "All God's Chillun' Got Rhythm," "Zaz-zuh-zaz" citations, and call-and-response between the White angel Gabriel and the troubled Black "folk" in shantytown. Harpo is eventually joined by Groucho and Chico who cannot help but "truck" in response to the jazz rhythms. Eventually some authority figures come in looking for the Marx Brothers and the three of them hide under a horse carriage while using the grease from the carriage wheels to "black up" for the ultimate disguise. Once concealed the three comedians leap out and join the jam, not to be discovered by the White authorities. Here the Gabriel variation offers a context for this disguise which in turn narratively excuses the blatant use of the Marx Brothers' blackface. Simultaneously, the Gabriel variation invoked here delivers a less overt message regarding the imagined sin of Black rhythm while reinforcing the salvation offered by the White body. Encoded in this latter message, however, is also a critique of White Jewish masculinity, effeminized through Harpo's speechless role and feminizing pantomimes. Here, once again, feminization of the Jewish male occurs, like Sander Gilman has argued, as a form of civil disempowerment, yet through such disparagement, Marx mediates between White masculinity and Blackness.[14]

The Gabriel variation, an extension of what Susan Manning has termed "metaphorical minstrelsy," or the "convention whereby white dancers' bodies ma[k]e reference to nonwhite subjects," was typically steered by a host of White Jewish comedians. Even though performers such as Marx, Jolson, and Cantor often engaged in imitation—and in the case of the latter two, blackface—their personification and abstraction of "Black heaven" distinguishes the Gabriel variation from other forms of mimicry.[15] The period in which these presentations of heaven appear overlaps with the metaphorical minstrelsy Manning identifies in a 1930s modern dance context and the widespread acceptance of performances of covert minstrelsy at large when delivered vis-à-vis the Jewish American body.

While "Who dat man?" captures most elements of a typical Gabriel variation, specifically in its valuation of syncopation by means of "hot" rhythms and a swung dance break, the number lacks the costumes typical of cinematic

236 BEHIND THE SCREEN

representations of Black heaven and many of Hollywood's more frequently used caricatures of Black life. Standard costumes include a mix of gospel choir gowns, wings, and halos while the backdrops tend to rely heavily on clouds, pearly gates, and Art Deco inspired architecture. Verbal and visual references to a canon of Black stereotypes including chicken, fried fish, watermelons, and dice infiltrate all parts of these scenes. Finally, and more covertly, the number presents a series of encoded references to both a primitivist framework and more overt references to Judaism: a pervasive use of gaudy African kings flaunting animal print, gold, marabou, and fur—a sort of "primitive chic"—in the case of the former, and a list of buried references to the Hebrews, Yiddish, King Pharaoh, and Jewish slavery in the case of the latter. All these ideas together comprise the Gabriel variation and allow for the use of blatant blackface, justified logistically as necessary if White performers are to share the stage with Black artists.

Many films made between 1934 and 1941, like *Races*, utilize the Gabriel variation, but Jolson's performance of "Save Me Sister" in *The Singing Kid* (1936) is exemplary.[16] To give this illustration some context, *The Singing Kid* is one of many Jolson films made about a star performer living his star-performer life thus requiring many "shows-within-the show." The more of these films Jolson made, the more opportunities there were for him to internally reference his own shows within these films. By 1936, he had amassed enough material to create an opening montage that is nothing but a series of solipsistic citations. The film begins with Jolson in blackface and large white gloves performing his original "Mammy" routine in front of the same drawn caricature of himself that was used in promotional materials to advertise *The Jazz Singer*. This scene transitions into a straw hat and overall-wearing Jolson in blackface singing George Gershwin's rendition of "Swanee" (1919), a reference to the actor's successful performance in *Sinbad* at the Winter Garden Theatre as well as his famous Plantation Act for Vitaphone. The montage cuts to his performance of "Rock-A-Bye Your Baby with a Dixie Melody," which he recorded in 1918 and first introduced in the Broadway show *Sinbad*.[17] Here he performs in a suit, downstage of a caricature of himself in blackface. This immediately cuts to Jolson in blackface and white gloves singing "California Here I Come" from his 1921 Broadway musical *Bombo*.[18] His backdrop in this scene references *The Honeymoon Express*, a show he performed onstage in 1913. This transitions seamlessly into "April Showers," a Jolson standard that he introduced in *Bombo* and subsequently popularized for Columbia Records. Jolson is dressed as Christopher Columbus's slave Gus, his *Bombo* character, still in blackface. The mood changes though as the montage cuts to Jolson's first reference without the use of burnt cork singing "About a Quarter to Nine" which Jolson sang in 1935 for the Hollywood musical *Go into Your Dance* aside Ruby Keeler.[19] The montage closes with Jolson belting the lyrics of "Sonny Boy," a reference to his performance in *The Singing Fool* [FIG. I.1, top],[20] a performance originally done in blackface, but sung without in this closing sequence.[21] This number is important because it establishes a citational framework for the film and foregrounds Jolson's career as one marked by burnt cork, even when the Code urges him to remove the mask.

The camera closes in on a magazine column featuring Jolson's character: "Al Jackson, America's favorite Stage and Radio Star, Chooses a Penthouse in the Clouds" by Louella Green immediately following the retrospective montage.[22] This article in the fictional *Show World* fades into a never-ending upward tilt of a prodigious Art Deco–styled skyscraper, so tall it appears to collide with the clouds. Atop this paradigm of modern architecture stands Jackson (Jolson) and Calloway (as himself) in a swinging call-and-response duet of "I love to Sing-a"[23]—as Jackson belts "Oh ain't it grand, to live in green" . . . Calloway responds with a combination of lyrics and scats interspersed with his now-classic way of conducting amid a swingin' dance routine, accented by his tightly curled bangs. The countless similarities between this scene and so many others staged by Warner Bros. since "Goin' to Heaven on a Mule" speaks to the popularity of both Jolson and Calloway during this era as well as the relevance of modern architecture to a swing aesthetic, a relationship present onscreen as early as the title number in *Ritz*. Thus, the Whiteness of the protagonist or "savior," swing aesthetic, lyrics, and modern architecture are crucial to the Gabriel variation, which ideologically cements the notion that modern swing requires some sort of heavenly intervention. Furthermore, that such a projection of heaven is interposed with a kind of "grandiose exteriority" might further allude to the subtext of Jewish identity in the majority of these Gabriel variations, an idea to which I will soon return.[24]

The Gabriel variation in this film begins with Jolson's transparent act of donning blackface in a backstage mirror, fetishizing the mask and reminding viewers that the act of masking is itself a spectacle. Such transparency is not a requirement of the Gabriel variation so much as it helps to frame what follows as merely a performance, an approach that, as we have seen, became increasingly more important as Hollywood enforced the Code. We then get a glimpse of Jolson dressed similarly to Bill Robinson backstage before the

238   BEHIND THE SCREEN

camera cuts to Calloway onstage singing "You Gotta Have that *Hi-Di-Ho* in Your Soul."[25] With Black choristers and later Black dancing couples in a jook-joint-like setting, this scene could have easily been taken from one of Oscar Micheaux's contemporaneous race films. However, when Jolson in blackface enters singing "The Swingin'est Man in Town," he disrupts the all-Black aesthetic, crediting himself as the superior "king of swing" in a manner reminiscent of Robinson's reputation as the "king of Harlem."[26] Jolson, sporadically tipping his bowler hat, mimics the tap dancing of Robinson. This reference is pure imitation in the way that Susan Leigh Foster in *Reading Dancing* has described the imitative mode of representation as a performance that unquestionably references the intended referent, rather than an example of the tribute guise.[27] Because Jolson's use of blackface in this scene goes beyond a mere synechdochizing–acting as more of a citation of self than of Robinson—his performance is mimetic rather than honorific. Furthermore, there is nothing covert about the problematic nature of this scene's narrative. Like so many of the films we have examined, "*Hi-Di-Ho* in Your Soul" showcases the White performer as the proprietor of an Africanist aesthetic, as if to assert that Black people would fawn over Jolson's use of Black rhythmic sensibilities. The tribute guise uses the White body as a vessel for appropriating an Africanist aesthetic in a much more covert way, yet Jolson's use of Robinson's image speaks to the tap dancer's popularity and hence frequency with which one observes his iconography during this period.

Once Jolson, dressed like Robinson, has narratively established himself as the "swingin'est man in town," the White actress Wini Shaw, dressed in a White gospel choir gown and made up with blackface, steals the screen with the opening notes of "Save Me Sister."[28] High on a pedestal she communicates with Calloway in the pit and with a large ensemble of Black performers below. They listen to Shaw's words intently responding with alternating "praise the lord" hands and a version of truckin' in-between her lyrics and Calloway's scats. Both the "swingin'est man in town" and the swing dancing populace awaiting heaven's pearly gates ask forgiveness "from that devil revelry; from the life of fancy free." We have seen this imagery before—most recently in "Goin' to Heaven on a Mule," and in *Pastures* (1936), but some of the references harken back to *Cakewalk Infernal*, like the smoke and mirrors, devil iconography, and White savior who recuperates the souls of Black people (and White) who have fallen prey to Black rhythm and dance, a message so powerful that it could even be conveyed without sound. Still, *Singing*

Kid delivers an even more covert message when we examine such imagery in the context of sound and the performativity of 1930s–1940s jazz culture.

Calloway's Crossover Appeal

While Cab Calloway achieved great success during his decade at the Cotton Club (i.e., his four-year residency from 1930 to 1934 and then sporadic performances until its closure in 1940), he attained even wider success through frequent (sometimes weekly) radio broadcasts, film appearances, and recorded repertoire. But Calloway's unique crossover appeal to audiences from diverse race and class backgrounds is perhaps at the heart of his incredible success. *The Singing Kid* both illustrates how Calloway performed to a racially diverse audience and typifies how the same performance might have been regarded differently by different listeners, offering Americans, as Nate Sloan convincingly argues in his essay "Constructing Cab Calloway," "multiple visions of the Black metropolis—the slummer's Harlem, the New Negro's Harlem, the migrant's Harlem, and the race rebel's Harlem."[29]

Sloan traces Calloway's diverse success back to two publicity stints: first his long residency at the Cotton Club and second his management by Irving Mills, who held a reputation as a "controversial figure known as much for his unethical business practices . . . as he [wa]s for his canny promotion." Despite such a repute, Mills offered his Black clients a "level of publicity that was seldom available to artists of color."[30] Mills was smart about how he "branded" his stars and prepared special marketing manuals for his clients that offered carefully crafted personas for publicity purposes; Mills constructed two personas for Calloway, one that appealed to White audiences and one that appealed to Black audiences.[31] Curated for White consumption was "The Harlemeaestro," a person whom Sloan poignantly describes as "an ambassador from Harlem subculture to white America . . . a Charon-like figure who catalogues in detail the alluring drugs, sex, and danger that animated the Harlem vogue, while remaining at a safe distance from that scene's racialized pleasures."[32] Mills played up Calloway's one-time aspiration of becoming a lawyer when appealing to his African American fan base. These stories focused on Calloway's intelligence and collegiate experience; music was a choice, not a "primitive product of his race" for the musician.[33] Such splitting between two diverse audiences allowed for a range of racially coded promotional materials that would also surface in his recorded

240 BEHIND THE SCREEN

repertoire. Sloan discusses how the key branding points that were meant to exoticize the singer were the very traits that "enabled Calloway to subvert his constructed persona and assert a self-fashioned identity even when performing in a segregated nightclub."[34] "Minnie the Moocher" perfectly expresses Calloway's double-coded performance repertoire and offers insight into why the celebrated musician held such crossover appeal.

Calloway wrote "Minnie the Moocher" at the suggestion of Irving Mills, who convinced the musician that he needed a musical identifier.[35] Calloway used the "harmonic structure and instrumental introduction of Louis Armstrong's recording of 'St. James Infirmary' and based the lyrics on 'Willie the Weeper,' a vaudeville tune about a drug-addled chimney sweeper that had been recorded by Frankie 'Half-Pint' Jaxon in 1927."[36] This combination retained its crossover appeal through its reliance on "local" practice in combination with "wild" vocalizations—"hi-de-ho" and "za-zuh-zaz"—and references to sex and illicit drugs. Furthermore, the lyrics themselves relied on slang that could be decoded by fellow Harlemites or completely obscure to his White listeners unaware of the double meanings. The performative qualities also served a dual function for his diverse audience: Calloway's signature "hi-do-ho" phrase invites in both Black and White listeners through its participatory nature. What might have read as humorous and nonsensical to White audiences—again an affirmation of the alleged "jungle" or "primitive" sound—was in fact engaging them in a game of call-and-response. Calloway's aptitude for this "game" allowed even his rehearsed recordings to sound improvised as if performed live from the Cotton Club. Thus, the "hi-de-ho" phrase that became Calloway's signature sound at the Club and also seeped into recordings and film allowed White listeners to "visit" Harlem without being present. It allowed for intimacy with Black music at a safe distance. More important, however, it allowed Calloway to reverse the terms of these White-owned, White-run businesses. With "Hi-de-ho," Calloway "dictates the terms of this engagement, maintaining ownership and control of the "hi- de-ho" game, which always remains playful enough to appear outwardly innocuous."[37]

Calloway's racially indeterminate physique also contributed to his crossover appeal. His hair, which he chemically straightened, was often used as proof that Calloway was not wholly Black. Promotional materials often played up his hair as being "quite unlike the tight wool that usually crowns the negro head" and he was "able to toss [it] about with amazing dexterity when he wishe[d] still further to emphasize the idea of ecstasy."[38] His hairstyle spoke to Black and White audiences alike. So did his embrace of the zoot suit, which allowed him to perform a kind of Blackness that diverse audiences could get behind. His embrace of White beauty standards was also a marker of his unique Black urban identity. As Robin D. G. Kelley suggests, Calloway's unique style allowed him "to negotiate an identity that resisted the hegemonic culture and its attendant racism and patriotism, the rural folkways (for many, the 'parent culture') which still survived in most black urban households, and the class-conscious, integrationist attitudes of middle-class blacks."[39] Thus what may have looked and sounded White to Calloway's White fans also occupied a potentially rebellious and liberating space for his African American fan base. Calloway stood somewhere in the middle, in-between, in-transit.

While arguably less "clownish" than his performance of "Kickin' the Gong Around," in *The Big Broadcast of 1932*, Calloway does himself no favors singing "You Gotta Have that *Hi-Di-Ho* in Your Soul" by agreeing to perform alongside Jolson's blackface and blatant appropriation of a jazz aesthetic.[40] The Black press overlooked the demeaning stereotypes to which this film played and instead emphasized Calloway as the film's star.[41] To many Black people, Calloway was not a sellout but instead a prototype for challenging race prejudice, which might best be illustrated in *Singing Kid*'s closing number.

Arthur Knight, in his poignant analysis of Jolson and Calloway's relationship in this film, offers an important critique: the finale, "You're the Cure for What Ails Me," sung by Calloway when Jolson enters the theater (without blackface), begs the question "Who is Calloway singing to and/or for?" Knight responds, "Calloway is singing *for* Al in every sense. . . . Al employs Calloway . . . the lyric Calloway sings expresses Al's feelings." But this *for* in fact works two ways: as a production "Jolson needs Calloway's new style to reinvigorate his career . . . [and] Jolson does Calloway good in aiding him in reaching a wider, whiter, more remunerative music market."[42] Furthermore, in giving Calloway a bit part rather than a character with emotional depth, Hollywood portrays Calloway as being fine with this exchange. His character holds the same kind of copacetic attitude as his contemporary, Bill Robinson, who seemed to also elevate the roles of White characters/actors at the same time Hollywood made it clear that these performances were representative of changing race relations. Thus, no matter how much Calloway's "brand" resisted the hegemonic culture and its attendant racism, his image appealed to a racist superstructure and would aid in Hollywood's rhythmic negotiations

242   BEHIND THE SCREEN

between an Africanist aesthetic and White performers. Calloway's appearance in films like *The Singing Kid* allowed White audiences to have a safe encounter with a more primitive sound as well as a chance to visit Harlem from a distance while at the same time elevating White performers like Jolson. These films' soundtracks provided new possibilities for how to convey the story of White Christian redemption from the peril of Black culture.

From Low Down Dribble to "High"-De-Ho

Sound had been rapidly developing since the silent *Infernal* in part because of the manufacturing boom and techno-futurist craze that dominated the teens, twenties, and early thirties. The mid-1930s were marked, culturally speaking, by swing and jazz, and as Joel Dinerstein argues, they embodied machine aesthetics as necessitated by a need for taking one's body back from the machine.[43] The techno-dialogic reveals "how the presence (or 'voice') of machinery became integral to the cultural production of A[frican] A[merican] storytellers, dancers, blues singers, and jazz musicians" and contains a combination of "West African rhythms, the industrial soundscape, European song structures, and African American musical practices," making the period between 1934 and 1942 on film particularly techno-dialogic in its use of the swing aesthetic.[44] Jazz music, as Duke Ellington famously described it, is a "matter of onomatopoeia" and helps explain why so many of the performances described in this chapter utilize not only a jazz aesthetic, but specifically a rhythm driven by the sonicity of skyscrapers and machinery, with an emphasis on scatting.[45] This model can be seen in "Slap that Bass" from *Shall We Dance* (1937), a tap dance featuring Fred Astaire, Dudley Dickerson, Steve Gibson, and Perry Anderson, all of whom but Astaire were uncredited.[46]

   Narratively, the techno-dialogic offers Hollywood opportunities to slip in these types of rhythmic negotiations between an Africanist aesthetic and the White dancing body. Dinerstein describes Astaire's dancing in "Slap that Bass" as a classic encoding of primitivism, where Astaire "visits" the lower classes—like the trip Harpo takes to shantytown in *Races*—for "raw instinctive passion" in rhythm. Dinerstein writes, "He first acknowledges the rhythmic genius of the African American workers by getting their stylized rhythms (and artistic affirmation) into his bones; then he's ready to sing a jazz-influenced popular song, converting raw material to refined popular art on the spot."[47] Here the "transaction" between Black and White artists occurs through the rhythm, much like the exchange functions for Powell in her tribute to Robinson or Astaire in "Bojangles of Harlem." Thus, more than how the techno-dialogic helps to explain the evolution of machine rhythms into popular culture (as Dinerstein seeks to do), I am interested in how this evolution assists in the transfer from something audible and Africanist to something visible and White. And moreover, this evolution operates with a similar ambivalence to that of the blackface mask that allows Hollywood to mark difference while also attempting to exploit it.

This aesthetic reassignment is also evident in the ways that the dialogue and lyrics in musicals of this era not only draw on jazz's musical codes but also operate on a perceived relationship between jazz and danger. As we saw in the lyrics sung by Astaire in "Bojangles of Harlem," the words "'Hot,' 'swing,' and 'jazz' were code words for improvised, highly syncopated music and music-making."[48] This was true not just of Irving Berlin's music or films in which Astaire appeared, but also of media across the board during the height of the swing era (roughly 1935–1945). In *Music Makes Me*, Todd Decker describes the significance of such language in Astaire films of this era, writing, "*Hot* was a descriptive word, and seldom spoken aloud in an Astaire film." Conversely the word "swing" was connected to the marketing of music and as such, writers would often try to slip the words into dialogue and song lyrics to help a film sell.[49] A good example of such coded language can also be seen in *Birth of the Blues* (1941) where Jeff (Bing Crosby) is criticized for his interest in jazz music. The film opens rehashing *The Jazz Singer*'s plot of a father shaming the musical interests of his son.[50]

Mr. Lambert: "Did you ever hear any white folks play that low down dribble? Doggone darkie music."

. . .

Jeff (as young boy): "This other music makes ya feel like the circus has come to town. It kinda turns you loose inside. You can stretch out and play what you feel."

Immediately the dialogue sets up jazz music as something distinctly Black and "loose." By the end of the film, the plot has offered another narrative indicating that White people are the experts of such an aesthetic. Jeff and his all-White jazz band, the Basin Street Hot-Shots, become the most popular jazz band on Bourbon Street; they improvise better than the locals and just as well as the performers in the film's other cameos such as Duke Ellington and

244   BEHIND THE SCREEN

Louis Armstrong. In this film (and countless others) Bing Crosby does for a jazz aesthetic in song what Astaire does for Black sound in dance.

During the height of swing's popularity, Astaire was able to mediate between the "dangerous" syncopated rhythms, which were tied to the Black primitive body, and the trendy swing rhythms of White America. That is to say, the music that White crooners like Crosby sang and White hoofers like Astaire danced to in these films was no different from what Black musicians and tap dancers were performing onscreen, but Hollywood was careful to use different descriptors to describe the dances of each actor according to his racial identity. An example of this can be seen in the dialogue of *Shall We Dance* in which Astaire (as Pete) is careful to distinguish the syncopated dancing that he performs as modern and different from what Black hoofers do:

> Pete: *Jazz went out with the flapper, Jeff.*
> Jeffrey: *Look here—you're not thinking of becoming one of those hoofer persons, are you?*
> Pete: *Oh, this is different. It's got swing, rhythm . . .*[51]

Establishing the "appropriateness" of an Africanist aesthetic as a symbol of modernity when performed by White bodies was necessary if White musicians and dancers were going to be successful onscreen and free from censorship. A history of this shift from swing as Black and hot to White and hep will be helpful.

Swing entered popular music vocabulary with the breakthrough of Benny Goodman's band in July 1935 after the band's engagement at the Palomar Ballroom in Los Angeles. Todd Decker and others have attributed this increase in popularity to a shift in musical taste "initiated by White teenagers listening to network radio, swing, like rock and roll and rap after it, was a musical marker that quickly became a marketing tool."[52] John F. Szwed writing in *Phylon* notes as early as 1966 that it "has been obvious for some time that White jazz musicians by and large have been *followers* [italics mine] of Negro innovators, yet have been given public credit for the innovations." He uses Benny Goodman as a perfect example of this phenomenon: Goodman's "very successful band was a carbon copy of Fletcher Henderson's earlier unsuccessful group."[53] Which is to say, as was the case with White tap dancers in Hollywood stealing the spotlight from their Black contemporaries, the White public often had an easier time accepting—or was perhaps more impressed by—Black music delivered vis-à-vis the White body, even if Goodman's swing (and a more general jazz aesthetic) was less "authentic." Shortly after

WITH A GLORY BE   245

Goodman's show at the Palomar Ballroom, the term "swing" began appearing in the White press.[54] *Swing* was a new word for *hot*, and "Hollywood swiftly embraced the term and the musicians associated with it."[55]

Swing had gone mainstream by 1936 and 1937, and by 1938 it had "acquired sufficient mass to become a national fad, the subject of articles and editorials in the country's most widely read periodicals and newspapers."[56] As a musical genre accepted into the mainstream, swing continued to populate both the White and Black moviemaking industries with writers doing whatever they could to work swing into the film's plot, however tangentially. This tendency to include swing allowed these Hollywood films of the era to showcase Black and White talent, but even more important, it served as a marketing device to sell music.

Whether rhythm was in the title or merely a part of these films' trailers, Hollywood producers knew swing's popularity would help box office sales while the musicians themselves knew that playing for these films would benefit the sale of their songs. Shorts like *Cab Calloway's Jitterbug Party* (1935), *Hi De Ho* (1934 and 1947), or *Meet the Maestros* (1938) spotlighted trending artists such as Cab Calloway and popular songs (e.g., "Zaz-Zuh-Zaz," "Minnie the Moocher," and "Hi-De-Ho Miracle Man"). Occasionally feature films would have little to do with music or dance and would include nightclub scenes for the sheer purpose of highlighting artists, as exemplified by the Mills Brothers' cameo in *Strictly Dynamite* (1934).[57] The directors of *Hollywood Hotel* (1938) echoed this trend by writing Goodman into the contract after the project had already been conceived of simply as a way to highlight his band's talents and feature his music.[58] Most commonly, however, films made during the height of the swing era worked "rhythm" or "swing" into their titles and plot lines and as such could showcase the talent of one artist or even several groups at once. Examples of this strategy can be found in films like *Sing as You Swing* (1937), *College Swing* (1938), or *Birth of the Blues* (1941).[59] Yet despite featuring Black artistry in these films, "whites and whites alone controlled the commerce of swing. From this unique position within the Hollywood studio system, Astaire was among the most empowered of these jazz-making whites."[60] Thus, as Matthew Morrison has applicably expressed through his theory of blacksound, American popular music, whether circulated on film, radio, or record, is "based in the construction and embodiment of 'whiteness' by ethnic white Americans through the foil of stereotyped and commodified scripts of blackfaced blackness."[61] The song (and dance) "Peckin'" from *New Faces of 1937* epitomizes this process of jazz-making Whites *literally* changing the face of Black vernacular artistry through their foil of blackfaced Blackness.

FIGURE 5.3 (*Top*) The Three Chocolateers (Albert Gibson, Esvan Scott Mosby, and Guss Moore) perform in the opening of "Peckin'" from *New Faces of 1937*. (RKO/Photofest); (*Bottom*) The uncredited Black chorines of "Peckin'" in the nightclub scene. (Private collection)

That Peckin' Order

The curtain opens to a chicken farm in perfect time with a swingier version of Ben Pollack and Henry James's soon-to-be famous tune.[62] *Two Black farmhands lean up against the fence, fatigued from a day's work, but the motion of nearby chickens feeding perks them up. The first stares intently at a (trained) Minorca rooster pecking on some feed and then begins mimicking the kinesis of its head and neck, back and forth. The second farmhand follows suit adding a sideways motion to his head bop and a bucking of his eyes. A third head bopper enters from stage right and joins the other two, knees bent and hovering. The three farmhands begin exaggerating their movements, all eyes now bucking, adding vocals, "just peckin' and peckin' and peckin' away . . ." The dancers (the uncredited Three Chocolateers) chug across the stage rhythmically mirroring the trills in the orchestra's brass section. [FIG. 5.3, top] Acting as if possessed by these rhythms, dancer one shuffles over to a tree trunk and mimes the action of banging his head while peckin'. The second climbs some tree limbs and moves similarly. The third simulates the action of cracking eggs on his teeth. Sheer peckin' madness ensues until the three gather single file to exit the barn. The music shifts as they enter a new space full of cooks (the uncredited Four Playboys) also inflicted with the peckin' "bug." They hang their straw hats on a rack and the cooks begin pursing their lips to produce trumpet-like sounds—not unlike the vocal percussionists in "Slap that Bass"—crescendoing their voices while the Three Chocolateers continue chugging their feet in perfect rhythm. The dancers don waiters' uniforms transforming into busboys. One of the Four Playboys hands them trays of roasted chickens that they will soon deliver to Black patrons in an adjacent room. The restaurant patrons too exhibit the itch, peckin' in lieu of speaking to one another. Their head bops nod in exuberant response to the steaming roasted chickens and to the three waiters who delivered them. As the camera zooms out, however, a menacing 25-feet-tall demonic bust with incandescent pupils watches over the establishment.*[63] *His eyes grow brighter as smoke emerges from his torso. From this smoke emerges a chorus of light-skinned chorines dressed in sparkling leotards and feathered bustles at the waist and nape. The sixteen women perform their own rendition of peckin', gliding around the stage in a series of chassés. [FIG. 5.3, bottom] The camera then cuts to an all-Black jazz orchestra also peckin'. It would appear that this six-piece jazz orchestra is providing this number's diegetic sound, but without any mention in the credits, it is hard to know who is responsible for the soundtrack. The camera cuts to a petite maid (Mildred Boyd) who gracefully pecks across the stage to enter an entirely new sound stage of White peckin'.*

248 BEHIND THE SCREEN

The maid arrives in the bedroom chambers of bride-to-be Patricia Harrington (Harriet Hilliard) and begins assisting Patricia with her veil. The peckin' tune gradually shifts into a swing version of Wagner's "Here Comes the Bride."[64] The maid passes the peckin' baton along with the bride's bouquet as Patricia makes her way to the adjoining bridal suite. Her bridesmaids follow her lead, bopping their heads in a procession she takes outdoors. A line of wedding guests await her arrival, bopping their heads to a swing version of Mendelssohn's "Wedding March."[65] The pastor dramatically pecks while bride and groom exchange a few words: "If there's one thing I can't stand it's independent women. . . . You need a good lesson . . . so in the first place, I'm gonna marry you." "The first place is good enough for me," giggles Patricia. The camera zooms out to show all the wedding guests gleefully tap dancing and then lindy hopping. The camera cuts away to the onscreen audience all peckin' in agreement and cuts away again to three men shoveling coal in each other's faces backstage such that they appear to be in blackface. The music continues and the words "THE END" dance across the screen in keeping with the song's swingin' finale. The abridged credits begin to roll.

The Three Chocolateers—Albert Gibson (or Gipson), Esvan Scott Mosby (later replaced by Eddie West), and Guss Moore (later replaced by Paul Black and then later Bethel "Duke" Gibson and ultimately Paul Black again)—were, according to the *Semi-Weekly Spokane Review* of March 9, 1934, "ebon-hued tap dancers, [who] work[ed] with the smoothness and precision of a machine with roller bearings and almost as ceaselessly. They switch from ensembles to solo work with no time out to catch the breath and leave the audience almost as breathless as they are. They are fast, furious and fancy." Yet despite their staggering reputation on stage, they often went uncredited onscreen.

Pivotal to the techno-dialogic transfer from Black sound to White screen, these three machine-like dancing prodigies were often singled out for their extraordinary antics and comedic elements. The three (in all of their iterations) fall into the category of "comedy dancers" according to Marshall Stearns, a style characterized by satiric pantomime, a more rhythmic and eccentric style of dance, and "making fun of each other as well as themselves."[66] Stearns attributes their razor-sharp and self-deprecating humor to several sources, including the "West African song of allusion (where the subject pays the singer *not* to sing about him), reinterpreted in the West Indies as the political calypso, in New Orleans as the 'signifyin'' song, and in the South generally as 'the dozens.'"[67] While known for many things,

The Three Chocolateers are most remembered for the song and dance trend "Peckin'" they helped make famous. Marv Goldberg cites one plausible origin story of their "barnyard novelty,"[68] writing that The Three Chocolateers appeared, "along with Pollack's orchestra, at Frank Sebastian's Cotton Club, in Culver City, California, where they did a dance to the ["Peckin'"] tune, imitating chickens. . . . Pollack's unit recorded the tune (as an instrumental) on December 18, 1936, although it wasn't released until around May of the following year. (The basic tune to "Peckin'," however, seems to have been the Charles "Cootie" Williams's trumpet solo portion of Duke Ellington's 1931 "Rockin' in Rhythm.").[69] The Three Chocolateers performed an uncredited version of "Peckin'" in Twentieth-Century Fox's *Can This Be Dixie* (1936).[70] The dance took off in early 1937 around the same time Calloway recorded a slow version with lyrics, which suggested that this "way low down" dance should supplant truckin' and the Suzy-Q: "*You talk about your truckin' when your peckin' is new, Well, here's a dance that you all should do . . . look at old Jim, he's pecking on his back!*" With lyrics likes these, Calloway, the crossover jazz musician, helped to bridge the racial gap between the Black dance that The Three Chocolateers performed at Frank Sebastian's Cotton Club and the song for which Benny Goodman received Hollywood billing. It was both the Calloway image and the way he sold the song that aided in this techno-dialogic transfer. His ability to market the song to a wide and diverse audience aided in the success of Benny Goodman and other White jazz musicians.

Calloway's marketing strategies for this song were as important as they had been for "Minnie," but rather than calling on "hi-de-ho," the dance itself became the prime participatory element, inviting in both Black and White listeners. Calloway recorded this version during a time when dance songs would spell out the specific dance steps one was supposed to copy on the dance floor. This made popular dance accessible to all and the music could sell itself through its proliferation in public spaces. As time progressed, these songs that described their dance steps would be replaced by songs that Broadway and Hollywood would pay White dancers to "choreograph," making popular dance mostly available to those who were White and those with money.[71] But, for a time, amid this transfer from Black people dancing a Black vernacular to White people transcribing Black dancing, to the erasure of Black people performing these Black vernacular forms, Black dance was both accessible and popular to America's diverse audience.

250 BEHIND THE SCREEN

As part of the growing accessibility of dance, the Peckin' craze swept ballrooms across the country and continued to gain esteem as many famous jazz orchestras recorded their own versions. The Johnny Hodges Orchestra recorded theirs in May of 1937 with Cootie Williams "reprising his 1931 trumpet performance, but also doing the vocal." Jimmy Dorsey's Orchestra released theirs in June with a vocal by Bing Crosby. Goodman recorded an instrumental version of the song on July 6, 1937, just a few days after RKO's release of *New Faces*.[72] The fact that Benny Goodman recorded a version of this and is often cited as the composer due to his association with the film speaks to the popularity of the song—Goodman was really the hippest sound for most White Americans living at this time—and also an example of what Karl Hagstrom Miller describes as "regimes of white supremacy and segregation." For Miller, these regimes target racialized bodies rather than sound such that the sonic guise here operates in a much more complex way than simply labeling some sound Black and some sound White. That a song borrowed from Cootie Williams's riff in Ellington's 1931 song and its corresponding dance—the creation of The Three "Chocs"—could reach "popular" status on Goodman's recording and RKO's advertising of it evidences Miller's claim that "the emergent musical color line eventually brought the logic of segregation into the realm of sound and style, linking sonic signifiers of race to the corporeal bodies and physical landscapes that Jim Crow already had been trying to contain for several decades."[73] As my description of this dance illustrates, the filmed version reinforces a register of associations between Blackness and "the help" while also yoking Black dance with the devil. The final scene overtly displays a kind of hand off of the dance, one that acknowledges its infectiousness but also iterates its acceptability as a dance once tied to Satan, but now betrothed to the sanctity of marriage; a "decent" dance.[74]

The success of "Peckin'" in *New Faces* launched Peckin' as America's biggest dance craze and gave The Chocs the exposure they needed to stay in the White public eye for the next decade. Following this performance, they had great success in Calloway's "Cotton Club Parade," continued to book gigs in Hollywood, and became the "new faces" of the "Skrontch" dance, as accompanied by Duke Ellington's song (later recorded by Calloway January 23, 1938) of the same name.[75] Yet despite the triumph of groups like The Three Chocs, Black cameos in Hollywood were becoming sparser and more invisible. The success of Black actors relied on being "discovered" by a notable White person in show business and generally meant relinquishing "ownership." The Chocs exemplify this process of relinquishing ownership of Black performance practices, "hav[ing] a history of being absorbed into popular entertainment, making them ineligible for copyright and available in the public domain."[76]

WITH A GLORY BE   251

Another popular—yet often uncredited—Black trio got their big break when Eddie Cantor employed them at the Palace. Tip, Tap, and Toe (originally Sammy Green, Teddy Frazier, and Raymond Winfield) then launched their Hollywood career shortly after George White "discovered" them about a decade later in 1936 and cast them in *Scandals*.[77] That same year Tip, Tap, and Toe were cast in Roy Mack's *By Request* and the following year the trio had a big number in Twentieth Century Fox's *You Can't Have Everything* to the Louis Prima hit, "Rhythm on the Radio."[78] This number showcased the trio's tap-dancing talents, especially their innovative use of the slide. Winfield's gliding is so smooth here it was "as if he had buttered feet on a hot stove."[79] Yet their role was small and the whole routine reads as an Orientalist parade of belly dancing choristers in some vaguely Middle Eastern palace, with Tip, Tap, and Toe's costumes referencing British colonialism in Africa.

During that same 1936–37 period, many Black trios would have small tap-dancing cameos in otherwise White run, White cast shows and Hollywood films. The Three Gobs (Mike Riley—later replaced by Eddie Dent—Eddie Johnson, and Clarence "Sonny" Austin), who had been performing as an act at least since 1930, would join Ellington and Calloway at the Cotton Club in 1931 and by 1936 would be pulled into the White circuit alongside Cantor at Philadelphia's Earl Theatre. Like The Three Chocolateers who became associated with Peckin', the Three Gobs—named the "cheerful chocolate children of rhythm," by the *New York Age* gained a reputation for their tap dancing take on the Suzy-Q.[80] Yet despite the success of these Black trios on the Hollywood screen, it was rare to find any kind of acknowledgment of their dancing in the White press, let alone the credits of films in which they appeared.[81] Furthermore, the manner in which Hollywood presented their dancing still exhibited Blackness within a framework of archaic stereotypes including blackface. The "Peckin'" number, for example, is bookended by blackface: right before "Peckin'," three actors on a train emerge from a tunnel covered in coal and in the film's final image the camera centers on these three actors shoveling coal in each other's faces. That the reference to Blackness is made clear here and in other films made in 1937, which take up syncopated dancing, is no coincidence.

By 1937, a swing aesthetic guaranteed box office success in some cities while it was hotly contested in others. Juxtaposing swing with stereotypical representations of Blackness and alongside representations of brownface, offered economic support from both sides. In plots that could not justify blackface narratively through disguise or as accident, but wanted to incorporate a swing aesthetic in dance, Hollywood screenwriters staged elaborate primitivist frameworks that relied on either the Gabriel variation or brownface (or sometimes both) to qualify the use of blackface. We see hints

252 BEHIND THE SCREEN

of this in the Orientalist tap routines performed by Tip, Tap, and Toe in *You Can't Have Everything*, and in the year 1937 alone, brownface would similarly surface in "Panamania" from *Swing High, Swing Low, Top of the Town* with its "Blame It on the Rumba" and the Gabriel variation in the film's closing "Jamboree," and many others.[82]

As discussed in chapter 2, many musicals made during Hollywood's Golden Age included some kind of Latin number, regardless of whether the plot warranted it. Tunes that rely on an Afro-Cuban beat yet use English lyric—regarded as "Latunes" by Gustavo Pérez Firmat—acted as a selling point for American audiences craving a close but safe encounter with the Other. These tunes helped to collapse anything down South into a singular atmosphere, one in line with an imagined version of Latin America, and one lacking concreteness or cultural specificity. Such approximations in song help "keep the appropriated object at a distance."[83] Yet these approximations became more approximate over time and what started as an effect of America's "rhumba craze," and condensing Latin America into an amorphous group of latunes and "brown" bodies, became an even looser application of brownface, one that lumped the Middle East and tropical islands into an opaque definition of safe exoticism. Such "brown" terrain could be visited en route to more distant and dangerous Black spaces.

Cantor's blatant use of burnt cork in "Swing Is Here to Sway" not only employs the swing aesthetic within a primitivist framework situated in Baghdad but also utilizes the Gabriel variation, makes use of the Bill Robinson effect in its physical citations of Robinson, and depends on the citational guise used in its aural citations of Cab Calloway and of Cantor's familiar nods at Jolson. While still taboo in many ways, directors could reconcile the use of hot rhythms and the laws of the Code if Black performers or White performers in blackface were the ones dancing to those "dangerous" syncopations and the frame was properly established.

> *Baba: Excuse me, who are these fellows? They're not even listening!*
> *Sultan: They're my new musicians from Africa.*
> *Baba: Africa? [to musicians] What part of Africa?*
> *Sultan: I'm afraid they don't understand you. You see, they talk a strange tongue.*
> *Baba: [to musicians] Parlez-vous Français? [No response] Se hable espanol? Capisce italiān? [No response]*
> *: Verstehse bissel Yiddish? [No response. Ali Baba has a flash of inspiration] Wait a minute!*

FIGURE 5.4 Two scenes in "Swing Is Here to Sway," from *Ali Baba Goes to Town*, 1937. (*Top*) Eddie Cantor sings in front of the Peters Sisters (Mattie, Ann, and Virginia Vee) and uncredited Black musical artists. (Twentieth Century-Fox/Photofest); (*Bottom*) Jeni Le Gon performs in front of the band. (Twentieth Century-Fox/Photofest)

254   BEHIND THE SCREEN

"Hi de hi de ho"-calls Ali Baba (Cantor)
"He de he de he"-responds a group of primitively dressed Black actors
"Hey de hey de hey"
"Ho de ho de ho"
Cantor and these "African primitives" engage in a simple call-and-response of
    Calloway's famous Hi-De-Ho scat phrase[84]
"Zaz-zuh-zaz."[85]

The call-and-response continues as Ali Baba causally applies burnt cork. The song shifts into "Hosanna," followed by a series of recognizable Negro spirituals. The combination of "Gabriel" plus a series of jazz solos invokes the now-familiar Gabriel variation—a mix of caricature, religious kitsch, and a melding of the swing tradition with Black heaven. As Baba struts to and fro across the stage he gradually picks up the tempo and transitions from somber spiritual to upbeat swing, a pattern we have now seen in The Singing Kid *and* A Day at the Races: *"There's gonna be a Harlem; there's gonna be a dance called 'truckin' and a dance called 'peckin' . . ." He proceeds to demonstrate each of the Black vernacular forms: truckin'; peckin'; Suzy-Q—"there's gonna be a Robinson, with happy, tappy, feet (he demonstrates a quick three-bar Robinson-esque tap phrase) before transitioning from the intro to the real meat of the song, "Swing is here to sway, you can't deny it; just grab your partner and dance . . ." The African primitives take over the chorus, alternating between song and vocal percussion. As the song slows, a twenty-year-old Jeni Le Gon makes her way onto the set wearing a Josephine Baker-style banana skirt, a bra made of shells and a feather headdress. The tempo speeds up to accommodate her lightning-fast toe-tapping, heavy on the over-the-tops and toe stands and interlaced with truckin', peckin', and Suzy-Qs. After two complete 32-bar tap dance choruses, Le Gon passes the baton off to the three Peters Sisters (Mattie, Ann, and Virginia Vee)[86] who are dressed in three variations of "exotic": the first offers a take on the grass skirt; the second, a jungle style zebra print; and the third an intricately patterned fabric, wrapped in chains. All three wear seashell moccasins on their feet and elaborate feather headdresses as hats. After they sing their close harmony rendition of "swing is here to sway" they break into a 40-bar shim sham, retaining the standard double shuffle, tack Annie, and half break sections but revising completely the crossover section and inserting a Frankie Manning–inspired four-bar "boogie back, boogie forward, shorty George" between the tack Annie and half breaks. In keeping with the song's vernacular themes, they intersperse moments of*

*truckin' and peckin' throughout. Baba interjects with a whistle hustling the
Sisters into a Suzy-Q exit. Baba then leads the "primitives" as if the leader
of a marching band in circles around the stage, an image that is hard to distinguish from Harpo's leadership in "Who dat man?" The camera cuts to the
village people who are quickly catching on to the contagiousness of the swing
and peckin' crazes. The camera cuts again to the Sultan (Roland Young) and
Princess Miriam (June Lang) who are also "caught" peckin'.*[87]

Hi-De-Ho: That Universal Language, That Language of the Future

Aloysius "Al" Babson (Eddie Cantor) happens upon the making of a big
Hollywood production of *Arabian Nights*. Accidentally overdosing on
some pills the resident nurse gives him, Babson falls asleep and dreams he
(now Ali Baba) becomes an advisor to the sultan (Roland Young). In many
ways a reworking of the *Roman Scandals* or *Kid Millions* plots from four/
three years prior, this dream sequence somehow justifies—or at least temporarily excuses—a conflation of many ancient Eastern things. The plot loosely
weaves in and out of the Middle East, sometimes settling on Arabia and sometimes on Baghdad, while occasionally referring to the ancient Romans and
Hebrews. Cantor's double coding is present throughout the film, both as it
regards his Jewish identity and as it involves an Africanist aesthetic. *Verstehse
bissel Yiddish?* Might be an obvious reference to his Eastern European roots,
while his love interest in princess Miriam and use of an inverted crescent/
star (likely signifying the Arab-themed Shriner's hat) on his fez might
only read as the alienation of a Jew in a predominantly Muslim country to
some viewers.[88] But neither of these encoded messages were lost during the
censors' review of the script and Joseph Breen strongly encouraged Colonel
Jason S. Joy, Twentieth Century Fox's director of public relations, to remove
the Shriner reference as well as the film's "repeated references to Allah and
the showing of Moslem ritual throughout." In a letter dated June 15, 1937,
Breen reminds Joy that "the Production Code specifically directs that 'no
film or episode may throw ridicule on any religious faith.'"[89] Breen's board
was scrupulous in their review of the film's references to sex (including visual
and/or audible references to nudity and polygamy), anything with "pansy
flavor," and anything that might offend the censors in Moslem countries.
Yet nowhere did correspondence letters between Breen and Joy remark on

256 BEHIND THE SCREEN

any of the film's racial slurs, including the blatantly offensive "Swing Is Here to Sway," which seemingly elided criticism due to its implementation of the citational and sonic guises shrouded in affected integration, political humor, and a primitivizing framework.

The film abounds with internal citations, both to Cantor's own films and to Jolson's Hollywood corpus. Cantor's famous retort to "what's your name?" is naturally, "Al baba- Just call me Al," and leading into "Swing Is Here to Sway," he addresses the crowd as his "fellow Baghdaddies and Bagmammies," while squatting down on one knee. And for viewers familiar with Cantor's work in vaudeville and films like *Roman Scandals*, his script is much funnier— "Deena, is there anyone feena?" will only read to those who remember his hit "Dinah, is there anyone finer?"

But more distracting than these layers on layers of citations and internal references is his deeply political humor. The crux of the plot rests in Baba's suggestion that the sultan have an election—let the people decide who rules.

> Baba: *You can go on being the head man, but instead of sultan you become a president . . . like they have in America.*
> Sultan: *Well, does he rule the country?*
> Baba: *Does he rule the country? Hunh! Ask the Republicans!*

Ali Baba is rife with references to US President Franklin Roosevelt's politics, specifically the Works Progress Administration (WPA) and inflation. Even though Roosevelt had won the recent 1936 presidential election in a landslide victory, Democrats met his New Deal with harsh criticism; Cantor did not shy away from comedic denigration of FDR's politics. While Cantor's popularity and political triumph within the plot of *Ali Baba* might also have been referencing the Bakr Sidqi Coup—the coup to overthrow Iraqi prime minister Yasin al Hashimi and the very first military coup against Arab countries—of 1936, it was mostly (if not completely) an attempt to mock the high taxes Cantor was now paying and a shrug at the Federal Projects (mainly theater and dance). In addition to Cantor's character organizing work programs, abolishing the army, and taxing the rich, the script contains many underhanded jokes aimed at inflation and FDR's failed court-packing plan.[90]

Amid all these political jabs sit buried an unprecedented number of instances of covert minstrelsy, primarily as swing is concerned. David Stowe has suggested the idea that crediting the economic recovery under way by

WITH A GLORY BE 257

1936 to swing's popularity, as the White press had done for decades, is "an interpretation that downplayed the role of the music itself in creating its own vogue."[91] I propose that the economic recovery that ensued from 1936 until the United States' involvement in World War II was not what gave way to the swing phenomenon but instead was an opportunity for the media to reframe syncopated rhythms as linked to both Blackness and modernity. While swing's embodiment of sonic energy and its image of progressiveness to White America might have lent itself to certain utopian visions of democracy and "populist producerist ideology," the acceptance of jazz into the mainstream was not proof that society was "growing ever more egalitarian" as Stowe and others have suggested.[92] It took the move of the Cotton Club downtown, Black artists catering to a White aesthetic,[93] and some corporeal reorganization in Hollywood to bring swing into visibility. Mendi Obadike reminds us that "the messages told through sound are linked to each other as much by our practices for engaging with sound as they are by the sounds themselves."[94] The sonic, citational, and protean guises in "Swing Is Here to Sway" engage with the swing aesthetic in such a way as to link *hot* music with the new *and* the archaic, the religious *and* the profane, Whiteness *and* the Other, such that swing would, over time, signify the former associations in these pairings while gradually rendering the latter extinct.

Time travel narratively justifies "Sway": Baba teaches the people of ancient Baghdad about what music and dance will be trendy in the future. In doing so he highlights the futuristic, modern properties of a swing aesthetic—"there's a great way comin' to ya, a thousand years from today, Hallelujah!"—while at the same time acknowledging that the African primitives who naturally understood "Hi De Ho" are somehow already versed in this tongue. He also offers what Harley Erdman has described as a kind of travelogue exoticism, a foreigner "living in the modern industrial West, yet somehow not of it."[95]

There is another transit narrative present in all the Gabriel variations I have examined thus far: the ascension that Cantor—like Harpo Marx and Jolson— makes to heaven narratively through his role as White savior undergirds a quiet and imperfect assimilation, where his trip to heaven is representative of a deeper, more personal journey toward identifying as White. Heaven is not a Jewish concept, nor is the archangel Gabriel. However, playing the part of Gabriel allows these Jewish performers yet another opportunity to engage with the American mainstream, a costume which, like blackface, reinforces his Whiteness through a temporary identification with Christianity. Thus, buried beneath Orientalism and blackface's hypervisibility, as well as swing's definitive audibility, sits a series of subtexts that can only be told in transit. Those things that can be seen and heard merely point to the distorted mirror through which Jewish performers come to recognize their own liminal identity and signify the more covert displacements Hollywood enacts between the White body and Black sound; brownface mediates this transition.

Ali Baba in blackface, who is already an imposter in Baghdad, at once acknowledges his Whiteness—we witness the act of "blacking up"—as privilege (i.e., White enough to black up) and authority of the form. Cantor as Ali Baba conducts his all Black "aboriginal" orchestra—the members of which he has just led in prayer—"Hallelujah"—and teaches his audience how to peck, truck, and Suzy-Q.[96] He can perform alongside these Black musicians because he sings in a fictional Baghdad wearing a Middle Eastern–inspired linen outfit and turban. [FIG. 5.4] This mythical kingdom protects Cantor's performance in blackface from censorship because of the narrative setting that takes place off American soil and his temporary brownface masquerade. Invoking the essence of Bill Robinson, Cantor elevates his own tap dancing by relying on the necessary failure of simulacrum. If he impersonates Robinson, his own creativity cannot be evaluated—yet another way he masquerades. The citations here act as low hanging fruit, professing to offer credit to those exceptional individuals in the most blatant way so that the overarching aesthetic appropriation goes unquestioned by mainstream audiences and legal mechanisms.

Organized within a narrative framework, the performances of Jeni Le Gon, the Peters Sisters, and the background vocal percussionists present the swing aesthetic alongside a series of Black caricatures. When Cantor as Baba presents swing as the music of the future, he offers swing within a primitivizing and Orientalizing framework, situated in the past but modernized. Here the techno-dialogic transfer occurs between vocalizations and body percussion vis-à-vis the Black body and Cantor's White body as some sort of time traveling messiah. His use of blackface in this iteration of the Gabriel variation, like Jolson's in both "Mule" and "Save Me Sister," constructs a White identity for himself while further commodifying a script of Blackness. This includes not just the dehumanizing properties that the Black artist's costumes portray but also the subtext of class and morality that their roles as deliverers communicate. Also, the intentional way these White performers present themselves as foils to the "raw instinctive passion" of swing sets up modern swing rhythm as distinct from Whiteness.

But the film's narrative interventions were not enough to convince southern audiences that swing music and Black artists should become mainstream "American" entertainment nor did they appreciate Cantor's political humor. In fact, some southern audiences were horrified by *Baba*'s modernism and the ways in which it corrupted America's youth. In letters addressed to the heads of Atlanta's two biggest theatres (Lucas and Jenkins Theatre and Fox Theatre), the city's board of review expressed its disapproval:

November 3d, 1937

Dear Mr. Lucas,

> I have just previewed Eddie Cantor's picture ALI BABA GOES TO TOWN. I asked that the negro women in the picture be eliminated. These are so offensive as to be nauseating, and as no Southern man or woman could fail to object to this I ordered these out.

> . . .

> Also it seems to be the best kind of Republican propaganda, for there has never been so keen a weapon as ridicule. Of course, as I said before, in no country on earth except in the United States would this kind of thing be allowed. I consider too that to ridicule the nation's highest officer in the way this picture does, is not a good thing to engender in the hearts of youth respect for government. Youth already exposed to much that is lacking in respect or reverence for high ideals.

> . . .

> Yours very truly,
> Mrs. Alonzo Richardson. Sec. to Bd. of
> Review of the City of Atlanta, Georgia

Yet even when integration was framed by primitivism and a swing aesthetic defined as antithetical to heaven, White southern audiences were still concerned about the ways Black people might corrupt the wholesomeness of America. This partially explains why Hollywood constantly struggled to produce pictures that would satisfy both northern and southern markets. It is conceivable that the industry found it easier and more economical to eliminate Black artists altogether than to face such resistance from one of its biggest markets. If so, juxtaposing Black artistry with racial caricature might have helped to soften the southern stance.

260 BEHIND THE SCREEN

It was rare to see female tap soloists perform in Hollywood films of this era; Le Gon's performance is an anomaly. Cantor announces her as "Minnie the Moocher," a fictional character with a national reputation as a cocaine-using "red-hot hootchie-cootcher," biasing her entrance before she even arrives.[97] Her scanty costume further sexualizes Le Gon's eighty seconds of screen time, [FIG. 5.4, bottom] materializing what Mary Ann Doane describes as "the *episteme* which assigns to the woman a special place in cinematic representation while denying her access to that system."[98] Prior to coming to Hollywood, Le Gon was a chorine with the Count Basie Orchestra and successful on the TOBA (Theater Owners Booking Association) circuit alongside the Whitman Sisters. RKO discovered Le Gon while she was performing show-stopping routines in Los Angeles. Her first screen appearance—beside Bill Robinson and Fats Waller in *Hooray for Love*—granted her the nickname of "Chocolate Princess" by the White press. MGM quickly signed her to a long-term contract and assigned her to work in *Broadway Melody of 1936* alongside Eleanor Powell.[99] After rehearsals had already begun, however, the studio decided that casting two female tap dancers was unnecessary; they dropped Le Gon in favor of Powell and sent Le Gon to London to perform in *At Home Abroad*.[100] Similar to the Three Eddies, who were met with far less racism overseas, Le Gon received great praise from the London press. Unfortunately, despite her dexterous dancing, White directors and producers in the United States often cast her as a servant or hired her to stage numbers behind the scenes, only to be given no visibility onscreen or in the credits. Thus, even without the use of burnt cork, Le Gon's life onscreen was constantly buried.

Something similar happens with the Peters Sisters who perform their vocal harmony with a tap dance in the same sort of primitive chic attire. [FIG. 5.4, top] Not much has been written about the sisters, and the print they received is the product of the White press. Like the Three Gobs, Cantor supposedly discovered the Sisters at an obscure nightclub in Los Angeles and immediately signed them to "the banjo-eyed comedian's picture" *Ali Baba*.[101] This does not account for the uncredited appearance of the Peters Sisters (all five of them) in *With Love and Kisses* a year earlier.[102] That same year, three of the sisters played a Hawaiian vocal trio in *Love and Hisses* and would go on to perform alongside Calloway, Ellington, Peg Leg Bates, and Three Chocolateers at the Cotton Club, with Jimmie Lunceford and the Miller Brothers and Lois Bright at the Apollo, and with Bill Robinson at the Zanzibar, just to name a few.[103] That the Peters Sisters had their own version of the Shim Sham is no surprise considering how frequently they performed with leading tap dancers of the day. Also, they were a part of Ellington's Cotton Club Revue when The Chocs debuted the Skrontch dance.[104] They were always on top of the latest dance trends. While not sexualized like Le Gon in Cantor's film, the trio were fetishized for their weight in subsequent reviews of the show and future performances: "The three Peters Sisters (who weigh over 700 pounds between them) have been signed to add musical weight to *Rebecca of Sunnybrook Farm*," wrote the *Times Union* shortly after the success of *Ali Baba*. A few years later the same paper wrote, "The Peters girls are nearly a ton of harmony."[105] Despite their talent, their artistry was often obscured by the way the media presented them as Hottentot attractions. Often uncredited in films as well, the Peters Sisters found much greater success in Europe. Although equally—if not less—talented, the (White) Boswell Sisters and the Andrews Sisters would far exceed the "success" of the Peters Sisters in America. The Peters Sisters, like Le Gon, were abandoned in favor of comparable White talent. And, as the Code became stricter and America came closer to entering the war, Black cameos showcasing Black artistry became scanter.[106]

While Hollywood was working to obfuscate the relationship between an Africanist aesthetic and Blackness, a handful of White entrepreneurs were circulating a similar narrative through the sale of their dance manuals. "Peckin'" was one of the last dance songs recorded in which the lyrics described the dance, and Cantor's "lecture demonstration" in "Sway" is also one of the last vernacular "how-to" examples onscreen. According to Marshall Stearns, the description of dances became less precise over time and "the emphasis was placed on the fancied origins, novelty, and popularity of the yet-to-be presented number."[107] This was true across the board, and as songs' instruction became less precise, so did these dances; they "survived and prospered through innumerable variations, reinterpretations, revisions, and revivals." Because the majority of these vernacular dances stemmed from Africanist origins, many White professionals had difficulty mastering the hip movements their Western training de-emphasized. Stearns attributes the success of Mae West, Gilda Gray, and Ann Pennington to their having mastered such movement qualities; at the same time, their dancing "allowed room for improvisation and at the same time had real character and style when performed to jazz rhythms."[108] But the success of these White professionals also relied on dressing such Africanist forms in brownface and delivering them via the White body either in dance manuals or on the Hollywood screen as we saw in *Honolulu*. Powell's hula tap dance is only the crest of a decade-long tradition of dressing other "Native" forms

262 BEHIND THE SCREEN

up in Africanist vocabulary and marketing them through the White body as authentically "Native."

Cross Dissolving Black with Brown

Brownface serves covert minstrelsy in several ways: in previous chapters I have explored how brownface becomes a symptom of situating films in a mythical kingdom; this fiction aided in absolving a film from international criticism as well protecting it from censorship review boards closer to home. I have also addressed how brownface has been used as an intermediary in the techno-dialogic transfer from Black aesthetic practices performed by Black artists to White performers presenting an Africanist aesthetic as their own; this is especially prevalent in films and songs created during America's rhumba craze, as the nebulous "Latin" body has offered Hollywood producers, directors, and choreographers a means of blurring the lines between Black culture and brown and has allowed them to move more freely within the Code's guidelines. That is, when brownface is used in conjunction with the female body, it makes the presentation of more sexual and "exotic" themes permissible.

Many of the latunes described earlier boast of some sort of tropical island where "palm trees sway in the breeze and waves lap against the shore in *clave*." The sun on these islands (or isles) gives you a glow rather than a sunburn, and "when you walk in the moonlight, you are bathed in perfume and sighs."[109] Such generalities allowed the general function of brownface to thrive, even if Hollywood modified the location; American territories were also common liaisons between "here" and "there."

Beginning in the late nineteenth century, the hula and the Hawaiian women associated with hula dancing were "spectacularized on colonial stages and became metonyms for the nation of Hawai'i."[110] These Native women performing hula for an imperialist gaze became primary "objects" in America's tourist economy representing what Adria L. Imada aptly describes as the "erotic pleasures of the new colony."[111] Edward Said has written extensively on the relationship between sexual subjugation and imperial possession; that America sexualized its new colony was an important part of the colonialist mindset and helped to construct a "Pacific" that was, as Bernard Smith describes it, "young, feminine, desirable, and vulnerable, an ocean of desire."[112] Imada notes that by the twentieth century, the "hula girl" helped to "domesticat[e] the Pacific for U.S. political, military, tourist, and economic interests."[113] Central to my argument surrounding Eleanor Powell's brownface in Honolulu is the idea that Hawaiian women have played an important role in shaping America's national image. This was particularly prevalent during World War II and was part of an effort to "conceal an illusory peace over a continuing military occupation."[114]

Powell's Tribute to the Hawaiian Islands in *Honolulu* upholds the image of the hula dancer as a young, sensual, and utterly feminine "vessel of desire."[115] Powell's masquerade as a Native Hawaiian allows the White female body to deliver this message of peace so as to keep the Native Hawaiian at a distance and not relinquish too much control in Hollywood. But like Powell's tribute to Bill Robinson performed earlier in the film, her tribute to the Hawaiian Islands involves several layers of disguise. Her multi-masking also allows her much more representational leeway at the height of the Hays Code scrutiny.

The island setting, "Native" soundtrack, and real "brown" bodies that surround Powell in *Honolulu* allow her hula tap dance to skirt censorship because of her geographic distance from the mainland. Although the Code dictated that certain subjects "should not be introduced when not essential to the plot," *Honolulu*'s mythical (Pacific) kingdom in conjunction with brownface made its "scenes of passion" and "seduction" seem foreign enough to be acceptable to the censors. Thus, even though these seductive hula dance scenes were neither essential to the plot nor even admissible under the Code in 1939 for their overtly sexual display of a woman's body, the foreignness of these scenes allowed them to evade the censors. Outsmarting the Code in this way also allowed Hawaii to maintain its image as "the staging ground not only for battle, but for the leisure of millions of soldiers, defense workers, and military administrators who came to the islands,"[116] an important depiction to present to reluctant draftees who would be called on the following year.[117]

The most covert function of brownface, however, is its ability to mediate between extremes—Black and White, here and there, us and them—allowing exceptional non-White performers finite opportunities for imperfect assimilation. As we saw in chapter 2, the brown body oscillates between two extremes, not achieving the freedom afforded by Whiteness and never inhabiting the same abject space bestowed on Blackness. Operating at the threshold of each, brownface facilitates the absorption of Africanisims into the American mainstream. Overlaying black(face) with brown also helps to create a kind of cross dissolve, or the fading in of one image with the seamless fading out of another. A degree of this seamless dissolution occurred when Cantor flirted with American Indian identity as a way to transform racial difference into ethnic difference, thereby staking a claim on his ability to assimilate and thus acquire a "true" American identity through his sonic and corporeal redface performance in films like *Whoopee!* Jewish blackface performers in general utilize brownface as a means of clouding more covert references to blackface while disguising a much more complex pattern of appropriating an Africanist aesthetic. Cantor's performance in *The Kid from Spain* and Jolson's performance in *Go into Your Dance* (1935) typify two examples of this use of brownface.[118] Cantor's use of brownface in *Ali Baba* similarly disguises Hollywood's appropriation of an Africanist aesthetic, and Powell's use of brownface on the Hawaiian Island both "justifies" her use of blackface on the ship and helps to blur her use of Africanisms in her hula tap dance; her hula dance was as much a conga as it was a tap dance.

"The Sheik of Araby" in *Tin Pan Alley* flaunts an extreme example of flattening many exotic locales into a conglomerate brownface, which then mediates between a Black aesthetic and a White. The very name "Araby" is a romantic term for the Middle East generally reserved for poems and literature about a somewhat vague portion of Eastern geography.[119] The scene opens at the Alhambra theater, a likely reference to the Andalusian palace begun by Abu Abdullah Muhammad ibn al-Ahmar. At least the theater offers a link between Spain and the title's relationship to Arab countries. The other foreign references minimize this effort: after pausing on the Alhambra's marquee, the camera cuts to a large, vaguely Middle Eastern palace. An uncredited Princess Vanessa Ammon—traceable only through one newspaper's critique of her performance—emerges from a pile of feathers.[120] She performs a strange combination of moves: imaginative interpretations of Balinese, Thai, and Cambodian dance vocabulary held together by a solid training in Dunham technique; her costume resembles a modified version of something possibly found on a Balinese *Sita* Sculpture but looks more like a bikini than something one would find in the *Ramayana*.[121] She strokes the bodies of two men sitting under a giant fruit platter before striking a statue-like pose. The camera then cuts to a close-up of these two men who, on cue, buck their eyes toward the camera. It quickly becomes apparent that these two Black men dressed in Ostrich-feathered turbans and underpants are the Nicholas Brothers who will help situate a swing aesthetic within this mythical Arabia. Here, their brownface (and that of Princess Ammon) seems to excuse the presence of their Black bodies onscreen in 1940, a time when most films were devoid of Black cameos; it also allows them an opportunity for imperfect assimilation. [FIG. 5.5]

FIGURE 5.5 The Nicholas Brothers in a scene from *Tin Pan Alley*, 1940. Jumping: Harold Nicholas, *left*, and Fayard Nicholas. Billy Gilbert in *back*; others unidentified. (Core Collection. Production files, Margaret Herrick Library, Academy of Motion Picture Arts and Sciences)

Through brownface, the Nicholas Brothers relativize themselves to the White norm. Their imperfect assimilation allows them to temporarily transcend what Frantz Fanon has referred to as their "epidermalization of inferiority," while simultaneously reinforcing old epidermal schema as it concerns a White gaze. If, as Fanon argues, a Black body can mask "White potentials,"

266   BEHIND THE SCREEN

a brown mask might offer a cover for presenting Black artistry under the guise of not-Blackness.[122] All the while, the Brothers are able to situate an Africanist aesthetic (vis-à-vis swing music and their syncopated tap dancing) within a mythical kingdom of "brown" people and cultures. Hollywood collapses the cultures of pseudo-Arab, Balinese, Thai, Cambodian, and even Hawaiian—the last suggested by the hula duet performed by Betty Grable and Alice Faye following the Brothers' tap dance—into an amorphous brown that exists somewhere along the road from White to Black. "The Sheik of Araby" is thus a romanticized portrayal of anything down there, to the East, or close to Africa (but technically not Africa) that allows Black performers to entertain, exposing costumes to slip past the censors, and for the "safe" delivery of Africanist rhythms through a White medium.[123] The transit narrative assists in this general remapping of an Africanist aesthetic by helping to enact the migration that occurs en route from here to there. Keeping these stories "in-between" keeps the transfer of Black sound to White body fluid and poised to absorb other musical styles into the aesthetic mix.

Consuming the Spectacular Sign

Popular entertainment of the mid-late 1930s in the United States that referenced African Americans evolved into a safer, more desirable obsession with Hawaii. Historian Howard Zinn writes that the first American officials sent to evaluate the potential of the Islands believed Hawaii was "'a ripe pear ready to be plucked.'"[124] Consequently films like *Honolulu* reinforced a layer of separation between the island and the mainland, the Native Hawaiian body and the White, the truth and the fiction.

As is clear from the hula dance manuals pervasive throughout the early twentieth century—especially those written by Gilda Gray—the hula dance became less representative of Native Hawaiian dance idioms and more marked by American stylistic choices as it crossed over into the mainland. Americans felt entitled to the island dance vocabulary and began reformatting it to suit their own aesthetic and political needs. Dance manuals retained only a hint of Native Hawaiian vocabulary, instead turning to an African American vernacular dance lexicon for inspiration. Using only elements of Hawaiian movement and dress, choreographers began labeling this colonial interpretation of Hawaiian hula "authentic," promising an American public something new, exotic, and not Black.

Gray notoriously denied that "the Negro had anything to do with" her dancing and yet all of her purported creations can be traced back to Black vernacular forms.[125] The language in Gray's manuals describes particular movements in the hula as "just like a Charleston," or resembling a Shimmy.[126] As is clear from dance manuals pervasive throughout the teens and twenties that claimed to teach "Native" dancing, the dances become less and less "authentic" as they left their place of origin and crossed over into the American mainland.

While Hawaii was a particular destination of interest, this argument could be made for any of America's territories. Americans felt entitled to the island dance vocabulary and began reformatting it to suit their own aesthetic and political needs. Using only elements of Native styles, choreographers began labeling these forms "authentic," promising an American public something new. Thus, in a manner akin to Powell's performance in *Honolulu*, Gray's circulation of Africanist forms vis-à-vis the "expert" White body forced notions of authenticity onto these forms so that each woman's iteration came to stand in for the real.

Powell's body produces a discourse around the feminine and the exotic. As in chapter 4, while dancing on the ship Powell first symbolizes an idealized White femininity; then, during the costume ball, she represents Black masculinity in her tribute to Robinson, not only solidifying a notion that the body can stand in as a material sign for categories of social status but, under the "sign of spectacular corporeality," promises that mere presence on the island and contact with Native Hawaiian culture will transform her body into a sign of "Native authenticity." While the film takes Powell's body as sign (for Native-ness) for granted, it also blurs the act of signifying and draws attention to its signified. What becomes invisible in Powell's performance is the colonial agenda to both appropriate Hawaiian culture and mask the elements of her dance that have already been lifted from the mainland's Africanist presence. Jane Desmond captures this process perfectly when she writes, "This sign simultaneously symbolizes bodily presence ('native,' 'woman') and cultural enactment (Hawaiian-ness) and stands for the 'destination image' of Hawaii."[127] Powell's presence in Hawaii qualifies her representation of the female Native, demonstrates her ability to enact Hawaiian-ness, and attracts viewers to her display of the exoticism.

Powell's tap dance, embedded in a Native hula dance, participates in the colonial annexation of Hawaiian culture; moreover, the inculcation of Hawaiian imagery into mainland dance practices claims to defy "strategies of

268   BEHIND THE SCREEN

containment" by purporting an island free of difference-making ideologies and practices. In configuring the Hawaiian Islands as colonized and exotic, *Honolulu* repeats an ongoing process of distinguishing *us* from *them and* further masks the cultural depth that is inherent to America's identity. *Honolulu* was not the only film Powell made that followed this formula. Several of her films make use of the transit narrative or situate her title numbers aboard a ship—"Swing the Jinx Away" from *Born to Dance* (1936), for example— perhaps using the liminality of transit—neither here nor there—to aid in justifying her heavy use of a swing aesthetic. But *Ship Ahoy* (originally called *I'll Take Manila*) reads almost as a carbon copy of *Honolulu*, substituting Puerto Rico for Hawaii and morse code for blackface.[128]

Morse Code, Less Paint

Much of *Ship Ahoy's* narrative resembles that of *Honolulu*. The film opens with another iteration of Powell's hula tap, performed on the mainland as part of a nightclub routine alongside Tommy Dorsey's Orchestra (featuring drummer Buddy Rich) rather than Andy Iona and his Islanders.[129] Shortly thereafter we learn of Powell's departure for Puerto Rico and once on the ship the camera cuts to an almost identical poolside scene to the one in *Honolulu*, only here Tommy Dorsey engages Merton Kibble (Red Skelton) in a dialogue about swing, establishing the swing aesthetic as something cool, as distinct from square.

> Dorsey: Don't tell me you're from Squaresville?
> Kibble: Where's Squaresville?
> Dorsey: Why, man, that's *everywhere.*
> Kibble: Oh, you mean I don't dig it. I'm not hep.
> Dorsey: Groovy!

This dialogue frames Powell's ensuing rhythm tap dance performed to "Tampico." Sonically both the song and Powell's dancing adopt elements characteristic of swing and Latin music, yet visually they read as White. Meanwhile the lyrics, which we hear later in the film as a reprised version, conflate a mix of cultural references to a range of "brown" territories and dance forms—Brazil, Marquita the Cheeta, the conga and the hula, for example—while also referencing Aunt Jemimah.[130] Then, in an almost uncanny duplication of certain main events in *Honolulu*, the camera cuts to a sign announcing a costume ball—the "Bal Caribbean"—which, like the one in *Honolulu*, offers an excuse for key cast members to masquerade as Hollywood personas. This pretense also provides a context for the obligatory nightclub scene, only instead of Powell performing a tribute to Robinson in blackface, a young Frank Sinatra croons and a youthful Stump and Stumpy (James Cross and Eddie Hartman) perform a high-energy tap dance. After the jazz tap number, Powell and Skelton exit the costume ball for some alone time—another parallel between the two films—the song "Moonlight Bay" plays in the background with the audible lyrics "we could hear the darkies singing" coloring the scene's romantic dialogue.[131] This sonic reference to "darkies singing" is succeeded by Powell's introduction to morse code tap dancing, where each dot and dash has a corresponding toe or heel tap and surreptitiously, she can send and receive messages.

The crux of *Ship Ahoy*'s plot is that Powell is unknowingly recruited by "the enemy" (unnamed Nazis perhaps) who have stolen a prototype explosive mine. Powell thinks she is working for the American government but when she finds out that she is not, she uses tap dance to disguise her morse code communication in the finale. As the ship docks in Puerto Rico, Powell presents the film's most extravagant number: the blending of several "Latin" and Spanish dance styles with tap dance and Powell's *matadora* costume make "Cape Dance" undoubtedly the 1942 substitute for *Honolulu*'s climactic hula tap. The concluding dance sequence at a Puerto Rico nightclub showcases Powell in a sparkling white power suit with a top hat and glistening high-heeled tap shoes. While each of these substitutions may seem small, each carries significant weight, and when read together, they are emblematic of the shift covert minstrelsy takes during the years following the bombing of Pearl Harbor.

***

The attack on Pearl Harbor impacted Hawaii's idyllic landscape and shifted Americans' attention away from Hawaii onto other territories and vague Pacific islands.[132] By the time MGM released *Ship Ahoy* in May 1942, both Hawaiian music, latunes, and jazz had become a part of the White American vernacular. Hollywood's strategies for representing jazz alongside references to the ill-defined "brown" body, helped to erase the visibility of Black artistry onscreen, permitting White musicians like Benny Goodman and Tommy

Dorsey to become some of its new faces. Not only would they begin to take the place of Calloway and Ellington onscreen, but dialogue like that in *Ahoy* further conditioned a White audience from seeing jazz music as being taboo to instead finding it cool, hep, and groovy. So too did the sound of jazz change from being dominated by a swing aesthetic to a new form that contained elements of Bebop and hints of Hawaiian instrumentation as well rhythms heavily influenced by Latin America.

Primitivizing frameworks like brownface as well as the Gabriel variation, together, provided covert minstrelsy important mechanisms of distraction necessary to complete the techno-dialogic transfer between the audibly Africanist and the visually White. While seemingly different approaches, both narrative devices offered vehicles of passage between a "dangerous" Black aesthetic and the White screen. Whether Eddie Cantor or Al Jolson in blackface were the agents through which Black music found White redemption onscreen, or Eleanor Powell's traveling body was a conduit between the US mainland and one of its territories mediating between Black dance and White vis-à-vis some Latin or "Native" form, their individual trips capitalize on an Africanist aesthetic at the expense of Black visibility. The branding of Cab Calloway as a crossover artist as well as popular Black vernacular "how-to" songs marketed to White people through film and dance manuals allowed everyone to participate in the jazz craze while further obscuring Hollywood's process. Through such narratives and marketing schemes White promoters would untether jazz from its past narratives of sin and repackage it as cool, White, and "American." This process not only kept Black artists out of the spotlight but also, as we have seen, scripted non-Black Others as safe exotics, hyper-feminized, sexualized, and "ripe for the taking," making it easier to capitalize on those bodies and aesthetics as well. This process supported a colonialist mindset and primed the screen for White, female bodies like Powell's to create an illusion of peace during the height of World War II. Thus, while a certain jazz aesthetic had landed, Powell's dancing was still very much in transit, writing America's script as she danced, her body creating its own layer of censorship during this particularly deceptive time in Hollywood.

Shortly after America entered the war, Roosevelt signed Executive Order 8985, which established the Office of Censorship and instructed director Byron Price to use "his absolute discretion" when censoring international communications.[133] As censorship tightened at the highest level, the film industry followed in its representations of race and world politics. The use of visible blackface, even in the context of a tribute, would be tolerated less and less. In *Ship Ahoy* the tap dance performance by Stump and Stumpy stands in for Powell's blackface tribute as the one Black specialty act during the costume ball. By this point, Powell had already proven herself as a competent rhythm tap soloist and there was less of a need for her to pay tribute to an icon like Robinson. But the lack of burnt cork in this film is not an indication of the disappearance of blackface.

The jazz aesthetic, figured as White yet juxtaposed to composite representations and instances of brownface, is presented in transit from the mainland to Puerto Rico. Even if jazz music and tap dance are read as White in this context, as long as they appear "in transit," they equivocate between nationalism and colonialism and if they are arranged beside sonic references to the minstrel stage, they occupy a liminal space between the past and present. Troubled by caricatures of Blackness, Powell's new "tribute" in the form of her morse code tap dance to "Moonlight Bay" is a less visible form of racial insult.

This finale, which takes place off the American mainland, broadcasts a false message of national unity. Since Powell has already established a set of signs—dot-dot-dash using toes and heels—during the earlier scene along-side Skelton with "darkies singing" in the background, the audience has now subconsciously paired her new means of communicating with old codes of behavior. Deborah Kapchan has described such a phenomenon as a facet of sound writing when "the interpretations we make of the messages carried in sound are also linked to messages carried in other media when those messages invoke the practices and qualities we associate with sound."[134] Having performed the film's earlier tap sequences in more revealing attire, Powell has already encoded female sexuality into her dancing body. The suit she wears in the finale allows her to transmit "genuine code" without disrupting Production Code guidelines to represent national institutions with the utmost respect. Here Powell's feet become techno-dialogic vehicles for transmitting a national message against an invisible backdrop of minstrel timbre. The pairing of morse code with racist lyrics simultaneously signifies the nineteenth-century minstrel stage while broadcasting the nation's unity against the "enemy" (unnamed but no doubt predicated on Nazi Germany). Yet, inverse to the frequency of occurrence, Powell's silences disguise a logic of segregation, signaling absence instead of presence, her White body assisting in deracinating rhythm tap while transmitting at a rate higher than that which the receiver is capable of decoding.

272 BEHIND THE SCREEN

AMERICA NEEDS YOUR MONEY,
BUY DEFENSE BONDS AND STAMPS EVERY PAY DAY

Notes

1. Lloyd Bacon, *Wonder Bar* (March 31, 1934; USA: First National Pictures), Film.
2. For more specific ways that this film ignored Code guidelines, see Jeffrey Spivak, *Berkeley: The Life and Art of Busby Berkeley*, Screen Classics (Lexington: University Press of Kentucky, 2011), 103.
3. The Black press took issue with a different set of issues. The *Defender* was upset that Jolson had recently tried to buy rights to *Green Pastures*, enraged at the recent news that Jolson would play the title role in *Porgy and Bess* and that he was also pleading to play Jones in *Emperor Jones*, and criticized the absence of Chilton and Thomas, the two Black performers who had performed in the stage tour of *Wonder Bar*, in the film. See "Al Jolson Buys Film Rights to Green Pastures," *Chicago Defender*, June 6, 1931, 7; "Al Jolson Given the Lead in 1933 Edition of *Porgy*," *Chicago Defender*, June 13, 1931; and "Al Jolson Pleads for Lead in 'Emperor Jones' on Stage," *Chicago Defender*, April 7, 1934, 9.
4. Mourdant Hall, "THE SCREEN: 'Wonder Bar'"; Al Jolson, Kay Francis, and Dolores Del Rio, *New York Times*, March 1, 1934.
5. Marc Connelly and William Keighly, *The Green Pastures* (August 1, 1936; USA: Warner Bros.), Film; Sam Wood, *A Day at the Races* (June 11, 1937; USA: Metro Goldwyn-Mayer), Film; William Keighly and Busby Berkeley, *The Singing Kid* (April 11, 1936; USA: Warner Bros.), Film; Leigh Jason, *New Faces of 1937* (July 2, 1937; USA: RKO Radio Pictures), Film; David Butler, *Ali Baba Goes to Town* (October 29, 1937; USA: Twentieth Century Fox), Film.
6. David Stowe, *Swing Changes: Big-Band Jazz in New Deal America* (Cambridge, MA: Harvard University Press, 1994), 13.
7. Joel Dinerstein, *Swinging the Machine: Modernity, Technology, and African American Culture Between the World Wars* (Amherst: University of Massachusetts Press, 2003), 116.
8. For more on the Harlem Riot, see chapter 4, n. 8.
9. Quoted in Spivak, *Berkeley*, 102.
10. Roark Bradford's collection, *Ol' Man Adam an' His Chillun*, was a collection of pseudo-African American folktales that depicted African Americans in a questionable manner, similar to Joel Chandler Harris's representation of African American life and the South in the *Uncle Remus* tales.
11. Quoted in George S. Schuyler, "Mr. Whitney and Mr. Lewis," *Pittsburgh Courier*, October 8, 1930.
12. Judith Weisenfeld writes that Connelly was particularly interested in the varying "attitudes toward dancing and other forms of movement, both socially and in the context of worship. After observing a range of churches, he was most impressed with

those that prohibited social dancing, since he felt their songs and movement in worship were much more energetic and affecting." Judith Weisenfield, *Hollywood Be Thy Name: African American Religion in American Film, 1929–1949* (Berkeley: University of California Press, 2007), 58 and 70.

13. G. S. Morris, "Thank God for Uncle Tom—Race and Religion Collide in *The Green Pastures*," *Bright Lights*, no. 59, February 2008.

14. Sander Gilman, *The Jew's Body* (New York: Routledge, 1991).

15. Manning notes that modern dancers who engaged in metaphorical minstrelsy did not engage in imitation as did blackface performers. See Susan Manning, *Modern Dance, Negro Dance: Race in Motion* (Minneapolis: University of Minnesota Press, 2004), 10.

16. Music by Harold Arlen; Lyrics by E.Y. Harburg; performed by Jolson, Shaw, and Calloway and Chorus.

17. Written in 1918 by Jean Schwartz with lyrics by Sam Lewis and Joe Young.

18. Music by Joseph Meyer and lyrics by Buddy G. DeSylva.

19. Music by Harry Warren and lyrics by Al Dubin.

20. Lloyd Bacon, *The Singing Fool* (September 19, 1928; USA: Warner Bros.), Film.

21. Music by Jolson, Buddy G. DeSylva, Lew Brown, and Ray Henderson in 1928.

22. This fictional journalist was likely a reference to Louella Parsons, an American movie columnist known as the "Queen of Hollywood Gossip" throughout the 1920s and 1930s. See Amy Fine Collins, "The Powerful Rivalry of Hedda Hopper and Louella Parsons," *Vanity Fair*, Conde Nast.

23. Music by Harold Arlen and Lyrics by E.Y. Harburg.

24. Harley Erdman, *Staging the Jew: The Performance of an American Ethnicity 1860–1920* (New Brunswick, NJ: Rutgers University Press, 1997), 26.

25. Music and Lyrics by Irving Mills and Cab Calloway but uncredited in the film.

26. Music by Harold Arlen and Lyrics by E.Y. Harburg.

27. Susan Foster, *Reading Dancing: Bodies in Motion in Contemporary American Dance* (Berkeley: University of California Press, 1988).

28. Music by Harold Arlen and Lyrics by E.Y. Harburg.

29. Nate Sloan, "Constructing Cab Calloway: Publicity, Race, and Performance in 1930s Harlem Jazz," *Journal of Musicology* 36, no. 3 (July 1, 2019): 399, doi: https://doi-org. libproxy.chapman.edu/10.1525/jm.2019.36.3.370

30. Ibid., 374.

31. Ibid., 374–75.

32. Ibid., 377.

33. Ibid., 378.

34. Ibid., 381.

35. Cab Calloway and Bryant Rollins, *Of Minnie the Moocher and Me* (Boston: Thomas Y. Crowell, 1976), 111.

36. Sloan, "Constructing Cab Calloway," 381.

37. Ibid., 384–85.

38. From Calloway Press Manual and quoted in Sloan, "Constructing Cab Calloway," 395.

39. Robin D. G. Kelley, *Race Rebels: Culture, Politics and the Black Working Class* (New York: Free Press, 1994), 165.

274   BEHIND THE SCREEN

40. In "Kickin' the Gong Around"—the title itself a slang phrase originally referencing opium—Calloway imitates the acts of snorting cocaine and shooting heroin.
41. Arthur Knight, *Disintegrating the Musical: Black Performance and American Musical Film* (Durham, NC: Duke University Press, 2002), 77.
42. Ibid., 76.
43. Dinerstein, *Swinging*.
44. Ibid., 126 and 117.
45. Ibid., 351, n. 30.
46. Mark Sandrich, *Shall We Dance* (May 7, 1937; USA: RKO Radio Pictures), Film.
47. Ibid., 245.
48. Decker, *Music Makes Me*, 117.
49. Ibid., 120.
50. Victor Schertzinger, *Birth of the Blues* (November 7, 1941; USA: Paramount Pictures), Film.
51. RKO S/447, SWD script, December 23, 1936 (blue pages dated January 6, 1937).
52. Todd Decker, *Music Makes Me: Fred Astaire and Jazz* (Berkeley: University of California Press, 2011), 119–20.
53. John F. Szwed, "Musical Style and Racial Conflict," *Phylon* 27, no. 4 (1966): 361.
54. Stowe, *Swing Changes*, 6. For a more in-depth account of this tour, see also Arthur Rollini, *Thirty Years with the Big Bands* (Urbana: University of Illinois Press, 1987), 34–70.
55. Decker, *Music Makes Me*, 119–20.
56. Stowe, *Swing Changes*, 8.
57. Elliott Nugent, *Strictly Dynamite* (May 11, 1934; USA: RKO Radio Pictures), Film.
58. Busby Berkeley, *Hollywood Hotel* (January 15, 1938; USA: First National Pictures), Film.
59. Redd Davis, *Sing as You Swing* (July 7, 1937; UK: Joe Rock Productions), Film; Raoul Walsh, *College Swing* (April 29, 1938; USA: Paramount Pictures), Film, Victor Schertzinger, *Birth of the Blues* (November 7, 1941; USA: Paramount Pictures), Film.
60. Decker, *Music Makes Me*, 51–52.
61. Matthew Morrison, "Race, Blacksound, and the (Re)Making of Musicological Discourse," *Journal of the American Musicological Society* 72, no. 3 (2019): 800.
62. Ben Pollack and Henry James wrote this song in 1936, and Eddie Cherkose wrote additional lyrics for it in 1937. Benny Goodman (a member of Pollack's band) re-recorded the tune with his orchestra later in 1937.
63. According to the Auburn (California) *Journal*, the "Genii" was twenty-five-feet tall, eighteen-feet wide, and weighed three tons. He had three horns, each six-feet long. The eyes of this creature contained two arc lights and steam pipes that would allow five men to spotlight the dancers and help emit smoke from the monster's nose. See Goldberg's R&B Notebooks—THREE CHOCOLATEERS, http://www.uncamarvy.com/3Chocolateers/3chocolateers.html, accessed December 23, 2020.
64. Known as the "Bridal Chorus" from Richard Wagner's *Lohengrin* (1850).
65. From Felix Mendelssohn, "A Midsummer Night's Dream," incidental music, op. 61 (1842).

66. Marshall Winslow Stearns and Jean Stearns, *Jazz Dance: The Story of American Vernacular Dance* (New York: Da Capo Press, 1994), 241.
67. Ibid., 242. Anderson also engaged in a similar dialectic with members of Ellington's band while singing.
68. Ibid., 246.
69. Goldberg's R&B Notebooks—THREE CHOCOLATEERS, http://www.uncamarvy.com/3Chocolateers/3chocolateers.html.
70. George Marshall, *Can This Be Dixie* (November 13, 1936; USA: Twentieth Century Fox), Film.
71. Stearns and Stearns, *Jazz Dance*, 103, 106–7, and 113.
72. Goldberg's R&B Notebooks–THREE CHOCOLATEERS.
73. Miller, *Segregating Sound: Inventing Folk and Pop Music in the Age of Jim Crow* (Durham, NC: Duke University Press, 2010), 15.
74. Stearns and Stearns, *Jazz Dance*, 114. Vernacular dances had long battled public opinion. Stearns and Stearns write, "In a typical dispatch to the New Orleans *States* in 1922, the Morality League denounced the 'cherry pickers, tack-hammers, cheek-pressers, hip-swingers, and lemon-rollers of the fierce jazz dance invaders' and pressed for an 'anti-vulgar dance ordinance.'"
75. Following the Harlem Riots of 1935, the Cotton Club moved down to Broadway and 48th Street and the shows presented there (to Whites only) were high-budget shows that lasted months.
76. Morrison, "Race, Blacksound," 792.
77. Stearns and Stearns, *Jazz Dance*, 272.
78. Roy Mack, *By Request* (November 9, 1935; USA: Warner Bros.), Film; *You Can't Have Everything* (August 3, 1937; USA: Twentieth Century Fox), Film.
79. Stearns and Stearns, *Jazz Dance*, 272.
80. Goldberg's R&B Notebooks—THE HARLEM HIGHLANDERS, http://www.uncamarvy.com/HarlemHighlanders/harlemhighlanders.html, accessed December 23, 2020.
81. I did not locate any White publications about the Three Chocolateers before an advertisement in the *Long Island Daily Press* dated October 18, 1939.
82. Ralph Murphy and Walter Lang, *Top of the Town* (April 18, 1937; USA: Universal Pictures), Film.
83. Gustavo Perez Firmat, "Latunes" *Latin American Research Review* 43, no. 2 (2008): 187.
84. This scat phrase originally appeared in Calloway's "Minnie the Moocher" (1931) and was then the title of Paramount's short by the same name (1934) starring Calloway and Fredi Washington. It appears again in Calloway's famous "Hi-De-Ho-Man" song (Calloway was eventually labeled the "Hi-De-Ho Man") and was later the title of a race film directed by Josh Binney and released by All American Entertainment (1947). The film features the Peters Sisters and the famous tap trio The Miller Brothers and Lois Bright.
85. Another musical reference to Calloway's hit by the same name in 1933.
86. An African American close harmony trio similar in style to the better-known White Boswell or Andrews Sisters.

276 BEHIND THE SCREEN

87. Because of the way they are dressed, this is clearly a citation of "Peckin'" from *New Faces*.

88. In the Old Testament, Miriam is the daughter of Amram and Jochebed and the sister of Aaron and Moses. She plays a big role in the story of Passover, which takes place in Egypt, complicating the film's conflation of Middle Eastern territories.

89. David Butler, *Ali Baba Goes to Town* (Twentieth Century Fox, 1937), MS Hollywood, Censorship, and the Motion Picture Production Code, 1927–1968: History of Cinema, Series 1, Hollywood and Production Code Administration, Margaret Herrick Library, Archives Unbound, https://tinyurl.com/njutrzh8, accessed April 27, 2021.

90. Even a sign in the background of a bazaar advertises: "learn to dance—Peckin'; Truckin' and Susy-Q in 10 easy lessons—a Federal Project." [39:30] For more on his court-packing plan, see William E. Leuchtenburg, "When Franklin Roosevelt Clashed with the Supreme Court—and Lost," *Smithsonian Magazine*, May 2005, accessed December 28, 2020, https://www.smithsonianmag.com/history/when-franklin-roosevelt-clashed-with-the-supreme-court-and-lost-78497994/.

91. From *Metronome* quoted in Stowe, *Swing Changes*, 25.

92. Stowe, *Swing* Changes, 11–13.

93. See chapter 1.

94. Mendi Lewis Obadike, "Low Fidelity: Stereotyped Blackness in the Field of Sound" (PhD diss., Duke University, 2005), 2–3.

95. Erdman, *Staging the Jew*, 25.

96. Sometimes called a heel twist or grind walk, the Suzy-Q is a step used in lindy hop, tap dance, and jazz.

97. While nobody knows exactly if "Minnie the Moocher" was based on a real person, the song garnered its own reputation based on the lyrics, which allude to her promiscuity and drug use.

98. Mary Anne Doane, "Film and Masquerade: Theorizing the Female Spectator," in *Femme Fatales* (New York: Routledge, 1991), 133.

99. Roy Del Ruth and W. S. Van Dyke, *Broadway Melody of 1936* (September 20, 1935; USA: Metro Goldwyn-Mayer), Film.

100. Constance Valis Hill, "Jeni Le Gon," in *Tap Dance in America: A Short History, Library of Congress Database*, https://www.loc.gov/item/ihas.200217630/, accessed December 29, 2020.

101. This is according to the *Binghamton Press* in an article written September 11, 1940.

102. Leslie Goodwins, *With Love and Kisses* (December 20, 1936; USA: Conn Pictures Corporation), Film.

103. *New York Sun*, February 26, 1938, March 19 and 24, 1938, and September 26, 1946. See also Sidney Lanfield, *Love and Hisses* (December 21, 1937; USA: Twentieth Century Fox), Film.

104. According to E. Moncell Durden, the Skrontch has many variations but is "basically going into a squared position on a diagonal while rotating the hips with independent knees. You do a hard swivel as you wind the hips down on one side and pop the booty back and slightly up on the other side" (Author's personal interview, December 30, 2020).

WITH A GLORY BE   277

105. *Times Union*, Albany, NY, October 25, 1937—though they seem never to have appeared in *Rebecca* alongside Shirley Temple and Robinson—and *Times Union*, Albany, NY, February 9, 1942.

106. Other exceptions include race films made during this period (like *Double Deal*), Le Gon's appearance in *I Can't Give You Anything but Love, Baby* (1940), Robinson in *It's Swing Ho-Come to the Fair!* (1939), and the uncredited Nicholas Brothers in *My Son Is Guilty* (1939), and a credited performance in *Down Argentine Way* (1940), as well as Theresa Harris's performance in *Buck Benny Rides Again* (1940).

107. Stearns and Stearns, *Jazz Dance*, 113.

108. Ibid., 114.

109. Firmat, "Latunes," 189.

110. Adria L. Imada, *Aloha America: Hula Circuits through the U.S. Empire* (Durham, NC: Duke University Press, 2012), 5.

111. Ibid., 12.

112. Bernard Smith, *Imaging the Pacific in the Wake of the Cook Voyages* (New Haven, CT: Yale University Press, 1992), 210.

113. Imada, *Aloha America*, 16.

114. Ibid., 17.

115. Barbara A. Babcock, "First Families: Gender, Reproduction, and the Mythic Southwest," in *The Great Southwest of the Fred Harvey Company and the Santa Fe Railway*, ed. Marta Weigle and Barbara A. Babcock (Phoenix, AZ: Heard Museum, 1996), 207–17.

116. Imada, *Aloha America*, 213.

117. A year and a half after *Honolulu* was released, Congress passed the Selective Training and Service Act of 1940 authorizing a draft across the country. By October of that year men between the ages of twenty-one and thirty-five were required to register with their local draft board. Despite relatively low standards, 5 million potential draftees were rejected for medical, educational, or emotional reasons. Many attribute this to long-term effects of the Depression. See William M. Tuttle Jr., *World War II and the American Home Front: Part Two* (Washington, DC: National Park Service, 2004), 57.

118. Archie Mayo and Michael Curtiz, *Go Into Your Dance* (April 20, 1935; USA: First National Pictures), Film.

119. James Joyce's short story "Araby" from his 1914 collection *Dubliners* is a *bildungsroman* about a boy who falls in love with a "brown figure" and ultimately must come to terms with his idealized notion of the East and the girl existing only in his imagination.

120. See "Tinful and Amusing Is 'Tin Pan Alley,'" *Rochester Times Union* (Rochester, New York), December 6, 1940, 19–A.

121. The only archival trace of Vanessa Ammon that exists outside of this film is a *Billboard* mention of her "stylized moves" in a Bali number performed at the Cotton Club, dated December 9, 1939.

122. Frantz Fanon, *Black Skin, White Masks* (London: Pluto Press, 1986).

123. Similarly, Tip, Tap, and Toe's performance in *You Can't Have Everything* is almost a literal writing of Fanon's ideas in its ability to reduce the dancing of Sammy Green,

Teddy Frazier, and Raymond Winfield to racist representations of colonial ideology. This layer of brownface allows Hollywood to mediate between cultural intimacy and keeping the Other at a distance.

124. Quoted in Howard Zinn, *A People's History of the United States* (New York: Harper Perennial Modern Classics, 2005), 312. America annexed Hawaii in July 1898 by joint reduction.

125. Ibid.,105.

126. Jane Desmond, *Staging Tourism: Bodies on Display from Waikiki to Sea World* (Chicago: University of Chicago Press, 1999), 75–76.

127. Ibid., 5.

128. Roy Del Ruth, *Born to Dance* (November 27, 1936; USA: Metro Goldwyn-Mayer), Film.

129. Dorsey's Orchestra plays "Hawaiian War Chant (Ta-HupWa-Ha-Hai)" written in 1936 by Johnny Noble and Prince Leleiohoku.

130. This song appears later in the film as "I'll Take Tallulah," but the music is identical.

131. Music written in 1916 by Percy Wenrich with Lyrics by Edward Madden. Sung by Frank Sinatra and the Pied Pipers in the film.

132. Some examples from 1942 alone include *Wake Island*, *Pardon My Sarong*, *Song of the Islands*, *Don Winslow of the Navy*, and *The Mad Doctor of Market Street*.

133. Louis Fiset, "Return to Sender," *Prologue Magazine* 33, no. 1 (Spring 2001), https://www.archives.gov/publications/prologue/2001/spring/mail-censorship-in-world-war-two-1.html, accessed from US Government National Archives on January 2, 2021

134. Deborah Kapchan, *Theorizing Sound Writing* (Middletown, CT: Wesleyan University Press, 2017), 3.

PRODUCED IN COOPERATION WITH WARNER BROS.
AND U.S. TREASURY DEPT. DEFENSE SAVINGS STAFF
IN TECHNICOLOR

FIGURE 6.1 Bugs Bunny performs "Sammy" by Irving Berlin in *Any Bonds Today*, 1942. (Private collection)

6

Hays Is for Horses

Cartoons' Crossover Appeal, Dis-figuration, and the Animated Bestiary, 1934–1942

A painted image of George Washington playing bass drum with a man to his right and left playing the side drum and fife, respectively, fades up on the screen, setting the tone for the spirited piece of American propaganda that will follow. A Betsy Ross flag waving in the background refers to a revolutionary time in United States' history while the ensuing melody sung by none other than Bugs Bunny speaks to the urgency of the present. "A tall man in a high hat, with the whiskers on his chin will soon be knocking at your door—and you oughta beeee in!" *The famous rabbit marches across the stage with an Uncle Sam's hat as he sings these words and alternates between nibbling and playing the piccolo-shaped carrot. His message continues:* "Get your savings out, when you hear him shout, *ANY BONDS TODAY!*" *He performs some familiar vaudeville steps, his lack of joints making it easier to master the legomania style.* "Any bonds today? Bonds of freedom, that's what I'm sellin'—any bonds today? Scrape up the most you can *(bell kick)*, here comes the freedom man *(Charleston)* asking you to buy your share of freeeeedom today *(truckin')*." *He finishes the stanza in a wide center split. He spins and after completing a few revolutions, POOF, re-presents himself in blackface. Adapting his voice to sound like Al Jolson, he continues his sales pitch:* "We all invest in the U.S.A" *(bending down on one knee),* "SAAAMMY! My Uncle Sammy," *he croons highlighting this famous spin on Jolson's lyrics. As he shakes his hands for emphasis, the resemblance between his white gloves and those appearing on the minstrel stage are unmistakable. Elmer Fudd and Porky Pig appear upstage, and while they join Bugs in song, Bugs uses his giant minstrel gloves to wipe away his makeup. The backdrop has also seamlessly changed to a sky of warbirds.* "Any stamps, any bonds Tooodayyyy?" *The three cartoons unite in a rough copy of a single basic time step.*[1]

Behind the Screen. Brynn W. Shiovitz, Oxford University Press. © Oxford University Press 2023.
DOI: 10.1093/oso/9780197553091.003.0007

282 BEHIND THE SCREEN

FOR DEFENSE BUY UNITED STATES SAVINGS BONDS
AND STAMPS

A few weeks before Eleanor Powell's body proved to be a convincing vehicle for transmitting national messages in *Ship Ahoy*'s morse code tap dance, Bugs Bunny was demonstrating similar techno-dialogic feats for the animated bestiary. A primary difference between Powell's image, as discussed in chapter 5, and that of Bugs Bunny was that Powell's message surrounding citizenship and the film's efforts to garner support for the war required high levels of decoding. Bugs Bunny's blatant blackface performance in *Any Bonds Today*, however, demonstrates the ways Hollywood producers framed narratives of patriotism in tandem with a kind of minstrel hauntology of the screen, an ode to the minstrel stage enmeshed in war propaganda, all masked by Bugs's leporid identity. Bugs's Africanist vocabulary together with his swift transformations between cartoon rabbit, Uncle Sam, and Al Jolson reiterate the efficacy of the protean and citational guises within an animated format. Together these images cheaply and quickly inundate American audiences with long-standing, deep-seated attitudes toward race; moreover, they speak to Hollywood's transition from live action to cartoon artistry as a way to capitalize on animation's governing principles to both economize and standardize in the face of less funding and more regulations during the war.

Seven months after Powell's performance in *Honolulu* and four months prior to the release of *Any Bonds Today*, the world entered a war more widespread and destructive than history had seen to date. Over 100 million people from thirty different countries were thrown into a state of "total war," forming two opposing camps—the Allies and the Axis—that erased the distinction between civilian and military resources. During the war, several mass killings marked it as the deadliest in human history. The Holocaust extended over four years (1941–1945) and resulted in the deaths of 11 million stigmatized Others—6 million of whom were Jews. The atomic bombings of Hiroshima and Nagasaki in August 1945 were responsible for the deaths of 129,000 people. The six-year war produced between 50 and 85 million fatalities and changed the world's social structure and political assembly. The world established the United Nations in October 1945 to promote global cooperation and prevent another war like the Second World War from ever recurring.[2]

Documenting this war and informing the public of its devastation continued to raise challenges for both Hollywood and the Office of War Information. Thomas Doherty notes, "The War Department, the Office of War Information (OWI), and Hollywood's studio heads colluded in keeping the awful devastations of combat from the home front screen— sometimes by outright fabrication, usually by expedient omission."[3] Everything from newsreels to films had to be censored so that the stories fed to Americans by the media were not necessarily in line with reality. The OWI believed that "properly directed hatred [was] of vital importance to the war effort." They pleaded with Hollywood to make war ideologies the subject of attack rather than individual rulers (e.g., Hitler) or entire nations (e.g., the Germans or Japanese). Yet they were highly supportive of films that commented on the militaristic system and incorporated war ideologies. Nelson Pointer notes, "Hatred of the militaristic system which governs the Axis countries and of those responsible for its further-ance definitely should be promoted."[4] Film thus became the mediator of discourse and social/political values: "Shocked and enlightened by the motion picture propaganda of the Nazis, obliged to obey new codes of conduct and send out life-and-death messages, the motion picture in-dustry became the preeminent transmitter of wartime policy and a light-ning rod for public discourse."[5] This included live action films like *Ahoy*, which united Americans against a common "enemy" while using song, dance, and romance to make light of the severity of the situation. Some production houses would directly engage with the war effort, pleading with viewers to "buy defense bonds and stamps every pay day" at the end of a feature. True propaganda, though, was generally funded by govern-ment agencies like the US Treasury or the War Production Board, as was the case with Warner Bros.' *Any Bonds Today* (1942) or Disney's *Out of the Frying Pan into the Firing Line* (1942), respectively.[6] The animated format of these films allowed for even more distance from the gravity of the circumstances in Europe and was generally successful in its didacti-cism.[7] That is, the cartoon format further removed viewers from the more confrontational images of gas chambers, emaciated bodies, and imploded cities that photojournalism could have conveyed. And while film—both live and animated—mediated public knowledge of the war and the op-posing Axis, Hollywood directors and writers also played major roles in interpreting and controlling certain citizens' bodies.

During this period, the United States continued to struggle with ra-cial equality. Many Black Americans were troubled by Roosevelt's "Four Freedoms" speech given in January 1941, as it seemed hypocritical to promise freedom for *all* men when Black men were still being alienated from the war effort. Philip Randolph's March on Washington led to Roosevelt's ban on discrimination in the defense industry, and the *Pittsburgh Courier* launched the Double V campaign by inciting their Black readers to give the war effort their all *while* calling on the government in 1942 to abide by the actual language of the Declaration of Independence (which promised to treat ALL men equally). This campaign stimulated people of color and liberal Whites to work together to instigate change and likely influenced Truman's official ban on discrimination in the Armed Forces in 1948.[8]

Considering the historical context, this chapter examines the radical aesthetic shift that animation technology made possible and explores how this transition not only aided in what was imaginable artistically, technically, visually, and sonically, but—and perhaps more important—also naturalized laws of the appropriate and ethical as governed by Breen's iteration of the Production Code. This argument especially concerns media representations of rhythm, Blackness, and sin. Much of what the Code deemed unacceptable in live action film for the censors was excused when the representation was not "real." Neither live action nor animated films were absolved of the guidelines set forth by the Hays Code, but animated films and shorts seemed to get away with a lot more "promiscuous" and controversial behavior than did live action films made during the same years. The same technology that allowed Hot Breath Harry's voice and image to be stereotyped to an extreme degree in the *Boogie Woogie Bugle Boy of Company 'B'* (1941) also allowed him to dance with a White woman at a time when such mixing was forbidden between live actors onscreen.[9] While cartoons from the 1930s and 1940s radically depicted the female body (e.g., Max Fleischer's Betty Boop cartoons) and cutting-edge politics (e.g., Disney's *Der Fuehrer's Face*) on the screen, I focus specifically on how animation technology utilized covert minstrelsy, or vice versa. The diminished use of blackface in live action film of the same period was in fact displaced onto Hollywood's animated productions, "deeply embedded in the visual, auditory, and performative traditions of the genre."[10] Bugs Bunny as Al Jolson could embolden patriotism in blackface under the same censorship laws that ultimately prevented Jolson from performing American-ness in burnt cork. That is, at a time when directors were democratizing racial politics on the live reel, antiquated notions of race relocated to the sketched unreal: the sonic, protean, citational, and tribute guises were deeply entrenched in Hollywood's mid-century animation aesthetic, as were the Bill Robinson effect, Gabriel and minstrel-show-within-a-show variations, southern repossession, brownface, redface, and jewface. In this penultimate chapter, all layers coalesce for a demonstration of how covert minstrelsy is most effective when its complete cast of intricate masks perform synchronously, each further obscuring the other.

While covert minstrelsy in live action films operates similarly to that of the animated screen, several things about the nature of a medium that comes to fruition purely through the imagination offer this genre several unique qualities and methods for sidestepping the Code. Four distinctions stand out to this end: first, children have always been the perceived intended audience for animated films. A guise in and of itself, the Production Code Administration (PCA) tended to be more lenient in its censorship as the cartoons were often identified as naïve.

Second, cartoons take on a series of protean qualities that humans cannot. Cartoons can be animals, inanimate objects, and a range of characters at once. Using Paul Wells's notion of "bestial ambivalence"—a paradigm that describes four categories of animated animals—I sketch the varying degrees of anthropomorphism that occur when animators give animals roles that traditionally belong to humans. Here the protean is constituted by any group of drawn caricatures used by their creators to aid in a *discreet* transmogrification that gives race or ethnicity a body on and through which to map a series of identifiers that may or may not be based in reality. Such a use of the protean guise may be seen in countless films including Disney's *Three Little Pigs*, which not only exemplifies bestial ambivalence but also illustrates the role of technology (sound and visual) and a necessary layering of racial and/or ethnic disguise in such types of protean transformations.[11] Here pen-and-ink allowed the Wolf to masquerade as a Yiddish peddler in jewface in 1933 and cutting-edge technology in 1947 made it possible to modify pieces of this costume to satisfy censorship review boards, without having to redraw the film from scratch or re-record its soundtrack.

Technology is the third layer that sets animation apart from live action film. This includes everything from color to sound to the artistic apparatus, and as such it will cover issues of depicting literal blackface, brownface and redface as well as explicate the special kinds of sound manipulation that become possible with animation. The sonic guise here, as in live action covert minstrelsy, depends on a film's soundtrack, dialogue, and intonation, but it also holds the power to use and re-use the same voice for multiple characters. A stellar example is Mel Blanc who voiced caricatures of Jolson,

286   BEHIND THE SCREEN

Cantor, African "Natives," American Indians, the Devil, and a barnyard menagerie including horses, pigs, chickens, cows, and even Bugs Bunny. And just as the voice could be severed from the image, so too could the body itself be split.

This mode of dis-figuration, as proffered by the protean guise, held a certain appeal: amputation, which serves as the fourth unique quality that animation possesses, allowed even more room for the imagination. The protean guise, along with the sonic, allows a single body part to either perform on its own, disappear, or re-assemble itself to another part of the body to create a new form, unrealistic by presentation—like a cubist Picasso painting—but believable in virtue of the expediency with which it morphed. Because animators control cartoons, this change can be made easily; and with animation technology, this transformation can appear seamless. Saidiya Hartman's notion of the fragmented Black body lends itself to this critique that, like the wounds of the Middle Passage, re-ruptures the fissures created on the nineteenth-century minstrel stage.

Framed by censorship laws, the remainder of this chapter rapidly builds on each of these concepts with every example constructed on the last through its use of the citational and tribute guises. With Friz Freleng's *Goin' to Heaven on a Mule* (1934), I explore the unique direction the citational guise takes within the field of animation.[12] Not only does this unique use of the citational guise expand the range of feasible quotations (i.e., the citation of entire films becomes possible, as it does in *Clean Pastures*, while entire film sequences could also be *sighted* as in *Sunday Goes a Meetin' Time*), but its ability to sever voice from visible image further nuances covert minstrelsy's sonic component, altering the citational soundscape at the most minute levels.[13] *Goin' to Heaven on a Mule* introduces this animated genre's use of the Gabriel variation and demonstrates how the art of animation lends itself more freely to concepts such as imitation, exaggeration, and buffoonery, since these very techniques helped to define cartoons and distinguish them from other artistic mediums.[14]

September in the Rain (1937) capitalizes on these citational possibilities and offers a complicated semiotic layer of product placement combined with racial fetish.[15] A similar narrative structure shows up in *Have You Got Any Castles?* (1938) which relies on what I see as a cutting and pasting of characters and ideas thus offering a patent specimen of the Bill Robinson effect as it applies both to the tap dancer and to Cab Calloway and other swing artists.[16] Everything comes together in *Mississippi Swing's* (1939) transit narrative (i.e., stories that produce their own slippage by taking place in the space between here and there), including the minstrel show-within-a-show variation (a minstrelized vocal quartet sings onboard the ship) and southern repossession (signaled by variety of visual, sonic, and narrative cues including the title). Despite the inherent lessons about imagined difference and a perceived racial hierarchy that these animated films taught, their racist overtones were often overlooked because of the genre's childishness. In a world where humans can become animals, animals can become raced, and body parts can detach from one object and re-attach to another almost instantaneously, all in the blink of an eye, it would have been difficult for the average White theatergoer to see these imaginary creatures as creating acts of violence, especially for their targeted audience of children.

Old Stereotypes, New Media

Race cartoons were most popular during the early 1930s—post-modern-sound technology and pre-enforced-Code era—roughly 1930 to 1934, but still extremely popular once the Breen administration took over censorship. These animated depictions of Black stereotypes evoked much earlier depictions of Blackness, reminiscent of both the minstrel stage and early advertising culture. Animators commonly drew characters with thick lips, put bones in the hair or noses of these cartoons, and, in keeping with a live action aesthetic of the period, regularly reproduced the images of Sambo, Mammy, and Uncle Tom. Like live action films, the Sambo figure sometimes took on the shape of a boy living in Africa and at other times manifested as someone attending to a plantation in the rural South, not only essentializing Blackness but also conflating ideas of a glorified South with those of "jungle fever." Ub Iwerks's *Little Black Sambo* (1935), for example, includes a scenario where a young caricatured Black boy, his "Mammy" mother, and their pet tiger-turned dog live in a southern makeshift home in the middle of the African jungle.[17] These cartoons become indexical markers of Black referents that span centuries and continents. Not all the decisions surrounding the presentation of racialized tropes through animated pictures were necessarily conscious on the part of the writers, and many representational choices effectively economized labor, even if they resulted in racial profiling. Christopher Lehman notes that attributes like oversized eyes, lips, and bodies animators often described as "inked" or "inky" were easy to draw due to their lack of

288 BEHIND THE SCREEN

intricate details (i.e., they were primarily drawn from black ink)—making it easy for animators to churn out cartoons, and thus episodes, more quickly; also, they had high appeal for White audiences who were accustomed to such images in print. Paul Terry's work in *Aesop's Fables* perfectly exemplifies such a model and, as Lehman writes, "contributed to the first of several cost-cutting animation techniques, allowing Terry to maximize profits throughout his three decades as a cartoon producer-director."[18] Thus, not only did racial caricature increase commercial value, but it also cut down on cost; drawing on blackface was a profitable endeavor for White artists.

Animators, because of their medium, enjoy the combined possibilities (and repercussions) of representation held by both live action film and print. In addition to depicting Blackness as all the archetypes mentioned above—a kind of primitivizing framework as discussed in chapter 5—a purely pen-and-ink existence allows animators the ability to quickly draw in and subtract different features as needed. The white minstrel glove that so many cartoon characters wear is just one example, and one that carries significant fetishistic weight. When animators pair other markers of the minstrel tradition such as blackface, tap dance, and/or a citation of Jolson's "Mammy" with the minstrel glove—as did the creators of *Any Bonds Today*—it becomes harder to ignore the references as anything but deliberate. Now add to this the idea that a single cartoon can take on many qualities within a limited number of frames: a cartoon can simultaneously reference the nineteenth-century minstrel stage *and* solicit its audience to buy "Bonds of freedom" or introduce a close-up of the Big Bad Wolf doing hambone (an Africanist rhythm technique that uses the body as a drum set) just a few seconds before he masquerades as "the big bad Jew." This all says that the protean guise becomes much more fluid in animated films than it ever can in live action film or print, and a single body can reference several tropes simultaneously, often conflating patriotism with racial caricature (e.g., *Bonds*) and villainizing Africanist forms as we will see throughout the remainder of this chapter. The use of animals in place of humans and their dexterous mutability is one way the protean guise operates in animated renderings of covert minstrelsy.

Becoming Animal

Animals, as narrative subjects, provide many things that a human subject cannot for human artists and audience members. However, because all attempts to create an animal on the screen are based purely on human observation and interaction, animators can never know the thoughts or feelings of animals, beyond the assumptions the cartoonists make about them. This limitation tends to result in an anthropomorphized version of animal cognition and behavior: even if it were to be based on real scientific evidence and observation, it is nonetheless convoluted by human projections and fantasies of the species in question, including assigning certain human attributes to them (e.g., emotions, thoughts, and sensations). This personification leans toward irony and, at times, absurdity, offering animators the perfect setup for humor and comedy. Animals as film protagonists provide something incredibly economical; animals supply an inexpensive and efficient solution to storytelling. Authors have been writing about animals for centuries, and consequently, a wealth of plots and storylines already exist for narratives starring animals. Using a story already in the public domain cuts down on the amount of work an artist has to invest in his storyline/character development, *and* it likely already strikes a familiar chord with the spectating audience. Finally, assigning personalities and traits to animals decreases the chance for human insult by distancing the human from the behavior, allowing the artist a way to deflect any potential criticism around racial representation. Shrouded in the feathers and fur of juvenile entertainment was thus a highly effective means of sidestepping the Code during its most stringent period.

Rather than marking the Black body—or any other racialized body—with projected significations, allocating human character traits to animals makes it more difficult for the assumed subjects of these stereotypes to voice a concern, thus making irrelevant the need for censorship review boards to expurgate such material. Anthropomorphizing animals and assigning various classes or races to particular species is never ultimately based on empirical observation and still maintains dire consequences for the assumed subjects of these personified animals. This practice mirrors what Alexander Weheliye terms "racializing assemblages," or the process of "taking race as a set of sociopolitical processes that discipline humanity into full humans, not-quite-humans, and nonhumans. This disciplining, while not biological per se, frequently depends on anchoring political hierarchies in human flesh."[19] As such, animated animals in these cartoons operated as naïve vessels for communicating and reinforcing dominant White narratives.

Paul Wells's concept of bestial ambivalence enables the represented animal to have metaphorical and totemic properties while simultaneously standing in as a critique of the natural world. Bestial ambivalence, or the idea that the represented (and for the purposes of this discussion, the animated) animal operates on "a set of oscillations within each text and does not remain static and fixed," makes the space between human and animal apparent at the same time it shows the similarities between the two species.[20] Wells acknowledges the following ambivalences: "aspirational human," "critical human," "pure 'animal,'" and finally the "hybrid 'humanimal.'" While all these ambivalences function in a theory of covert minstrelsy, this chapter looks specifically at the hybrid "humanimal" as a type of protean guising; the humanimal operates only on the symbolic level, consequently offering animation a subset of covert minstrelsy not possible in live action film, other than in specific examples where a humanimal might appear in painted props and set design. That is, we cannot observe the humanimal out in the world; the being exists only in our imagination and operates at the metaphorical and symbolic level. Creatures thus come to represent an array of meaning depending on the specific context from which their story emerges. Animation is but one place this range of narratives can perform, and as such, it reiterates *and* creates its own system of sociocultural symbolism, sometimes running parallel to the "literal one" and at other times taking a significant departure from real life.[21]

Using animals in lieu of humans in animation offers many benefits. One advantage is that the representation of an animal becomes a blank canvas (or cel in this case) endowed with the power of absorbing whatever humans need of them most; the act of drawing an animal thus always results in an imitation of the form itself. Such an imitation becomes increasingly more complex as an animator anthropomorphizes an animal for the sake of the plot. As soon as an artist starts to assign a class, a gender, and a race to an animal, the animated representation quickly becomes an imitation of an imitation of an imitation. Kevin Sandler in his exploration of Warner Bros. animation remarks, "Gender imitation in animal characters does not copy that which is prior in humans since gender is already a fiction; it copies what is already assumed to exist in humans. . . . By repeating this imitation, the animators create an illusion of a talking gendered animal while reproducing the illusion of gender itself."[22] Anthropomorphism therefore reiterates various social ideologies as fact, rather than fiction, consequently blurring the distinction between the real and the unreal. According to this model, animated characters become "phenomenological creations, predicated on the flux of meaning caused by the relativity of representational possibility."[23] Therefore the animated animal becomes a powerful vessel for meaning making, capable of moving through multiple discourses simultaneously. The challenge is, as a viewer, recognizing the various discourses at play and distinguishing the real from the unreal, the metaphorical from the literal, and replications from imitations and exaggerations.

The act of donning (or drawing) certain abstractions—for example, coats and tails, beaks, gloves, or masks—lends itself to a minstrel practice partially because of the way it operates on an ambivalent axis. The animal is almost-but-not-quite human, almost-but-not-quite animal. This ambiguous status causes a rupture in the signifying chain. Jonathan Burt, who writes on the significance of animals in film, argues that "giving [the animal] ambiguous status that derives from what might be described as a kind of semantic overload, the animal is also a marked site where the symbolic associations collapse into each other. . . . the animal image is a form of rupture in the field of representation."[24] Like other performances of masking, there is something non-threatening in the cartoons' pen-and-ink existence; yet animation also destabilizes the reality of certain racial stereotypes and social stigmas. The "costume" itself encourages hiding in the same way the blackface mask of the past promoted an inherent slippage in the art of representation while the multiplicity of symbolic associations contained in animated versions of racial masquerade create a semantic overload in much the same way that early sound film overwhelmed the senses and created a temporary blindness for audiences who were newly experiencing the medium. Ambivalence in these cartoons thus operates on multiple registers simultaneously, not least of which is the irony of animating a human stereotype by way of anthropomorphization. An audience confronted by so many oppositions and inherent conflicts is bound to get caught up in the readings that are *most* visible and the codes that present themselves most superficially.[25]

An animal's utility involves the irony contained in ambivalent action as well as the incongruity that surfaces when opposing personality traits define an animated character. As I mentioned earlier, the more familiar an audience is with a particular plot or story line, the easier it is for them to engage. Employing familiar narratives thus saves the artist time with both plot and character development and allows more time for working out the small idiosyncrasies and gags that make a cartoon stand out from the original story.

The economy of comic effect also acts as a disguise for cartoons. The animal, because it can signify multiple things simultaneously, becomes a rich source for animators seeking gag victims, jokesters, and absurd

292   BEHIND THE SCREEN

representations. Humans tend to see themselves as removed from the animal kingdom, so an animal that makes a fool of itself onscreen, is the victim of physical or emotional abuse, or even becomes the brunt of a joke will be less likely to offend its audience than if these same offenses were directed at a human representation.

Deciphering the opposing personality traits for which animals and humanimals become vessels can be difficult, especially when the dichotomies themselves tend to create the comic irony and absurdity incumbent on audience engagement. The representations on the animated screen become "comic excesses" and or depictions that are "culturally charged," saying as much about the animal caricatures as they do about the humans drawing them.[26] These representations form the foundation of a good joke and since cartoons thrive on irony and comic excess, the formula encourages ambivalent performances, where the jokes carry "an implied set of assumptions upon which the comic event is structured."[27] The incongruity that emerges when an animator entertains certain recognizable tropes inherent in human life but interprets them through bestial symbolism lays the foundation for a joke predicated on a set of assumptions about animal life at the same time that it mocks the absurdity of thinking in such a way. Such a joke comments on society while simultaneously assigning roles to particular members of the animal kingdom. Animation in this way can "visualize the space between the intention of the gag, the execution of the gag, and what might be termed its socio-comic outcome."[28] But rarely do we as viewers choose to do such a meta-analysis of the sounds and images that fly across the screen. Even if the audience is aware of the irony at play in such joke-making, it would be incorrect to assume that participants break down every gag into its ambivalent schema. Instead, audiences tend to accept the sounds and images with which they are presented and laugh accordingly without asking *why* such presentation evokes laughter. Because these cartoons tend to target children, the speed with which sounds and images fly by makes it difficult for even those so inclined to disentangle.

Who's Afraid of the Big Bad Jew

Films like *Three Little Pigs* present characters who, through the protean guise, oscillate between the actual and the symbolic, creating an ambivalence for viewers not unlike that present on the nineteenth-century minstrel stage. By using a well-known story in its successful 1933 short, Disney cut down on the time it had to spend storyboarding, assured of audience familiarity. But to make its version stand out, Disney would have to enliven its characters and develop the dialogue. Because the story already sets the Wolf up as the antagonist, his character was a logical source for absorbing whatever prejudices the creative team held. The Wolf as "pure animal"—a natural born predator—offers an already organic relationship to the film's "edible" pigs. But when the Wolf disguises himself as a Yiddish-speaking peddler with attributes of the caricatured Jew, he symbolically ruptures the behavioral relationship between wolf and pig and instead primes the cartoon for a critique of ethnic behaviors and human values disguised as natural.

The Fuller "Brosh" man with a Yiddish-speaking accent, green eyes, giant nose, and Orthodox beard is the second of two disguises the Wolf wears to try and fool the pigs. [FIG. 2.4] When his first disguise as a sheep fails with Fifer and Fiddler, he opts for a subterfuge with layered symbolic significance. The sheep costume was supposed to succeed because of natural animal relations; sheep and pigs can cohabitate amicably, so a sheep at the door should not threaten a pig in the same way that a wolf would. Similarly, in 1933, the Fuller Brush man was someone for whom people always opened the door, perhaps due to the company's reputation for hiring extremely personable salesmen who catered to each person's needs and the lifetime guarantee for all the company's products promised by the founder Alfred Fuller.[29] Thus Disney utilized a reference that would have been familiar to its primarily White, middle-class audience. The Fuller Brush man would have (comically) been the only disguise more convincing than a sheep to a "practical" pig. The first layer of irony thus surfaces when the audience assumes that farm animals and the White middle class value the same sorts of things; the comic event is based on this implied assumption.

The second layer of irony emerges when the animators globalize the concept of a traveling salesman, an occupation often associated with the Jew. Alfred Fuller had family ties to the Mayflower and his prototypical salesmen did not fit the image of the Jewish peddler. Here the creators of the Wolf's disguise are at once highlighting the absurdity of a Jewish Fuller Brush man while they are activating the stereotype. The medium allowed animators to add specific attributes to the Wolf's disguise to exaggerate such a stereotype: the Jew with the large hook nose and beady eyes is a stereotype that goes back centuries and can thus be easily interpreted by a large audience.[30] Combine this age-old stereotype with a swindler-type role, beard, and

294   BEHIND THE SCREEN

Yiddish accent, and the Wolf's disguise mobilizes what Robert Dawidoff has termed "jewface," a caricatured performance of the Jew that was a vaudeville mainstay in the late nineteenth century.[31] Add to this masquerade the protean transformation the Wolf's mask undergoes during the "unmasking," when the mask itself transforms into a caricature of Groucho Marx, overloading the audience with Jewish references. Here animators collapse his jewface into Groucho glasses. His beard becomes a bushy mustache, and the large prosthetic nose becomes more exaggerated when his thick-rimmed glasses fall off. Additionally, Groucho's notoriously bushy eyebrows magically appear. The joke is punctuated, however, when these eyebrows morph into horns, validating a long-standing misconception that Jews have horns. In a matter of just a few seconds, the Wolf has become a vessel for communicating a multitude of Jewish stereotypes, in the fashion of the protean guise.

The irony of animating a human stereotype by way of anthropomorphizing an animal creates a kind of humanimal, capable of collapsing all kinds of symbolic associations to create humor through the absurd at the same time it incriminates the Jew. Because censorship was not tightly monitored when the film was released in 1933, such representations went unsuppressed, especially because jewface was presented as a costume, narratively excused as a blackface disguise would have been in an Eddie Cantor film produced during the same period. To complicate matters, such anti-Semitic propaganda appeared at the same time that news about persecution of the Jews began coming out of Germany, the significance of which was not lost on Walt Disney. The film would go through many alterations in the years following, as censorship rules around what constituted "appropriate" shifted with the global rise of antisemitism.

The corresponding *Three Little Pigs* book published the same year used an image of the Wolf in horn-rimmed glasses instead of printing the image of the jewfaced-peddler. Disney was aware that print could not be altered after the fact, unlike film. The text in this 1933-edition nonetheless kept the dialogue from the original film intact, likely because it would have been hard for censors to claim anything without the presence of certain auditory cues. Tracing the various modifications made to the animated film not only clues us in to the kinds of things censor review boards were looking for at various moments but also offers valuable insight into the significance of various technologies.

Following the Holocaust, the Hayes Office demanded that the sequence be revised. In a re-release made in September 1947, director Jack Hannah changed the visuals to align with those found in the book, but he chose to keep the original dialogue track. Because this scene is twenty seconds in length, the revision required animators to edit only a fraction of the film's frames. Despite the removal of most of the stereotypically Jewish imagery, however, the horn-rimmed glasses combined with linguistic profiling and a very klezmer-like leitmotif playing in the background, makes the performance of jewface explicit. The wide circulation of the original cartoon and the unexpurgated dialogue without the original image leaves viewers with an *impression* of jewface.[32]

In 1948 the Hayes Office again demanded that the sequence be revised, this time sonically. True of all of the Silly Symphonies Disney produced, *Pigs* contained operetta-like dialogue which "usually rhymed and all but indistinguishable from song—extended the musical emphasis."[33] This rhythmical dialogue could be "planned in advance, to the frame, and then recorded at the same time as the music, after the film was otherwise complete. In such cases, the animators worked with exposure sheets that broke the dialogue down into frames, permitting them to animate the mouth movements accurately even though they could not hear the voices."[34] The Yiddish accent was removed in this 1948 revision and the Wolf's second line of dialogue changed to, "I'm working my way through college." However, the klezmer-like leitmotif remained and traced viewers back to the original, especially with other, earlier versions of Disney's *Pigs* still circulating in print. Thus, after multiple revisions, the new masks (both the Wolf in horn-rimmed glasses and the substitution of lyrics from "semples" to "college") with which audiences were confronted continued to contain the specters of jewface even if not so explicit as before.

As discussed above, anthropomorphizing reiterates various social ideologies as fact rather than fiction, and this muddies distinctions that can be made between the real and the unreal. Animals thus became a more excusable outlet for animators wishing to utilize blatant racial and ethnic caricatures as censorship laws tightened, since it would have been hard for anyone to make a concrete argument that a cartoon's racism/ethnic caricature was pointed at any one person or group of people. While each studio did something different with these animals and developed its own unique style, the use of animals and their aesthetic evolution became an important constituent in the art of film animation itself. Hence developing one's skill as an animator included learning how to capture and represent the animal onscreen. From the mid-1930s up until about 1943, most animators tried to emulate

296 BEHIND THE SCREEN

Disney's model of "hyperrealism" when it came to drawing animals. This, Wells argues, was, "underpinned by Disney's own conviction that animals had very real personalities, expressed through their bodies, which it was the responsibility of the animator to understand, embrace, and re-create."[35] But as studios started to break away from this mold, the need for artists to confine their representations to real-world physics diminished and left open immense space for what Eisenstein has called "plasmaticness," or the ability for a cartoon to defy the laws of gravity and immutability.[36] This shift marked a return to an older animation aesthetic (e.g., early forms of Mickey or Felix the Cat), but it was informed by new technology and artistic advances. The films discussed in the following sections focus on human caricatures that sometimes cross over into the realm of humanimals as a way of dehumanizing certain groups of people. Technology, the protean and sonic guises, as well as the coupling of blackface with other forms of ethnic/racial caricature will become no less important in the following examples. However, employing the citational and tribute guises as analytical lenses will yield an even more layered critique of covert minstrelsy within cartoons of this era.

Code Switching through the Protean Guise

When it comes to animation, the protean guise describes a reconfiguration and successive substitution of the "body" that performs, allowing for the concealment of everything else going on in the production. This re-constituted body often takes the form of an anthropomorphized animal such as Bugs Bunny performing Al Jolson or the Wolf performing jewface. Here the animator uses the attributes of a real animal—e.g., feathers, fur, quills, tails, whiskers—as well as a character's status as "cartoon" to mask a set of social caricatures vis-à-vis bestial ambivalence and "costume." This practice is not specific to animation but in part gains its influence from animation's governing principles of exaggeration and appeal, the perceptual phenomenon of persistence of vision, cartoons' association with youthful naiveté, and finally, the characters' purely pen-and-ink existence that allows for all sorts of abstract and delusive iterations. The semantic overload that the protean guise makes possible also conceals obvious minstrel tropes and Africanisms, narratively, sonically, and even visually.

As previous examples have demonstrated, covert minstrelsy commonly utilizes multiple kinds of racial and ethnic caricature simultaneously. *Pigs* highlights this process of layering on the visual level, but other cartoons from this period offer insight into how covert minstrelsy could be achieved concurrently on multiple levels. In Van Beuren's *Molly Moo-Cow and the Indians* (1935), animators created a soundtrack of Foster's "Oh Susanna!" with what became standard "Native" music: a tom-tom beating in the background, often with a cow bell accent, and likely some version of screaming or howling, thought to emanate from the mouth-tapping chants of the American Indian caricature.[37] Fleischer Studios produced *Big Chief Ugh-Amugh-Ugh* (1938) as part of its *Popeye the Sailorman* series.[38] The "Indians'" noses are disproportionately large, and the chief is inexplicably larger than the rest of his clan, as was common in most animated depictions of American Indians. The short film opens with all of the "Indians" howling around the fire to a repetitive song, "Ugh-Amugh-Ugh." Each clansman is dressed in a feather headdress, moccasins, a skirt, and has a bare chest. The chief's voice sits at the bottom of the vocal register, and his sentences register as half English, half gibberish, much like the strange gallimaufry Chief Black Eagle speaks in *Whoopee!* The cartoon is played by Gus Wickie, a baritone frequently used by Paramount, often employed as the voice of the villain in *Popeye* shorts and the man behind animated hippos and elephants. With a constant tom-tom beating in the background, all these visual symbols become tied to the red body and a particular sound.

The same year, Warner Bros. produced *Jungle Jitters*, blurring the line visually and sonically between what constituted the American Indian and what constituted the Native African onscreen.[39] Animators designed the "teepees" out of raffia, and the skin of most of the characters was colored somewhere between a red and a brown, with an occasional charcoal black body thrown into the mix. This juxtaposition further intensifies the ethnic ambiguity at play. These nonspecific "Natives" perform generic circle dances to the beat of a tom-tom while howling like animated caricatures of American Indians in most cartoons, yet these cartoon characters also stomp their feet as if performing a South African gumboot dance.[40] Moreover, the characters are neither fully animal nor fully human. Thus, in addition to conflating two Natives into one nonspecific "ethnic" stereotype, Warner Bros. blurs the line between "Native" and animal. Fleischer reuses "Ugh-Amugh-Ugh" in his 1940 short, *The Dandy Lion*.[41] The first minutes of the film are a fictional take on the significance of animals to American Indian life, beginning with a young child who tries to hunt a bird with a bow-and-arrow. Later, several of the elders shoot down a vulture. The short also includes a red braid–wearing Mammy

298   BEHIND THE SCREEN

figure, shown washing her son in a wood basin. When her child brings home a lion, she becomes hysterical. All these cartoons reiterate the stereotype that the American Indian is violent and bloodthirsty. Secondary to the violent stereotype in these cartoons is the "Indian's" proclivity for acting crazy. Rain is also a recurring theme: in Walter Lantz's *Boogie Woogie Sioux* (1942), salvation from a deadly desert drought comes when "Tommy Hawk and His 5 Scalpers," a traveling jazz band of redfaced African Americans arrives with magical music. When Tommy Hawk's swingin' boogie beat finally brings rain, he saves the tribe.[42] Thus these red-colored characters, no matter how entangled in Africanisms or minstrel caricatures they appear, preserve certain power dynamics while making the White studios look progressive.

Through examples such as *Pigs* and *Chief Ugh-Amugh-Ugh*, one can observe the significance of the soundtrack, especially as it pertains to voiceovers. While soundtracks play an important role in live action film, the animation medium allows the voice to travel independently of the body who speaks; the voice has the ability to circulate information while keeping its processes invisible. As Lisa Gitelman observes, "The success of all media depends at some level on inattention or 'blindness' to the media technologies themselves (and all of their supporting protocols) in favor of attention to the phenomena, 'the content,' that they represent for users' edification or enjoyment."[43] These sound technologies can provide entertainment for viewers without necessitating a discussion of their particulars, and it is precisely this ability that lends itself to covert minstrelsy. Such media detach the human voice from its body; technology allows words and melodies to transcend the flesh, in effect making it possible for the public to hear without seeing. Thus, the circulation of media that inscribe voice even in the absence of a body are simultaneously material and semiotic; they represent the ongoing negotiation of meaning within their particular social and historical contexts.[44]

In this sense, we might offer a first definition of amputation as it pertains to animated films: a phenomenon wherein technology allows the human voice to be modified to the point of unrecognizability and also altered in a way that allows the same voice to stand in for many players simultaneously. This is what allowed Mel Blanc to be the voice of Bugs Bunny and the voice of Al Jolson and even the voice of Bugs Bunny citing Jolson's "Mammy" in *Bonds*. But amputation in animation also applies to animation's visible parts and is tied to both a form of synecdochizing the raced body and rupture. In Powell's tribute to Robinson in *Honolulu*, I showed how her body operates as a signifier of both Whiteness and standard of American entertainment. The transaction between her dancing and Robinson's offered a rupture in the way the artistry of other Black dancer's bodies could be read. On the animated screen, this split appears quite literally when feet/shoes (or in the case of jazz music, hands/gloves) become the new vessels of Black artistry. Caricatures of Black artists then become onlookers in awe of the Africanist performance(s) of these body parts. I return to an analysis of this understanding of amputation shortly, but first, here is a simpler, sonic manifestation of amputation as it overlaps with black and white animation during the pre-Code era.

Goin' to Imaginary Heaven on a Cartoon Mule

A succession of familiar tunes fills the screen: an unidentified facsimile of the Hall Johnson Negro choir interspersed with exaggerated diegetic pings accompanies the cotton-picking montage reminiscent of King Vidor's film Hallelujah; *a prototypical modern swing soundtrack complements the animated machines of a cotton processing plant. The screen cuts to an Uncle Tom–like caricature, half man, half primate, sleeping behind the horse stables. The sound seamlessly transitions from the modern swing groove to a swung variation on some well-known Stephen Foster tunes. As the Uncle Tom cartoon—let's just call him Al—stands up to take a drink, a white angel and a black devil appear out of thin air, wrestling with one another about who will be the more persuasive. The black devil clearly gets the best of Al as we see him guzzle down a growler full of spirits that immediately sends him into a stupor evidenced by certain sound effects and the blurring of film cells that follows. The screen dissolves into black. As an iris slowly expands to reveal Al, we recognize Jolson's hit from a few months prior: "When I pass away, on that judgment day, I'm goin' to heaven on a mule." Al rides through heaven until reaching the pearly gates of "pair-o-dice" where his entrance is greeted by Sambo-like cherubs and animated caricatures of the Lord, Gabriel, a gambling Emperor Jones, and other nondescript Black protestants performing a jamboree-like dance. The screen then cuts to an animated version of* Wonder Bar's *depiction of a Harlem bustling with swing—lindy hoppers hold up traffic and local folk cakewalk across the street. Al rides up to the Milkyway Café. He makes his grand entrance shuffling to the music of four Black vocal harmonists. He tap dances all the way to a central table; there is a*

300 BEHIND THE SCREEN

giant watermelon which he eats contentedly while watching two Fats Waller caricatures with angel wings duel on a set of pianos. Al joins the jam using the leftover watermelon scraps as a harmonica but even the hot rhythms are not enough to deter him from the adjacent "gin orchard." The Lord quickly interrupts Al, who is laughing like a hyena from drunkenness. The Lord orders two giant bodyguards to escort Al out of heaven, down the chute of Hades. The nightmare ends and Al finds himself right back where he started, beside the horse stables. He throws away his jug of alcohol sending the message to viewers that alcohol leads you on the path to sedition. As the cartoon ends, Al re-enters, conveniently just as his spirits are seen falling from the sky. He catches the spirits mid-air and whistles a sigh of relief. "So long folks."

Black and white films like Friz Freleng's *Goin' to Heaven on a Mule* (*GHM*) were cheaper to make than their Technicolored counterparts, and their very black and whiteness would later be used as justification to keep racist films in circulation, as many film distributors argued that only their use of a brown skin color actually made these films racist.[45] Yet this description makes it clear that there was a lot more at play than the skin color in these cartoons. This animated short, like so many of its contemporaries, was one of many that imagined the southern plantation as contiguous with the jungle, Black heaven, Harlem, and the Jazz Age. Because of the film's medium, the characters take on totemic properties; their humanimal existence affords them the ability to double signify: their human attributes offer a citation of the actors in *Wonder Bar*'s finale while the characters' primate-like qualities suggest a jungle origin, encoding both the Gabriel variation and a classic primitivist framework into the script. The soundtrack alone signifies both the South (in its use of a Hall Johnson–like choir) and Harlem (in its bursts of swing music), while the narrative speaks directly to Black heaven and the Jazz Age.

Like "GHM" from *Wonder Bar* and most illustrations of the Gabriel variation, the soundtrack of the animated short version of *Goin' to Heaven* locates sin in urban contexts. This particular depiction of sin equivocates in its identification of where that sin originates—horse stables, plantations, Africa—and whether Al Jolsons disguised as Uncle Toms are equally capable of falling prey to such hedonism as are "real" Black folk; however, the portrayal ultimately suggests that locations like the Milkyway Café, which house gambling, swing music, tap dance, and alcohol, breed sin and are somehow unique to those who get tangled up in Black culture. While sending a somewhat mixed message about the correlation between alcohol, Black heaven, swing music, and hell, the ambiguity with which this cartoon ends makes sense in the context of the industry's turnover in Production Code administration.

This short was released in May 1934, just two months after the live action version of "GHM," in *Wonder Bar*, and two months before the MPPC was officially enforced by Breen's administration. Many elements of this cartoon enact the building pressure from the Catholic Church to be meticulous in films' depictions of religion. In fact, this cartoon foreshadows representations of religion in Connelly's *The Green Pastures* even more clearly than what we see in Jolson's rendition of Black heaven in *Wonder Bar*. While very much a citation of *Wonder Bar*'s finale, this animated version in combination with Jolson's performance establishes a cinematic definition of a Black version of the Bible as seen through a White consciousness. These two iterations of "GHM" thus help justify what Judith Weisenfeld describes as the artifice of films like *Pastures*, which she argues "points us to an imagined, fantastic world and . . . is mediated through images reminiscent of the world of black collectibles, the romanticized images of black mammies, uncles, and 'pickaninnies' preserved in ceramic kitchen items that seek to reassure whites by domesticating blacks."[46]

Several film scholars have identified ways in which Connelly's film adaptation of *Pastures* managed to reconcile two extreme opinions operating on censorship review boards. On the one hand, Warner Bros. had to appease the Black community by not including blatantly offensive caricatures of Black life. On the other hand, the script was up against a considerable amount of backlash from White religious figures who felt that it offered inaccurate representations of religion. Anything perceived by the church as even remotely related to hell was off limits unless it was placed within a didactive framework. Many countries went so far as to ban the release of *Pastures* because its God was Black.[47] Addressing White religious leaders' concerns was clearly a greater priority than attending to the film's depiction of Black life. The result was to change God's character to "De Lawd" and to offer a carefully worded intertitle to the beginning of the film.[48] The "De Lawd" label distinguishes this Black man playing the part of God from that of a real (White) God. [FIG. 5.1] A rumor that Warner Bros. was considering casting Jolson in blackface to play the part of De Lawd further speaks to Hollywood's quest to appeal to the religious men of Breen's administration.[49] But this point also acknowledges that the film version of *Pastures* was looking to "GHM"—both Jolson's live action version and the later animated

FIGURE 6.2 Two models that uphold the ceramic kitchen in order to "reassure whites by domesticating blacks": (*Top*) Fish Fry scene from *The Green Pastures*, 1936. (Private collection); (*Bottom*) Cast of the stage production Lew Leslie's *Blackbirds of 1930*, with backdrop depicting Aunt Jemima, 1930. Photo by White Studio © (New York Public Library for the Performing Arts)

short—as a source. The film *Pastures* presented De Lawd as lacking agency "with regard to the salvation of humanity" and used "various strategies for distancing itself from sacred Scriptures"; both of these make a mockery of Black theology by representing it as parochial and limited. But *Pastures* was not alone in this treatment of Black people and religion.[50] The two versions of "GHM" set a cinematic precedent for framing Black theology as childish and laden with minstrel stereotypes and help to justify later presentations of Black Biblical narratives as "acceptable," no matter how fictitious, because they were truer to life than Jolson's performance in blackface or that of a minstrel-mouthed Uncle Tom who dreams up Black heaven in a drunken stupor. Depicting Blackness as fundamentally connected to religion generally troubled the censors, but for reasons yet to be determined, this obviously racist cartoon slipped in just at the cusp of the transition and elided the notorious "censored eleven": eleven Looney Tunes that were suspended from syndication in 1968 for their outdated racialized content.[51] As we saw with *Pigs*, animation lends itself to unique forms of retroactive editing in both image and sound. Once cartoons became more accessible to the public, censorship-worthy material that had previously been overlooked was attended to by United Artists, the company responsible for distributing all Looney Tunes and Merrie Melodies. Some cartoons were removed from circulation altogether, such as the "Censored Eleven." Other cartoons had scenes edited out, as was the case with Hanna and Barbera's *Gallopin' Gals* (1940), which had one scene involving a dark horse removed from reruns of the cartoon in later years.[52] And some cartoons, as evidenced by MGM's *Tom and Jerry* episode *Mouse Cleaning* (1948), not only changed the visuals but re-dubbed the cartoons' voices.[53] Over the course of a decade, animators edited the fully exposed Black Mammy present in *Puss Gets the Boot* (1940) to show just her legs.[54] So if editing individual scenes and re-dubbing voices was possible, why did *GHM* slip through the cracks, even ex post facto? Understanding this cartoon through its less obvious, more covert masks offers some clues.

Cartoons made in the image of a feature film such as the animated *GHM* short become *simulacrum* (in the Baudrillardian sense), offering viewers more "truth" than copy.[55] In this view, the original, which was a fiction to begin with, becomes the sole means of validating the realness of the copy. Thus, the citational guise works to reinforce the illusions put forth in the live action version and further shrouds the stereotypes by offering extra layers of deceit provided by the irony and absurdity that the characters' pen-and-ink existence makes possible. On the visible level, the characters in *GHM*

304   BEHIND THE SCREEN

are half man/half primate painted in black and white. While on the narrative level, this short cites *Wonder Bar*'s finale, the once White actors in blackface become humanimals shaded dark, with anthropomorphism reiterating various social ideologies and stereotypes as fact rather than fiction. The signified meaning is not lost on an audience because of the citational context, but this citational context enables Warner Bros. to write this cartoon off as a comical reinterpretation of something that had already passed the censors.

Similarly, the soundtrack to this cartoon utilizes sonic simulacra to cite the original *GHM* and other soundtracks that accompany the Gabriel variation in live action film. This process is akin to what Baudrillard describes as "no longer a question of imitation, nor duplication, nor even parody. It is a question of substituting the signs of the real for the real."[56] The person voicing Jolson comes to stand in for animated representations of Jolson, making it impossible for the real Jolson to ever escape his performance of caricatured Blackness; the parodied voices of characters like De Lawd become the animated versions of Black likenesses, establishing new precedents for a cast of voices that stand in for Blackness. This simulacrum takes away not only the autonomy of representation on a visual level but also reattributes vocals (both as a stereotyped dialect and as animal-like) to Black artists and caricatures of those Black artists. The animated versions of these characters thus lose touch with an original sonicity, becoming a *precession* of simulacra where the (unreal) cartoons visibly and aurally precede and regulate the real.[57] In this fashion, even though Warner Bros. released *GHM* on the cusp of an administrative transition in Code regulations, several variations of covert minstrelsy were already being normalized on the animated screen by the time the film was released.

Offering Black theology as childish and laden with Black stereotypes—a pattern we see in live action film throughout the Golden Age—becomes even more pronounced when the medium itself is classified as juvenile, as is the case with cartoons. *GHM* would only signal the beginning of infantilizing representations of Black religion with *Sunday Go to Meetin' Time* and *Clean Pastures* following close behind. In both these color cartoons, the Gabriel variation continues to justify the ever-increasing popularity of a swing aesthetic, Black vernacular forms like tap dance and truckin' become an even more common movement source for the films' churchgoing swingers, and technology would assist in leaving the real authors of these Africanist dance and musical forms detached from such visible, animated re-presentations. That is, where Black artistry went uncredited in live action films of this era,

HAYS IS FOR HORSES   305

cartoons gave real voices to Black simulations, blurring the line between White labor and Black and exaggerating the intensity of the picture.

Muddying the Waters with Clean Pastures and Castles

As the title sequence appears on the screen, an uncredited chorus sings the Calloway classic "Save Me Sister" that we heard last year during Jolson's performance in The Singing Kid. *The title screen fades, and a series of marquees flash up on the screen: JAZZ; CHOP SUEY; BAMA CLUB; HARLEM; NITE LIFE; SKAT; TRUCKIN'; DINAH; DANCE, words which by this point in the book should all carry semiotic significance. Several light-brown-skinned choristers resembling Josephine Baker cross dissolve with the flashing marquees. Had this been a live action film, their scantily dressed bodies would not have made it past Breen's censorship board. But the hue of their skin combined with their pen-and-ink existence allows them to be overlooked. Cut to a large black hand rolling a pair of dice and another black hand shaking up a cocktail. Bring on the martini and the jitterbuggers. This is HARLEM. Zoom out. Way out into outer space. High up in the clouds sit the golden gates of "Pair-O-Dice." Cut to a caricature of "De Lawd" who appears to be the same Lawd in GHM reading the front page of the Financial section: "Pair-O-Dice Preferred Hits New Low as Hades Inc. Soars." The uncredited chorus sings "Only Half of Me Wants to Be Good" in the background while De Lawd, saddened by the statistics, shuffles to his switchboard and rings the angel Gabriel. Cut to a hybrid caricature of Stepin Fetchit as Oscar Polk or Oscar Polk as Stepin Fetchit lazily lounging on a cloud playing his horn in the foreground as we hear Stephen Foster's "Old Folks at Home" in the background. [FIG 6.3, top right] "Yes sah," Gabriel receives the call from his "massa." As he scratches his head and continues to speak in a slowed, garbled dialect, his ears pop out and he is temporarily transformed into "pure" monkey, no longer humanimal disguised as Oscar Polk masquerading as Stepin Fetchit. Summoned by De Lawd, Gabriel descends on Harlem, very slowly. The camera cuts the tempo of his flight in half and he speaks as if intoxicated. Again, we see the opening marquees flash up on the screen.*

Gabriel, now on a platform in the middle of bustling Harlem, cries out: "Come here, right over this way. I got sump'n to tell y'all." The camera pans and then zooms in on the sign to his left: "Pair-O-Dice NEEDS YOU! Opportunity; Travel; Watermelon; Music" accompanies De Lawd's big face

306 BEHIND THE SCREEN

and pointer finger, an obvious allusion to James Montgomery Flagg's World War I recruitment poster. As Bill Robinson—recognizable by his bowler hat and famous walk—makes his way up the street, Foster's "Old Folks at Home" accompanies the dancer's humming and syncopated riff-walk. [FIG. 6.4, top left] The dance he performs with his hands accentuates the minstrel gloves he is wearing and the big smile he wears draws attention to his exaggerated lips and eyes. As Robinson exits the frame, a caricature of Al Jolson in blackface (voiced by Mel Blanc) with giant lips and minstrel gloves enters singing "I Love to Sing-A." He drops to one knee. [FIG. 6.3, middle left] A black marionette falls from the sky: "Sonny Boy," sings Jolson. "Hullo stranger," responds the marionette in a thick Yiddish accent, a reference to Sam Hearn's Schlepperman character on the Jack Benny Show. The black-colored Yiddish impersonator evaporates into thin air and Jolson makes his way into the Kotton Klub. Gabriel lethargically calls after him, "You can't go in there. I is suppose-ta keep ya outta those places." Tilt up to Black heaven.

"What's the matter with hiiiiiim," calls a caricature of Fats Waller to his posse of jazz musicians, caricatures of Jimmie Lunceford, Cab Calloway, and Louie Armstrong, respectively. "R*H*Y*T*H*M" [FIG. 6.3, bottom left] The quartet of jazz musicians surrounds De Lawd and offers a didactic melody about the power and necessity of rhythm: "Boss you'll have to re-a-lize, to get your folks to Pair-o-Dice, your kids you'll have to mod-ern-ize—"... "Rhythm in your soul!" "Rhythm in your feet!" "Rhythm on the range!" "Rhythm on the street!" Jump cut. Cab Calloway conducts his orchestra in "Swing for Sale" atop the same platform from which Gabriel preached. Harlem residents old and young come flocking from their brownstones to congregate around Calloway's infectious scatting. Cut to a caricature of the radio-famous Mills Brothers, evident because of the animated radio microphone and the quartet's ability to sound like musical instruments through song. Cut to Fats Waller on piano. His angel wings (cut from GHM) grow from his back as second limbs and they too begin playing keys on a second piano behind him. Cut to a caricatured Louis Armstrong on vocals and trumpet. Cut to the golden gates of Pair-O-Dice where all the aforementioned jazz greats parade through heaven like a New Orleans brass band. Meanwhile a group of familiar dancers—the same animations and choreography from Sunday Go to Meetin' Time—*follows the band. Cut to a Harlem dressing room where new Harlemites get haloed, an animated copy of this same scene from* The Green Pastures. *Looking very pleased at this new idea of heaven because of its ever-increasing population, De Lawd places a "no vacancies" sign on the door. But a devil disguised as an*

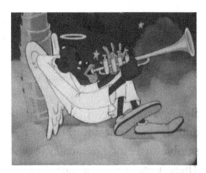

FIGURE 6.3 (*Top left*) The Mills Brothers drawn as frogs in *Old Mill Pond*, 1936; (*Top right*) Caricature of Oscar Polk citing Stepin Fetchit as a monkey in *Clean Pastures*, 1937; (*Middle left*) Citation of Jolson singing "Sonny Boy" alongside Sam Hearn's Schlepperman character in *CP*; (*Middle right*) Citation of Jolson surrogating Rastus on Dream of Wheat box in *September in the Rain*, 1937; (*Bottom left*) Citation of Fats Waller as an angel in *Clean Pastures*; (*Bottom right*) Citation of Fats Waller and Louis Armstrong standing in for the Gold "Rust" Twins in *September in the Rain*. (Private collection)

angel, speaking like Al Jolson (also voiced by Mel Blanc) sneaks in at the very end clearly critiquing what heaven has apparently become in the eyes of De Lawd: never trust the jazz rhythms, drinking, and gambling of Harlem for they are the devil in disguise.

By 1937, caricatures of *Goin' to Heaven on a Mule, Sunday Go to Meetin' Time*, and the live action film *Green Pastures* comprised Friz Freleng's small ensemble of Black characters used in his popular eight-minute animations. These were a mix of caricatures of famous Black performers like Stepin Fetchit, Bill Robinson, Fats Waller, and Cab Calloway; imitations of Black roles like De Lawd, Gabriel, and Emperor Jones; visible illustrations of famous Black archetypes like Zip Coon, Ol' Black Joe, and Uncle Tom; and citations of famous White performers notorious for their racial and ethnic caricatures like Al Jolson, Eddie Cantor, and Sam Hearn. These cartoons often blurred the lines between real human, archetype, fantasy, and primate (e.g., monkey, ape, or orangutan). Behind these images were an even smaller cast of voices: Mel Blanc, Gus Wickie, Wini Shaw, Danny Webb, and the uncredited 4 Blackbirds distorted their voices in such a way that each could play a character from every one of these categories while also playing such famous personalities as Bugs Bunny, Woody Woodpecker, and Goofy (to name just a small sample). Yet despite the layers upon layers of distortion present in *Clean Pastures*, the film ultimately passed the censor review board in 1937.

Due to the derisive nature of the cartoon's images, sound, and narrative, *Clean Pastures* was temporarily held up with the Production Code Administration. However, the holdup had nothing to do with race; instead, it was because of the cartoon's mockery of religion. In a letter to Leon Schlesinger, Breen mentioned the portions of the film set in Pair-O-Dice, saying, "I am certain that such scenes would give serious offense to many people in all parts of the world."[58] Yet despite its religiously controversial nature, Warner Bros. was able to convince the PCA to compromise because *Clean Pastures* (*CP*) included a large number of references to famous contemporary Black entertainers, and because it was one of the few colorized cartoons of the day. The PCA saw these two attributes as advantageous and agreed to green light *CP* after modifications were made to the soundtrack.[59]

The crossover appeal that jazz musicians Calloway, Armstrong, Waller, and Lunceford held is what enabled these Black artists to be depicted as angels, in-between figures who are "neither fully white nor fully black—the minstrel figure whose ideal blackness is painted on, and which rests uneasily above its ostensibly material body."[60] [FIG. 6.3, bottom left and FIG. 6.4, right column] Moreover their liminal expression acknowledges the general ambivalence these White production houses held around presenting "hot" rhythms alongside religion. And because African Americans were generally excluded from positions of power in Hollywood, the way these representations manifested was well outside their control. The films could project jazz music within a "dangerous" urban environment led by hedonistic Black musicians, whose apish portrayals were becoming as prominent to the image of Black jazz as Cantor's blackface was becoming intrinsic to his identity offstage.

Like Jolson's "Mammy," drawings of crazy-haired Calloway "Hi-do-Ho"-ing and doobie-smoking Fats Waller became iconic imagery of the decade spanning 1934 to 1944. Similar imaginings would be used in *September in the Rain*, released the same year; *Have You Got Any Castles?*; and *The Isle of Pingo Pongo* in 1938, as well as *Tin Pan Alley Cats* in 1943, with each new caricature building on the ones made earlier.[61] Justified through the citational guise and the fact that incorporating caricatures of Black artistry had become synonymous with inclusivity—especially if the Black artist being integrated was also someone who was one of the day's "exceptional" Black artists slowly integrating the theatrical space as artists Calloway and Robinson were doing in live action film—these films skirted the Code. And, moreover, "integration" in this context was no less damaging than the inborn fallacy of integration in *Ritz's* title number. Thus, we must revisit the Bill Robinson effect as it applies to animation, and also distinguish the unique way in which the citational guise operates in tandem with the protean in cartoons and is separate from pure caricature, which we see frequently in a medium whose basic principles involve exaggeration and imagination.

Caricature versus Racial Caricature versus Citation

In general, caricatures are clownish representations. The products of covert minstrelsy, however, constitute minstrelized mis-representations. Caricatures critique and exaggerate actual physical characteristics—or in the special case of racial caricature, exaggerate popular stereotypes in circulation; citations,

310   BEHIND THE SCREEN

however, tend to falsify the real as a way of shrouding an Africanist aesthetic in imagery—in some way tied to the nineteenth-century minstrel stage so that Black artistry gets mired in a master/slave dialectic. In animation, the citational guise must be accompanied by the protean—quick, shrewd, and sudden—or else it may be viewed as just caricature. Several cartoons during this same era used physical parody in Hollywood as the basis of their plots and as the subjects of their comic thrust.[62] In films like *Hollywood Capers* (1935), *Coo-Coo Nut Grove* (1936), *Hollywood Bowl* (1938), and *Hollywood Steps Out* (1941), famous personalities collide in celebrated Hollywood hotspots and fictional movie premieres. Prominent performers are presented—sometimes crudely—in more of a roast format, where the non-racialized idiosyncrasies of these notorious individuals become the plot.[63]

To distinguish the citational guise from pure caricature, we can examine two figures who were often featured in these films: Jimmy Durante and Clark Gable. Out in the world, these two actors were known for their very distinct facial features: Durante referred to his own nose as the "schnozzola," and the cosmetic surgery Gable had had on his disproportionately large ears was widely spoken about in the tabloids. Animation's governing principle of exaggeration makes it easy to portray Durante and Gable comically without the burden (or risk) of racial reification. Their exaggerated physical attributes—noses, ears, and in the case of Greta Garbo, enlarged feet—become clownish representations, comically hyper-realized. This manner of representation is different from the minstrelizing and complete re-imagining that occurs with depictions of Black artists such as Eddie "Rochester" Anderson, Robinson, Calloway, or Waller, whom I discuss in terms of the Bill Robinson effect. Such minstrelization is also different from common citations of blackface performers that commonly occur in cartoons of this era, such as those involving Al Jolson or Eddie Cantor, which are—though more nuanced than live action—literal *illustrations* of the citational guise. In the case of these latter representations, the artists in question are singled out for their race or their contributions to racial masquerade. Moreover, their presence in these cartoons is generally brief, more a cameo than a character part. Their fleeting existence lends itself to the protean guise allowing for quick conversions between plain caricature, racial hyperbole, and bestial ambivalence, which when done well and simultaneously, was seemingly invisible enough to evade censors. That is, caricatures are grounded in existent attributes of a single person versus the artifacts of covert minstrelsy that are based on categorical racial stereotypes. Furthermore, citations and tributes tend to assess a

FIGURE 6.4 (*Top left*) Citation of Bill Robinson in *Clean Pastures*, 1937; (*Top right*) Cab Calloway drawn as a frog conducting in *Old Mill Pond*, 1936; (*Middle left*) Citation of Robinson performing his stair dance in *Have You Got Any Castles*, 1938; (*Middle right*) Citation of Calloway fashioned as an angel conducting in *Clean Pastures*; (*Bottom left*) Citation of Robinson performing his stair dance in *You're an Education*, 1938; (*Bottom right*) Citation of Calloway reimagined as a bird conducting in *Swooner Crooner*, 1944. (Private collection)

312   BEHIND THE SCREEN

person's performative qualities rather than physical properties that are fixed and unchanging, even if modifiable as in the case of Gable's cosmetic surgery.

When real humans are re-imagined as animals—Fats Waller as an ape, for example—the human form is dehumanized; no longer can the clownish adjective apply, because a clown, always, is human. In the case of *CP*, all the jazz musicians have been monkey-ified for lack of a better term. Bill Robinson is the only citation in this cartoon that has not crossed over into the realm of humanimal—and this is precisely why his cartoon image consistently belongs in a category unto itself, namely, the Bill Robinson effect, straddling a fine line between citation and tribute. Even though Robinson's performance in *CP* is true to life—Foster's tunes, the humming, and his famous syncopated riff-walk—his image has been minstrelized. While Robinson is never depicted as an animal (with the exception of his amphibian debut in *Old Mill Pond*), animated citations of him are never completely flattering: blackened, wide eyed, large-mouthed, and jolly, these citations embellish his wardrobe and embroider his performance in a way that draws more on Black stereotypes than on Robinson's ontological contours.

In a manner akin to what Irving Berlin's lyrics attempt to do in the original version of "Puttin' on the Ritz," most of *CP* endeavors to create a snapshot of Harlem life, in effect collapsing all Africanisms, Black impersonators, and decadent lifestyle choices into the same frame. At the same time, the animation medium allows for a flattening of time and space— which physics make impossible for live action film. Here the "Kotton Klub" can literally sit beside the Milkyway Café; outer space is heaven is Harlem. And just as pen-and-ink allows for the compressing of geography, so too can old stereotypes be tangled up in new: Bill Robinson becomes Long Tail Blue; the animated Cab Calloway, a more contemporary spin on Zip Coon.

The inclusion of a Bill Robinson type in all these animated films offers an obligatory signification of the swing aesthetic. Unlike the animated example I explored in chapter 3 from *Old Mill Pond*, however, the caricatures of Robinson from 1937 onward are more human than animal, yet his exaggerated facial attributes might as well belong to a class of aves or amphibians. Early on in *CP*, a caricature of Robinson enters the stage doing the famous riff (*heel toe scuff toe toe, heel toe scuff toe toe, heel toe scuff toe, toe scuff toe, toe scuff toe toe*) section of his "Doin' the New Lowdown" routine to the tune of "Swanee River." His face is blacker than coal, his teeth bigger and whiter than those of an elephant, his hands sporting the same oversized minstrel gloves we continue to see. [FIG. 6.4, top left]

Exceptionalism and synecdochization set the Bill Robinson effect apart from strict imitation. This very short clip of Robinson in *CP* reveals itself visually as an archetypal snapshot of disjointed elements of the icon's step/ sonic vocabulary and wardrobe—riff walk, humming, and bowler hat— and a general likeness of his face, exaggerated to the point of caricature. The white circles drawn on his coal black face, emphasize his dimples, likely a reference to the copacetic smile for which he was so well known. His hands are adorned with minstrel gloves, his body covered in a clownishly colorful suit; neither of these accurately represent his form-fitting, neutral palate. Animation allows this version of Robinson to become the new popular representation of Black dandyism on the American stage, designed in part to mitigate the threat posed by "real" Black tap dancers to White performers working in Hollywood at the same time. By collapsing Robinson's image into a series of disjointed parts that coalesce under something as general as tap dance, Robinson becomes an archetype akin to what Long Tail Blue offered the minstrel stage in the 1830s.

Benjamin Miller has analyzed the complexity of Long Tail Blue (a minstrel archetype) through a nuanced reading of both song lyrics and visual imagery. While recognizing that the elaborate costume of real Black dandies was a "symbol of a self-conscious manipulation of authority," he argues that such an interpretation is complicated by corresponding representations of blackface dandyism, which, to use Monica Miller's words are "an attempted denigratory parody of free blacks' pride and enterprise."[64] This blackface version of the dandy pursues White women and gets into trouble with the law. He is essentially the "upwardly mobile dandy brought down a peg or two."[65] While the real Black dandy is a "dignified and respectable man of property who is ready to put his equal citizenship with White men to the test by taking his place in a 'teeming metropolis,'" the blackface version is demonized.[66] Thus at the same time Blue represents upward mobility through his dandyism, he also "serves as a synonym for social transgression."[67]

The real Bill Robinson was both an icon of upward mobility and a marker of social progressiveness, at least as perceived by White people in America in the 1930s. He had climbed his way to the top in film, become internationally recognized as the man who danced with Shirley Temple—thus successfully "integrating" the screen—and was always dressed with class. He in many ways epitomized Black dandyism through his self-conscious manipulation of the White public's perception of Blackness. He had also made headlines for

314   BEHIND THE SCREEN

his gambling addiction and minor run-ins with the law. Between the way the media played up Robinson's social transgression and the manner in which cartoons of this era depicted him, animated imagery of Robinson offers his dandyism a similar opposition as Long Tail Blue offered Black dandyism a century earlier.

The cartoons from this era that portray some semblance of a Bill Robinson figure may offer the dancer a level of visibility not afforded to most Black artists at this time, yet this visibility comes at the expense of demonizing his art as sinful and his legacy as steeped in minstrelsy. As Benjamin Miller has noted was the case with Blue, Robinson's features were amplified to "repress the perceived challenge posed by discourses and performances of black liberty."[68] As White tap dancers like Fred Astaire and Eleanor Powell rose to fame, Robinson's body became more schematized and his talents situated within a context of turpitude. Consequently, these cartoons complemented a "narrative of white liberty that undercut any potential arguments for cross-racial working-class solidarity, abolition, cross-racial sexual relationships, or black rights."[69] On the surface, Robinson appeared to be changing the national image without consequence when in fact behind the screen his reflection merely rendered a new version of Blue. That, as Barbara Lewis has so clearly articulated, was the case with Blue: Robinson "with his obvious ambitions, made [White] people exceedingly uncomfortable."[70] Robinson's onscreen achievements threatened the success of White tap dancers; his cartoon image fashioned him as darker than he was and made his face grotesque, helping to counter the (real) Bill Robinson's more dignified image and what such upward mobility meant for White dancers working in Hollywood at this time. But Robinson was not the only exceptional Black artist given screen time at the expense of reading Black character and Africanist trends in music and dance as depraved. As earlier expressed, animators were drawing several "crossover" Black jazz musicians into these moralistic narratives regarding the sinfulness of swing.

Cab Calloway made more appearances in the cartoons of this era than even Robinson. Known for being particularly animated in his real-life conducting, his image was an easy source of impersonation. In addition to "Hi-De-Ho" and related audible scat-phrasing, caricatures of Calloway generally included a wide mouth, wild and crazy hair (the "conk"), and some version of fanatical conducting.[71] [FIG. 6.4, right] It is precisely the ways in which his image was presented as disheveled and comical—often referred to as "clowning" by the press—that arguably make him a logical (and modern) replacement for the image of Zip Coon, a nineteenth-century archetype of the minstrel stage known for exhibiting qualities of both the buffoon and the dandy.[72] Tavia Nyong'o and Douglas Jones have made convincing arguments for the ways in which "the discourse of blackness under blackface" has usurped Black freedom to support White working-class freedoms.[73] In a manner akin to the process of distorting Robinson's artistry and identity through animation at a time when White tap dancers were seizing the screen, animators fetishized Calloway's body in a way that stripped his crossover appeal of any subversive potential, significantly impacting public perceptions of Black jazz in the popular sphere. Moreover, these films used the voices of other Black artists—as was the case of using LeRoy Hurt's (of the 4 Blackbirds) uncredited vocals during *CP*'s big number "Swing for Sale"—so that a single Black voice would stand in for several. One voice might speak for the Mills Brothers, Calloway, *and* Calloway's entire band.

While references to Calloway were as pervasive as allusions to Robinson during this period in both live action and animation, suggestions of Calloway—visible, aural, and embodied—all tend to fall within the realm of citation rather than the special case of the Bill Robinson effect. Calloway was often depicted as a creature other than human [FIG. 6.4, right top and bottom], and his image was rarely collapsed into being that of the only exceptional swing artist. Unlike animated depictions of Robinson that generally offered commentary through the darkening of his skin, a difference Barbara Lewis notes is a "difference occasioned by an increase in pigment, the result of environment," Calloway's image was "depicted as part of the animal kingdom, a separation sanctioned by nature, not just nurture."[74]

I do not wish to imply that Cab Calloway's image upheld all the same truths as did the Zip Coon archetype of the nineteenth century. Lewis has theorized that part of Zip Coon's function was to undermine the upwardly mobile dandy. That is, on the nineteenth-century stage, Zip Coon "converted the respectability of Long Tail Blue into an outrageous and blasphemous black buffoon."[75] Zip Coon teaches that the stately clothing is just a masquerade; underneath the Black male is deformed and subhuman. Calloway's cartoon image did no such thing for Robinson's on the twentieth-century stage, but the ways in which his manager Irving Mills marketed Calloway as the "Harlemaestro," and the subsequent attention he received from the White press, which played up his "primitivist spectacle on display," promoted the

316   BEHIND THE SCREEN

idea that underneath Calloway's fancy clothes was an "untutored avatar of 'natural' black expression," further cementing the idea that Black people were in some way subhuman, or at least less human than White men.[76]

In most of Calloway's "appearances" his illustration is accompanied by other exceptional crossover jazz musicians, making it possible to distinguish between the Calloways and the Wallers, Luncefords, or Armstrongs. Portrayals of Calloway in these films are citations rather than caricatures because of the ways in which his mouth takes on properties of the minstrel stage and the manner in which animators, through their exaggeration of his conducting, for example, assess the musician's performative qualities rather than those properties that are fixed. Depictions of both Robinson and Calloway utilize a handful of physical falsifications (e.g., Robinson's enlarged eyes and Calloway's mouth drawn as a slice of watermelon) as well as sound and movement to expose certain minstrel tropes without alluding to them through obvious markers like blackface. Juxtaposing Calloway's or Robinson's image alongside that of Jolson's in blackface further cements these properties.

This same audiovisual footage from "Swing for Sale" would be re-used by Warner Bros. a year later in the animated short *Have You Got Any Castles?* which builds its premise around a series of classic books that come to life. Such a plot not only lends itself to all kinds of racial caricature (e.g., the kneeling globe depicted behind Pearl S. Buck's Pulitzer Prize–winning book, *The Good Earth*, mumbles gibberish with a very thick caricatured Chinese accent) but also offers a narrative context for citational and sonic guising tied together by free association and word play. That is, the imaginings that follow are obvious displays of both implicit and explicit bias, furtively shielded by the cartoon's plot and a series of covert guises that justify their presence and add "insider" humor. The film's very title is a reference to the Johnny Mercer song sung by Priscilla Lane and later Buck and Bubbles in *Varsity Show* (1937).

In *Castles*, the Bill Robinson effect is built into John Buchan's famous novel, *The Thirty-Nine Steps*. [FIG. 6.4. left middle] After zooming in on the title, the cartoon pans downward to expose Robinson's brown dancing body. His body is still fully intact, as is his famous bowler hat and suit, but again animators have added to his costume the oversized minstrel gloves. His skin is noticeably lighter than in earlier cartoon citations, and his lips and teeth seem to have shrunk in size since last year's *CP*. Changes have been made to his face, however, to include pudgier cheeks, a rounder nose, and a plastered smile, adjustments that read more clown-like and once again speak to the derogatory archetyping that plagued his image as he transformed from Black dandyism to Long Tail Blue. *You're an Education* (1938) used the same image of Robinson (though his suit was changed from green to blue) in a "Steppes of Russia" routine five months later. [FIG. 6.4, left bottom] Following this glimpse of Robinson, the camera pans directly down to capture another Pulitzer Prize–winner, *So Big*, with a caricature of Greta Garbo standing in for Shirley Temple. Small in comparison to her oversized shoes, she, like Temple, performs a sand dance in the shadow of her teacher, completing the integrationist image of Robinson dancing with someone White.

The thickly layered sonic and citational guises swathed in witty word play present themselves when the screen tilts up to catch sight of Marc Connelly's book *The Green Pastures*. It quickly becomes clear that using *CP* is also an economical move on the part of Warner Bros. since the next 35 seconds of animation have been lifted directly from *CP*: a split second of the scantily dressed, light-skinned chorines; a close-up of Calloway's baton in his disproportionately large hands and turgid lips belting "I've got swing for sale!" Once again, LeRoy Hurt's voice stands in for the haloed-Mills Brothers and Cab Calloway. Cut to blonde-haired Heidi, of 1881 Swiss fame, who comically belts the sounds *Heidi Heidi Heidi Ho*. Other parodies ensue—a caricature of William Powell from *The Thin Man* series that transforms into a political caricature after visiting the *White House Cookbook*; a whistling "Whistler's grandmother" who sings on the cover of an art history book; an Andrews' Sisters–like song that accompanies the dancing of three *Little Women* characters; a very zaftig Old King Cole of nursery-rhyme fame who is White but sings like Nat King Cole of the then-"King Cole Swingsters."[77] The Andrews Sisters impersonators add the line, "He waved his scepter with a swing" after Cole's solo, and the camera cuts away to a very phallic image of *Rip Van Winkle*'s long beard lying between his legs. When *Van Winkle* awakes, he jumps into the book next to his and chops off the white hair of a very decrepit Uncle Tom, atop Harriet Beecher Stowe's famous title, using the slave's white cotton-like hair as ear plugs so he can fall back asleep. A very caricatured American Indian musician drums on the cover of *Drums along the Mohawk* while a very stereotypical naked (South-East Asian) Indian plays an Indian brass horn in front of the Taj Mahal and two asps. This Indian looks almost indistinguishable from the Aladdin who appears later in the cartoon, implying the perceived visual similitude of all Indians and Arabs. All these racial caricatures appear five months later in *You're an Education. Education*

318   BEHIND THE SCREEN

shares a similar plot but substitutes travel brochures for books, making it even easier to utilize distracting mechanisms such as brownface and redface to further camouflage the cartoon's more blatant synecdochization and commodification of Blackness.

Citation, not Tribute

Through the films of Eddie Cantor, we saw how the protean guise often camouflages the impact of particular racial encounters when they emerge in rapid physical and aural succession. The narrative premise of *Castles*—and *Education*—lends itself to bombarding an audience with images and sounds in rapid succession; these simultaneously offer a surplus of caricature, racial stereotyping, and naturally, a cavalcade of citations, leaving a large window of opportunity for animators to subtly remark on all aspects of culture through magical realism, parody, satire, word play, and irony. The protean situated within this context is thus wrapped up in the logic of animation and relies on the visual working in tandem with the sonic and citational guises.

A major difference between live action tributes to Bill Robinson and animated citations of him is that in the former, an actor from the film will dress up as the person he/she is impersonating, pay tribute, and then undress; this action is an important part of the meaning-making process for audience members. If Eleanor Powell did not make her application and removal of blackface makeup intentional when she paid tribute to Robinson in *Honolulu*, the audience might have mistaken Powell for being Black. However, when the quotation of someone exists within the world of the unreal to begin with, the perceived fear of misidentification is mitigated, since the character literally appears out of nowhere.

In a world that is sketched and colored, the possibilities for representation are endless. Additionally, the very act of obscuring the process might in fact confirm the realness of the performance. That is, if there is no costume—no mask—then the person who preceded the caricature slowly dissolves. The repeated use of certain visible characteristics (e.g., coal black skin, gigantic lips, and oversized gloves) become as ingrained for spectators as an actor's idiosyncrasies. Furthermore, animation lends itself to the art of deconstruction and juxtaposition, making it possible to transform racial caricature into something as innocent as word play and to downsize the weight of disembodiment to mere slapstick, as in the corporeal deconstruction that animators use on the cover of *The Invisible Man*, or the thought-provoking placement of Rip Van Winkle next to Uncle Tom, which allows animators to interpret and re-interpret history in the most covert of ways. It is here that we see an example of the second order of the Bill Robinson effect materialize—a narrative revision in which authors evoke a historical figure through a biased lens. When crucial details of a person's biography are omitted, the subject of this re-telling transcends time and thus the social stigmas he endured while alive. Combine this re-telling and flattening of history with clever product placement and it becomes easy to sell your short to the PCA.

The Signifying Chain

An uncredited Wini Shaw opens September in the Rain *as she voices a bottle of blueing which claims to "keep your clothes white and clean." A turbaned fakir comes to life on a tin of coffee that faintly reads "air-tite dated" as the music from his Turkish zurna charms a snake that appears from a tube of Tootsie toothpaste. A box of Old Maid Cleanser features a Klompendansen Dutch girl—a symbolic spin on the once popular "Old Dutch Cleanser" which transitions seamlessly into a rubber glove using its digits to stand up and dance around the counter to a piece of Scottish-inspired music. The same bagpipe soundtrack accompanies a shelf of "Carmel" cigarette boxes whose camels walk in time with the music's downbeats. Across the shelf sits a box of Threaded Wheat. Its cascading waterfall surrounds a factory—a stylized insinuation of Shredded Wheat's industrial unit locale in Niagara Falls—and drips off the cardboard to become the rain on a blue cannister of unnamed salt with a caricature of Ruby Keeler as the Morton's girl in a yellow raincoat, standing and singing in the rain. A caricature of Dick Powell standing in as the biscuit boy from a box of "Uneedum" crackers—a twist on the National Biscuit Company's "Uneeda Bakers"—also dressed in a raincoat, jumps off his box to join the Morton's girl; together Keeler and Powell sing "By a Waterfall" in the rain, an homage to their famous 1933 duet in* Footlight Parade. *The camera cuts from salt and biscuits to Al Jolson's breakfast advertisement. The same caricature of Jolson that appeared in* Clean Pastures *surfaces here singing "September in the Rain," on the front of a box of "Dream of Wheat," which complicates Jolson's performance of Blackness, since here he appears to be Black rather than in blackface. Dream of Wheat also cites previous an-imated caricatures of Jolson, especially through song and movement, and*

320 BEHIND THE SCREEN

furthermore plays on Emery Mapes's barely literate "Rastus" caricature that was the symbol for the Cream of Wheat company for over two decades.[78] *This loaded signifier sets Jolson up to sing "Mammy" facing the direction of Aunt "Emma" Pancake Flour who is both a caricature of Ethel Waters and a reference to Aunt Jemimah; she sings "Sonny Boy" back to Jolson. [FIG. 6.3, right middle] Jolson then speaks of his "southern home," an excuse to bring in a "Cabin Syrup" dwelling while Foster's "Old Folks at Home" plays in the background. Cut to citations of Ginger Rogers and Fred Astaire on boxes of "Domingo" and "Tareytown" cigarettes, respectively. In keeping with Tareyton's real slogan to "fight" rather than "switch" where models donned black paint under their eyes, Astaire's cigarette box emphasizes the cigarette's cork tips and acknowledges that "There's a Funny Thing About Them," likely referencing the donning of black paint that Astaire had done just a year earlier. Astaire and Rogers dance down a box of Park Avenue cigarettes, up a staircase of matchbooks, and over to a box of Lucky "Blows." As they finish their set, the music changes and the camera cuts to a box of Gold "Rust" Washing Powder, which features two black "twins"—caricatures of Fats Waller and Louie Armstrong. [FIG. 6.3, right bottom] This allusion to Fairbank's all-purpose Gold Dust washing products and the brand's well-known trademark, the Gold Dust Twins, Goldie and Dustie, is problematic for many reasons, not least of which is the idea that all Black musicians are identical. Waller's and Armstrong's images are the same caricatures we witnessed in* Clean Pastures, *re-used and repurposed—wearing tutus.*[79] *Armstrong shouts, "Swing it, brother," to a Paul Whiteman lookalike disguised as a "Bisquit" chef who adds some percussion along with the arm of a "Strong Arm Baking Soda." Waller then leaps over to a box of piano wax where he begins to play the "Nagasaki" tune on piano; Armstrong soon joins him on vocals while two roosters on a box of chicken feed peck in response to the music. The film ends on this note with Waller jamming on the piano, Armstrong soloing on trumpet, Aunt Emma jumping off the box and dancing wildly, and close-ups of other boxes of happy, singing caricatures of Black chefs.*

With so many citations at play, *September's* animations make it difficult to untangle the real from the unreal. The human becomes the caricature; the caricature becomes the advertisement; the advertisement becomes the joke; and the joke becomes the object of our projections. Like the ways the directors of the book sequence in *Castles* or the travel brochures in *Education* create meaning out of deconstruction, imitation, and juxtaposition, *September's* creative team relies on these elements of humor in combination with advertising culture to exploit the body in such a way as to blur the line between commodity, irony, and fetish.

A kind of twice- or thrice-removed replica realism forms the basis of these plots. In the case of live action tributes, the White performer (e.g., Astaire or Powell) fabricates parts of Robinson's character and in the process loses not only the aura of Robinson's representational politic but also the whole quality of his dancing. The blackface attempts to stand in for Robinson's corporeality and the staircase seeks to surrogate his performative ontology. Animation complicates the tribute guise because it removes real flesh from the picture, making it hard to distinguish between imitations of the real and facsimiles of the mask. Rarely are we exposed to the act of putting on blackface, and when we are, the act of donning becomes part of the gag—the protean magic (Bugs Bunny in *Bonds*), the explosion (Mickey Mouse in *Mellerdrammer*), the melted chocolate (the vocal harmony group in *Toyland Broadcast*). Thus, the protean in animation removes the intentionality behind blackface application making it easier to cite than to pay tribute. Moreover, animation requires a much more economical use of time and movement than does live action, making copies of copies appealing for several reasons.

Recycling many of the images from *CP* and all of the songs from other Warner Bros.' films, *September* was incredibly economical. *September* required a lot less time and money to create, and it helped market other films, cartoons, and sheet music owned and distributed by Warner Bros. In fact, it is the recycling of previously used animation cels and sound bytes that allowed a film with such egregious racial and ethnic profiling to pass Breen's administration. In addition to all of its internal references and recycled material from *CP*, *September* is a remake of a 1934, pre-Code black and white, Friz Freleng short, *How Do I Know It's Sunday*.[80] The major difference between these two films is that in the former, product placement of items such as Scream of Wheat, Aunt Mima Pancake Flour, and Gold Dust Washing Powder look more similar to the original packaging, with fewer letter substitutions and no cross citational play between household commodities and names; pre-Code rules allowed for such product (re)placements. But even *Sunday* likely obtained inspiration from an earlier show.

Hollywood directors and producers could cite earlier moments in theatrical history as justification for the inclusion of particular racial imagery, especially if that imagery stemmed from an allegedly Black source. Pictures of the set design for Lew Leslie's all Black revue *Blackbirds of 1930* look eerily familiar. [FIG. 6.2, bottom] Here it is conceivable that the creators of *Sunday* derived inspiration from *Blackbirds* and used its all-Black cast as justification for such racial fetish, which would have been enough to satisfy the loosely monitored Code in early 1934. Here racial caricature is based on a form of commodity fetishism that was used in a Black context onstage, though conceived of through a White consciousness behind the scenes. By citing this theatrical moment, animators benefited artistically and logistically while also further fixing old stereotypes of print through the moving image. By 1937, substituting caricatures of Jolson for Rastus, Waters for Mima, and Waller and Armstrong for the Gold "Rust" Twins acts as yet another discourse of Black archetypes masquerading under blackface. In a manner similar to the replacing of Robinson for Blue and Calloway for Zip Coon, caricatures of White actors in blackface and exceptional Black artists stand in for older models of Blackness, sentimentalizing outdated print capitalism through sonic and kinetic citations.

The fact that the bodies of Jolson (as Black), Waters, Waller, and Armstrong can so easily be substituted for other identifiable commodified Black imagery and the notion that their individual voices can be surrogated by a single Black voice should say something about the significance of rupture to an Africanist aesthetic and fragmentation to the Black body.

While Astaire's and Powell's performances ask their audiences to see Black people as substitutable and re-attributable—a request that operates purely on the symbolic level—the disarticulation in *September* behaves literally and figuratively, requiring that the sonic, protean, and citational guises work together to achieve such substitution. Furthermore, rather than slipping in an Africanist aesthetic under the pretense of "integration," blackface, brownface, redface, jewface, or hypersexualized White femininity, an Africanist aesthetic in *September* surfaces through the caricatured body parts (heads, hands, and eyes, for example) of Black artists whose very disembodiment markets White cultural capital.

Rupture and Racial Fetish

Dismembering heads to place on the boxes of wheat cereal and pancake mixes was only one of the ways animators presented the Black body as fragmented. Fats Waller's hands (and sometimes wings) almost always detach themselves from his cartoon body in order to play the piano free-hand.

Animators often unfasten a character's (minstrel) gloves to either play music or perform a tap dance, as Disney did in *Thru the Mirror* (1936).[81] In films like *Coal Black and de Sebben Dwarfs* (1943) or *Tin Pan Alley Cats*, animators disconnect the singing mouth, further accentuating imagined differences between Blackness and Whiteness while bringing out illusory connections between a slice of watermelon and Black oral cavities.[82] But most common for films featuring Black caricatures during this period was to detach the feet or shoes from the caricatured Black dancer, imbuing the extremities with power while simultaneously taking away that authority from the dancer. The boogie beat of the hands or the syncopated counts of the feet become *dismembered entities.*

Such dismemberment stands in stark contrast to the ways that White performers were portrayed in these same cartoons. Fred Astaire and Ginger Rogers stay whole in *September*'s cigarette duet. In *Red Hot Riding Hood* (1943), *Swing Shift Cinderella* (1945), and *Little Rural Riding Hood* (1949),[83] for example, the White jazz singer/jazz tap dancers' bodies remain whole, unlike the corporeal transformations the Gold Rust Twins endure in *September,* or the jazz musicians undergo in *CP* and *Castles*. The disparity between Black and White representation here echoes Saidiya Hartman's idea that acknowledging the Black body necessarily entails remembering the fragmented, or "amputated," body produced through slavery. Viewing the amputated Black body in these cartoons "entails a remembering of the pained body, not by way of a simulated wholeness but precisely through the recognition of the amputated body in its amputatedness, in the insistent recognition of the violated body as human flesh."[84]

Unlike the Bill Robinson caricatures in *CP* and *Castles*, the "Robinson" presented in Terrytoons' *Mississippi Swing* (1939) bears absolutely no resemblance to the real man other than the color of the cartoon's skin. Instead, this depiction is one of an old decrepit Uncle Tom, hobbling onstage with a cane. We know this cartoon is supposed to signify Robinson because of the staircase that awaits him in center stage and the very rhythmically complex (for a cartoon at least) tap dance that follows. The soundtrack makes a dramatic shift from the "Swanee River" tune that plays for the majority of the cartoon to the song "Old Black Joe" that Hollywood has reattributed to Robinson in recreations of his stair dance in films like *Honolulu* (1939). Unlike most of Terrytoons' work, the tap dance routine performed by the Uncle Tom version of Bojangles exhibits close attention to detail both musically and from a movement perspective: animators managed to attempt foot articulation that

324   BEHIND THE SCREEN

was in synch with the more rhythmically complicated stair dance. But two thirds of the way in, Bojangles's shoes jump off his feet and begin tapping down the staircase on their own. They continue to shuffle off the stage, off the "showboat," and finally into the ocean. Uncle Tom/Bojangles stands in awe of his dancing feet, exposing what Hal Foster might call " 'magical commodities' containing the repressed promise of a utopian cathexis between the work of art and society, between the artist and the viewer-consumer."[85] As the Black caricature stands in admiration of the tap dancing shoes, the narcissistic thingification of Black artistry in Hollywood reveals itself. The dancing shoes in these cartoons become the "mystical 'icons' of capital," where "people and things exchange semblances: social relations take on the character of object relations, and commodities assume the active agency of people."[86] Such splitting at once renders the Black body as fragmented and Black artistry as stripped of its agency. *Mississippi Swing*, like so many of these cartoons, not only restages the event of rupture through a disembodiment of the protagonist's tap-dancing shoes but also reopens the wounds of the Middle Passage by re-fracturing the site of subjection through its amputation and synechtochization of Blackness.

Such violence is "allowed" to appear onscreen because its cruelty is cloaked in several layers of covert minstrelsy: situated within the context of a minstrel show-within-a-show onboard a southern-repossessed showboat in transit: Bill Robinson as Uncle Tom collapses exceptional Black artistry into caricature producing a schism in the way Robinson's body and art can be read. Here the audience is not only asked to see Black people as substitutable and re-attributable, but they are also encouraged to detach an Africanist aesthetic from Black artistry, thereby making it easier to re-assign Whiteness to forms such as swing music and tap dance. De-emphasizing swing/tap dance's Africanist roots indicates an erasure of jazz's complicated ties to slavery, minstrelsy, and centuries of derogatory print capitalism.

***

Most cartoons made during 1934–1942 inundate viewers with images— some funny, some violent, and some too layered to judge. From wolves masquerading in jewface to jazz musicians parading as monkeys, cartoon images become simulacra of simulacra, copies of copies, fallacies built atop one another. Animators collapse stereotypes and artistic proclivities into single, often dehumanizing images that shift so rapidly that real humans quickly dissolve into fragmented pieces, attributes, and figments of the imagination. Racial caricature as such reveals a latent desire to rid the screen of its difficulty to represent Black artistry without representing the stigma of Blackness while retaining the "entertainment" quotient (i.e., films that dispose of overt blackface but still engage Black culture and caricatures of Black American life, as well as tropes of "Native" and Jewish identity). Banking on racial and ethnic stereotypes, these animated films satisfied censors while taking advantage of a kind of Black exteriority, dismissing "real" Black corporeality in favor of its cultural capital.

Hollywood would continue to sever Black artistry from the bodies of artists themselves, re-assigning an Africanist aesthetic to White surrogates and animated simulacra. Despite the tightening Code and the war efforts of Black individuals against a common enemy during World War II, Hollywood's landscape continued to shift in terms of its laws surrounding the appropriate and the tasteful: covert minstrelsy in the years following World War II may have looked different, but its message was more potent than ever. A surge in films made with all-Black casts and the continued decreasing popularity of visible blackface sent one message to anyone *watching* on the surface. More deeply embedded uses of the sonic, citational, and protean guises would further challenge integration onscreen and at home.

Notes

1. Since the early nineteenth century, Uncle Sam has been a popular symbol of the US government.
2. Donald Sommerville, *The Complete Illustrated History of World War Two: An Authoritative Account of the Deadliest Conflict in Human History with Analysis of Decisive Encounters and Landmark Engagements* (Leicester: Lorenz Books, 2008), 5.
3. Thomas Doherty, *Projections of War: Hollywood, American Culture, and World War II* (New York: Columbia University Press, 1993), 2–3.
4. Quoted in >IBT>Doherty, *Projections of War*, 122.
5. Ibid., 5.
6. The Army Air Force, Navy, and Bureau of Aeronautics also supervised animated films for training and instructional purposes. Examples can be seen in Robert Clampett, *Any Bonds Today* (April 2, 1942; USA: Leon Schlesinger Studios and the US Department of the Treasury), Film; Ben Sharpsteen, *Out of the Frying Pan into the Firing Line* (July 30, 1942; USA: Walt Disney Productions and War Production Board), Film.
7. Examples include *The Thrifty Pig* (1941), *Scrap Happy Daffy* (1942), and *Ding Dong Daddy* (1943).

8. Henry Louis Gates, "What Was Black America's Double War?," in *The Root*, May 24, 2013, 1.
9. Walter Lantz, *Boogie Woogie Bugle Boy of Company 'B'* (September 1, 1941; USA: Walter Lantz Productions), Film.
10. "Nicholas Sammond, "Gentlemen, Please Be Seated, Racial Masquerade and Sadomasochism in 1930s Animation," in *Burnt Cork: Traditions and Legacies of Blackface Minstrelsy*, ed. Stephen Johnson (Amherst: University of Massachusetts Press, 2012), 165.
11. Burt Gillett, *Three Little Pigs* (May 27, 1933; USA: Walt Disney Animation Studios/Productions), Film.
12. Friz Freleng, *Goin' to Heaven on a Mule* (May 19, 1934; USA: Leon Schlesinger Studios and Warner Bros), Film.
13. Friz Freleng, *Sunday Goes a Meetin' Time* (August 8, 1936; USA: Leon Schlesinger Studios), Film; Friz Freleng, *Clean Pastures* (May 22, 1937; USA: Leon Schlesinger Studios), Film.
14. Disney artists Ollie Johnston and Frank Thomas defined twelve principles of animation that they believed guided Disney animators from the 1930s onward. The tenth of these principles is exaggeration, or alterations made to a character's physical features or actions, or an overall filter for the plot itself. Exaggeration is based on reality but presented in a wilder, more extreme way. See Ollie Johnston and Frank Thomas, *The Illusion of Life: Disney Animation* (New York: Disney Editions, 1983).
15. Friz Freleng, *September in the Rain* (December18, 1937; USA: Leon Schlesinger Studios), Film.
16. Friz Freleng, *Have You Got Any Castles?* (June 25, 1938; USA: Leon Schlesinger Studios), Film.
17. Ub Iwerks and Shamus Culhane, *Little Black Sambo* (February 6, 1935; USA: Celebrity Productions and Ub Iwerks Studio), Film.
18. Christopher P. Lehman, *The Colored Cartoon: Black Representation in American Animated Short Films, 1907–1954* (Amherst: University of Massachusetts Press, 2007), 13.
19. See Abstract to Alexander G. Weheliye, *Habeas Viscus: Racializing Assemblages, Biopolitics, and Black Feminist Theories of the Human* (Durham, NC: Duke University Press, 2014).
20. Paul Wells, *The Animated Bestiary: Animals, Cartoons, and Culture* (New Brunswick, NJ Rutgers University Press, 2009).
21. Wells writes, "Creatures in all cultures become metaphorically charged with a range of narratives, identities, and sociocultural symbolism that creates a parallel world to the literal one." See Wells, *The Animated Bestiary*, 53.
22. Kevin S. Sandler, *Reading the Rabbit: Explorations in Warner Bros. Animation* (New Brunswick, NJ: Rutgers University Press, 1998), 159.
23. Wells, *The Animated Bestiary*, 60.
24. Jonathan Burt, *Animals in Film* (London: Reaktion, 2002).
25. By "superficial" I mean to suggest those codes that reside on the outermost layer of performance; at the same time I wish to imply a superficiality that exists in costumes and makeup which seek to cover up something deeper.
26. Wells, *The Animated Bestiary*, 197.

27. Ibid., 101.
28. Ibid., 102.
29. Alfred Fuller made each of his salesmen sign a pledge that promised, "I will be courteous; I will be kind; I will be sincere; I will be helpful." Furthermore, Fuller taught his men to wear oversized overshoes so if they were to be invited inside, "they could quickly and easily step out of the wet, snowy shoes." See "History" on Fuller Brush Co. website, https://fuller.com/pages/fuller-brush-history, accessed January 27, 2021.
30. Toni Wein, *Monstrous Fellowship: "Pagan, Turk and Jew" in English Popular Culture, 1780–1845* (Oxford: Peter Lang, 2018), and Sara Lipton, *Dark Mirror: The Medieval Origins of Anti-Jewish Iconography* (New York: Metropolitan Books, 2014).
31. Robert Dawidoff, "Some of Those Days," *Western Humanities Review*, 41, no. 3 (1987): 263–86.
32. Klezmer is an Ashkenazi Jewish traditional form of instrumental music from Central and Eastern Europe.
33. Michael Barrier, *Hollywood Cartoons: American Animation in Its Golden Age* (New York: Oxford University Press, 1999), 117</IBT<.
34. Ibid.
35. Ibid., 94.
36. Martin Lister, *New Media: A Critical Introduction* (London: Routledge, 2003).
37. Burt Gillett, *Molly Moo-Cow and the Indians* (November 15, 1935; USA: Van Beuren Studios), Film.
38. Dave Fleischer and Willard Bowsky, *Big Chief Ugh-Amugh-Ugh* (April 25, 1938; USA: Fleischer Studios), Film.
39. Friz Freleng, *Jungle Jitters* (February 19, 1938; USA: Leon Schlesinger Studios), Film.
40. The African gumboot style, also known as Isicathulo, is native to the Zulu people of South Africa. See Kariamu Welsh Ashante, *African Dance: An Artistic, Historical, and Philosophical Inquiry* (Trenton, NJ: Africa World Press, 2002), 19. By showing this connection I do not mean to imply that the cartoon was based on Isicathulo but instead to show how animators (and others) often generalize and collapse the concept of "Native" movement.
41. Dave Fleischer and Shamus Culhane, *The Dandy Lion* (September 20, 1940; USA: Fleischer Studios), Film.
42. Alex Lovy, *Boogie Woogie Sioux* (November 30, 1942; USA: Walter Lantz Productions), Film.
43. Lisa Gitelman, *Always Already New: Media, History and the Data of Culture* (Cambridge, MA: MIT Press, 2006), 6.
44. Gitelman, *Always Already*, 6.
45. In February 1949, the Jewish Labor Committee (JLC) in California joined forces with the NAACP to help bring attention to Hollywood executives regarding animated racist caricatures. The sale and distribution of the colorized version of *Little Black Sambo* in Macy's department stores and by Castle Films is a perfect example of converting color cartoons back to black and white to appease the NAACP. See Lehman, *The Colored Cartoon*, 89–90.
46. Judith Weisenfeld, *Hollywood Be Thy Name: African American Religion in American Film, 1929–1949* (Berkeley: University of California Press, 2007), 72.
47. Ibid., 84.

328 BEHIND THE SCREEN

48. The intertitle would read: "God appears in many forms to those who believe in Him. Thousands of Negroes in the Deep South visualize God and Heaven in terms of people and things they know in their everyday life. *The Green Pastures'* is an attempt to portray that humble, reverent conception." *New York Amsterdam News*, March 14, 1936.

49. Weisenfield, *Be Thy Name*, 66.

50. Ibid., 77.

51. These eleven were *Hittin' the Trail for Hallelujah Land, Sunday Go to Meetin' Time, Clean Pastures, Uncle Tom's Bungalow, Jungle Jitters, The Isle of Pingo Pongo, All This and Rabbit Stew, Coal Black and de Sebben Dwarfs, Tin Pan Alley Cats, Angel Puss,* and *Goldilocks and the Jivin' Bears.*

52. Joseph Barbera and William Hanna, *Gallopin Gals'* (October 26, 1940; USA: Loew's/ M-G-M Cartoon Studio), Film.

53. Joseph Barbera and William Hanna, *Mouse Cleaning* (December 11, 1948; USA: Loew's/M-G-M Cartoon Studio), Film.

54. Joseph Barbera and William Hanna, *Puss Gets the Boot* (February 10, 1940; USA: Rudolf Ising Productions, Loew's/M-G-M Cartoon Studio), Film.

55. Jean Baudrillard, *Simulations* (New York: Semiotext(e), 1983).

56. Ibid., 4.

57. Ibid.

58. Joseph I. Breen to Leon Schlesinger, May 11, 1937, Assorted papers from the Warner Bros. Archive at the University of Southern California.

59. According to Lehman, the PCA "operated under a double standard." This can be seen in the apparent contradiction between those images and songs they found to be acceptable and those they chose to deny. See Lehman, *Colored Cartoon*, 42–44.

60. Sammond, "Gentlemen, Please Be Seated," 167.

61. Tex Avery, *The Isle of Pingo Pongo* (May 28, 1938; USA: Leon Schlesinger Studios), Film; Robert Clampett, *Tin Pan Alley Cats* (July 17, 1943; USA: Leon Schlesinger Studios), Film.

62. If this book were any longer, I would go into immense detail on what I am calling the "walk-of-fame" variation. I plan to explore this in a future article.

63. Jack King, *Hollywood Capers* (October 19, 1935; USA: Leon Schlesinger Studios, Warner Bros.), Film; Friz Freleng, *CooCoo Nut Grove* (November 28, 1936; USA: Leon Schlesinger Studios, Film; Elmer Perkins, *Hollywood Bowl* (1938; USA: Walter Lantz Productions), Film; Tex Avery, *Hollywood Steps Out* (May 24, 1941; USA: Leon Schlesinger Studios, Warner Bros.), Film.

64. Monica Miller, *Slaves to Fashion: Black Dandyism and the Styling of Black Diasporic Identity* (Durham. NC: Duke University Press, 2009), 81.

65. Benjamin Miller, "Twisting the Dandy: The Transformation of the Blackface Dandy in Early American Theatre," *Journal of American Theatre and Drama* 27, no. 3 (Fall 2015).

66. Miller proves this through imagery in various lithographs that sketch Long Tail Blue as having horns or snake-like attributes. See Miller, "Twisting the Dandy," 7.

67. Ibid., 8.

68. Ibid., 1.

HAYS IS FOR HORSES   329

69. Ibid., 1.
70. Barbara Lewis, "Daddy Blue: The Evolution of the Dark Dandy," in *Inside the Minstrel Mask: Readings in Nineteenth Century Blackface Minstrelsy*, ed. Annemarie Bean, James Hatch, and Brooks McNamara (Hanover, New Hampshire: Wesleyan University Press, 1996), 265.
71. Lehman notes, "The script for the film, as approved by him [Freleng], crudely identifies Calloway's scatting as African American by twice calling for his caricature's 'coon shouting.' See Lehman *Colored Cartoon*, 41.
72. See, for example, "Duke, Cab Original," *Pittsburgh Courier*, April 29, 1933, A2.
73. Tavia Nyong'o, *The Amalgamation Waltz: Race, Performance, and the Ruses of Memory* (Minneapolis: University of Minnesota Press, 2009), 122; Douglas Jones Jr., "Black Politics but Not Black People: Rethinking the Social and 'Racial' History of Early Minstrelsy," *TDR: The Drama Review* 57, no. 2 (2013): 25.
74. Lewis, "Daddy Blue," 265.
75. Ibid., 269.
76. Nate Sloan, "Constructing Cab Calloway: Publicity, Race, and Performance in 1930's Harlem Jazz," *The Journal of Musicology* 36, no. 3 (2019): 378.
77. *Have You Got Any Castles?* was released before Nat King Cole became a big solo artist (c. 1943).
78. The image of formerly enslaved "Rastus" was himself a caricature based on Joel Chandler Harris's Uncle Remus characters and helped to solidify the notion of the happy Black servant as did advertisements featuring Aunt Jemima and Uncle Ben. In the late 1920s, Cream of Wheat replaced the drawing of Rastus with a photograph of Frank L. White, a Chicago-based chef from Barbados.
79. The original twins were a drawing of two young Black children pictured side by side. In 1903 as part of a national campaign, the image of the twins became more caricatured, their gender complicated by tutu costumes. In the 1920s the twins became the featured performers of a popular radio program starring Harvey Hindemeyer as "Goldie" and Earle Tuckerman as "Dusty," two White actors who performed in blackface. See Jane Elizabeth Dailey, Glenda Elizabeth Gilmore, and Bryant Simon, eds., *Jumpin' Jim Crow: Southern Politics from Civil War to Civil Rights* (Princeton, NJ: Princeton University Press, 2000), 16.
80. The cartoon also borrows elements from two 1935 Freleng shorts, *Billboard Frolics* and *Flowers for Madame*.
81. David Hand, *Thru the Mirror* (May 30, 1936; USA: Walt Disney Productions), Film.
82. Robert Clampett, *Coal Black and de Sebben Dwarfs* (January 16, 1943; USA: Leon Schlesinger Studios), Film.
83. Tex Avery, *Red Hot Riding Hood* (May 8, 1943; USA: Loew's, MGM Cartoon Studio), Film; Tex Avery, *Swing Shift Cinderella* (August 25, 1945: USA: Metro Goldwyn-Mayer), Film; Tex Avery, *Little Rural Riding Hood* (September 17, 1949; USA: Loew's, MGM Cartoon Studio), Film.
84. Saidiya V. Hartman, *Scenes of Subjection: Terror, Slavery, and Self-Making in Nineteenth-Century America* (New York: Oxford University Press, 1997), 74.

330 BEHIND THE SCREEN

85. Hal Foster, "(Dis)agreeable Objects," in *Damaged Goods: Desire and the Economy of the Object*, ed. Brian Wallis (New York: New Museum of Contemporary Art, 1986), 13.
86. Emily Apter, *Feminizing the Fetish: Psychoanalysis and Narrative Obsession in Turn-of-the-Century France* (New York: Cornell University Press, 1991), 11, and Foster, "(Dis)agreeable Objects," 13.

Coda

Enlisting the Tropes

Covert Minstrelsy in Action, 1942–1954

January 11, 1943

Colonel Jason S. Joy
20th Century-Fox
10201 West Pico Blvd.,
Los Angeles, Calif.,

Dear Colonel Joy:

We have read the temporary script dated January 6, 1943, for your proposed picture, THANKS PAL, also some pages of changes (3–34) dated January 9th, and are happy to report that the basic story seems to meet the requirements of the Production Code.

We will be happy to read all of the lyrics for this production, whenever you have them ready.

Page 44: In this lyric DIGA DIGA DOO, the following lines are unacceptable and should be changed:
        "Love and mamas there are free,"
        "And when you love it is natural to Diga Diga Doo Diga Doo"
        "How can there be a Virgin Isle."

Page 45: Great care will be needed with the various dances, throughout this picture, to avoid anything questionable. In particular we call your attention to the dance on this page. As written, it suggests the kind of dance that might be questionable unless it is handled with extreme care, so as to avoid any suggestive elements.

Behind the Screen. Brynn W. Shiovitz, Oxford University Press. © Oxford University Press 2023.
DOI: 10.1093/oso/9780197553091.003.0008

332   CODA

[a segment of this letter has been clipped]

Cordially yours,
Joseph I. Breen[1]

In an early Code correspondence between Joseph I. Breen and Twentieth Century Fox's Director of Public Relations, Colonel Jason S. Joy, Breen advises Joy to modify some of the lyrics for "Diga Diga Doo" and to take extra precautions with its accompanying choreography due to the nature of its story and jazzy rhythms. The rules surrounding sexual conduct onscreen and specifically fears surrounding how the Catholic Church might read jazz music and dance had not changed much since Will H. Hays appointed Breen to lead the PCA in 1934; for the duration of the Code, jazz would always be "hot" and hot would forever be dangerous when its rhythms were performed by Black artists. In fact, reading Breen's correspondence with Hollywood directors alongside the films themselves reveals the period between 1942 and 1945 as exhibiting a kind of social regression: the films made during this era expose both the pervasiveness of covert minstrelsy and the contradictions many Black artists faced behind the screen.

Future correspondence during *Thanks Pal*'s pre-production phase would continue to stress the importance of handling this picture's choreography with extreme "care" due to the nature of the film's soundtrack as if jazz music necessitated overtly sexual dancing. The film also ran into many wardrobe problems: Breen continuously urged Joy to modify the women's costumes:

February 18, 1943

Dear Colonel Joy:

We have received costume changes Nos. 9, 7, and 11, worn by Lena Horne in your proposed picture STORMY WEATHER.

Changes Nos. 9 and 7 are acceptable. However, change No. 11 is not acceptable, as it seems to expose too much of Miss Horne's breasts.

You understand, of course, that our final judgment will be based upon the finished picture.

Cordially yours,
Joseph I. Breen[2]

CODA 333

February 23, 1943

Dear Colonel Joy:

With regard to the wardrobe stills of Cleo Herndon for your proposed picture THANKS PAL (STORMY WEATHER) we suggest you raise it in front, so as to avoid any danger of her breasts being exposed from any possible camera angle.

With every good wish, I am,

Cordially yours,
Joseph I. Breen[3]

Despite some censorship hurdles along the way, no doubt exacerbated by its all-Black cast and "licentious" soundtrack, *Stormy Weather* lived up to its White expectations, which according to the *Hollywood Reporter* was sure to "Mop up at Boxoffice."[4] Producers were banking on its Black actors and Africanist aesthetics to please trade reviewers and audiences in most states, claiming that nobody needed a "crystal ball, an Ouija board, or a voodoo charm to aid in the prediction" that *Stormy Weather* would be an all-around success, an "extravaganza in every sense of the wor[]d."[5] Thus, at the height of the war, Americans at home were returning to the tried and true comfort of "Negro" entertainment; the alleged inclusion of Black performers in Hollywood was highly visible, yet a quiet narrative of racial difference was still crystal clear.

Running parallel to and at odds with James G. Thompson's Double V Campaign was a push in Hollywood to showcase Black artistry (both the artists and their vernaculars) rather than simply casting Black performers in menial roles.[6] On the surface, films like *Stormy Weather* and *Cabin in the Sky*—both released in 1943—did seem to address some of the discrimination Black actors experienced in Hollywood in a notable way. The rhetoric used to both advertise and memorialize these films, however, perpetuated as much loss as it did a victory. The White press's appraisal of *Stormy Weather* as sure to "mop up" alluded to a long-standing correlation in Hollywood between Black performers and "the help," and the Ouija board and voodoo charm references in the review were hinting at a kind of "black magic." Both themes, along with the limpid notes of the film's opening cakewalk, thus reveal the all-Black cast as a veneer of onscreen equality and bolstered key tropes dating back to the nineteenth-century minstrel stage.

334   CODA

For *Stormy Weather*'s Black audience, it was easier to see through such a façade. While the film was heavily praised by the White press, Black news outlets gave *Stormy* significantly less attention than they did *Cabin*—released just three months earlier—and its coverage of the film was very mixed. For one thing, *Stormy* was released amid race riots across the country, kicked off by the infamous zoot suit riot in Los Angeles earlier that summer. Cab Calloway, known for his embrace of the zoot suit, and the film's zoot-suited ensemble dancers were not exactly good press in 1943, when the summer race riots were initially spawned as a reaction to the manufacturing and wearing of these wide-cut suits.[7] The Black press's coverage of these more urgent matters no doubt overshadowed film coverage. It might also have even been a conscious choice, not to draw too much attention to the film's glorification of zoot-suit culture. Furthermore, the film's all-Black cast made it "acceptable" for screening in some of the South's often-restricted cities, but in many ways the film's wider-accessibility was a detriment. As Arthur Knight notes was the case with *Cabin*, a southern audience often forced filmmakers "to balance progressive and conservative impulses and demands, both in terms of form and content."[8] This helps to explain the mixed reviews the film received from the Black press as well as the diverse academic appraisal of the film's various acts. While I recognize that multiple interpretations of the film's individual numbers exist, each arguably as complex as Bill Robinson or Cab Calloway's image, I am specifically interested in how imagery such as that found in the opening cakewalk, "African Dance," and "Diga Diga Doo," evaded the censors.

This final chapter tracks the ways in which the Code seemed to tighten around issues of Black sexuality during World War II while easing up on what was appropriate in depictions of race, despite increasing pressure on the Production Code Administration from the Black press and vocal organizations like the NAACP. The all-Black cast film, like *Stormy Weather*, was but a pretense that real integration was occurring. Less glaring were the all-Black large ensemble numbers featuring exceptional Black entertainers within films that were otherwise White, giving consumers a false sense of progress. "The Cabin in the Sky Girl, Lena Horne" and "She's Hot, Hazel Scott" became publicity catchphrases for *I Dood It* (1943),[9] which exploited Black artistry while still failing to give these artists roles that were integral to the plot or any meaningful compensation for their labor. That Hollywood relied on these song and dance scenes to save otherwise "inhumanely onerous" films and yet still treated esteemed performers without any sort of equanimity speaks

CODA   335

volumes.[10] Meanwhile, Eddie Cantor's use of visible blackface would forever be excused since his mask had become ineradicably linked to his flesh. His typical blackface schtick is recuperated in films like *Show Business* (1944) and *If You Knew Susie* (1948),[11] which not only re-utilize his celebrated banjo-eye look but also recycle many of his musical hits and salvage old stock footage.

But the most popular musical trend throughout this World War II–era was to capitalize on Irving Berlin's successful American songbook as a means of re-establishing entertainment, and specifically the minstrel show, as patriotic. *Holiday Inn* (1942) and *This is the Army* (1943) do exactly that: in a grand finale so outrageous that its contents could only be classified as aesthetic camp, the musicals of this era engage with minstrelsy on every possible level.[12] If we write off these routines and films as *just* bad art or kitsch—as a lot of "serious" scholarship tends to do—we miss an opportunity for "serious admiration and study" of an important and ambivalent wartime representational politic.[13] When all of covert minstrelsy's layers interact in synchronicity, not only do the most visible elements (e.g., blackface) pass as "American," but their invisible features are forever sealed in the American songbook. I wish I could say that this story of covert minstrelsy from 1927 to 1954 closes out on a high note, but the grand finale here is really just minstrelsy repackaged as "White Christmas."[14] Instead, I conclude much where I began, with Berlin's music, new optical technology, and female sex appeal as means of covering up one social narrative so that some members of the nation can feel good about the state of the "union."

The curtain opens to expose a giant cake stacked high with brown-skinned chorines dressed in daisy bonnets in the foreground against a backdrop of two even larger American flags. Similar to the Goldwyn Girls' charade in The Kid from Spain, *these women have minstrel faces painted on the back sides of their bonnets, parts of the costume that seem to have been omitted from Production Code files, either never approved or since vanished. [FIG. C.1, top] Unlike Goldwyn's girls, however, their costumes come high up above their breasts leaving no room for even the slightest hint at cleavage. In the opening shot, the audience only sees the racial caricature, bopping side to side with a big plastered-on grin. Meanwhile the male ensemble encircles the female chorus, the tails of their long minstrel coats flapping with each high-stepping kick. The emcee—James "Jim" Reese Europe played by actor Ernest Whitman—interrupts "Camptown Races" to invite members of the audience to join the cakewalk. Bill Williamson (Bill Robinson) trying desperately to*

FIGURE C.1 (*Top*) The opening image of the cakewalk in *Stormy Weather* (*SW*), 1943 (Private collection); (*Middle left*) Ensemble member Lucille Battle (uncredited) poses for a wardrobe still to be approved by the PCA for the cakewalk costume in *Stormy Weather*. (Margaret Herrick Library); (*Middle right*) Uncredited ensemble member poses for a wardrobe still to be approved by the PCA for the "Diga Diga Doo" costume in *Stormy Weather*. (Margaret Herrick Library); (*Bottom*) Production still featuring Bill Robinson, Lena Horne, and Emmett 'Babe' Wallace from "Diga Diga Doo." (Private collection)

win over Selina Rogers (Lena Horne) invites her to join him on the dance floor. The minstrel caricatures continue to haunt the stage in the background as Williamson and Rogers continue, unfazed, with their dialogue.

Diga Doos and Diga Don'ts

There is nothing covert about *Stormy Weather's* opening cakewalk, but the PCA seems to have turned a blind eye to the back sides of these bonnets. As one sees in the photo on the middle left, [FIG C.1] Lucille Battle models only the front side of the costume for review. And since no person was in black-face per se, the use of such makeup did not need to be justified. The entire film is a series of nods toward blackface without the use of literal burnt cork, except for F. E Miller and Johnny Lee's "indefinite talk" routine performed in blackface.

To be fair, the film as a whole purportedly seeks to showcase some of Hollywood's leading Black performers while also "paying tribute" to iconic Black artists and revues who/which paved the way for Black stars Lena Horne, Bill Robinson, and Cab Calloway's success. Thus, if a number like the cakewalk is specifically "citing" Black history by alluding to shows like *Shuffle Along* (1921), *Blackbirds of 1928*, and *The Cotton Club Parade of 1933*, the minstrel bonnets are appropriate (re)presentations; minstrel caricature *is* a significant component of early twentieth-century Black performance.

Stormy Weather's cakewalk is further complicated, like so many of the numbers in this film, because more than one interpretation is always at play. It holds what Jayna Brown has called "multi-signifying power." Complex racial mimesis sits at the heart of the cakewalk's many origin stories, the most common of which locates its development on slave plantations as a means of the Black enslaved parodying the styles and mannerisms of White plantation owners. As a kind of "forced entertainment with satirical meanings hidden in full view of the masters," the cakewalk was born out of resistance.[15] This multi-signifying power holds true on the concert stage as well for performers like Aida Overton Walker who, like Cab Calloway, managed to obtain cross-over status by asserting herself (and her performance) through strategic marketing and talent. Walker learned how to "deliver the hyperreal, the domain of desires" to an audience seeking her own reification.[16]

That *Stormy Weather's* all-Black cast film was produced and managed by a White creative team situates the film in the same sort of contrived

338   CODA

"marketplace" as Walker and Calloway; the notorious Irving Mills (Calloway's manager) was even the film's production advisor. Thus, we can assume that this cakewalk, like many of *Stormy*'s dance numbers, embraces the ability to multi-signify, especially considering the presence of Jim Europe, Stephen Foster's "Camptown Races," and the camp-like nature of these chorines' costumes.[17] But even if we accept this film as offering both a narrative and a counter-narrative, the question remains, how is it that such blatant racial caricature even made it past the censors? Beginning with the opening cakewalk, we can track a whole history of covert minstrelsy, connecting each loosely related scene featuring Bill Robinson (and his tap dancing) like dots along a map of this sneaky practice's numerous guises and variations.

Immediately following the cakewalk is a classic example of southern repossession. Dressed in a plantation worker's clothes, Robinson performs a sand dance alongside the Tramp Band aboard a Memphis riverboat passing through New Orleans. The clothes he wears here are almost identical to those he wore in *Dixie* and *The Littlest Rebel*, conceding that not much about racial representation really changed between 1930 and 1943. The subsequent "Diga Diga Doo" and "African Dance" numbers epitomize the primitive chic and even put the extreme costumes in *Ali Baba* to shame.[18] [FIG. C.1, middle right and bottom]

How and why did all of this outdated material make its way into this all-Black film in 1943? Twentieth Century Fox spins the whole film as a tribute—"a tribute to the Negro race and the contribution it has made to entertainment," according to *Trade Showing* and "a tribute the great trouper Bill Robinson" according to *Weekly Variety*.[19] But if the critics of this so-called tribute thought that they were doing the "Negro race" any favors by describing such talent as "mopping up" and "barbaric"—well, they were not. *Trade Showing* writes of Dunham, "Katherine Dunham and her group lend barbaric rhythm to the spectacle dance numbers."[20] Spectacle this film was, politically correct, it was not, even for its time. Most curious of all is how material that is so clearly racist went "unnoticed" despite the PCA's meticulous demands for wardrobe and lyric revision around issues of sexuality. The Production Code files of films made during the same period featuring White dancers were not nearly as scrupulous in their demands for covering up the female body, even when tap dance or other predominantly Africanist forms were used. Just look at Eleanor Powell's high-slitted hula skirt and bra she wears in her tribute to the Hawaiian Islands in *Honolulu*. The Black artists who performed Africanist rhythmic traditions in Hollywood faced a double standard when it came to their image and the rhetoric surrounding that representation.[21] During the war and for years thereafter, White women who performed blacksound could flaunt their sexuality, while Black artists who performed the same blacksound had to cover themselves up completely.

Setting Up Camp during the War

As was the case during the Great Depression, Hollywood held a certain responsibility to the American people during the Second World War: films were regarded as a necessary form of entertainment, not meant to be didactic so much as a source of distraction and amusement, and like the minstrel show of the nineteenth century, they were a way of bringing Americans from varying economic classes and backgrounds closer together. Of course, certain members of the nation were still being left out of such recourse. I offer one possible explanation for why the films made between 1942 and 1945 exhibit a form of social regression with regard to race.

Many of the musicals made during this window exemplify a kind of covert minstrelsy gone wild: not only do a large percentage of them contain visible blackface, but they, like many of the cartoons made in the mid-1930s, exhibit all the tropes, guises, and variations that define the practice. I would like to suggest that these musicals fall into a category of aesthetic camp, as defined by Susan Sontag in her eminent notes on the subject. Sontag offers a series of criteria rather than a strict definition of camp that seem to convene around notions of artificiality, style at the expense of content, and a certain degree of outdatedness. The spaciousness of Sontag's criteria lends itself particularly well to covert minstrelsy, but if we want to be more specific, Mark Booth proposes a narrower yet still applicable definition of the practice: "To be camp is to present oneself as being committed to the marginal with a commitment greater than the marginal merits."[22] My supposition that covert minstrelsy during this era epitomizes a camp aesthetic is based both on Booth's definition and Sontag's broad criteria. The willfully hackneyed nature of some of these musicals made during the war are—I propose—what allowed them to be overlooked by the censors.

Like minstrel performances that signify on multiple registers simultaneously, camp vacillates between "shameless insincerity" and the "provocative."[23] Broadcasting such mixed signals must have made it difficult to criticize such material during the war when part of minstrelsy's allure was

340   CODA

tied to White patriotism. That is, its elements of cultural "slumming" were so tied to American entertainment and thus a particular narrative of nostalgia that for it to be *a*-patriotic was almost impossible. This might partially explain the PCA's oversights during this period despite the material being *blatantly* tactless and racially offensive. Before continuing this train of thought, though, allow me to offer some of Sontag's key points:

"Camp sees everything in quotation marks"[24]: **the Citational guise**
"Camp taste identifies with what it is enjoying"[25]: **the Tribute guise**
"Camp is the glorification of 'character' ": **the Bill Robinson effect**
"What camp taste responds to is 'instant character' "[26]: **the Protean**
"[Camp] incarnates a victory of 'style' over 'content,' 'aesthetics' over 'morality,' of irony over tragedy"[27]: **Irving Berlin's music**
The combination of "travesty, impersonation, and theatricality"[28]: **primitive chic**
"Camp proposes a comic vision of the world"[29]: **the Gabriel variation**
"Camp is playful, anti-serious": **Eddie Cantor**

The collision of all these aesthetic qualities repeatedly occurs in the World War II–era Hollywood musical. Placing certain ideas in the context of parody, satire, or even camp tends to absolve the creator of social responsibility. During the war, the PCA exerted most of its energy on protecting the image of America's foreign allies (i.e., the signatories to the 1941 Declaration of the United Nations) and was particularly cautious around the topic of religion, which included both an attentiveness to anti-Semitic slurs and a hypervigilance surrounding the depiction of sexuality (and specifically Black sexuality) so as not to offend the Catholic Church. Aesthetic camp provided a framework for deactivating the seriousness of racism that still pervaded the United States while also offering Americans "the spirit of extravagance" that proved to be a necessary distraction during the war.[30] To the average White American, these films were good because they were "awful" and they were made even better if they could also deliver robust nationalism, no matter what the cost. Thus, it is not that camp is political—this would in fact contradict Sontag—so much as it offers a progressive form of presenting the old (limitless) imagination.

An orchestra of White jazz musicians dressed in plantation costumes like those frequently worn by Al Jolson, plays the opening of notes of "Abraham,"

FIGURE C.2 (*Top*) Bing Crosby, Marjorie Reynolds, and ensemble performing "Abraham" in *Holiday Inn*, 1942; (*Middle*) Eddie Cantor, George Murphy, Joan Davis, Constance Moore, and ensemble performing "Dinah" in *Show Business*, 1944; (*Bottom*) Vera-Ellen, John Brascia, Bing Crosby, Rosemary Clooney, Danny Kaye, and ensemble perform "Mandy" in *White Christmas*, 1954. (Private collection)

one of many Irving Berlin's hits in Holiday Inn. *Bing Crosby hobbles onstage dressed like Abraham Lincoln but incongruously caked in blackface (like the musicians) and wearing white minstrel gloves. The lyrics he sings commemorate the sixteenth president and celebrate him as the man who "set the darky free." The camera cuts backstage to Louise Beavers in one of her distinctive Mammy roles also singing words of praise to two pick-like children eating apple scraps. It becomes clear that "Abraham" sung as a Negro spiritual, as it is, elicits an ironic biblical undertone. We have heard notes of this history before—in* Wonder Bar, *for example—where Black oppression is reversed by Abe Lincoln, Abraham, or Gabriel, a story puzzlingly always told by White men in blackface. The camera cuts back to the stage, zooming out to show off the Inn's blackened wait staff (dressed very similarly to the female cakewalk performers in* Stormy Weather *with daisy-like bonnets and polka dots); they sing and dance in praise of Lincoln as well. Marjorie Reynolds (dubbed by Martha Mears) also in blackface and dressed as a Little Eva caricature continues the tribute. Reynolds sits down after her solo, eyes fixed on Bing Crosby who will finish out this strange reworking of the Gabriel variation. The camera zooms in, capturing in the same frame Bing Crosby in his blackface tribute to Abraham, the White jazz orchestra in their citation of Jolson's plantation act, a combination of southern repossession and early blackface cinema, and a prominent American flag. "That's why we celebrate... Abraham. Abrahaaaaam." [FIG. C.2, top]*

Named the "lightheartedly patriotic musical" by the *New York Times, Holiday Inn* is a perfect example of the kind of outlandish patriotism Hollywood exhibited during the War.[31] While the same means are used to "justify" the visible blackface—e.g., southern repossession, the show-within-a-show formula, the Gabriel variation, the citational, the tribute, the sonic, etc.—it happens all at once in the most ludicrous manner. It converts the more serious matters of slavery and the Civil War into costumes and props, something frivolous. Which is not to say some of the more covert means of justifying this scene to the PCA do not appear. The dialogue between Jim Hardy (Crosby) and Linda Mason (Reynolds) that precedes "Abraham" marginalizes blackface, narratively writing it off as a more sullied art, yet still tied to the roots of American entertainment and thus applicable:

Hardy: *"I thought it over and I think your number would go over better in blackface."*

Mason: *"I look terrible in this stuff. I don't even know how to put it on."*

Hardy: *"Oh, I'll put it on. I broke in as a boot black, you know?"*

Mason: *"Ohhhhhh. For a month and half I've been thinking about how pretty I was going to look tonight. Here's my punishment for thinking so well of myself."* [FIG. I.1, bottom]

This dialogue—which implies that even in 1942, blackface always made a number "better" for the average White audience *and* carried a kind of degenerative or debased art stigma—was evidently enough to satisfy the PCA, and the film was just over-the-top *enough* that the White press completely bought into such aesthetic kitsch. The *Times* described it as "all very easy and graceful; it never tries too hard to dazzle."[32] Such aesthetic camp as a form of American jingoism during these years was pervasive.

With the goal of boosting morale during the war, Michael Curtiz adapted Irving Berlin's 1942 Broadway musical *This Is the Army* for the screen. In it, Jerry Jones (George Murphy), a song and dance man, is drafted into the army for World War I and stages a revue called *Yip Yip Yaphank*. Twenty-five years later, Jerry's son, Johnny (Ronald Reagan), stages another musical that includes Berlin's now-famous minstrel song "Mandy." Sontag's description of camp as "a mode of seduction—one which employs flamboyant mannerisms susceptible of double interpretation: gestures full of duplicity with a witty meaning for cognoscenti and another, more impersonal for outsiders" fully materializes in this version of "Mandy."[33] The large-scale tap dance number that ensues is ALL these things:

The lights come up on a man in full blackface, lips exaggerated, eyes outlined in contrasting white paint, white gloves, and a zoot-inspired minstrel suit. He serenades his audience with the opening notes of "Mandy" crooning them in front of a gigantic banjo while an ensemble of uniformed Army men line the raked steps with military precision. Soon, more men dressed like the first appear, along with a dozen men dressed as "Island" women, precursors to next year's rollout of Miss Chiquita. Donned in the most lavish pink and green satin dresses and brownface, they couple with the minstrel men to perform a classic soft-shoe, momentarily breaking into a recognizable Virginia essence step while the soundtrack seamlessly shifts to Stephen Foster's "Swanee River." It is loud, colorful, and unabashedly inappropriate, yet when the music returns to "Mandy" and the curtain starts to close, the crowd goes wild. George Murphy greets the performers backstage: "And you kids were worried about a minstrel

344   CODA

number being too old fashioned. Why it worked just as well tonight as it did in the old show."

You might recall from chapter 4 that "Mandy" performed by George Murphy and Eddie Cantor in *Kid Millions* was originally written by Berlin in 1918 for the army-themed musical revue *Yip Yip Yaphank*, which followed the format of a traditional minstrel show. We thus find ourselves back in the command of the citational guise justifying blackface through the minstrel show-within-a-show, which is both a citation of a previous minstrel show and a reference to Murphy's history with the song. In the 1943 version, the gender play and brownface in combination seem to make the use of blatant minstrel makeup more palatable to White audiences while the camp created by these coincident masquerades vindicates the cross-dressing elements from censorship scrutiny. This dance, along with the rest of the film was, according the *New York Times*, "the freshest, most endearing, the most rousing musical tribute to the American fighting man that has come out of World War II," and a "warmly reassuring document on the state of the nation."[34] Furthermore Murphy's salutation as the performers exit the stage is a reminder of the ways in which Hollywood saw the minstrel show as nostalgic and thus patriotic, partially explaining its strong presence during the war.

What we might view as aesthetic camp today was viewed by Hollywood and the White press in the early 1940s as catchy, patriotic, and in good taste: it "never commits a breach of taste by violently waving the flag.... [I]t offers a reason for celebration."[35] At once shamelessly facile and sincere in its homage to American history, the "Abraham" and "Mandy" numbers exhibited the current need for démodé disguise. Like *Holiday Inn* and *This Is the Army*, *Show Business* also proved to be a success, despite its outdated content. Occurring right at the climax of the film is "Dinah," performed by Cantor and Murphy in minstrel masks and Constance Moore and Joan Davis, in blackface. [FIG. C.2, middle] This is a typical show-within-a-show set in the South. "Dinah" is also performed by two men who were notorious in Hollywood for performing in minstrel shows-within-shows. As we have now seen in countless films, the men utilize the full minstrel mask with exaggerated lips and eyes while the women merely don black face paint. Cantor's use of burnt cork seems to justify not only his own mask, but those of his fellow thespians; "Dinah" was so tied to Cantor that it would have been unthinkable not to perform this piece as a minstrel song. All these features ostensibly mollified the PCA during the war, which is why I posit a correlation between aesthetic camp and an ambivalent nationalism that Hollywood expressed during this era. Thus, it is not that the censors let up so much as the minstrel show, and specifically blackface, transformed into a discourse of White patriotism that was consequently excused during the war when placed in camp's quotation marks. Thus, camp covers a collective trauma, hiding what Saidiya Hartman refers to as an "inescapable prison house of the flesh or the indelible drop of blood." Aesthetic camp that utilizes the blackface mask as a form of White patriotism involves a historical branding that continuously reiterates, inscribes, and re-ascribes the tortured Black body at the same time that it seeks to silence that pain.[36]

Missing Blackface

The use of highly visible blackface in film greatly diminished in the years immediately following World War II. In large part this was due to the vocality of groups like the NAACP and other progressive organizations for which the Double V campaign had had some (even if small) impact. In films like *If You Knew Susie*, we see the ways in which the narrative allowed for the presence of highly nostalgic and visible blackface at the same time it would begin to write a new, albeit *superficial*, narrative of blackface for the nation. As it had in animation, blackface became part of the gag.

Susie begins with "My How the Time Goes By," the most over-the-top tap dance in blackface performed since "Mandy," this time danced by Sam and Susie Parker (Cantor and Joan Davis). Before the curtains open, an oversized animated caricature of Cantor sings the opening lyrics while doing a dance solely with its minstrel gloves and shifty eyes, overstressing the already exaggerated features of a minstrel costume. [FIG. C.3, bottom] Following the big dance number, the off-camera audience is immediately taken backstage where we learn that this is Susie's last performance on the vaudeville circuit. She and Sam are to retire for a better life. Like the critique of blackface embedded in Reynold's *Holiday Inn* performance, Davis's dialogue comments on the outdatedness of blackface, as if discussing blackface as something she was *forced* to do her whole career absolves her of her social responsibility: "There I was rubbing and rubbing and finally I realized that never again will I have to take off *blackface*." Everyone backstage laughs, including Cantor who comes over to give his wife a kiss. The gag is predictable as he besmirches

FIGURE C.3 (*Top*) Duke Ellington and "the boys" perform live in London, 1930. (Private collection); (*Middle left*) Adelaide Hall performs "To Have You, To Hold You" in *An All-Colored Vaudeville Show*, 1935; (*Middle right*) Joe Louis, James "Stump" Cross, Harold "Stumpy" Cromer (uncredited), and Black ensemble in "That's What the Well-Dressed Man in Harlem Will Wear," 1943; Opening caricature of Eddie Cantor in "My, How the Time Goes By" from *If You Knew Susie*, 1948. (Private collection)

his wife with the paint he has yet to remove, subtly commenting on the omnipresence of his (Cantor's) mask. The film was not much of a success, but it was confirmation that Cantor would always be synonymous with blackface, and blackface, whether visible or not, would always haunt American entertainment. The *New York Times* commented on this film, " 'If You Knew Susie' is just the proof needed, if, at this late date, there are a couple of doubting Thomases doubting Eddie Cantor is not indestructible . . . [this film] is proof that Mr. Cantor is as solid as the Rock of Gibraltar and just as changeless."[37] And the attachment to blackface would remain just as changeless.

The major differences between the films made during the war and those just after is that there was not the same need for the country to come together around a nostalgic pastime such as blackface in such a blatant way. This is not to say that highly visible blackface disappeared overnight; instead, it slowly began fading while the invisible components of covert minstrelsy would move into center stage. Accordingly, we see a rise in the sonic guise, a more frequent use of painted minstrel imagery in the background [FIG C.3] and a large number of biopics that pay tribute to famous blackface performers (e.g., *The Al Jolson Story* (1946) and *The Eddie Cantor Story* (1953)). By the end of Breen's run as the "watchdog of movie morals" in October 1954, most visible instances of blackface had been expurgated.[38]

* * *

Irving Berlin's *White Christmas* was released within a week of Breen's departure, making it one of the last films he oversaw from start to finish. *White Christmas* is notable for several reasons: for one, it was the first film to be released in VistaVision, a silent studio camera that used twice the surface area of standard 35mm film allowing for a clearer picture on bigger screens.[39]

The film also introduced some new hit songs—"Sisters" and "Gee, I Wish I Was Back in the Army," for example, and reprised several of Berlin's classics, including three from *Holiday Inn*. In addition to the Oscar-winning (1942) "White Christmas," Paramount resurrected "Abraham," and "Mandy." But between the film's new widescreen format and use of Technicolor, these reprised numbers looked very different from their appearance in previous iterations. So, what then did the *New York Times* mean when it claimed that Paramount "has done 'White Christmas' up brown"? Was the Africanist presence somehow detectable despite these dance numbers' lack of "brown" bodies? It seems the lack of "brown" in these numbers was something of a letdown to the press, as suggested in quotes like this: "Oddly enough, the

348   CODA

confection is not so tasty as one might suppose. The flavoring is largely in the line-up and not in the output of the cooks."[40]

Nothing like its rendition in *Holiday Inn*, "Abraham" is a sprightly tap dance duet choreographed by Robert Alton and performed by Vera-Ellen and John Brascia. Full of highly syncopated jazz rhythms (one of Alton's trademarks) accented by snaps, claps, and knee swivels as well as the isolations for which Jack Cole became so well-known, this routine epitomizes a 1940s/1950s theatrical jazz aesthetic clearly inspired by *bharata natyam* and lindy hop, but also completely absent of East Indian and Black dancers.[41] Because nothing about this version publicizes "minstrelsy," it would be difficult to make any sort of connection between this extremely speeded-up version and the Abraham Lincoln minstrel show in *Holiday Inn* unless one were well versed in covert minstrelsy's guises. Perhaps "brown" was a reference to the way the creative team tried to decorate a jazz aesthetic White. This is even more glaring in "Mandy," part of the film's apogean "Minstrel Show," which merely covers up visible blackface and a camp aesthetic with White female sexuality, or a fragmented simulation thereof. [FIG. C.2, bottom]

The spotlight shines on Bing Crosby and Danny Kaye, both wearing black tuxedos with red shirts and matching gloves. Behind them, a white backdrop with large, abstract caricatures of the two prominently displaying their red minstrel gloves. As Crosby and Kaye continue singing, the backdrop lifts and reveals two brazenly painted red minstrel gloves plucking banjo strings on the back wall and one dozen men in green satin tuxedos onstage. Twelve scandalously dressed women then appear costumed like Christmas gifts, their large bows both covering and drawing attention to their bottoms. As the ensemble members rattle their tambourines, Rosemary Clooney becomes the interlocuter and engages Crosby and Kaye (Mr. Tambo and Mr. Bones) for the minstrel show's olio. "That's a joke, that was told, in the minstrel days we miss. When Georgie Primrose used to sing and dance to a song like this: MANDY. Ooooohhh, Ooooohhh, MANDY!" A very svelte Vera-Ellen rises from upstage, her long legs made even longer by the camera's calculated upward tilt and her strappy stilettos. The lines are clean. Her legs are bare. Her long red glitter gloves accent her long-sleeved, high-necked silver-trimmed, white-sequined leotard. "MANDY." She flirts with the men in green tuxedos as she makes her way down the long flight of red stairs to eventually join Crosby and Kaye as the centerpiece in this minstrel show's afterpiece. Crosby and Kaye then pass Vera-Ellen off to John Brascia for another spicy theatrical jazz duet. Eventually the two are rejoined by the full ensemble. The entire cast closes out the number with song, dance, and red tambourines on which are painted the attributes of a "sexy woman." The members of the chorus strike their red tambourines on the 2s and the 4s, accenting the Africanist pulse with those painted plastered-on smiles and lustful gazes, the face of the modern minstrel show. [FIG. C.2, bottom] *Preserving more than a century of saturation, this is minstrelsy in Vista Vision.*

Writing on the dynamic between style and substance within a camp context, Mitchell Morris challenges Sontag's "style over content" proclamation, instead suggesting that "substance, when it breaks the style, is what matters most.... [C]amp claps its hands loudly to show that it believes in essences."[42] The camp of *White Christmas* draws blatant attention to its illusions and to use the words of Richard Dyer, "It is in the recognition of [such] illusion that camp finds reality."[43] While intensely saturated, the essence of this film (and others made during this era) is distinct in its illusion. And for this, the White press applauded loudly.

While I imagine Bosley Crowther, writing for the *New York Times*, meant something quite different by his review of *White Christmas*, his assessment encompasses exactly what a theory of covert minstrelsy hopes to dismantle. He writes, "The colors on the big screen are rich and luminous, the images are clear and sharp, and rapid movements are got without blurring—or very little—such as sometimes is seen on other large screens."[44] The colors were indeed vibrant, a glaring reflection of the ways Hollywood has long projected nineteenth-century minstrel logic through a modern lens. By the time *White Christmas* premiered, Hollywood had perfected this charade, rendering White performers the celebrated ventriloquists of an Africanist aesthetic. To the passive consumer, these performances—and acts of transfer—occur too rapidly to process. Yet, if one tracks this history of racial caricature on the big screen from the beginning and recognizes the several guises at play, even the images (and imagery) projected through this new technology read clear and sharp. The careful spectator of these films will slow these sequences down, uncover the countless artists who contributed to their making but never once received credit, see through the soundtracks' cracks and fissures, and strip away the citations. On the surface, these films tell one story; behind the screen these narratives break down, and the picture's brilliance fades.

350 CODA

Notes

1. Stone, Andrew. *Stormy Weather* (20th Century-Fox, 1943). January 7, 1943–February 22, 1950. MS Hollywood, Censorship, and the Motion Picture Production Code, 1927–1968: History of Cinema, Series 1, Hollywood and Production Code Administration, Margaret Herrick Library.
2. Ibid.
3. Ibid.
4. "'Stormy Weather' Certain to Mop Up at Boxoffice," *Hollywood Reporter* (Hollywood, CA), May 27, 1943.
5. Ibid.
6. The Black newspaper, the *Pittsburgh Courier*, launched the Double V, or Double Victory, campaign in 1942. The first "V" was a symbol the United States and its allies had adopted to represent "victory over aggression." The Courier was demanding a second "V" for the African Americans who risked their lives fighting for their country. The second "V" stood for the rights of Black people who should be treated as first class citizens.
7. When war rationing went into effect, people caught wearing these suits were seen as criminals, which quickly became a way of incriminating marginalized groups, since those wearing these suits were largely from Black and Mexican-American communities living in Los Angeles and New York City. The Zoot Suit riot began when a series of racially violent acts ensued between American servicemen and Latinx zoot-suiters in Los Angeles.
8. Arthur Knight, *Disintegrating the Musical: Black Performance and American Musical Film* (Durham, NC: Duke University Press, 2002), 149.
9. Vincente Minnelli, *I Dood It* (September 1943; USA: Metro-Goldwyn-Meyer), Film.
10. "'I Dood It,' a One Man Comedy, the Same Being Red Skelton, with an Assist from Eleanor Powell, Opens at Paramount," *New York Times,* November 11, 1943.
11. Edwin L. Marin, *Show Business* (December 8, 1944; USA: RKO Radio Pictures), Film; Gordon Douglas, *If You Knew Susie* (February 7, 1948; USA: RKO Radio Pictures), Film.
12. Mark Sandrich and Robert Allen, *Holiday Inn* (September 4, 1942; USA: Paramount Pictures), Film; Michael Curtiz, *This Is the Army* (August 14, 1943; USA: Warner Bros.), Film.
13. Susan Sontag, *Notes on "Camp"* (UK: Penguin Random House, 2018), 7.
14. Michael Curtiz, *This Is the Army* (October 14, 1954; USA: Paramount Pictures), Film.
15. Jayna Brown, *Babylon Girls: Black Women Performers and the Shaping of the Modern* (Durham, NC: Duke University Press, 2008), 130.
16. Thomas Postlewait, "The Hieroglyphic Stage: American Theatre and Society, Post–Civil War to 1945," in *The Cambridge History of American Theatre, 1870–1945*, vol. 2, ed. Don B. Wilmeth and Christopher Bigsby (Cambridge: Cambridge University Press, 1999), 161.
17. James Reese Europe is an interesting figure who deserves more attention than I have the space to give him (or his character) here. Historically it makes sense to put him in

CODA 351

this scene as both he and Bill Robinson were assigned to the 369th Infantry known as the "Harlem Hell-Fighters" band of the American Expeditionary Force. He has long been associated with racial uplift due to the tremendous success he had introducing Black music to the upper echelons of New York society, including the Vanderbilts and Astors. He also accompanied Irene and Vernon Castle with his own "society orchestra." It is precisely these associations, along with his partnerships with notable blackface performers, Ernest Hogan and Bert Williams, that further complicate his appearance in this cakewalk. For an excellent article on Europe and his contributions to jazz music, see R. Reid Badger, "James Reese Europe and the Prehistory of Jazz," *American Music* 7, no. 1, Special Jazz Issue (Spring 1989): 48–67.

18. The "African Dance" number is a perfect example of a performance that has been viewed critically and with opposition by the Black press and academics alike. Many scholars have critiqued the "African Dance" and the title song "Stormy Weather" as "provid[ing] a vehicle through which a counter-tradition of Black modernism and performance could be articulated." Hannah Durkin has argued that insofar as Bill Robinson represented "the innately rhythmic, highly sexualised jungle 'primitive'" in the "African Dance," he in fact "embodies a dialectical interplay of cultural imagery that facilitates complex—even contradictory—interpretations." That is, even if "African Dance" upholds an onslaught of racial stereotypes, the number itself allows Robinson to exceed Hollywood's limiting framework. Most notably, as Durkin argues, "it replaces notions of crude and comic physicality and artlessness with light-footed artistry and exceptional bodily control" reconfiguring a nineteenth century concept of Black masculinity so pervasive on the minstrel stage. Katherine Dunham's performance in "Stormy Weather" has been evaluated similarly: Katherine Dunham, whose technique was a combination of classical ballet vocabulary and movement learned in Haiti, Jamaica, Trinidad, and Martinique, in fact "offered a modernist revision of the racial aesthetic of the black nightclub tradition and restaged the history of black performance." See Hannah Durkin, "'Tap Dancing on the Racial Boundary': Racial Representation and Artistic Experimentation in Bill 'Bojangles' Robinson's *Stormy Weather* Performance," *IJAS Online*, No. 2 (2010): 98–99, 101; and Shane Vogel, "Performing 'Stormy Weather': Ethel Waters, Lena Horne, and Katherine Dunham," *South Central Review* 25, no. 1 (Spring 2008): 93–113.

19. "Stormy Weather," *Weekly Variety* (Hollywood, CA), May 27, 1943.

20. "Stormy Weather," *Trade Showing* (Hollywood, CA), June 2, 1943.

21. The Production Code files for *Cabin in the Sky* refer to the dancing as "orgiastic." See Production Code Administration Records, *In Re: "Cabin in the Sky," October 28, 1940,* p. 2. Letter. From Margaret Herrick Library, *The Production Code Administration Records, Cabin in the Sky, 1943,* https://digitalcollections.oscars.org/digital/collect ion/p15759coll30/id/1952 (accessed May 1, 2021).

22. Mark Booth, "Camp-Toi! On the Origins and Definitions of Camp," in *Camp: Queer Aesthetics and the Performing Subject: A Reader,* ed. Fabio Cleto (Edinburgh: Edinburgh University Press, 1999), 69.

23. Ibid.

24. Sontag, *Notes on "Camp,"* 9.

25. Ibid., 56.

352 CODA

26. Ibid., 21
27. Ibid., 24–25.
28. Ibid., 10.
29. Ibid., 26.
30. Ibid., 16.
31. "Irving Berlin's 'Holiday Inn' Co-Starring Bing Crosby and Fred Astaire, Has Navy Benefit Premiere at Paramount," *New York Times*, August 5, 1942.
32. Ibid.
33. Sontag, *Notes on "Camp,"* 13.
34. "The Screen," *New York Times*, July 29, 1943.
35. "Holiday Inn," *New York Times*, August 5, 1942.
36. Saidiya V. Hartman, *Scenes of Subjection: Terror, Slavery, and Self-Making in Nineteenth-Century America* (New York: Oxford University Press, 1997), 57–58.
37. "'If You Knew Susie,' New Feature at the Palace, Shows Eddie Cantor Cutting Usual Capers," *New York Times*, February 23, 1948.
38. "Joseph I. Breen, Film Code Chief," *New York Times*, December 8, 1965.
39. Martin Hart, "The Development of VistaVision: Paramount Marches to a Different Drummer," American Widescreen Museum, last revised November 2006, http://www.widescreenmuseum.com/widescreen/vvstory.htm.
40. Bosley Crowther, "'White Christmas' Bows at the Music Hall," *New York Times*, October 15, 1954.
41. For more on Jack Cole's unique style, see Teal Darkenwald, "Jack Cole and Theatrical Jazz Dance," in *Jazz Dance: A History of the Roots and Branches*, ed. Lindsay Guarino and Wendy Oliver (Gainesville: University Press of Florida, 2014), 82–88.
42. Mitchell Morris, *The Persistence of Sentiment: Essays on Pop Music in the 70s* (Berkeley: University of California Press, 2012), 207.
43. Richard Dyer, "Entertainment and Utopia," in *Only Entertainment*, ed. Richard Dyer (London: Routledge, 1992), 20.
44. Bosley Crowther, "'White Christmas' Review," *New York Times*, October 15, 1954.

APPENDIX

Excerpts from the Production Code (1934–1954)

The following excerpt is taken from "A Code to Govern the Making of Motion Pictures: The Reasons Supporting It and the Resolution for Uniform Interpretation" published by the Motion Picture Association of America and printed in 1955.[1]

PREAMBLE

The Motion Picture Production Code was formulated and formally adopted by The Association of Motion Picture Producers, Inc., (California) and The Motion Picture Association of America, Inc.* (New York) in March, 1930.**

Motion picture producers recognize the high trust and confidence which have been placed in them by the people of the world and which have made motion pictures a universal form of entertainment.

They recognize their responsibility to the public because of this trust and because entertainment and art are important influences in the life of a nation.

Hence, though regarding motion pictures primarily as entertainment without any explicit purpose of teaching or propaganda, they know that the motion picture within its own field of entertainment may be directly responsible for spiritual or moral progress, for higher types of social life, and for much correct thinking.

During the rapid transition from silent to talking pictures they realized the necessity and the opportunity of subscribing to a Code to govern the production of talking pictures and of reacknowledging this responsibility.

On their part, they ask from the public and from public leaders a sympathetic understanding of their purposes and problems and a spirit of cooperation that will allow them the freedom and opportunity necessary to bring the motion picture to a still higher level of wholesome entertainment for all the people.

*Until December 14, 1945, the Motion Picture Producers and Distributors of America, Inc.
**The Code as presented in this edition contains all revisions and amendments through 1954.

354 APPENDIX

THE PRODUCTION CODE

GENERAL PRINCIPLES

1. No picture shall be produced which will lower the moral standards of those who see it. Hence the sympathy of the audience shall never be thrown to the side of crime, wrongdoing, evil or sin.
2. Correct standards of life, subject only to the requirements of drama and entertainment, shall be presented.
3. Law, natural or human, shall not be ridiculed, nor shall sympathy be created for its violation.

PARTICULAR APPLICATIONS

I. CRIMES AGAINST THE LAW*

These shall never be presented in such a way as to throw sympathy with the crime as against law and justice or to inspire others with a desire for imitation.

1. **Murder**
   a. The technique of murder must be presented in a way that will not inspire imitation.
   b. Brutal killings are not to be presented in detail.
   c. Revenge in modern times shall not be justified.
2. **Methods of Crime** should not be explicitly presented.
   a. Theft, robbery, safe-cracking, and dynamiting of trains, mines, buildings, etc., should not be detailed in method.
   b. Arson must be subject to the same safeguards.
   c. The use of firearms should be restricted to essentials.
3. The illegal drug traffic, and drug addiction, must never be presented.

*See also Special Regulations on Crime on pages 7 and 8.

II. SEX

The sanctity of the institution of marriage and the home shall be upheld. Pictures shall not infer that low forms of sex relationship are the accepted or common thing.

1. **Adultery and Illicit Sex**, sometimes necessary plot material, must not be explicitly treated or justified, or presented attractively.
2. **Scenes of Passion**
   a. These should not be introduced except where they are definitely essential to the plot.
   b. Excessive and lustful kissing, lustful embraces, suggestive postures and gestures are not to be shown.
   c. In general, passion should be treated in such manner as not to stimulate the lower and baser emotions.

APPENDIX   355

3. **Seduction or Rape**
   a. These should never be more than suggested, and then only when essential for the plot. They must never be shown by explicit method.
   b. They are never the proper subject for comedy.
4. **Sex perversion** or any inference of it is forbidden.
5. White slavery shall not be treated.
6. Abortion, sex hygiene, and venereal diseases are not proper subjects for theatrical motion pictures.
7. Scenes of **actual childbirth**, in fact or in silhouette, are never to be presented.
8. **Children's sex organs** are never to be exposed.

III. VULGARITY

The treatment of low, disgusting, unpleasant, though not necessarily evil, subjects should be guided always by the dictates of good taste and a proper regard for the sensibilities of the audience.

IV. OBSCENITY

Obscenity in word, gesture, reference, song, joke, or by suggestion (even when likely to be understood only by part of the audience) is forbidden.

V. PROFANITY

Pointed profanity and every other profane or vulgar expression, however used, are forbidden.

No approval by the Production Code Administration shall be given to the use of words and phrases in motion pictures including, but not limited to, the following:

Bronx cheer (the sound); chippie; God, Lord, Jesus, Christ (unless used reverently); cripes; fairy (in a vulgar sense); finger (the); fire, cries of; Gawd; goose (in a vulgar sense); hot (applied to a woman); "in your hat"; Madam (relating to prostitution); nance; nuts (except when meaning crazy); pansy; razzberry (the sound); S.O.B.; sonof- a; tart; toilet gags; whore.

In the administration of Section V of the Production Code, the Production Code Administration may take cognizance of the fact that the following words and phrases are obviously offensive to the patrons of motion pictures in the United States and more particularly to the patrons of motion pictures in foreign countries:

Chink, Dago, Frog, Greaser, Hunkie, Kike, Nigger, Spig, Wop, Yid.

It should also be noted that the words "hell" and "damn", if used without moderation, will be considered offensive by many members of the audience. Their use, therefore, should be governed by the discretion and the prudent advice of the Code Administration.

VI. COSTUMES*

1. **Complete nudity** is never permitted. This includes nudity in fact or in silhouette, or any licentious notice thereof by other characters in the pictures.
2. **Undressing scenes** should be avoided, and never used save where essential to the plot.
3. **Indecent or undue exposure** is forbidden.
4. **Dancing costumes** intended to permit undue exposure or indecent movements in the dance are forbidden.

*See also Special Resolution on Costumes on page 8.

VII. DANCES

1. Dances suggesting or representing sexual actions or indecent passion are forbidden.
2. Dances which emphasize indecent movements are to be regarded as obscene.

VIII. RELIGION

1. No film or episode may throw **ridicule** on any religious faith.
2. **Ministers of religion** in their character as ministers of religion should not be used as comic characters or as villains.
3. **Ceremonies** of any definite religion should be carefully and respectfully handled.

IX. LOCATIONS

The treatment of bedrooms must be governed by good taste and delicacy.

X. NATIONAL FEELINGS

1. **The use of the Flag** shall be consistently respectful.
2. **The history**, institutions, prominent people and citizenry of all nations shall be represented fairly.

XI. TITLES

The following titles shall not be used:

1. Titles which are salacious, indecent, obscene, profane or vulgar.
2. Titles which suggest or are currently associated in the public mind with material, characters or occupations unsuitable for the screen.
3. Titles which are otherwise objectionable.

APPENDIX   357

XII. SPECIAL SUBJECTS

The following subjects must be treated within the careful limits of good taste:

1. **Actual hangings** or electrocutions as legal **punishments** for crime.
2. **Third degree** methods.
3. **Brutality** and possible gruesomeness.
4. **The sale of women,** or a woman selling her virtue.
5. **Surgical operations.**
6. **Miscegenation.**
7. **Liquor and drinking.**

Note

1. The full pamphlet can be accessed through the Core Collection Pamphlets located at the Margaret Herrick Library, Academy of Motion Picture Arts and Sciences, http://catalog.oscars.org/vwebv/holdingsInfo?bibId=7534.

Index

For the benefit of digital users, indexed terms that span two pages (e.g., 52–53) may, on occasion, appear on only one of those pages.
Figures are indicated by *f* following the page number

42nd Street, 112n.5, 132, 142–43
4 Blackbirds, the (Geraldine Harris, David Patillo, LeRoy Hurt, and Richard Davis), 144–45, 147–48, 308, 314–15, 317–18

"About a Quarter to Nine" 237
acousmatic, 13, 15, 88, 152–53
as related to Blackness, 13, 87
Aesop's Fables, 287–88
affected integration, 19, 21, 255–56, 322
See also integration
Africanist Aesthetic, 10–11, 12, 17, 18, 24, 49–53, 56–57, 58, 59, 62–64, 80, 97–99, 100–1, 109–10, 111, 149–50, 155, 171, 176, 191–92, 193–94, 203, 208–9, 212–13n.44, 221, 222–23, 231, 232, 233, 234, 237–38, 240, 241–43, 244, 254, 255–56, 261–62, 263–64, 265–66, 267, 268, 269–70, 271, 282, 288, 304–5, 309–10, 314, 322, 324, 325, 333, 338–39, 347–49
Aesthetic of the cool, 12, 167n.101, 198–99, 203–4, 219–20, 268, 269–70
call-and-response, 12, 50–51, 52–53, 155, 171, 240, 254, 269, 271
contrariety, 12, 56–57, 58
ephebism, 12, 52–53, 56–57
flexibility, 12
groove, 12, 153, 299–300
high affect juxtaposition, 12, 56–57
improvisation, 12, 33, 35, 50–52, 183, 184–85, 240, 243–44, 261–62
polycentrism, 12, 52, 109–10, 281
polyrhythm, 12, 18, 24, 49–53, 56–57, 62, 149–50, 193–94, 233, 237–38, 242–43, 288, 338–39, 348–49

See also Gottschild, Brenda Dixon; Thompson, Robert Farris
Alexander, Danny, 134–35
"Alexander's Ragtime Band," 50
Alhambra theatre, 264
Ali Baba Goes to Town, 18, 230, 252–59, 260–61, 263–64, 338
Al Jolson Story, the, 347
all-Black cast film, 23–24, 126, 127–28, 130–32, 134, 139, 140, 233–34, 334–35
See also *All-Colored Vaudeville Show;* *Cabin in the Sky; Harlem is Heaven;* race film; *Stormy Weather*
All-Colored Vaudeville Show, 134
"All God's Chillun' Got Rhythm" 234–35
Allen, Gracie, 190, 191–92, 194–95, 221–22
Altman, Rick, 33–34, 37–38, 59–60, 66n.22
Alton, Robert, 348
ambivalence, xv–xvi, 4, 7–8, 19, 50, 54, 55, 69n.80, 82–83, 125–26, 162–63n.49, 182, 224, 242–43, 285, 289–90, 291, 292–93, 296, 308–9, 310–12, 335, 344–45
American Indian, 5–6, 88, 89–90, 114n.33, 114–15n.34, 219n.ii
caricatures of, 16, 83, 87, 88–89, 90–91, 93–95, 115n.35, 263–64, 285–86, 296–98, 317–18
See also "playing Indian"; redface
Amos 'n' Andy, 83–84, 85–86, 90–91
amputation, 31–32, 185, 286, 298–99, 323–24
Anderson, Ivie, 234–35
Anderson, Perry, 242
Andrews Sisters, 19, 260–61, 317–18

360 INDEX

animal dances, 52, 198–99
    See also Peckin'
Ann-Doane, Mary, 92–93, 104, 260
Anthropomorphism, 11, 25, 285, 288–91,
    294, 295–96, 303–4
anti-Semitism, 2–3, 83–84, 114n.23, 121,
    293–95, 340
Any Bonds Today, 280–83
Apollo Theatre, 49, 175, 260–61
appropriation, 7–8, 93, 98–99, 176, 180–81,
    182–83, 197–98, 212–13n.44, 237–38,
    241, 252, 258, 263–64, 267
Aristo Films, 132
Armstrong, Louis, 240, 243–44, 282–83,
    306–9, 316, 321–22
    caricatures of, 306–8, 316, 319–20,
        321–22
Art Deco aesthetic, 69n.76, 204, 215–16n.75,
    227–28, 232
Astaire, Fred, 1, 12–13, 16–17, 24, 47–48,
    60–62, 142–43, 179–82, 183–90,
    186*f*, 192, 193–94, 197, 205–6,
    207, 211n.34, 213n.47, 216n.81,
    231, 242–44, 245, 314, 319–20, 321,
    322, 323
    in blackface, 1, 16–17, 24, 179–82,
        183–90, 197, 205–6, 243, 314
    See also *Puttin' on the Ritz; Swing Time;*
        techno-dialogic
At Home Abroad, 260
audio-vision, 40–41
    See also Chion, Michel
Aunt Jemima, 268–69, 319–20, 329n.78

Babes on Broadway, 142–43
Baghdad, 18, 252, 255–56, 257, 258
Baker, Houston, 69–70n.89
Baker, Josephine, 39–40, 69n.80, 113n.10,
    116n.66, 117n.74, 134, 254–55
Ball, Lucille, 172*f*, 173–74
    See also Goldwyn Girls; *Kid Millions*
Bañagale, Ryan, 62
Baphomet, 31–32
Battle, Lucille, 336*f*, 337
    See also *Stormy Weather*
Baudrillard, Jean, 157, 303–4
Beavers, Louise, 340–42
bebop, 269–70

becoming (state of), 6–8, 19, 76, 180–81
    See also "primal scene"
Benjamin, Walter, 157
Bennett, Joan, 48–49
Bentley, Gladys, 214n.50
Berkeley, Busby, 17–18, 21–23, 77, 95–96,
    112n.5, 219–20
    choreography and use of the camera,
        21–23, 75–77, 87, 91–95, 99, 103,
        104, 107, 109, 111, 115n.42, 115n.44,
        118n.87, 118n.88, 142–43, 223–24,
        228, 232–33
    on selecting women (*see*
        Goldwyn Girls)
Berlin, Irving
    biography, 50
    music, 21, 35, 47–48, 49–52, 56–58, 59–61,
        62, 63, 177–78, 200–1, 210n.9, 243, 312,
        335, 340–42, 343, 344, 347–48
bestial ambivalence, 285, 289–90, 292,
    296, 310–12
Betty Boop, 284–85
Bial, Henry, 81
Big Bad Wolf, 18, 121, 285, 288, 292–96
Big Broadcast of 1932, The, 73, 241
Big Chief Ugh-Amugh-Ugh, 296–98
Big Sea, 58, 70n.96, 70n.100
Bill Robinson effect, 11, 23–24, 128–29,
    138–39, 153–59, 176, 180, 183–89,
    191, 192–99, 203–9, 252, 286–87,
    309, 310–22, 340
    See also Robinson, Bill (caricatures of);
        stair dance; tribute guise (definition)
"Bill Robinson Stomp," 144
    See also *Harlem is Heaven*
Biographon, 33–34
Birth of the Blues, 243, 245
Black and Tan Fantasy, 134–35
Blackbirds of 1926, 124–25, 138–39
Blackbirds of 1927, 125, 137, 138–39
Blackbirds of 1928, 138–39, 140, 153,
    159n.2, 337
Blackbirds of 1930, 321–22
Black Bottom (dance), 52, 53–54
Black chorines, 246*f*, 247–48, 260, 317–
    18, 335–38
    See also *Harlem is Heaven*; LeGon, Jeni;
        Stormy Weather

Black consciousness, 129–30, 158, 233–34
  See also double consciousness
blacksound, 10, 13, 24–25, 38–39,
    112–13n.9, 149–51, 230, 245, 338–39
  See also Morrison, Matthew
Black heaven, 24–25, 227–39, 252,
    300, 304–5
  See also Gabriel variation; *Green
    Pastures,* the (film); *Green Pastures,*
    the (play)
Black sensibility, 12, 24, 63, 132, 134,
    149–50, 193–94
  See also Africanist aesthetic
Black Tuesday, 126
  See also Depression, Great
"Blame it on the Rumba," 251–52
Blanc, Mel, 285–86, 298–99, 305–8
Blues (musical style), 50–51, 70n.98,
    112–13n.9, 163n.58, 242
Blue Skies, 60–61, 62, 200–1, 211n.35
  See also "Puttin on the Ritz"
Bogle, Donald, 129–30
"Bojangles" 58, 60–61, 130–31, 135, 162n.34,
    165n.70, 183–89, 195, 207, 323–24
  See also "Bojangles of Harlem";
    Robinson, Bill
"Bojangles of Harlem," 1–2, 24, 60–61,
    179–90, 216n.81, 242–43
Boles, John, 150–51
Bombo, 236–37
Boogie Woogie Bugle Boy of Company 'B',
    19, 284–85
  See also *affected integration; Andrews
    Sisters*
Boogie Woogie Sioux, 297–98
Booth, Mark, 339
Born to Dance, 190, 267–68
Boswell Sisters, 260–61, 275n.86
Boyd, Mildred, 247–48
Boy Scouts of America, 53–54
Boys Town, 205–6
Bradford, Roark, 233–34, 272n.10
Brascia, John, 348
Breen, Joseph I., 2–3, 16–17, 24, 25, 26,
    110, 111, 142–43, 159, 221–22,
    228–30, 255–56, 287–88, 301–3, 305,
    308, 321, 331–33, 347
  See also Production Code

Broadway, 48–49, 58–61, 64n.2, 68n.58,
    70n.98, 71n.105, 81, 117n.74, 125,
    138–39, 231, 236–37, 249, 343
Broadway Gondolier, 73
Broadway Melody of 1936, 212n.40, 260
Brooks, Daphne, 7, 10
Brooks, Shelton, 199–200, 202, 203
Brown, Jayna, 162–63n.49, 337
Brown, Sterling, 130
Bubbles (Sublett), John, 170f, 171, 188,
    210n.13, 210n.14, 212n.36, 316
Buck and Bubbles (comedy duo Ford Lee
    Washington and John Sublett), 170f,
    171, 316
  See also John Bubbles
buck-and-wing, 136, 152–53
buck dance, 39–40, 79, 80, 112–13n.9, 148
Bugs Bunny, 280f, 281–82, 284–86, 296,
    298–99, 308, 321
  See also "Any Bonds Today"
Bureau of Indian Affairs (BIA), 89–90,
    114–15n.34
Burns, George, 190–91
Burt, Jonathan, 291
Butterbeans, 134–35
By Request, 251

"Cabin in the Cotton and the Cotton in the
    Cabin," 146–47
Cabin in the Sky, 333, 351n.21
call-and-response. *See* Africanist aesthetic
cakewalk, 31–35, 43, 52, 53–54, 177–78,
    299–300, 331, 333–34, 337–38
  in music, 50–51, 333–34
Cake-Walk Infernal, Le, 31–35, 43, 53–54,
    238–39
"California Here I Come," 236–37
Calloway, Cab, 231, 234, 239–42, 251,
    260–61, 270, 308–9, 337–38
  caricatures of, 286–87, 305–9, 310–12,
    311f, 314–16, 317–18, 321–22 (*see
    also* Bill Robinson effect; Zip Coon)
  fashion, 240–41, 334
  in film, 231, 237–39, 241–42, 245,
    269–70, 274n.40, 334
  music, 13, 113n.10, 227–28, 232, 234,
    240, 245, 248–49, 250, 252–55,
    275n.84

362 INDEX

Calloway's Jitterbug Party, 245
Cameraphone, 33–34
Camp aesthetic, 20, 25–26, 335, 337–38, 339–45
  and cross-dressing, 344–45
  as tied to queer agency, 20
  See also Susan Sontag
"Camptown Races," 215n.74, 335–38
Can This Be Dixie, 248–49
Cantor, Eddie, 5–7, 16, 18, 19, 21–23, 22f, 129–30, 142–43, 157–58, 178–79, 205–6, 235, 251, 263–64, 270, 294, 308–9, 318, 340
  in *Ali Baba Goes to Town*, 252–58, 253f, 260–62, 263–64
  bio, 81–82, 95
  caricatures and citations of, 125–26, 158, 285–86, 308, 310–12, 347
  in films of the 1940s, 334–35, 344–47
  Jewish identity, 80–81, 82–83
  in *Kid Millions*, 172f, 173–80, 182, 344
  in *Roman Scandals*, 79–80, 104, 105f, 106–11, 144
  in *The Kid from Spain* 75–76, 96–103, 263–64
  in vaudeville, 81
  in *Whoopee!*, 83–91, 93
"Cape Dance," 269
Career Girl, 206, 216n.79
caricature (definition), 309–18
"Carioca," 98–99
Castle, Irene and Vernon, 350–51n.17
Catholic Church, 2–3, 53–54, 62, 95–96, 177, 228–30, 301–3, 332, 340
censored eleven, 301–3
chair Dance, 112–13n.9, 213n.45
Chaplin, Charlie, 194–95
Charleston (dance), 18, 49, 70n.96, 75–76, 97, 99, 107–8, 109–10, 111, 222–23, 267, 281
Charters, Spencer, 83–84
Cheng, Ann Anlin, 55–56, 69n.80
Cherniavsky, Eva, 55, 197
Chewy Gooey Gum ad, 46f, 47, 54, 69n.78, 76–77, 134, 187
  See also Wrigley's
Chief Caupolican, 83
  See also Chief Black Eagle

Chion, Michel, 17, 40–41
  See also audio-vision
Chocolateers, 209n.5, 247–51, 260–61, 269
Chocolate Kiddies, 124–25, 160n.4
choreography (Susan Foster definition), 207–8
Choreosonic, 128
Christy Minstrels, 174, 201, 215n.74
Chronophone, 33–34
Cinderella (1922), 39–40
citational guise (definition of), 11, 13–15, 16–17, 21–23, 85, 143, 205–9, 309–18
citizenship, 42, 282, 313
Civil War, 19, 42–43, 50–51, 63, 126, 145, 147–48, 342
Clarabelle Cow, 15, 20
Clean Pastures, 286, 304–9, 319–22
Clooney, Rosemary, 341f, 348–49
Club Alabam, 124–25
Coal Black and De Sebben Dwarfs, 322–23
Cole, Jack, 348
College Swing, 245
comedy dancers, 141–42, 248–49
Come Take a Trip in My Airship, 36
commedia dell'arte, 4
composite brownface, 97, 101, 271
conga (dance), 224, 263–64, 268–69
Conk (hairstyle), 234, 314–15
  See also Cab Calloway
Connelly, Mark, 233–34, 301–3, 317–18
Coo-Coo Nut Grove, 309–10
"coon" song, 45, 166n.81
  See also popular music; Ragtime
Cooper, George, 137, 138–39, 164n.63
copacetic (attitude), 198–99, 241–42, 313
Copacetics, the (group), 112–13n.9, 213n.45
copyright, 183, 194, 197, 214n.52
Cortez, Ricardo, 228
Cotton Club (Harlem), 49, 58, 71n.103, 231, 239–40, 251, 256–57, 260–61, 275n.75
  caricatures of, 305, 312
  "Cotton Club Parade," 250, 337
  "Cotton Club Revue (Ellington), 260–61
Cotton Club (Frank Sebastian's in Los Angeles), 248–49
Count Basie Orchestra, 163n.58, 260

Covans, the Four, 48, 163–64n.61
Covert minstrelsy (defined) , xvii–xviii, 2,
    10, 11–17
"Cowboy Song, the," 92–93
Crawley, Ashon, 128
Crisis, The (magazine), 1–2
Cromer, Harold (Stumpy of Stump and
    Stumpy), 346*f*
    See also *This is the Army*
Crosby, Bing, 9*f*, 145–46, 194–95, 243–44,
    250, 340–42, 341*f*, 348–49
cross-dressing, 344
    racial, 6–7, 42 (*see also* Rogin,
    Michael)
crossover appeal, 231, 239–42, 248–49,
    270, 308–9, 314–15, 316
    See also Calloway, Cab
Cruz, Jon, 130–31
Cuba, 101–2
    dance, 98, 224
    music, 97–99
    rhythms, 97–98, 111, 252
    See also Latunes
cultural pastiche, 97

Dahomey, 31–32, 64n.2
    French colonization of, 64n.3
dance manuals, 71n.114, 222–23, 239–40,
    261–62, 266–67, 270
Dandy Lion, the, 297–98
Darby, Ken, 194–95, 214n.53
Darktown Revue, 131–32, 162n.40
"Darktown Strutters' Ball, the," 199–200,
    202
Davies, Marion, 145–46
Davis, Joan, 210n.18, 344–47
Dawes Act (1887-1933), 89–90, 93–95
Day at the Races, A, 230, 234–35
Decker, Todd, 184–85, 212n.38,
    243, 244–45
DeForest, Lee, 36
DeFrantz, Thomas F., 12
de lawd, 234, 301–3, 304, 305–6, 308
Del Rio, Dolores, 228
Depression, Great, 2–3, 47–48, 76, 77,
    81–83, 87, 93–96, 103, 104, 126,
    130–31, 142–43, 160n.17,
    277n.117, 339
Desmond, Jane, 222–23, 267

dice (symbolism), 142–44, 188, 227–28,
    235–36, 299–300, 305–6, 308
    See also gambling
Dickerson, Dudley, 242
diegetic audience, 139–40, 194–95
diegetic sound, 194–95, 247–48, 299–300
"Diga Diga Doo," 331, 332, 334, 337–39
"Dinah" (song), 72*f*, 73, 79, 82–83, 256,
    305, 344–45
Dīnār, 79, 96–97
Dinerstein, Joel, 230–31, 242–43
Disney (Films), 13–15, 39–40, 117n.83, 121,
    144–45, 214n.53, 282–83, 284–85,
    292–96, 322–23
"Dixie" (song), 15
Dixiana, 139, 154–55, 214n.52
Dodson, Jon, 194–95
Doherty, Thomas, 110, 282–83
"Doin' the New Lowdown," 123, 132,
    138–39, 140, 148, 312
Don Juan, 36–37
"Don'ts and Be Carefuls," 34–35
doppelgänger (film narrative), 180–81,
    190–91, 194, 212n.43
D'Orsay, Fifi, 145–46
Dorsey, Jimmy, 250
Dorsey, Tommy, 268, 269–70
double coding, 5–6, 78–79, 81, 82–83, 231,
    232, 239–40, 255–56
double consciousness, 158, 202–3
Double V campaign, 25–26, 283–84, 333,
    345, 350n.6
Down Argentine Way, 98–99, 277n.106
Doyle, Buddy, 178–79
dozens, the, 248–49, 275n.67
Drums Along the Mohawk, 317–18
Du Bois, W.E.B., 70n.92, 140–41, 161n.20,
    166n.81
Dunham, Katherine, 338–39, 351n.18
Dunham technique, 219–20, 264
Durante, Jimmy, 70n.98, 146, 158, 310–12
Durden, E. Moncell, 276n.104
Durkin, Hannah, 351n.18
Dyer, Richard, 349
Dyson, Michael Eric, 20–21

eccentric dancing, 123, 159n.1, 171,
    248–49, 281
    See also legomania

364 INDEX

Edison, Thomas, 113n.15
effeminacy, 21–23, 81–83, 84, 103–4,
  107, 234–35
Egypt, 19, 173–74, 182, 276n.88
Eidsheim, Nina, 10
  See also sonic blackness
Ellington, Duke, 113n.10, 234–35, 242,
  243–44, 248–49, 250, 251, 260–61,
  269–70
Ellison, Ralph, 6
Elmer Fudd, 281
Elstree Calling, 123–25, 160n.5
Emmett, Dan, 15, 145
Emperor Jones, The, 227–28, 272n.3,
  299–300, 308
Erdman, Harley, 257
Eternal Jew, the (ewige Jude, der), 121n.i,
  121
Ethiopian, 107
  as "authentic," 107, 117–18n.85, 137
  character in Roman Scandals, 106–7
  Ethiopian Serenaders, 107
Etting, Ruth, 109, 164n.65
Europe, James Reese, 335–37, 350–51n.17
Exile, the, 132
expatriation, 123–24

Fanon, Frantz, 265–66
Faye, Alice, 222–23, 265–66
femininity, 104, 173–74, 191–94, 207–8,
  215–16n.75, 267, 322
fetishization, 6–8, 103, 157–58, 180–81,
  210n.16, 260–61, 314–15
Feuer, Jane, 139–40
Fiddler pig, 121, 293
Fifer pig, 121, 293
Firmat, Gustavo Pérez, 97–99, 252
Five Hot Shots, 134–35
flash dance, 123, 124–25, 134–35, 179,
  192–93, 213n.48
Fletcher, Dusty, 141–42
Fleischer Brothers (Max and Dave), 36,
  37, 39–40, 65n.16, 65n.21, 73,
  284–85, 296–97
Flying Down to Rio, 98–99
Follies Pickaninnies, the, 177–78
Footlight Parade, 132, 142–43, 319–20
Forkins, Marty, 164n.65

Foster, Stephen, 13, 41, 132, 135–36,
  140–42, 144, 145, 147–48, 158–59,
  166n.80, 166n.81, 199–203, 206, 208,
  215n.65, 215n.66, 215n.67, 215n.68,
  215n.74, 296–97, 299–300, 305–6,
  312, 319–20, 337–38, 343–44
Foster, Susan Leigh, 207–8, 213–14n.49,
  237–38
"Four Freedoms" speech, 283–84
Four Kings of Harmony, 73
Four Musicians of Bremen, The, 39–40
Four Playboys, the, 247–48
Fox Pictures, 65n.16, 129–30
foxtrot rhythm, 141–42, 211n.34
Francis, Gussie, 124–25
Francis, Kay, 228
Franklyn, Irwin, 139
Freleng, Isadore "Friz," 286, 300, 308, 321
Fresh Hare, 144–45
Freud, Sigmund, 158, 212–13n.44
fried chicken references, 227–30, 232,
  235–36, 247–48
Frolics, The, 81
Fuehrer's Face, Der, 284–85
Fuller Brush Man, 121, 293–94, 327n.29
Fuller, Loie, 31–32, 64n.4

Gable, Clark, 310–12
  in animation, 310–12
  in film, 60–61
Gabriel variation (definition), 24–25,
  228–30, 233–38
gag, 15, 19, 20, 321, 345–47
gambling, 16–17, 24, 141–42, 143–44,
  162n.34, 184, 185–87, 213n.45,
  227–30, 232, 299–301, 306–8, 313–14
Garbo, Greta (caricatures), 310–12, 316–17
Garland, Judy, 142–43
gender, 21–23, 48, 76, 77, 80, 81–83, 92–93,
  103–4, 107, 111, 127, 145–46, 192,
  205, 207, 208, 213–14n.49, 290–91,
  329n.79, 344
Gentleman Be Seated, 190
George White's Scandals, 142–43, 146,
  158, 251
Georgia Rose, 132
Gershwin, George, 138–39, 236–37
Gibson, Steve, 242

Gibson (Gipson), Albert (of the Three Chocolateers), 245–50, 246f
Gilman, Sander, 82–83, 90–91, 234–35
Girl from Chicago, the, 162n.33
Gitelman, Lisa, 298
Gleason, James, 48–49
Going Hollywood, 145–46
Goin' to Heaven on a Mule (cartoon), 286, 299–305
"Goin' to Heaven on a Mule" (song), 227–30, 237
See also *Wonder Bar*
"Go Into Your Dance," 236–37
Goldberg, Marv, 248–49
Gold Diggers of 1933, the, 142–43
Gold Dust Twins (Goldie and Dustie), 319–20, 321–22
Goldwyn Girls, 18, 21–23, 22f, 74f, 75–78, 91–95, 94f, 98–99, 101–2, 103, 104, 109–10, 111, 118n.87, 118n.88, 132, 134, 146–47, 172f, 173–74, 219–20, 335–37
Gone with the Wind, 147–48
Gonzales, Anita, 12
Goodman, Benny, 212n.38, 231, 244–45, 248–50, 269–70, 274n.62
Good News, 52, 68n.58
Gorbman, Claudia, 202
Gottschild, Brenda Dixon, 12, 28n.30, 52–53, 56–57
See also Africanist aesthetic
Grable, Betty, 74f, 222–23, 265–66
Gray, Gilda, 261–62, 266, 267
Great Ziegfeld, the, 178–79
Greenbaum, Jules, 33–34
Greenlee and Drayton, 137
Green Pastures, the
citations of, 301, 308, 317–18 (see also *Clean Pastures*)
Film, 230, 233–34, 272n.3, 301, 308, 328n.48
Play, 233–34, 272n.3
Green, Sammy (of Tip, Tap, and Toe), 251, 277–78n.123
Gregory, Paul, 83
groove, 12, 153, 299–300
See also Africanist aesthetic

Hall, Adelaide, 124–25, 134, 146–47, 160n.9, 346f
Hall, Mordaunt, 228–30
Hallelujah!, 129–30
Hall Johnson Negro choir, 299–300
Hambone, 288
Hannah, Jack, 294–95
Happy Harmonies, 155
Harlem, 45, 47–56, 57–58, 70n.99, 71n.103, 71n.105, 71n.107, 132, 135–36, 140–41, 160n.9, 175, 183, 184, 187–88, 189, 191–92, 213n.45, 240, 254–55, 312
cartoon caricatures, 299–300, 305–6, 312, 315–16
feel in music (Berlin), 49–50, 56–57, 62, 184–85
feel in music (Calloway), 240, 241–42
references to Lenox Avenue, 47–48, 58, 60, 61, 227–28, 232
in vogue, 56–64, 70n.98, 187–88, 239–40
See also Apollo Theater; Cotton Club; "Bojangles of Harlem"; Hoofer's Club
Harlem chronotope (Massood), 139
Harlemeaestro, 239–42, 315–16
See also Calloway, Cab
Harlem Hell Fighters, 350–51n.17
"Harlem Honeymoon," 141–42
Harlem Hot Shots, 160n.3
Harlem is Heaven, 132, 135–36, 138–39
Harlem Renaissance, 48, 49, 56, 57–61, 67–68n.57, 70n.98, 71n.105, 98, 139, 140–41
Harlem Riot (1935), 175, 209–10n.8, 231, 275n.75
Harman-Ising, 155
Hartman, Saidiya, 286, 323, 344–45
Have You Got Any Castles? (cartoon), 286–87, 309, 316–17
"Have You Got Any Castles?" (song), 171
Hawaii, 18, 19, 176, 182, 191, 193, 194, 209, 212–13n.44, 219–24, 260–61, 262–64, 265–68, 338–39
See also *Honolulu*; hula; tourism
Hays Code, the, 1–3, 21–23, 24, 25, 212n.42, 221–22, 263, 284–85, 287–89, 300–1, 309, 325, 332
See also Production Code

366 INDEX

Hays, Will H., 1–3, 24, 332
Hearn, Sam (as Schlepperman), 305–8, 307*f*
Hearts in Dixie, 129–30
Heimlich, 212–13n.44
Henderson, Fletcher, 163n.58, 244–45
Herman, Woody, 112–13n.9
Heyward, DuBose, 138–39
Hi-de-ho, 227–28, 234, 240, 245, 249, 254, 255–62, 275n.84, 314–15
   See also Calloway, Cab
Hi-de-ho 1937 (film), 245
Hi-de-ho 1947 (film), 245
Hieronymus Bosch, 31–32
"High brown," 58, 59
Hilliard, Harriet, 247–48
Hitler, Adolph, 2–3, 282–83
Holder, Roland, 132
Holiday Inn, 335, 340–42, 344–48
Hollywood Bowl, 309–10
Hollywood Capers, 309–10
Hollywood Hotel, 245
Hollywood Reporter, 1, 149–50, 333
Hollywood Steps Out, 309–10
Holocaust, 282, 294–95
Honeymoon Express, the, 236–37
Honolulu, 18, 19, 24, 176, 180–205, 206–8, 209, 210n.18, 212n.39, 212n.43, 219–24, 261–63, 266, 267–69, 277n.117, 282, 298–99, 318, 323–24, 338–39
   See also hula tap dance; Powell, Eleanor
Hoofer's club, 183, 191–92, 213n.45
Hooray for Love, 155, 156*f*
   citations of, 155, 260
   See also *Old Mill Pond*
Horne, Lena, 332–33, 334–37, 336*f*
Horsey, Chick (Layborn) (Three Eddies), 122*f*, 123–25, 137
"*Hosanna*," 254–55
How Do I Know it's Sunday, 321
Howe, Irving, 50
Hudgins, Johnny, 124–25
Hughes, Langston, 58–59, 60–61, 67–68n.57, 70n.96, 70n.100, 71n.105
hula, 39–40, 107–8, 191–92, 219–24, 262–63, 265–66, 267–69, 338–39
   hula tap dance, 219–24, 261–62, 263–64, 268

humanimal, 289–90, 292, 294, 295–96, 300, 303–4, 305, 312
Hunt, Eleanor, 83
Hurston, Zora Neale, 67–68n.57, 233–34

I Ain't Got Nobody, 73
Idiot's Delight, 60–61
   See also "Puttin' on the Ritz"
I Dood It, 334–35, 350n.10
If You Knew Susie (film), 210n.18, 334–35, 345–47
"If You Knew Susie" (song), 178, 346*f*, 347
   See also *Great Ziegfeld, the*
"I love to Sing-a," 237
Imada, Adria L., 262–63
"I'm a Naughty Girl," 103
imperfect assimilation, 5–6, 18, 90–91, 104, 257–58, 265–66
improvisation, 12, 33, 35, 50–52, 183, 184–85, 240, 243–44, 261–62
   See also Africanist aesthetic
indefinite talk, 337
Indian New Deal, 89–90
Indian Reorganization Act (IRA), 89–90, 114–15n.34
Ingram, Rex, 226*f*
In Old Kentucky, 36, 147–48, 154–55
integration, 8, 19, 21, 41–43, 53–54, 55–56, 63–64, 77–78, 149, 152–53, 255–56, 259, 309, 322, 325, 334–35
   See also affected integration
interlocuter, 37–38, 141–42, 143, 173–74, 176–77, 194–95, 348–49
in the pocket, 12
   See also groove
Invisible Man, the, 318–19
Iona, Andy, 268
Isle of Pingo Pongo, the, 309
"I Want to Be a Minstrel Man," 173–74, 182
Iwerks, Ub, 287–88

Jack Benny show, 305–6
"Jamboree," 251–52
Jaxon, Frankie "Half-Pint," 240
Jazz Singer, The, 13–15, 21, 35–39, 40, 41–44, 45, 62, 63–64, 129–30, 142–43, 233, 236–37, 243
jewface, 5–6

Jewish, 2–3, 91–92, 257–58, 293–94
  as caricature, 87, 292–96 (see also
    Three Little Pigs)
  as identity, xv–xvi, 6–7, 21–23, 42, 50,
    67n.45, 82–83, 88–89, 90–91, 234–35,
    237, 255–56, 324–25
  music, 41, 294–95, 327n.32
  performance, 5–6, 16, 18, 21–23, 81,
    82–83, 84, 87, 88–89, 90–91, 231–32,
    255–56
  performers, 6–7, 78–79, 81, 90–91, 234,
    257–58, 263–64 (*see also* Cantor,
    Eddie; Jolson, Al)
  slavery, 82–83, 235–36
  See also anti-Semitism
Jewish Labor Committee, 327n.45
Jim Crow (figure), 1–2, 3–4, 8, 12–13,
    42–43, 58, 85, 107, 126–27,
    134, 250
Johnny Hodges Orchestra, 250
Johnson, Rita, 190–91
Johnson, Stephen, 8
Jolly N[sic]Bank, 54–55
Jolson, Al, 5–7, 9f, 38–39, 47–48, 85–86,
    164n.62, 215n.74, 235, 256, 257–58,
    263–64, 272n.3, 347
  bio, 41, 42, 43–44
  caricatures and citations of, 13–15, 14f,
    21, 45, 86, 87, 88–89, 90–91, 188–89,
    197, 205–6, 232, 270, 281–82, 284–86,
    288, 296, 298–306, 307f, 308, 310–12,
    316, 319–20, 321–22, 340–42
  in *The Jazz Singer*, 35, 41, 42–44, 45,
    102–3, 129–30, 142–43, 233
  in *The Singing Kid*, 236–39, 241–42,
    258, 305
  in *Wonder Bar*, 227–30, 232, 258
Jones, Douglas, 314–15
Jookin', 52
Joy, Jason S., 255–56, 331–33
Judaism. *See* Jewish
Jungle Jitters, 297–98
Jungle sound, 211n.34, 240, 287–88

Kahn, Gus, 199–200
Kalinak, Kathryn, 13, 40–41
Kapchan, Deborah, 39–40, 271
Katz, Mark, 34, 38–39

Keeler, Ruby, 236–37, 319–20
"Keep Young and Beautiful," 107, 109–10,
    118n.87, 149
Keighly, William Jackson, 233–34
Keith Circuit, 137, 164n.63
  See also vaudeville
Kelley, Robin D.G., 240–41
Kern, Jerome, 184
Kheshti, Roshanak, 145–46
Kibbee, Guy, 228
"Kickin' the Gong Around," 241
Kid Boots, 81, 113n.10, 113n.15, 125
Kid From Spain, The, 18, 21–23, 75–77,
    81–82, 95–104, 111, 130–31, 134,
    263–64, 335–37
Kid Kabaret, 81
Kid Millions, 19, 110, 173–80
King for a Day, 141–45
King Rastus Brown, 165n.68
Ko-Ko's Paradise, 39–40
Klezmer music, 41, 294–95, 327n.32
Knight, Arthur, 43–44, 241–42, 334
Krasner, David, 117–18n.85, 211n.33
Kraut, Anthea, 116n.66, 183, 214n.52
Kristeva, Julia, 7–8
Krueger, Lorraine, 206, 216n.79
Ku Klux Klan (KKK), 126–27

Lacan, Jacques, 188, 212n.37
Lane, Priscilla, 316
Lang, June, 254–55
Lantz, Walter, 297–98
LaRedd, Cora, 134, 163n.52
Latunes (Firmat), 97–99, 111, 252, 262,
    269–70
"Leader Doesn't Like Music, the," 194–95
Lee, Johnny, 337
legomania, 123, 281
Le Gon, Jeni, 253f, 254–55, 258, 260
Lehman, Christopher, 287–88, 328n.59
Leitmotif, 41, 202–3, 294–95
  See also Jewish music
Le Roy, Hal, 227–28, 229f
Leslie, Lew, 138–39, 140, 321–22
Levering Lewis, David, 57–58, 67–68n.57
Lewis, Barbara, 4, 86, 314, 315
Lincoln, Abraham (references), 141, 227–28,
    232, 340–42, 344–45, 347–48

368 INDEX

Lincoln Motion Picture Company, 131, 132
See also Race film
lindy hop, 52, 211n.34, 232, 234–35, 247–48, 276n.96, 299–300, 348
Linn, Bud, 194–95
"Listen to the Mockingbird," 199–200, 202
Little Black Sambo, 287–88, 327n.45
Little Colonel, the, 147–48, 149–50
Littlest Rebel, the, 147–48, 149–50, 167n.102
Little Eva (minstrel archetype), 15, 340–42
Little Rural Riding Hood, 323
Locke, Alain, 57, 67–68n.57, 130, 139, 140–41
Long Tail Blue, 4, 312, 313–17
Lott, Eric, 6–8, 67n.43, 67n.44
Louis, Joe, 346*f*
Lou-Scha-Enya, 83
Love and Hisses, 222–23, 260–61
Love and Kisses, 260–61
"*Love's Old Sweet Song,*" 141–42
Lucky Star, 221–22
See also *Honolulu*
"Lulu-Belle," 59, 200–1
Lulu Belle (1926), 59, 71n.105
Lunceford, Jimmy, 260–61, 308–9, 316
caricatures of, 306–8, 316

Mack, Roy, 251
Magee, Jeffrey, 50–51, 56–57
magical Negro, 151
Malone, Jacqui, 12
See also Africanist aesthetic
"Mamãe Eu Quero," 98–99
mambo, 98–99
Mammy (figure), 174–75, 287–88, 297–98, 301–3, 340–42
"Mammy" (*Jazz Singer* song), 21, 35, 38–39, 43, 44, 45, 47–48, 233
citations of, 13–15, 14*f*, 45, 85–86, 87–89, 102–3, 111, 188–89, 205–6, 227–30, 232, 236–37, 288, 298–99, 309, 319–20
See also *Jazz Singer, the*; Jolson, Al; "Sammy"
mammy singer, 114n.27, 146

"Mandy," 177–78, 179, 180–81, 200–1, 343–47, 348–49
See also *Kid Millions*; *This is the Army*; *White Christmas*
Manifest Destiny, 89–90
Manners, Joseph, 79
Manning, Frankie, 254–55
See also lindy hop
Manning, Susan, 10, 235, 273n.15
Many Happy Returns, 163–64n.61
Marais, Stéphane, xv, 7–8, 27n.21
Marx Brothers, 194–95, 234–35
Chico, 194–95
Groucho, 120*f*, 121, 194–95, 293–94
Harpo, 194–95, 234–35, 257–58
Marx, Karl, 157, 210n.16
masculinity, 82–83, 104, 199, 221–22, 223–24, 234–35, 351n.18
"Massa's in de Cold, Cold Ground" (Foster), 129–30, 147–48, 215n.66
Massood, Paula J., 139
master/slave dialectic, 7–8, 109, 149, 150–51, 200, 309–10
Mathews, Charles, 3–4, 16
McDaniel, Hattie, 130–31, 174–75
McFadden, Margaret, 81–82
McMains, Juliet, 5–6, 98
McPhail, Douglas, 194–95
McPherson, Tara, 126–27
McQueen, Thelma "Butterfly," 130–31
medley (music), 132, 140–41, 144, 147–48, 171, 199–200, 202–3
Meet the Maestros, 245
Melancholy Dame, the, 132
Méliès, Georges, 31–32
See also *Cakewalk Infernal, Le*
Memories and Melodies, 147–48
Mercer, Johnny, 171, 316
Merman, Ethel, 172*f*, 173–74, 179
Merrie Melodies, 301–3
metaphorical minstrelsy (Manning), 10–11, 235, 273n.15
Metro-Goldwyn-Mayer (MGM), 129–30, 147–48, 155, 189–90, 191–92, 194, 197–98, 199–200, 201, 202, 208, 212n.42, 260, 269–70, 301–3
Mexico, 96, 99, 100
See also *Kid From Spain, the*

Meyers, Moe, 20
Micheaux, Oscar, 23–24, 117n.74, 127–28, 131–32, 162n.33, 162n.40, 237–38
Mickey Mouse, 14f, 15, 295–96
  in *Mickey's Mellerdrammer,* 13–15, 20, 144–45, 321
Middle Passage, 286, 323–24
Milburn, Richard, 199–200, 202, 203
Miller, Ann, 206
Miller, Benjamin, 313, 314
Miller Brothers and Lois (Danny, George, and Lois Bright), 134–35, 260–61
Miller, Flournoy (F.E.), 134, 163n.51, 337
  as Miller and Lee, 210n.17, 337
  as Miller and Lyles, 163n.51
Miller, Karl Hagstrom, 140, 145, 250
Miller, Marilyn, 177–78
Mills Brothers, the, 72f, 73, 147–48, 245, 306–8, 307f, 314–15, 317–18
Mills, Florence, 117n.74, 124–25, 138–39
Mills, Irving, 239–40, 315–16, 337–38
"Minnie the Moocher" (song), 239–40, 245, 260, 275n.84, 276n.97
  See also "Hi-De-Ho"
minstrel archetypes. *See* Jim Crow; Little Eva; Long Tail Blue; Topsy; Uncle Tom; Zip Coon
minstrel gloves, 15, 43, 121, 123, 188–89, 195, 197, 205–6, 236–37, 281, 291, 305–6, 312–13, 316–17, 318–19, 322–23, 340–42, 343–44, 345–47, 348–49
minstrel show-within-a-show, 11, 23–24, 127–28, 131–32, 142–43, 144–45, 166n.88, 174, 176–82, 284–85, 286–87, 324, 342, 343–49
minstrelsy (definition and origins), xiii, 2, 3–11, 143–44, 174
Miranda, Carmen, 98–99
miscegenation, 63–64, 167n.101
Mississippi Swing, 19, 144–45, 286–87, 323–24
modernism, 55, 258–59, 351n.18
Molly Moo-Cow and the Indians, 296–97
"Moonlight Bay," 268–69, 271
Moore, Constance, 341f, 344–45
Moore, Gus (Three Chocolateers), 246f, 248
Moreland, Mantan, 117n.74, 134, 163n.51

Morris, Mitchell, 349
Morrison, Matthew, 10, 13, 112–13n.9, 149–50, 245
morse code, 231–32, 268–72, 282
Moten, Fred, 151–52, 204–5
Motion Picture Producers Association (MPPA), 177–78
Motion Picture Producers, and Distributors of America (MPPDA), 1–2, 44, 53–54, 88, 95–96, 110, 111, 135
Motion Picture Production Code. *See* Hays Code; Production Code
Mouse Cleaning, 301–3
Mulvey, Laura, 99
Murphy, George, 172f, 173–74, 179–80, 212n.42, 341f, 343–44
Musical Beauty Shop, the, 153
Muslim (Moslem), 255–56
  See also *Ali Baba Goes to Town*
Mutoscope, 33–34
"My Baby Just Cares for Me," 86–87, 93
"My How the Time Goes By," 345–47
My Old Kentucky Home (cartoon), 36, 37, 41
"My Old Kentucky Home" (song), 135–36, 202–3
mythical kingdom (concept), 95–104, 182, 220–21, 258, 262, 263, 265–66

"Nagasaki," 282, 319–20
National Association for the Advancement of Colored People (NAACP), 1–2, 23–24, 137–38, 174–75, 228–30, 327n.45, 334–35, 345
national integration, 21, 41–43
  See also integration
Native Hawaiian, 18, 191, 193, 209, 219–24, 262–63, 266–68, 270
Negro dialect, 3–4, 19, 45, 99–100, 106–7, 140–42, 145–46, 149–50, 201–2, 232, 234
Negro Spirituals, 41, 129–30, 140, 201–2, 232, 234, 254–55
"Negro type," 3–5, 20–21, 107
  See also Jim Crow; Long Tail Blue; Zip Coon

370 INDEX

New Deal, 110, 126–27, 230–31, 256
New Faces of 1937, 209n.5, 230, 245, 250–52, 276n.87
New Negro, The (Locke), 57, 64n.2, 139, 239
New York Age, 251
New York Times, 342, 344, 345–47, 349
Nicholas Brothers (Fayard and Harold), 12–13, 19, 134, 173–74, 179–80, 264–66, 265f, 277n.106
nickelodeons, 33–34
"Nobody Knows the Trouble I Seen," 269
Noel, Hattie, 141–42
"No More Love," 109
Norman, Richard, 131
North, Michael, 100–1
Norton, E.E., 33–34
nostalgia, 10–11, 42–43, 63, 115n.35, 201–2, 304–5
Nyong'o, Tavia, 314–15

Obadike, Mendi, 13, 87, 256–57
Office of War Information, 282–83
"Old Black Joe," 19, 135–36, 141–42, 166n.81, 166n.83, 199–200, 202–3, 215n.66, 232, 308, 323–24
"Old Folks at Home," 147–48, 199–201, 202, 215n.66, 305–6
    See also "Swanee River"
Old Mill Pond, 155, 156f, 159, 307f, 312
olio (minstrelsy), 24, 143–44, 174, 177, 348–49
one man dance, 123, 160n.3
On With the Show, 48
Orientalism, 97, 219–20, 222–23, 251–52, 257–58
Orpheum circuit, 137, 164n.63
Oswald the Lucky Rabbit in Bright Lights, 39–40
Othello (play), 3
Other, the, 2, 7–8, 10, 16, 19, 42–43, 54–55, 77–78, 81–83, 84–85, 87, 88–91, 93, 98–99, 104, 111, 151, 187, 200, 212–13n.44, 220–22, 224, 252, 256–57, 270, 277–78n.123, 282
Out of the Frying Pan into the Firing Line, 282–83, 350n.6
Out of the Inkwell series, 65n.21

Pacific (constructions of), 262–63
Palace Theater, 137, 164n.66, 251
Palmy Days, 95, 104, 118n.86
"Panamania," 251–52
Pan, Hermes, 192, 207, 216n.81
pansy craze, 104, 255–56
Parsons, Louella, 273n.22
passing parade, 75–76, 93–95, 219–20
    See also Berkeley, Busby; Goldwyn Girls
patriotism, 10–11, 25–26, 95–96, 137, 164n.65, 240–41, 282, 284–85, 288, 304–5, 342, 344–45
Pearl Harbor, attack on, 220–21, 269–70
Peckin' (dance), 198–99, 230–31, 245, 247–55
    See also Three Chocolateers
Peg Leg Bates, 260–61
Pennington, Ann, 261–62
Perry, Lincoln, 85
    See also Stepin Fetchit
persistence of vision, 18, 296
Peters Sisters, the (Mattie, Ann, and Virginia Vee), 134–35, 222–23, 253f, 254–55, 258, 260–61, 275n.84
Phonograph, 33–34, 47–48
phonograph effect, 34, 38–39, 55–56
pickaninnies, 146–47, 164n.62, 177–78, 205–6, 301
Plantation (club), 113n.10, 124–25
Plasmaticness, 295–96
"playing Indian," 16, 88–89, 90–91, 111
    See also redface
political calypso, 248–49
Polk, Oscar, 305
popular music, 13, 24, 42–43, 45, 49–51, 66n.22, 112–13n.9, 166n.81, 210n.9, 212n.38, 242–43, 244–45, 250, 270, 335
    See also coon song; ragtime
Porgy and Bess, 138–39, 188, 272n.3
Porky Pig, 281
Pornotroping, 55
    See also Spillers, Hortense
Powell, Dick, 228, 319–20
Powell, Eleanor, 12–13, 231, 260, 314, 321, 322
    in *Honolulu,* 18, 19, 24, 176, 179–82, 187, 189–209, 212n.36, 212–13n.44, 215n.63, 215–16n.75, 218f, 219–24, 261–64, 267–68, 298–99, 318, 338–39

in *Ship Ahoy,* 231–32, 242–43, 268–71, 282
Practical pig, 121, 293
Preer, Evelyn, 132
Price, Byron, 270–71
Prima, Louis, 251
primal scene (dressing and undressing), 6–7, 9*f*, 99–101, 107, 210n.16, 258, 340–43, 345–47
   See also gag
primitive chic, 19–20, 235–36, 260–61, 338
primitive sound, 241–42
Primrose, George, 136, 177–78, 348–49
Princess Vanessa Ammon, 264
Pringle, Aileen, 48–49
Producers Appeal Board (PAB), 95
Production Code, xviii, 1–3, 10, 19, 24–25, 34–35, 43–45, 48, 63–64, 77–78, 86–87, 93–95, 98–100, 108, 110, 126–27, 142–44, 145–46, 154, 159, 174–76, 177, 200–1, 221–22, 224, 228, 231, 255–56, 271, 284–85, 300–1, 308, 309, 331–32, 334–37, 338–39
   See also Hays Code; Motion Picture Production Code
Production Code Administration (PCA), 2–3, 16–17, 24, 44, 110, 228, 285, 308, 318–19, 332, 337, 338–40, 342, 343, 344–45
Prohibition, 95
propaganda, 121n.i, 259, 281, 282–83
PTA, 1–2, 53–54
Puerto Rico, 267–68, 269, 271
   See also *Ship Ahoy*
Puss Gets the Boot, 301–3
Puttin' on the Ritz (film), 35, 45, 47–64, 134
"Puttin' on the Ritz" (song), 21, 35, 47–64, 174, 191, 312

"Queen of the Taps," 190, 206
   See also Powell, Eleanor
queer aura, performance of, 20

race film, 23–24, 126, 127–28, 129–36, 139
   See also Micheaux, Oscar
racial caricature (definition of), 5–6, 18–19, 309–18

ragtime, 31–32, 35, 41, 50–51, 135–36
   See also popular music
Rahn, Muriel, 141–42
Rastus, 307*f*, 319–20, 329n.78
Ray, Tiny (Earle), 122*f*, 123–25
   See also Three Eddies, the
Reagan, Ronald, 343
Rebecca of Sunnybrook Farm, 260–61
Rector, Eddie, 164n.62
redface, 5–6, 18, 21–23, 78–79, 88–91, 93–95, 96, 97, 103, 263–64, 284–86, 296–98, 317–18, 322
Red Hot Riding Hood, 323
Remington, Mayme, 164n.62
replica realism, 157, 321
Reynolds, Marjorie, 9*f*, 340–43, 341*f*
Rhumba/Rumba, 97–99, 111, 184
   See also Cuba
Rhumba craze, 231, 252, 262
"Rhythm on the Radio," 251
Rice, Thomas "Daddy," 3–4
Rich, Buddy, 268
Richman, Harry, 46*f*, 47–49, 54
"Ring de Banjo," 147–48
Rip Van Winkle, 317–19
RKO Pictures, 131, 134–35, 139, 212n.38, 216n.81, 250, 260
Robinson, Bill, 7, 12–13, 23–24, 127, 128–29, 130–31, 134, 140–41, 147–48, 158–59, 164n.62, 164n.63, 164n.65, 165n.68, 165n.69, 165n.72, 174–75, 183, 196*f*, 231, 241–42, 260–61, 309, 313–280, 323–24
   bio, 136–39
   caricatures of, 11, 19, 23–24, 128–29, 135, 138–39, 144–45, 153–59, 156*f*, 168n.114, 176, 180, 183–89, 191, 192–99, 203–9, 252, 261–62, 286–87, 305–8, 309, 310–22, 334, 340
   citations of, 79–80, 82–83, 85–86, 234, 237–38, 252, 258, 323–24
   in *Harlem is Heaven,* 132, 133*f*, 135, 138–39
   in *King for a Day,* 131–32, 133*f*, 141–45
   relationship with Shirley Temple, 128, 148, 149–51, 158–59, 167n.101, 167n.102, 173–74, 179–80, 214n.52, 313–14

372 INDEX

Robinson, Bill (*cont.*)
  in *Stormy Weather*, 335–39, 336*f*,
    350–51n.17
  See also Bill Robinson effect; stair dance
Robinson, Rad, 194–95
"Rock-A-Bye Your Baby With a Dixie
    Melody," 236–37
Rogers, Ginger, 319–20, 323
Roman Scandals, 77, 79–80, 81–83, 84,
    86–87, 95–97, 104–6, 109–10, 111,
    112n.8, 113n.10, 118n.87, 135, 144,
    149, 255–56
Rooney, Mickey, 205–6
Roosevelt, Franklin D., 126–27, 160n.17,
    230–31, 256, 270–71, 283–84
Rosalie, 190
Rossen, Rebecca, 113n.21
Rubin, Martin, 92
rumbera films, 97, 98
  See also rhumba
Rutherford, Jack, 83
Ryan, Peggy, 216n.80

Said, Edward, 262–63
Sammond, Nicholas, 15
Sanders, Ronald, 50
Sandler, Kevin, 290–91
Sartre, Jean Paul, 157
Savage, Barbara, 10, 106–7
  See also aural blackface
"Save Me Sister," 236–37, 238–39, 258, 305
Scatting, 242, 306–8, 329n.71
  See also *Hi-de-ho*
Schenck, Joe (Van and Schenck), 177–78
Schlesinger, Leon, 308
"Schnozzola," 310–12
  See also Jimmy Durante
Scott, Hazel, 334–35
September in the Rain, 286–87,
    309, 319–20
Shall We Dance, 242, 244
Shaw, Wini, 238–39, 308, 319–20
"Sheik of Araby, the," 264–66, 265*f*
Shimmy (dance), 39–40, 177–78, 222–23,
    267
Shim Sham, 49, 68n.59, 211n.34, 254–55,
    260–61
  See also Tack Annie

Ship Ahoy, 222–23, 231–32, 267–68,
    269–71, 282
shorty George (dance), 254–55
Show Business, 334–35
Shuffle Along, 58, 70n.96, 71n.105, 337
shuffle walk, 19, 79, 86, 148
  See also Stepin Fetchit
signifyin' song, 248–49
silent film, 17, 32–38, 43, 45, 149
silent film music, 37–39, 40–41,
    66n.22, 66n.36
Silly Symphonies, 120*f*, 121, 295
simulacra, 135, 157–27, 304, 324–25
  See also Baudrillard, Jean; Bill
    Robinson effect
Sinatra, Frank, 268–69
Sinbad, 236–37
sing-alongs, 36, 37, 65n.17, 72*f*, 73
Sing as You Swing, 245
Singing Fool, the, 236–37
Singing Kid, the, 230, 236–37, 239, 241–42,
    254–55, 305
Sissle, Noble, 134
Skelton, Red, 268–69, 271
Skrontch (dance), 250, 260–61, 276n.104
"Slap that Bass," 242–43, 247–48
slavery, 32, 55, 57, 80, 102–3, 137–38,
    145, 150–51, 197–98, 235–36, 323,
    324, 342
  slave role, 80, 81, 82–83, 84, 96–97,
    106–10, 149–50, 151, 198–99,
    317–18
  See also *Roman Scandals*
Sloan, Nate, 239–40
Smash Your Baggage, 134–35
Smith, Bessie, 214n.50
Smith, Jeff, 187, 201–2
Snead, James, 102
Snow White and the Seven
    Dwarves, 194–95
social mobility, 6–7, 129, 313–14
soft-primitivism (safe exotic), 223
  See also *Honolulu*
soft-shoe, 79, 136, 177–78, 343–44
"Song of the Setting Sun, the," 93, 95
sonic blackness (Eidsheim), 10
sonic color line (Stoever), 100
"Sonny Boy," 236–37, 305–6, 319–20

INDEX 373

Sontag, Susan, 20, 339–40, 343, 349
Sothern, Ann, 172*f*, 179
sound synchronization, 10, 17, 39–45
sound technology, 39–45
soundtrack, 11, 13, 35, 39–40, 41, 66n.27,
    139–40, 145, 184, 187–90, 199–203,
    241–42, 247–48, 263, 285–86,
    296–97, 298, 299–301, 304, 308,
    323–24, 332, 333, 343–44, 349
South African gumboot dance, 297–98,
    327n.40
southern repossession, 19, 23–24,
    126–28, 145–48, 149–50, 202,
    286–87, 340–42
Spillers, Hortense, 55, 197–98
Sportin' Life, 188
Sport Parade, the, 134–35
Stair dance, 19, 85–86, 132, 135–36,
    137–41, 144, 148, 149–50, 151–52,
    153, 154, 155, 157, 159, 163–64n.61,
    165n.68, 167n.102, 175, 183, 187,
    193–94, 197–99, 201–5, 206–8,
    214n.52, 215n.63, 216n.79, 323–24
    See also Robinson, Bill
Stearns, Marshall and Jean, 137–38,
    183, 210n.14, 248–49, 261–62,
    275n.74
Stepin Fetchit, 13, 111, 114n.25
    citations of, 85, 86, 106, 107, 305, 308
    in film, 130–31, 163n.54
    See also Perry, Lincoln
"Stetson," 93
St. Denis, Ruth, 219n.i, 219–20
"St. James Infirmary," 240
St. Louis Blues, 130
Stoever, Jennifer, 100
stop time, 132, 135–36, 141–42, 153,
    165n.70, 171, 216n.79
stop trick, 33, 64n.6
    See also substitution splice
Stormy Weather, 165n.78, 332–34, 336*f*,
    337–39
Stowe, David, 230–31, 256–57
Strictly Dynamite, 245
Strike up the Band, 142–43
Stuart, Gloria, 106
Studio Relations Committee (SRC), 44, 95,
    96–97, 110

Stump and Stumpy (James Cross and
    Eddie Hartman), 268–69, 270–71
    See also Cromer, Harold
subception, 13, 28n.33, 39–40, 199–200,
    201–2, 203
substitution splice, 33, 64n.6
    See also stop trick
Sunday Goes a Meetin' Time, 286
Suzy-Q, 230–31, 248–49, 251, 254–55,
    258, 276n.90
"Swanee" (Gershwin), 236–37
Swanee River (film), 215n.74
"Swanee River" (song), 135–36, 141–42,
    195, 199–200, 312, 323–24, 343–44
    See also "Old Folks at Home"
"Swing for Sale," 306–8, 314–15, 316
Swing High, Swing Low, 251–52
"Swingin'est Man in Town, the," 237–38
"Swing is Here to Sway," 252–58
"Swing the Jinx Away," 267–68
Swing Time (film), 1, 24, 60–61, 180–81,
    183–89, 207, 212n.38, 216n.81
Swooner Crooner, 311*f*
Synchroscope, 33–34
syncopation, 21, 49–52, 62, 63, 123, 141–
    42, 216n.79, 230, 234, 235–36, 252
synecdoche, 88–89
Szwed, John F., 244–45

tack Annie, 227–28, 254–55
Tashman, Lilyan, 48–49
Tate, Greg, 4–5
Technicolor, 17–18, 147–48, 300, 347–48
techno-dialogic, 230–31, 242–43, 248–49,
    258, 270, 271, 282
Temple, Shirley, 19, 148, 316–17
    Relationship with Bill Robinson, 128,
    148, 149–51, 158–59, 167n.101,
    167n.102, 173–74, 179–80,
    214n.52, 313–14
Terry, Paul (Terrytoons), 287–88, 323–24
Thanks Pal, 331, 332, 333
    See also *Stormy Weather*
That's the Spirit, 134
Theater Owner's Booking Association
    (T.O.B.A.), 163n.58, 164n.63, 260
Thirty-Nine Steps, the, 316–17
This is the Army, 177–78, 335, 343–45

374 INDEX

Thompson, Robert Farris, 12, 56–57
  See also Africanist Aesthetic
The Three Dukes, the (Leslie "Bubba" Gaines, Arthur "Pye" Russell, and James "Hutch" Hudson), 163n.60
Three Eddies, the (Albert Gibson, Esvan Scott Mosby, Eddie West and Guss Moore, Paul Black, Bethel "Duke" Gibson), 7, 122f, 123–26, 127–28, 135, 136–37, 138–39, 157–58, 160n.4, 160n.8, 260
Three Gobs (Mike Riley, Eddie Dent, Eddie Johnson, and Clarence "Sonny" Austin), 251, 260–61
Three Little Pigs, 18, 120f, 121, 285, 292–96
Three R's, the, 126–27, 160n.17
  See also New Deal
Thru the Mirror, 322–23
Tip, Tap, and Toe, 251–52, 277–78n.123
Tin Pan Alley, 50–51
Tin Pan Alley (film), 222–23, 264
Tin Pan Alley Cats, 309, 322–23
  See also censored eleven
Tomkins, Donald, 52, 68n.58
  See also *Varsity Drag*
Top of the Town, 251–52
Topsy (minstrel archetype), 15
tourism, 222–23
Toyland Broadcast, 144–45, 321
Trade Showing, 338–39
transit narrative, 19, 24–25, 176, 182, 212–13n.44, 219–24, 230, 231–32, 257–58, 267–68, 286–87
trickster trope, 134
Trip to America, A, 3–4
truckin' (dance), 184, 185, 230–31, 238–39, 248–49, 254–55, 276n.90, 281, 304–5
Tucker, Earl "Snakehips," 138–39
"Turkey in the Straw," 19, 145, 151, 152–53
Twentieth century-Fox, 194, 214n.52, 248–49, 251, 255–56, 332, 338–39

Uncle Sam, 281–82, 325n.1
Uncle Tom, 15, 19, 167n.101, 215n.65, 227–28, 232, 287–88, 299–303, 308, 317–19, 323–24
Uncle Tom's Cabin, 144–45, 215n.65
Underworld (film), 209n.5

Unheimlich, 212–13n.44
United Artists, 47–48, 55, 108, 301–3

Valiquet, L.P., 33–34
Valis Hill, Constance, 160n.3, 163n.51, 165n.68
Vallée, Rudy, 86–87, 114n.27, 117n.80
Van, Gus (of Van and Schenck), 177–78
Van Beuren, Amadee J., 296–97
Van Vechten, Carl, 70–71n.101
Variety, 70n.98, 161n.30
Varsity Drag (dance), 49, 52, 68n.58
Varsity Show, 171, 210n.13, 316
Vaudeville, 5–6, 33–34, 35, 48–49, 80, 81, 90–91, 112–13n.9, 124–25, 136, 138–39, 143–44, 160n.5, 160n.8, 163n.51, 164n.63, 164n.66, 165n.68, 240, 256, 293–94, 345–47
ventriloquism, 6–7, 85–91, 285–86, 298–99, 308, 314–15
Vera-Ellen, 206, 348–49
vestigial minstrels, 15
Vidor, King, 130, 161n.30, 327n.39
VistaVision, 17–18, 347, 348–49
Vitaphone, 36, 65n.16, 236–37
vocal transmogrification, 5–6, 11, 86–87, 285
voice throwing, 11, 16

Wagner, Richard, 32, 202–3, 247–48
Walker, Aida Overton, 31–32, 69n.85, 337
Walker, George, 31–32, 69n.85
Waller, Fats, 308–9
  caricatures of, 155, 299–300, 306–8, 309, 310–12, 316, 319–20, 321–23
  in film, 155, 260
  music, 155
"Waltz in Swing Time," 184
war bonds, xvii, 281, 282–87
Warner Bros., 36, 37, 43–44, 48, 65n.16, 118n.88, 131–32, 134–35, 171, 178–79, 228, 232–33, 237, 280, 282–83, 297–98, 301–4, 308, 316, 317–18, 321
Warren, Harry, 118n.86, 199–200
Washington, Fredi, 275n.84
watermelon references, 138–39, 227–30, 232, 235–36, 299–300, 305–6, 316, 322–23

INDEX 375

Waters, Ethel, 113n.10, 163n.54
caricatures of, 319–20
Webb, Chick, 163n.58
Weheliye, Alexander, 289
Weisenfeld, Judith, 272–73n.12, 301
Wells, Paul, 285, 289–90, 295–96
West, Mae, 194–95, 261–62
"What a Perfect Combination," 100–2, 104
When Yuba Plays the Rumba on the Tuba, 73
White Christmas, 177–78, 335, 347–49
White consciousness, 11, 21–24, 126, 127–28, 130–31, 301, 321–22
White privilege, 2–3, 32, 221
White saviors, 230, 234, 237, 238–39, 257–58
White spectatorship (audience, gaze), 1, 23–24, 37–38, 57–59, 137–38, 139–41, 158–59, 174, 193–94, 265–66
See also Harlem; *Harlem is Heaven, Puttin' on the Ritz*
White, George, 142–43, 146, 158, 251
Whiteman, Paul, 319–20
Whitey's Lindy Hoppers, 234–35
See also Lindy Hop
Whitman, Ernest, 143–44, 335–37
Whitman Sisters, 260
"who dat," 234–39
Whoopee!, 18, 21–23, 77, 81–91, 93, 263–64, 296–97
Wickie, Gus, 296–97, 308
Williams, Bert, xv–xvi, 7, 69n.85, 124–25, 164n.63, 177–78, 350–51n.17
Williams, Cootie, 248–49, 250
Williams, Henry "Rubberlegs," 134–35, 163n.58
See also Butterbeans
Williams, Stringbean, 209n.5
"Willie the Weeper," 240
Willkie, Wendell, 174–75
Winfield, Raymond (of Tip, Tap, and Toe), 251, 277–78n.123
With Love and Kisses, 260–61

Wonder Bar, 227–33, 299–304, 340–42
Wong, Anna May, 123–24
Woody, Charles, 123–26, 160n.4
See also Three Eddies
Works Progress Administration (WPA), 256
World War I, 137, 343
World War II, 2–3, 20, 25–26, 114–15n.34, 126, 143, 164n.65, 174–75, 177–78, 194, 206, 213n.48, 220–21, 231, 256–57, 262–63, 270, 282–87, 334–35, 339, 340, 344, 345
"Would You Like to Buy My Violins," 194–95

Yiddish references, 227–28, 232, 235–36, 252, 255–56, 285, 292–95, 305–6
accent, 121
chutzpah, 90–91
pipiks, 79, 82–83
punum, 90–91
putz, 82–83
theater, 5–6, 50
See also Big Bad Wolf; Eddie Cantor; jewface
Yip Yip Yaphank, 177–78, 210n.9, 343, 344
YMCA, 1–2, 53–54
Young, Robert, 190, 221–22
Young, Roland, 254–55
You're an Education, 316–18
"You're the Cure for What Ails Me," 241–42

Zanzibar, 260–61
"*Zaz-zuh-zaz*," 234–35, 240, 245, 254
Ziegfeld, Florenz, 81, 92–95, 113n.18, 114n.27, 178–79
Ziegfeld Follies, 81, 125, 142–43, 177–78
Zip Coon, 15, 42–43, 85, 107, 134, 151, 308, 312, 314–16, 321–22
Žižek, Slavoj, 2
Zoot suits, 240–41, 334, 343–44, 350n.7
Zoot Suit Riot, 334, 350n.7

Printed in the USA/Agawam, MA
March 5, 2024

862203.006